Enriching the Value Chain

IT Best Practices Series

This book is published as a part of the IT Best Practices Series—a collaboration between Intel Press and Addison-Wesley Professional, a division of Pearson Education. Books in this series focus on the information technology challenges companies face in today's dynamic, Internet-based, business environment, as well as on the opportunities to improve IT performance and thereby gain a competitive edge. Some of the books explain proven strategies to help business executives and managers develop needed capabilities. Other books show technical professionals exactly how to implement specific solutions. The series overall reflects Intel's Best Practices Program, developed with leading researchers, vendors, and end-users to meet the challenges and opportunities described. These Best Practices recognize that companies must be agile and adaptable in the face of diverse and rapidly changing technologies, and, in particular, must be prepared and able to integrate multivendor, e-Business tools. Thus, the theme of this series is: *Making it all work together*.

Books in this series include:

The Adaptive Enterprise:
IT Infrastructure Strategies to Manage Change and Enable Growth
—Bruce Robertson and Valentin Sribar

Securing Business Information:
Strategies to Protect the Enterprise and Its Network
—F. Christian Byrnes and Dale Kutnick

Enriching the Value Chain:
Infrastructure Strategies Beyond the Enterprise
—Bruce Robertson and Valentin Sribar

For detailed information about these and other books, as well as announcements of forthcoming books in the series, visit the Intel Press and Addison-Wesley Professional Web sites:

www.intel.com/intelpress
www.aw.com/cseng

Enriching the Value Chain

Infrastructure Strategies Beyond the Enterprise

Bruce Robertson
Valentin Sribar

INTEL
PRESS

Addison-Wesley
Pearson Education

Boston • San Francisco • New York • Toronto • Montreal
London • Munich • Paris • Madrid
Capetown • Sydney • Tokyo • Singapore • Mexico City

Intel is a registered trademark of Intel Corporation. Many of the designations used by manufacturers and sellers to distinguish their products are claimed as trademarks. Where those designations appear in this book, and the publisher was aware of a trademark claim, the designations have been printed with initial capital letters or in all capitals.

The authors and publisher have taken care in the preparation of this book, but make no expressed or implied warranty of any kind and assume no responsibility for errors or omissions. No liability is assumed for incidental or consequential damages in connection with or arising out of the use of the information or programs contained herein. This book is sold with the understanding that the publisher is not engaged in professional services. If professional advice or other expert assistance is required, the services of a competent professional person should be sought.

Pearson Education offers discounts on this book when ordered in quantity for special sales. For more information, please contact:

Pearson Education Corporate Sales Division
201 W. 103rd Street
Indianapolis, IN 46290
(800) 428-5331
corpsales@pearsoned.com

Copyright © 2001 and 2002 Intel Corporation and META Group

All rights reserved. No part of this publication may be reproduced, stored in a retrieval system, or transmitted, in any form, or by any means, electronic, mechanical, photocopying, recording, scanning, or otherwise, without the prior written consent of the publisher. Printed in the United States of America. Published simultaneously in Canada.

For information on obtaining permission for use of material from this work, please submit a written request to:

Publisher, Intel Press
Intel Corporation
5200 NE Elam Young Parkway JF4-326
Hillsboro, OR 97124-6461
E-mail: intelpress@intel.com

ISBN 0-201-76730-9

Text printed on recycled paper

1 2 3 4 5 6 7 8 9 10—CRW—0605040302

First printing, January 2002

Contents

Preface xi

Chapter 1 Beyond e-Business   1
    Why Infrastructure (Suddenly) Matters   3
    Getting It Right   4
    The Importance of Being Adaptive   5
    The Clash of Cultures   7
    What's the Solution?   9
    Understanding Adaptive Infrastructure   10
    Measuring the Benefits   19
    Summary   21

Chapter 2 Laying the Foundation   23
    How to Catalog Components   24
        Physical Components   25
        Functional Components   28
        Interface Components   32
        Other Components?   34
        Other Layers?   35
    Developing Adaptive Services   36
        Understanding the Concept   37
        Applying the Model   38
        Benefits of Adaptive Infrastructure Services   38

Shifting Services to the Infrastructure   39
Decoupling the Lifecycles   40
Examining the Network Model   42
Service Interfaces and Service Level Agreements   44
Where to Create Service Boundaries   45
Keeping it Real   46
Design Guidelines   48
How to Apply Services to New Applications   49
Summary   51

Chapter 3   Identifying and Using Patterns   53

What Are Patterns?   54
Designing for the Future   55
Asking Who, Where, and What?   56
How Detailed Should It Get?   57
Understanding the Major Patterns   59
Transact Patterns   60
Publish Patterns   63
Collaborate Patterns   68
Key Patterns for e-Business   71
Web Publish Pattern   71
3/N-Tier Transact Pattern   75
What Patterns Do You Need?   79
Subdividing Patterns   80
Should Patterns for e-Business Be Different?   81
Applying Multiple Patterns   82
Summary   82

Chapter 4   Infrastructure Planning and Design   85

The Business/IT Project Lifecycle   86
Step 1: Setting Strategy   86
Step 2: Choosing Strategic Activities   87
Step 3: Matching Activities to Patterns   87
Step 4: Refining Patterns and Project Plans   88
Step 5: Implementing and Operating   88
The Importance of People Skills   89
Assessing the Skills Required   90
Increased Pressure to Deliver   91
New Types of Relationships   92

Developing Relationship-based Management   94
New Business Roles   95
Effective Recruiting   95
Retaining Employees   97
Understanding Infrastructure Planning   98
Details of Project Planning   100
Packaging Infrastructure   102
Designing Patterns   104
Summary   112

Chapter 5   Security Services   115

Isolation Infrastructure Service   116
Understanding Firewalls   116
Architecting the Demilitarized Zone (DMZ)   120
Intrusion Detection and Threat Management   128
SSL and Encryption Hardware   134
Refining Pattern Designs for Isolation Infrastructure   138
Identity Infrastructure Service   139
Web SSO: Simple Web-Centric Authentication   139
Public Key Infrastructure (PKI)   146
Directory Server   153
Building a Complete Identity Infrastructure   156
Refining Pattern Designs in Identity Infrastructure   161
Summary   163

Chapter 6   Physical Components   165

Network Layer   166
Overview of Networking Technologies   166
Scale-Out Design for Performance and Availability   167
Network Load Balancer   170
Caching Server   175
Content Delivery Network (CDN)   182
Internet Access and Transport Services   186
Extranet Service Providers (ESPs)   193
Hosting Services   195
Refining Patterns in the Network Layer   201
Storage Layer   206
Storage Area Network Interconnect   209
Network Attached Storage Solutions (NAS)   209

Backup/Recovery Architectures 212
Storage Options in the Server Layer 213
Refining Patterns in the Storage Layer 216
Server Layer 218
Server Evolution 219
Scale-Up Versus Scale-Out 219
Scaling Out Web Services 221
Server Consolidation 221
Refining Patterns in the Server Layer 225
Summary 226

Chapter 7 Functional Components 227

Database Layer 228
Important Design Issues 228
Trends in Database Technologies 231
Scale-Out Solutions and Clustered Database Options 233
Refining Patterns in the Database Layer 236
Integration Layer 239
The Integration Server (Message Broker) 240
The Inter-Enterprise Integration (IEI) Server 249
Refining Patterns in the Integration Layer 253
Application Server Layer 256
Understanding Application Servers 256
Choosing Application Servers 258
.NET versus J2EE 263
Refining Patterns in the Application Server Layer 266
Summary 270

Chapter 8 Interface and Management Components 273

Presentation Layer 274
Web Server 274
Wireless Application Protocol (WAP) Server 275
Wireless Service 278
Voice 281
Interactive Voice Response (IVR) 282
Refining Patterns in the Presentation Layer 284

API Layer   285
  Understanding APIs   285
  Refining Patterns in the API Layer   289
Management Layer   289
  Service Level Management (SLM)   290
  Web Application Monitoring Strategy   291
  A Note on Metrics   293
  Refining Patterns in the Management Layer   295
  Using a Test Lab to Increase Performance   296
Summary   297

Appendix A   Component Catalog   299

Index to Components   300

Glossary   345

Index   365

Preface

Competition in the future, even today in certain industries, will not be company against company but supply chain against supply chain. Companies will be only as strong as the weakest link in their supply chain. The winners will be companies that can build electronic B2B relationships rapidly and manage those relationships seamlessly.

To cope in this new world, businesses need more *agility*. But to get this agility, they need a well-designed IT infrastructure that is highly reusable and adaptive. An agile, adaptive infrastructure can help businesses turn on a dime and capture new opportunities as they arrive.

Enriching the Value Chain: Infrastructure Strategies Beyond the Enterprise explains how adaptive infrastructure techniques can create a more focused, organized approach to delivering and supporting high-agility applications for e-Business and beyond. Along the way, the book recommends best practices for dealing with architecture and technology issues within the infrastructure in a way that can lead to success.

Moreover, the book highlights the e-Business-centric infrastructure strategies that will become key internal strategies as well. The days of separate e-Business infrastructure design and delivery are waning, to be replaced by more codependent and jointly developed internal and external infrastructure solutions.

From an infrastructure perspective, the "e" is actually disappearing so that *e-Business* will become just plain *business*. Soon, creating a design for internal corporate infrastructure will involve nothing more than dropping a few requirements from high-level e-Business designs. If these internal solutions later need to be reused externally, the infrastructure will already be in place for a simple incremental upgrade to the e-Business level. And e-Business infrastructure will not be all that different from what we now think of as traditional enterprise computing.

Acknowledgments

Books written for the IT Best Practices Series draw on the talents of many contributors, reviewers, and advisors.

In particular, the authors would like to acknowledge the following key contributors to the book. Thanks to Peter Burris for his seminal thoughts and for his active support of both the IT Best Practices program and the book series. Brian Hellauer and Donna Maciver tirelessly translated raw analyst research into structured and readable manuscript content.

We thank the following individuals who were important advisors: Dan Fineberg, who conceived the IT Best Practices program of which the book series is a key part; Rich Bowles for defining the IT Best Practices Series within the overall program and driving it from concept to reality; Jerry Braun for supporting the program, even when economic conditions made scarce resources even more precious. Finally, we give special recognition to Deb Catello for her conscientious and high-quality content reviews and to Chris Thomas for his leadership in identifying key tenets and themes.

The concepts presented in *Enriching the Value Chain* represent the distillation of several years' worth of META Group research. The authors would like to thank the people whose contributions in specific areas provided such a wealth of information to support this effort. The META Group Global Networking Strategies analysts were: Mark Bouchard, Don Carros, Peter Firstbrook, Chris King, Chris Kozup, Jerald Murphy, Leif-Olof Wallin, Earl Perkins, Jean-Louis Previdi, Tom Scholtz, David Thompson, Elizabeth Ussher, Larry Velez, and David Willis. Server Infrastructure Strategies analysts were: Philip Dawson, Sean Derrington, Nicholas Gall, Charles Garry, Morgan Gerhart, Phil Goodwin, Luis Leamus, Kevin McIsaac, Brian Richardson, Mark Shainman, Carolyn White, and William Zachmann. Additional analyst contributors from Service Management Strategies were: Corey Ferengul, Glenn O'Donnell, and Herb Van Hook.

Other individuals contributed to our project by keeping us in touch with our audience through their feedback on various parts of the books. We recognize and thank these special reviewers: Pierre-Andre La Chance, Chief Information Officer at Kaiser Permanente's Northwest Region Center for Health Research, for his reflections on the significance of processes within his organization; Steve Borte, Director of Services at ObjectFrontier, for his suggestions and his candid perspective as a seasoned IT professional; Cloy Swartzendruber, senior consultant and independent contractor, for his in-depth review of the content and his detailed feedback on the book's approach to the subject.

Finally, thanks to Ryan Bernard and his staff at Wordmark and Associates for their diligent efforts while turning our manuscript into a book. For editing and proofing the numerous drafts, thanks to: Rikki Mitman, Stephanie Donovan, Laurie Feinswog, Deborah Long, Donna Marcotte, Vicki Radovsky, and Diana Gabriel.

—Bruce Robertson
Vice President for Adaptive Infrastructure Strategies, META Group

—Valentin Sribar
Senior Vice President and Co-Research Director, META Group

Chapter 1

Beyond e-Business

In the late 1990s, e-Business took the world by storm. The potent combination of the Internet's global connectivity, innovative Web interfaces, and standards such as Transmission Control Protocol/Internet Protocol (TCP/IP) and HTML captured the collective imaginations of business leaders and consumers alike.

e-Business was supposed to revolutionize entire industries, change how goods were purchased, services delivered, and brands defined. Potentially, e-Business impacted every facet of the organization, including business models, processes, applications, staffing, infrastructure, relationships, product development, purchasing, and sales.

Not only was e-Business expected to transform companies and industries, it was supposed to accelerate the rate of change. Business cycles that previously took years were supposed to happen in days. The business and investment worlds' traditional fixation on revenues and profits changed to a focus on time-to-market and "capturing eyeballs" of users on Web sites.

Businesses and government organizations spent huge amounts of money on e-Business initiatives, applications, and infrastructure. By the beginning of 2000, the e-Business mania had resulted in ludicrous stock valuations and a propensity to put the letter "e" in front of everything.

Within another year or two, however, much of the e-Business world came crashing down. Most of the so-called dot-com companies had gone out of business, stock valuations plummeted, and budgets were cut across industries. e-Business had followed the traditional cycle of overly hyped expectations and excessive spending that is associated with business boom cycles.

Figure 1.1 illustrates the gap that developed between e-Business expectations and reality. The technology investment curve shows how expenditures were even more extreme on either side of the rise and fall of expectations.

Looking from the past to the future, the right side of Figure 1.1 shows that many of the e-Business changes will be permanent and that technology investment will settle somewhere in the gap between boom and bust.

Leading organizations realize that many of the benefits and changes of e-Business are long-term. However, these benefits must be leveraged by the entire organization instead of existing as a separate appendage. This realization merges e-Business initiatives back into broader corporate initiatives. Likewise, e-Business infrastructure will be viewed as part of a larger infrastructure whole.

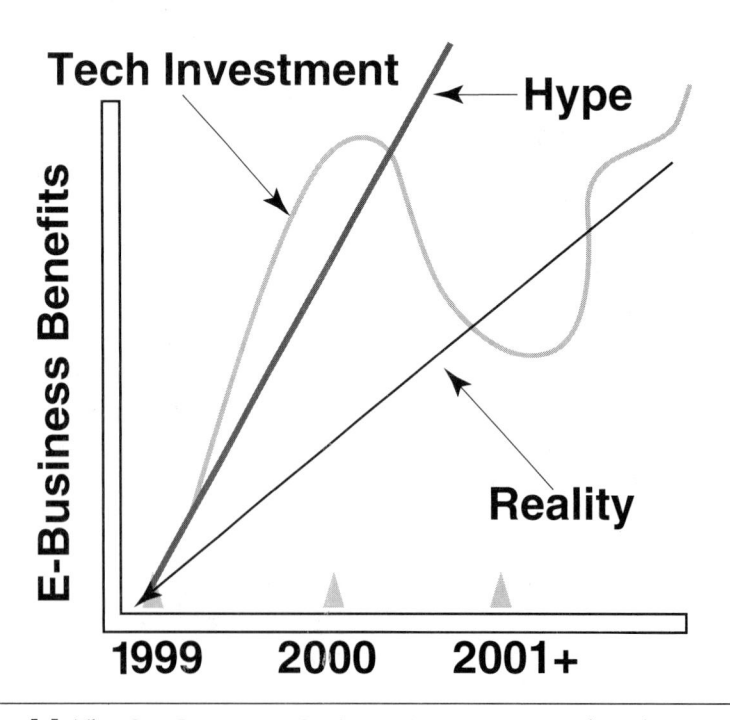

Figure 1.1 The Gap Between e-Business Expectations and Reality

Now that we are thinking "beyond e-Business," competition is not company against company but business chain against business chain. These chains include suppliers, partners, distributors, logistics providers, regulators, and even competitors. Companies can be only as strong as the weakest link in their chain. The winners will be companies that can build up, or tear down, electronic business-to-business (B2B) relationships rapidly and seamlessly.

Beyond e-Business, enterprise borders will change, or even disappear. Leading organizations will provide open access to infrastructure services, data, and applications. Partners, suppliers, customers and, in some cases, even your competition, or "co-opetition," will be able to peer into your corporate nervous system, including your traditional systems—not just the ones with an "e" in front of them.

In theory, all of this realignment is for the better, removing time and costs from key business processes. If not handled correctly, however, it could be detrimental, undermining your security and overall brand.

In this new era, customer expectations are rising mercilessly in terms of the speed and reliability they expect across all points of interaction. Just as people don't like to wait in line at a store or to be on hold waiting for a call center agent, studies show that Web customers will wait only eight seconds for a page view. Unfortunately, the customers do not care that you have no control over your call volume or their connection speed.

Not only are your external customers' expectations rising, so are the expectations of your internal customers and business leaders. They can't watch the news or read a magazine without being reminded about the possibilities when e-Business and traditional concepts are combined effectively.

Why Infrastructure (Suddenly) Matters

The pressure to move beyond e-Business places a great strain on infrastructure components such as networks, security, servers, and middleware. If your front doors aren't robust, highly available, and secure, your company risks major losses.

Innovations such as the Internet, wireless applications, call centers, and even the automated teller machines (ATMs) of the 1980s have made applications and infrastructure increasingly visible to customers and to the general public. Today, much of your organization's reputation and brand identity depends on the quality of your infrastructure, not just on your applications.

With the Internet as a common currency in the business world, lack of integration, robustness, or agility on your part becomes immediately and embarrassingly obvious to key customers—no matter where they are in the world. In the past, when you made mistakes, only your employees knew. Now, if your systems fail, the whole world may know. CNN might broadcast a report on how your Web site hasn't been up for five hours! That's definitely not good advertising for the company's brand.

An infrastructure that frequently fails, that doesn't support the traffic load, or that can't provide a reasonably integrated view of your complex organization can cost your company immediately in lost sales and lost goodwill. When you realize what's at stake, you begin to see why savvy, agile organizations are investing more to make sure that their infrastructure doesn't lag far behind their business vision and applications. Unfortunately, once your lack of robustness and agility is exposed, you can't change things very quickly. Having an adaptive infrastructure will ensure that you don't get caught flat-footed when your time comes to shine on the world's commercial stage.

Getting It Right

As time goes by, more businesses are buying, commissioning, and even renting applications in one form or another. Meanwhile, fewer companies are building their applications internally from scratch. In such situations, an adaptive infrastructure strategy becomes crucial to providing a versatile, flexible, and agile foundation for application deployment.

As your organization outsources more of its applications work, what's left for IT to do is to *get the infrastructure right*. From a practical standpoint, if you are implementing a database back-end, what differentiates your effort isn't the application itself, but how quickly you get it running and how well it works. In many cases, these problems aren't application issues; they're infrastructure issues.

As infrastructure becomes more important and increasingly separated from purely application issues, the resulting adaptive infrastructure solutions should exhibit several key traits:

- Efficiency. The ability to provide reusable components that are priced reasonably and can be quickly tailored for application development projects.

- Effectiveness. The easy integration of all components in a way that supports their robust operation.

- **Agility.** Good planning and design processes that allow you to develop new applications quickly and to repurpose or upgrade existing infrastructure to support new application requirements.

If you outsource the responsibility for running the infrastructure, your company must have at least one group that makes sure applications can run effectively on the outsourced infrastructure. This group must include infrastructure planners and designers, whose ability to manage separate service providers will be key in making your infrastructure efficient, effective, and agile. Of all the challenges you face in the burgeoning world beyond e-Business, this one is especially crucial.

The Importance of Being Adaptive

Organizations maturing beyond e-Business are no longer concerned about being on the bleeding edge, or being the latest and greatest. They are trying to be leaders in a world where their own competitors are also increasingly both agile and pragmatic. To support this capacity for change from an infrastructure perspective, you simply won't have time to reinvent the wheel or to rebuild your entire information technology (IT) infrastructure from scratch. Instead, you will have to learn how to adapt many of the infrastructure components you already have.

Assuming you don't have the time or resources to replace every system, integrating legacy systems will be a crucial strategy when trying to meet time-to-market deadlines. You must integrate applications with multiple points of interaction, such as Web browsers, interactive voice response units (IVRs), personal digital assistants (PDAs), and mobile phones, so that data is appropriately synchronized and so that various points of interaction represent your brand faithfully.

Early e-Business initiatives focused on the front-end—with applications such as online stock trading, online auctioning, and industry portals. Now, companies that are moving beyond e-Business apply these concepts across the front- and back-ends of enterprise processes.

Therefore, business-to-business (B2B) integration increasingly becomes a key infrastructure solution. Companies are moving beyond electronic document interchange (EDI) and adopting solutions based on extensible markup language (XML) to facilitate the flow of transactions between business processes and across organizations. You will realize the benefits of a fully adaptive approach when your company can easily change business partners or processes without undue cost or conversion time.

What is Infrastructure?

What does the term "infrastructure" really mean? In the physical world, infrastructure often refers to public utilities, such as water, electricity, gas, sewage, and telephone services. Often, these utilities are layers of a total structure. As shown in Figure 1.2, that total structure includes e-Business infrastructure. Each layer has the following characteristics:

- Shared by a larger audience than the structure it supports.
- More static and permanent than the structures it supports.
- Considered a *service*, including the people and processes involved in support, rather than just a physical structure or device.
- Often physically connected to the structure it supports.
- Distinct from the structures it supports in terms of its lifecycle (plan, build, run, change, exit).
- Distinct from the structures it supports in terms of its ownership and the people who execute the lifecycle.

The notion of separate ownership and lifecycles is crucial to the concept of infrastructure. e-Business repeated many of the traditional battles over ownership of applications and infrastructure between line-of-business groups and central IT departments.

In many companies, marketing ran the e-Business function, but was not typically involved in the daily routine of system upgrades and maintenance. Instead, they asked IT to take over responsibility for keeping the applications running. In organizations that are maturing beyond e-Business, IT does more than just keep things running. They own the entire lifecycle and fix broken processes by applying IT best practices to make them better.

What is Infrastructure? *(continued)*

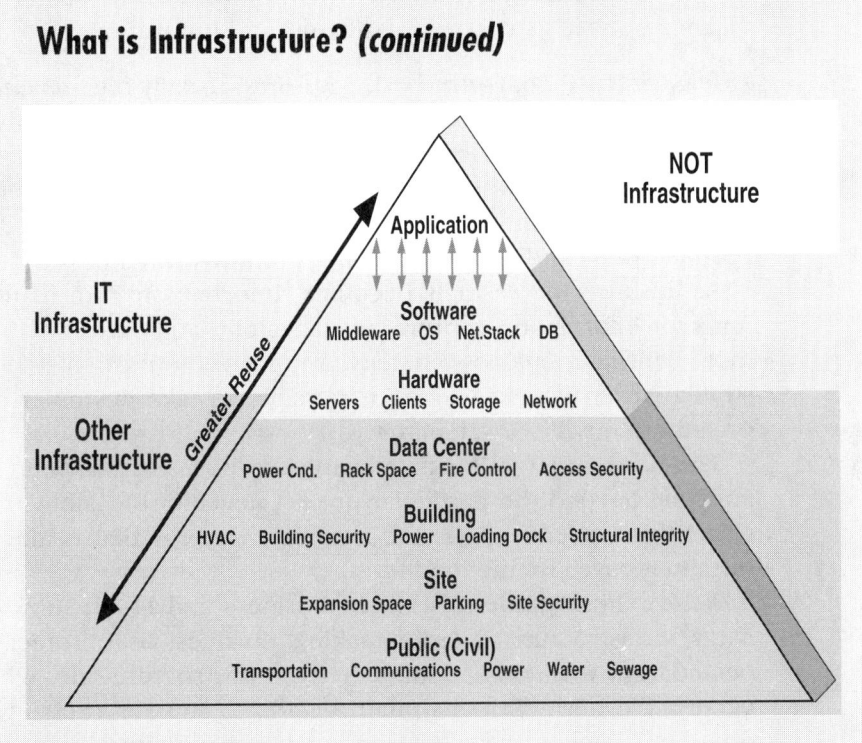

Figure 1.2 Understanding Infrastructure

Pyramid diagram showing (top to bottom): Application, Software (Middleware, OS, Net.Stack, DB), Hardware (Servers, Clients, Storage, Network), Data Center (Power Cnd., Rack Space, Fire Control, Access Security), Building (HVAC, Building Security, Power, Loading Dock, Structural Integrity), Site (Expansion Space, Parking, Site Security), Public (Civil) (Transportation, Communications, Power, Water, Sewage). Application is labeled NOT Infrastructure; Software and Hardware are IT Infrastructure; lower levels are Other Infrastructure. An arrow labeled "Greater Reuse" points upward.

The Clash of Cultures

So you want a more adaptive infrastructure but don't know how to make it happen? IT people realize all too well how difficult selling infrastructure improvements into the organization can be. In companies with less enlightened management, any IT department trying to create an adaptive infrastructure encounters two common yet fundamental reactions.

Stability is good. People often feel it's good to have an infrastructure that is stable, unchanging, and predictable. While this goal is admirable, an infrastructure must also be flexible, even breakable, to be fully leveraged by business. Existing e-Business applications are often unstable, and infrastructure is often the culprit. In the world beyond e-Business, making infrastructure more stable, but still flexible, requires a careful balance between structure (standards) and innovation (adaptability).

Infrastructure costs are bad. Business usually regards infrastructure as a cost to be minimized or as a necessary evil. Until recently, however, e-Business costs were exempt from this problem: No budget was too large if the project was e-Business. In the post e-Business world, companies are scrutinizing projects carefully to make sure they deliver true business value and an adequate return on investment (ROI).

As business increasingly becomes "informational" in nature, the systems for information capture, management, and delivery become even more central to business strategy. If infrastructure can support business strategy, even if only making it possible to take customer orders, the organization will see value in it.

The hard part will be convincing the business to spend money on anything beyond the particular project needs of the moment. To counteract this tendency, you need a funding strategy that is more responsible and focused on the long term.

A clear misalignment between business and IT organizations dominates infrastructure decision-making. Business is chronically disconnected from what is happening on the infrastructure side. When this rift occurs, the business units might decide to support their own application development projects using outside consultants, without considering whether the infrastructure is in place to support the planned applications.

Not surprisingly, this disjointed style of solution delivery often creates applications that don't perform nearly as well as originally intended and that are too complex and costly to implement. Such applications can even degrade the performance of other applications, because developers don't understand the complexities and dependencies of a shared network infrastructure within the organization. e-Business was no different; its larger-scale issues simply put more pressure on IT to get things right for all applications, rather than just one at a time.

In e-Business, each new application tended to be based on the "latest and greatest" solution, which required endless and extensive variations in infrastructure. This approach was counterproductive and tended to increase the complexity of managing the entire infrastructure. The need to support every variation often leads to mediocre support at best—or expensive and ineffective outsourcing at worst.

In the world beyond e-Business, given the renewed interest in affordability, business must make choices about what really makes a difference, and then IT must deliver it. This situation is actually better for infrastructure planners, since vague goals are replaced by specific projects with explicit service level requirements, which in turn should make planning easier.

What's the Solution?

Obviously, with pressures coming from so many directions, you need an organized way to handle everything. This book provides a number of strategies to help you cope, but in a nutshell here are the key concepts:

Plan your infrastructure end-to-end. When you plan your infrastructure, you can't just plan a piece at a time and hope it all works together. An adaptive infrastructure requires more extensive planning efforts. Chapter 3 explains how infrastructure *patterns* can help you do a more thorough planning job.

Design for adaptiveness. Your infrastructure shouldn't just meet today's requirements; it should be ready to scale, adapt, change, or grow to deal with challenges on the horizon. Once you identify your challenges, you must face them squarely and start designing for them immediately. A later section of this chapter explains how adaptive infrastructure works.

Make infrastructure reusable. A key reason for building an adaptive infrastructure is to make design standards and the physical components of your infrastructure reusable. Reinventing the wheel for every application only makes your infrastructure increasingly unmanageable and slows time-to-market. This book explains how to identify key infrastructure patterns within your organization, and how to structure them to leverage a set of reusable adaptive infrastructure services appropriate for the post e-Business era.

Find out what works, and do it. It's important to move from a strategy of "trying everything" to a strategy of "finding out what works," and then doing those things repeatedly, while optimizing to improve quality and reduce cost. Much of this approach requires stronger processes, more focus on delivery of working solutions, and a little less focus on keeping up with new technology.

Focus on people and process. Many IT people seem to focus on making product choices or architecture choices, while ignoring the people and processes needed to be successful. You can make great technology choices, but if you don't have the right people and processes, your technology choices will be useless and you won't get the success you need from them. Chapter 4 discusses people and process issues in considerable detail.

Choose the right technology and products. Of course, striking a balance doesn't reduce the need to select the best technologies and products for your infrastructure and application delivery needs. The latest best-of-breed solution isn't always the right one for your organization. The IT world presents a new best-of-breed product every time you turn around, so it's impossible to stay on top of a strategy that always focuses on best-of-breed products.

Balance immediate needs with long-term goals. Few people have the luxury of stopping the train to redesign the tracks. There simply isn't time to do that in today's fast-paced world, and the costs would be horrendous. To be successful, you must be able to change what you are doing *while you are still doing it*. You must strike a balance that helps you transform while you are performing.

This book shows you how to make the balancing act work correctly, and it provides a few specific approaches that might work for you. These recommendations include tying infrastructure solutions to new business plans, using incremental building strategies, and committing to new costs only as needed to handle incoming business opportunities—not buying for opportunities that never materialize.

Understanding Adaptive Infrastructure

Having a truly adaptive infrastructure gives your business the agility it needs and makes your job of planning and designing infrastructure easier as time goes on. The concept of adaptive infrastructure is discussed in greater detail in another book in this series, *The Adaptive Enterprise*. However, the following discussion will acquaint you with the basics.

A New Way of Thinking

Obviously, developing an adaptive infrastructure isn't something that happens overnight. To create major change within your organization, you must start by changing yourself—by adopting a new way of thinking and a philosophy to guide you toward your goals.

Look at adaptive infrastructure as a set of components, patterns, and services, along with the people and processes necessary to tie them together. These organizing principles are the key principles that drive much of the content in this book (see Figure 1.3).

- Platform is an organizing concept that groups individual component technologies into technical domains or *layers*.
- Patterns are organizing concepts that you can use to quickly match business requirements with end-to-end infrastructure designs.
- Services are "infrastructure applications" that shift responsibility out of the application domain into the infrastructure domain. Services provide a set of physically shared components, such as a network or a credit card processing service, that multiple applications can leverage.

The diagram in Figure 1.3 shows how all the elements of adaptive infrastructure work together in an organized way to support applications. If applications are the physical manifestation of real business processes, all the elements of infrastructure must work together successfully to ensure their flawless performance.

Having an adaptive infrastructure doesn't mean that you cater to every application on its own terms. This approach only creates more "stovepipes" within the organization. Instead, you can make both the application and infrastructure development processes more manageable by defining consistent and repeatable "patterns" that you can manage

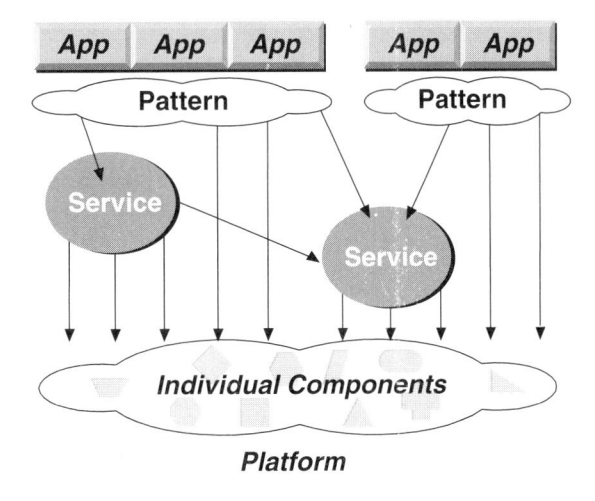

Figure 1.3 Key Elements of Adaptive Infrastructure

more effectively. These patterns are built on a foundation of key services that you have clearly identified as crucial to your business operation. These services, in turn, are based on individual infrastructure components working together as part of an adaptive infrastructure platform.

On one level, the first step in building an adaptive infrastructure is to identify and catalog all these elements: the patterns, platforms, and services, along with the people, processes, and packaging that will make your efforts successful. Once you organize the problem this way, you can avoid the dilemma of having to start from scratch each time a new application rolls out. Thus, you can avoid asking yourself questions such as "What exactly do I need for service levels?" or "Which component do I select?" Instead, you have pre-built solutions that you can tailor at a moment's notice, providing your organization with better agility.

Everything that you need to create an adaptive infrastructure strategy boils down to the six fundamental concepts discussed on the following pages. These concepts set the tone for your infrastructure planning efforts and form the core strategies of this book.

1. Identify and Catalog Technologies

If your decision-making attitude is "I bought from Vendor X, so now everything is solved," you're probably thinking the wrong way about the problem. To manage infrastructure well, you must first identify and catalog all your IT *components* into functional categories: common application run-time targets. These targets should maximize component reuse and systems integration and provide a base level of shared services.

By organizing your hundreds of components into categories, you can make them much easier to manage. Most components tend to fit rather neatly into the layers of stacked infrastructure identified in Figure 1.4.

In this figure, notice that the dividing line between applications and infrastructure intentionally runs through the center of the application infrastructure layer. Components in the infrastructure layers are all purchased, not physically built, such as a particular server. Components in the application layers could be developed internally, particularly if custom development would provide a potential competitive advantage. In the middleware layer, where these two worlds intersect, systems integration becomes a crucial element.

Chapter 2 provides more detail about these layers and the organizing principles behind categorizing and managing component technologies. For a complete component catalog, see Appendix A.

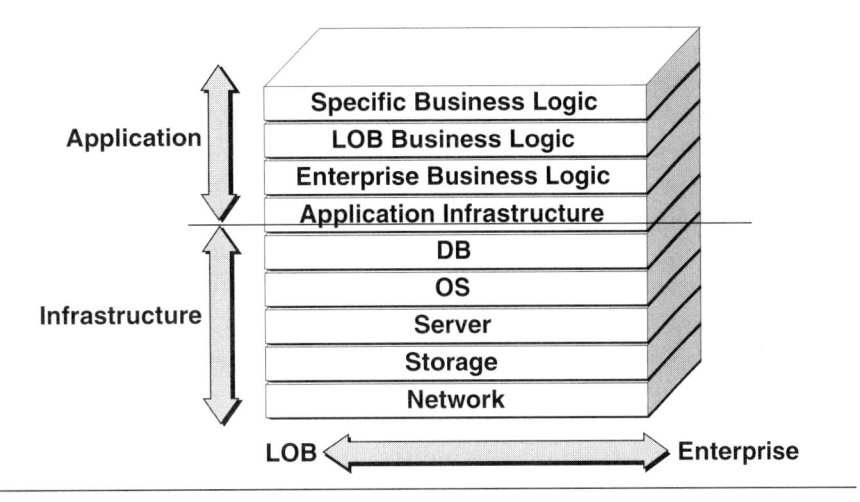

Figure 1.4 The Infrastructure Stack

2. Develop Reusable Infrastructure Patterns

One important way to resolve some of your problems is to simplify complexity wherever you can. The best way to simplify is to identify modular *patterns* within your infrastructure that can be supported, augmented, nurtured, and reused to ensure success. Using these end-to-end sets of infrastructure components from many platform layers, you can clarify and unify technology, planning, and operational processes, as well as personnel experiences.

It's a losing proposition when you react to the wide variety of application development requests by trying to maintain expertise in every type of infrastructure that might be needed to support an endless variety of applications. To make things more manageable, select a few key patterns to build your expertise around, then use these patterns to support business projects in a repeatable way that makes things easier and less expensive for everyone. In other words, simplify and prioritize.

Chapter 3 introduces a set of nine key patterns typically found in IT infrastructure, but the chapter focuses on the two patterns most essential to bringing e-Business into the next era: the Web Publish pattern and the 3/N-Tier Transact pattern. Chapter 4 explains how to refine design for these key patterns. The remaining chapters in this book provide considerable detail on refining each of the e-Business pattern designs for the new era.

3. Develop Adaptive Infrastructure Services

The next step in organizing your infrastructure is to organize components from platform layers into *services*. A service exists when someone delegates the responsibility for performing a process to a service provider.

In the outside world, service providers include people such as bank tellers and plumbers. In the e-Business world, Internet service providers (ISPs) and application pattern service providers (ASPs) were quite common. As the world moved beyond e-Business, surviving providers were integrated with traditional telecom and outsourcing service providers into broader, more financially stable shared service providers. Within your own company, your IT department might also be considered a provider of infrastructure services.

Unlike a component, which is focused on technology only, an adaptive infrastructure service is a shared set of technologies, along with a common set of processes and people skills. This combination is implemented once and reused by multiple applications. While a service may not represent the entire end-to-end infrastructure for an application, it can be reused by infrastructure patterns like any other component.

To be truly efficient and reusable, services must be decoupled and become separate processes from the person or system that interacts with them. By defining services in this way, you can start removing the stovepipes from your e-Business infrastructure, evolving toward the new era.

The network itself is an ideal example of this concept. Today, no one thinks of the network as part of an application; it's a service on which the application runs. No one builds a unique network just to host a single application. Not too long ago, however, such an arrangement was painfully common.

Now most organizations use a single network service, namely TCP/IP, to support all applications. e-Business made this concept even clearer. Some networks dedicated to specialized applications still do exist, such as the wireless networks used in the package delivery industry. However, these types of dedicated networks are relatively rare.

4. Use Good Tools in Well-Designed Processes

Once you have identified patterns, platforms, services, organizational issues, and old problems that must be fixed, you should sit down with a robust set of tools and processes and start the journey back toward organization and clarity:

Infrastructure Pattern Matching (IPM). If you're an infrastructure planner, what the business really wants from you—in addition to credibility and leadership—is the ability to estimate the cost, schedules, and risks associated with new projects. IPM helps by providing systematic answers to three fundamental questions: Who are the users, where are they, and what work is being performed? Answering these questions helps you define service-level commitments, predict costs, and identify the core technology issues that affect application scalability.

Periodic and Annual Processes. Having structured, repeatable processes with concrete outputs or deliverables makes a difference in terms of the speed, quality, and cost of everything you do. Figure 1.5 shows two kinds of processes that you will execute on a repeated basis. One is periodic or *strategic* infrastructure planning, used to review your standard infrastructure patterns and services on a regular cycle, such as annually. The other is per-project or *tactical* infrastructure planning, which is done for each application or new technology being introduced into the organization.

The last four chapters of this book take you through a pattern design process for each of the major components. The goal is to design a reusable blueprint for post e-Business infrastructures, yet in a way that gets at least one project planned as well. With a robust set of tools and a well-defined set of processes, your team can respond to application support requests in a repeatable, structured way within hours, rather than weeks or months. In the process, you will generate enormous credibility for the adaptive infrastructure concept and for your whole IT organization.

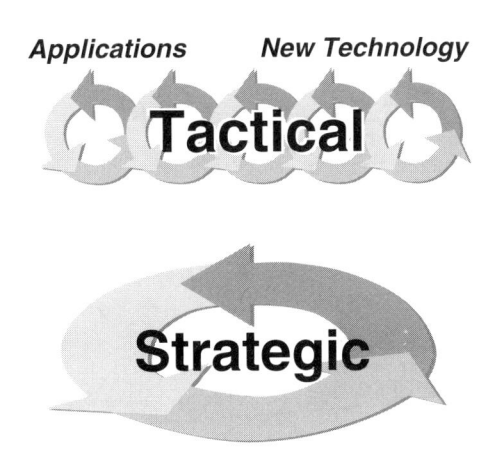

Figure 1.5 Tactical Versus Strategic Processes

Portfolios. Anyone who uses Quicken or Microsoft Money knows that half the battle in financial management involves keeping your planning portfolios up-to-date. Waiting until tax time to update your portfolios can be extremely painful. The key is to apply discipline and a set of easy-to-use tools to continuously update your portfolios.

Figure 1.6 shows how the same portfolio concept can be applied to infrastructure planning. Infrastructure portfolios keep you organized as you identify, catalog, and manage your patterns, platforms, and services on an ongoing basis.

Once you develop a set of infrastructure portfolios, people will know where to find all the details about components, patterns, or services, as they are needed.

5. Get Organized

For infrastructure planning to work, it has to be more than just a "good idea." It has to become an essential part of your business.

The only realistic way to incorporate infrastructure planning into your business is to create new roles and responsibilities, job titles, and even new groups or departments where necessary. Someone must own

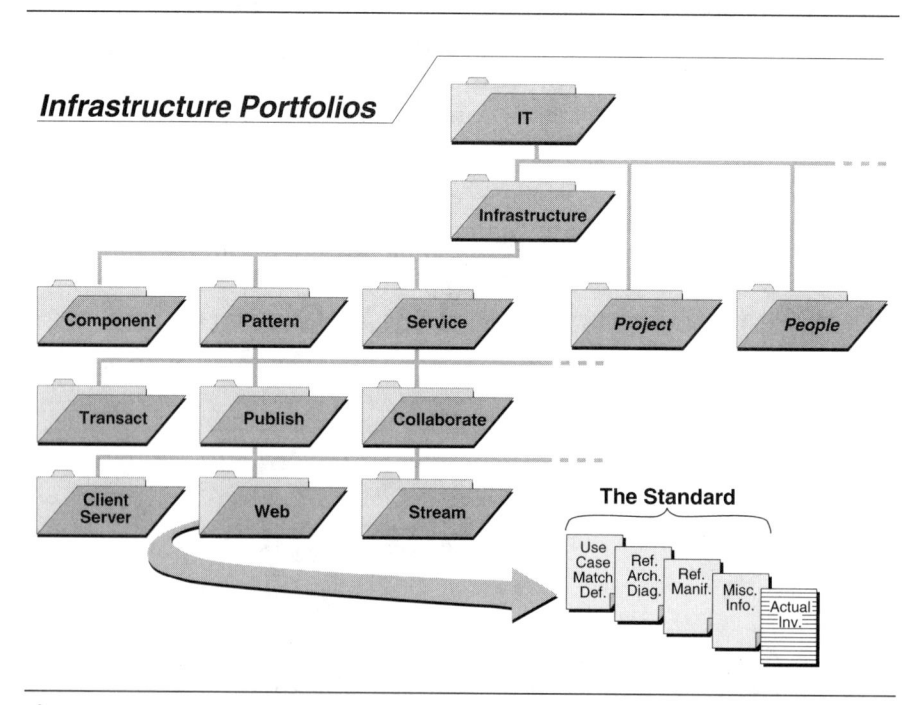

Figure 1.6 The Concept of Portfolios

infrastructure planning and development processes, and make sure that these processes are performed regularly as needed.

What's more, infrastructure planning roles must be clearly separated from traditional roles related to application development and operations. Figure 1.7 shows how separating these roles provides a certain balance to the organization and allows each group to focus on its own strengths, particularly with regard to shared services having separate lifecycles.

- Infrastructure developers are responsible for designing, implementing, and managing the interfaces between enterprisewide resources and the infrastructure shared by multiple applications.

- Application developers provide project-related interface requirements to the infrastructure developers, who ensure that interfaces are implemented efficiently, securely, and with management controls.

At a group level, having a team of infrastructure planners and developers can help prioritize an array of infrastructure projects. They can make sure that infrastructure standards, including components, patterns, and services, are available and reused correctly for application development projects. This group can also identify potential areas for reuse, not only of technologies, but also of project management methodologies, documentation, and the processes and people involved.

Within their more refined focus, infrastructure planners can recognize when unique components are required, and what they will cost.

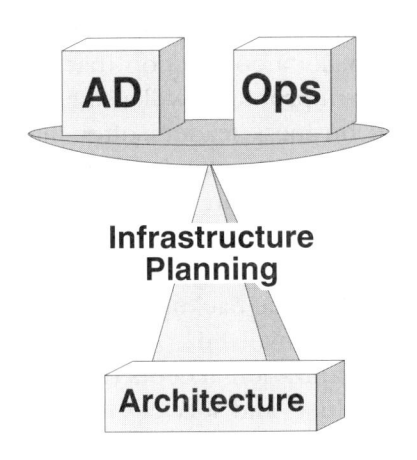

Figure 1.7 Balancing the Organization

Planners can also shift the focus from an emphasis on particular technologies to continuous improvement of the delivery process.

Chapter 4 gives more detail on how to organize people and processes into distinct roles and responsibilities that work well in traditional processes, in e-Business projects, and in the world beyond e-Business.

6. Describe Value Through Packaging

You can study a wide array of engineering principles, design methodologies, and pattern approaches. You can create your own infrastructure development group and achieve perfection in all your processes. But you'll never fully succeed unless you can sell your approach to the business and show the value of what you're doing.

Business unit managers who hold the purse strings must understand the *value* of what you are proposing. Only when they see value will they be willing to loosen the purse strings and give you the investment dollars and management support that you need.

One of the most important techniques you can use to sell the value of adaptive infrastructure to upper management is the concept of an "infrastructure product," which is an ongoing, reproducible, and repeatable set of services that your organization can deliver into the business.

For example, in a retail environment, line executives will sign on much quicker for a world-class system that sustains a particular retail function than they will for a world-class systems administration function. Retail executives will always see more value in their in-store processes. So your emphasis should be on packaging and pricing infrastructure products that support those efforts. Don't just solve your own infrastructure problems; solve your customer's problems, too. At the very least, make a connection that shows how the work you must do to fix your own problems will also end up solving their problems.

In addition, business leaders often have specific applications that they will pay extra to see delivered well. Once you have the quality-of-service issues covered, you can create premium subscription services for applications, while ensuring that these services are actually handled in a premium fashion. Such applications can then support additional IT expenses such as online backup and around-the-clock support, because of the extra charges involved.

Once your organization accepts the concept of infrastructure as a set of packaged products and services, infrastructure planning becomes an ongoing process of refinement. It becomes more a matter of adding to the service levels offered to the business. As you add more infrastructure and applications, the entire conglomeration starts behaving in an almost organic fashion. The objective is to optimize ongoing investments, while maintaining a balance between what the infrastructure delivers and what applications require.

Measuring the Benefits

Understanding exactly what is "adaptive" about adaptive infrastructure can be a complex task. Figure 1.8 shows the various measurements used to quantify the agility and range of your adaptive infrastructure.

Scalability. Scalability means building in some headroom so that your infrastructure doesn't have to be changed repeatedly as the user base for an application increases. Scalability is a relatively easy but potentially expensive way to be adaptive. Later sections of this book will highlight best practices that can be used to achieve scalability without spending too much up front, primarily by assuring that incremental scalability is a feature of the architecture and technology choices.

Presentation independence. Another dimension that affects virtually every organization is presentation: the way information is presented to users or business partners. Historically, the presentation layer has shown

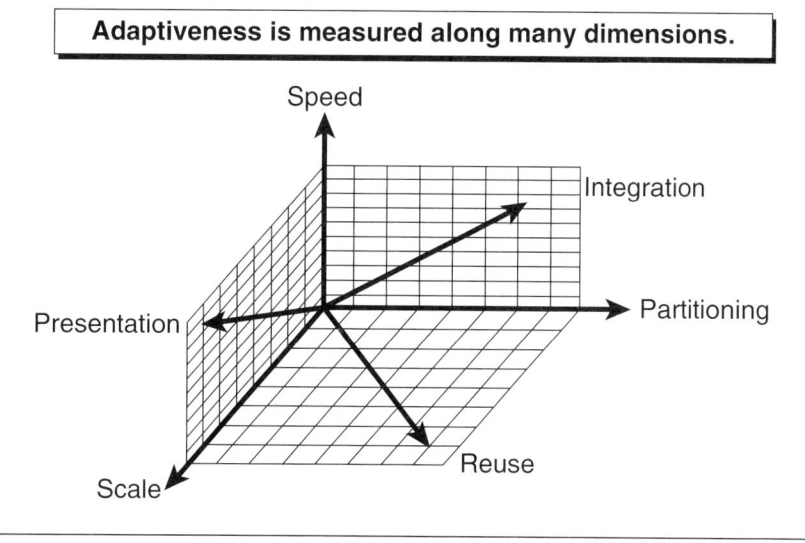

Figure 1.8 Measuring Adaptive Range

little adaptability. Organizations now spend much time and effort converting more traditional 2-Tier, "smart PC" applications into Web-based applications.

Unfortunately, designing Web-only presentation solutions is equally limiting. Other presentation methods, such as wireless devices (mobile phones or PDAs) and interactive voice response units (IVRs), can't support a full-page Web display and will require expensive and time-consuming development efforts. If consistency across multiple points of interaction is important to your brand, your designers should make sure it can be achieved without significant infrastructure replacement efforts and without rewriting code.

Presentation independence alone, however, doesn't guarantee sufficient adaptability. Infrastructure planners should be very focused on the front end, but if the application-to-application integration issues aren't addressed simultaneously, the result is taller stovepipes with applications that don't fit the adaptive infrastructure concept.

Partitioning. The ability to partition functionality and complexity within the infrastructure is another benefit of adaptability. If the infrastructure cannot be partitioned effectively, the resulting complexity spreads throughout the organization and eventually becomes unmanageable. For success, you must manage the interfaces between applications and between infrastructure components effectively, both for applications used within the enterprise and for those used by external partners.

Integration/reuse. Infrastructure integration and reuse are also measures of adaptability. The typical organization requires a dramatic increase in the reuse of infrastructure code, other technology components, and skills to increase adaptability and speed of deployment. Reusable code is the opposite of legacy code. Whereas most legacy code is difficult to maintain, enhance, and integrate, the most adaptive code has clean, well-documented interfaces. These interfaces enable bits of code to be changed or added without requiring major changes in other code.

Increasingly, you must describe the value proposition for infrastructure directly to the business users in terms of the discrete service levels that they want delivered. By turning to a discussion of service levels, you can influence business users to consider more than just the immediate impact of a single application. You must convince the business to consider the value of adaptability, because it will take more money, effort, and time to deliver than single implementations.

Summary

The following points summarize what's been discussed in this introductory chapter.

- Success depends on having an appropriate focus. You should focus on delivery of infrastructure products, not technological prowess. Any IT organization will find it difficult to differentiate itself based on how effectively it handles systems administration. Delivering basic technology services is like having the lights come on when you hit a switch. The real value you can provide is not in making the lights work, which is expected regardless, but in delivering sharable support services for applications in a way that promotes reuse, cost savings, and agility. This approach means planning for the future, not just catching up to current requirements.

- An "infrastructure product" mentality helps simplify options and drive competencies. Thinking in terms of infrastructure products leads to a delivery mentality. Creating tangible infrastructure products reduces the amount of uncertainty. You should focus on core infrastructure patterns, services, and processes. Then you should look for ways to reuse assets and expertise while emphasizing consistent delivery through people and process improvements. As an example, you might consider hosting a Web service internally so that your business units can share infrastructure resources such as network, server, middleware, and security. Or, you might add value by moving e-Business applications to a chosen outsourcer effectively and efficiently.

- Developing adaptive infrastructure requires cultural change. Successful implementation of adaptive infrastructure will change the relationship between business users and IT, but it should also change a key piece of IT culture: the application developer community. Your efforts will create a new class of workers: Infrastructure planners and developers who will have application developers as their customers.

- IT should team with the business in developing strategic investment priorities for infrastructure beyond e-Business. The typical IT department can develop a suitable infrastructure plan anytime. Developing a plan that reflects and accommodates developments within the business, and then updating and managing that plan, will require close coordination with business managers.

- Reuse is the linchpin of adaptive infrastructure. The concept of reuse does not apply just at the application level. Instead, you must foster reuse at the interface level, among application components, and through directly shared, infrastructure-focused services. A number of adaptive infrastructure concepts facilitate reuse, including adaptive infrastructure services, infrastructure pattern matching, predictive cost modeling, and the role of the infrastructure planner.

Chapter 2

Laying the Foundation

Now that you understand the basics of adaptive infrastructure, the question naturally arises: "How do I start developing an adaptive infrastructure suitable for e-Business and beyond?" As mentioned previously, developing an adaptive infrastructure involves breaking down raw infrastructure into three distinct domains:

- Platforms help you organize your infrastructure components into a basic technology-oriented catalog.
- Patterns help you organize the same components into complete end-to-end solution sets used to satisfy application requirements.
- Services help you package and deliver infrastructure in a way that provides high-level business value for multiple applications.

These three domains arise out of the "raw infrastructure" but are interconnected and work together as a group (see Figure 2.1).

This chapter helps you start organizing infrastructure at the *platform level* by grouping infrastructure components into a distinct set of layers. It also explains how to further organize these components and layers into *services* to provide more complete value to the organization. Many components mentioned in this chapter are already appropriate for the era beyond e-Business, addressing internal and external needs concurrently, while others are more e-Business oriented. You will encounter

How should IT infrastructure deliverables be formulated?

- "Raw Infrastructure" → **Services** — Common Delivery
- → **Patterns** — Common Organization
- → **Platforms** — Common Technologies

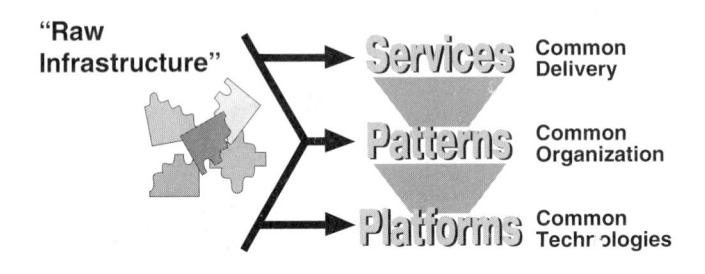

Figure 2.1 The Three Basic Levels of Adaptive Infrastructure

these components again in later chapters as this book explores the concepts of *patterns* and *refined infrastructure designs*.

How to Catalog Components

To organize technology at the platform level, it helps to divide all of your infrastructure components into a set of layers, as shown in Figure 2.2.

Organizing your components into layers based on technology groupings allows your expertise to be focused effectively, rather than being

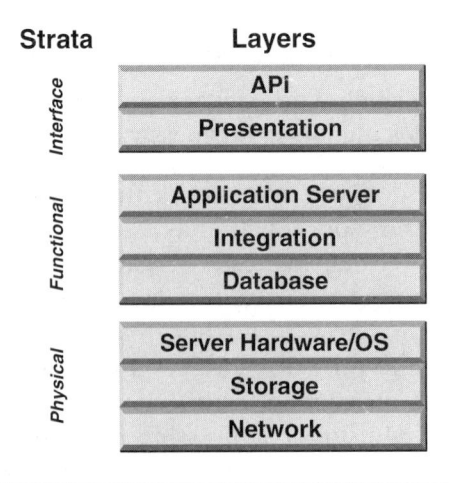

Strata	Layers
Interface	API
	Presentation
Functional	Application Server
	Integration
	Database
Physical	Server Hardware/OS
	Storage
	Network

Figure 2.2 Layers in the Adaptive Infrastructure Platform

distracted by the sheer complexity of it all. Inevitably, your list of infrastructure components will keep changing as often as technology changes. As new technologies arrive, your platform model will help you determine how they can be harnessed, by comparing the function of the new technology to the layers and components in your current platform.

Failing to organize your components this way leaves you with the prospect of planning your infrastructure piecemeal, with too much emphasis on individual technologies and not enough on integration. You might have optimized parts, but not an optimized whole.

To see what a component catalog looks like, turn to Appendix A. You can use this example as part of your initial portfolio of components.

Notice the sheer size of this list. With scores of components and hundreds of example products, the list embodies the complexity of the problem you are trying to solve. Cataloging all of these components will not be a simple task. But it is the unavoidable first step that you must take toward making your infrastructure more adaptive and manageable.

The reason is simple: You can't take 100 items and understand them all without organizing them into categories. Having categories will help you map your technologies to the patterns and services that are so important in developing and delivering adaptive infrastructure.

Physical Components

The physical part of your platform includes server hardware devices and operating systems, any storage infrastructure that you support, and the network infrastructure itself. These layers are outlined on the following pages and explored in greater detail in Chapter 6.

The Network Layer

The network layer is primarily concerned with locating and communicating among entities in a secure and manageable way. This layer provides a universal protocol (TCP/IP) that is essential to an adaptive infrastructure platform. Components in the network layer include transport services (wires, optical fibers, offerings from carriers), firewalls and other security components, routers, switches, proxy servers, caching servers, load balancers, and virtual private network solutions. Alternately, you could separate security into its own layer, if you prefer. Figure 2.3 summarizes the network layer components.

Several important trends may affect the network layer. The continuing evolution of optical fiber, traditional wire, and wireless technologies promises to increase transmission capacities by at least an order of mag-

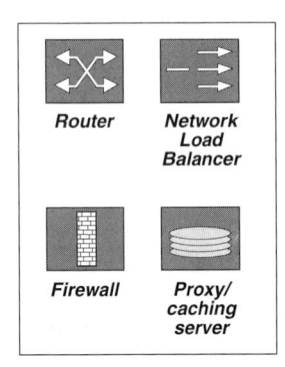

Network Layer Components (Hardware/Software):

Examples:
- Firewalls, intrusion detection systems
- LAN/WAN hardware (e.g., routers, switches)
- Proxy/caching server
- Content delivery network (CDN)
- Network load balancer

Figure 2.3 The Network Layer

nitude every 18 to 36 months. Router and switch improvements promise to not only increase capacities, but also to improve quality of service and traffic handling capabilities. These developments point strongly to a future where traditionally separate voice and data networks converge onto a common TCP/IP infrastructure, analogous to the convergence of traditional and e-Business infrastructures.

Finally, the ongoing trend toward deregulation and consolidation of telecommunications service providers promises to improve service availability and costs, but not without major dislocations and disruptions as unstable business models fail.

The Storage Layer

The storage layer is primarily concerned with handling the need for short-term and long-term storage of data within the organization. This includes the backup and redundancies that are vital to data security and disaster recovery. Figure 2.4 summarizes the storage layer components.

When organizing components in the storage layer, you should consider several broader issues:

- What is your most important need: processing power or storage?
- Where are your systems typically underutilized?
- Where do capacity problems occur more frequently?

In many organizations, storage is where the most performance problems occur. Storage is a major hardware and software component of the shared services infrastructure. Some organizations chose e-Business infrastructure as the site for their initial Storage Area Network (SAN)

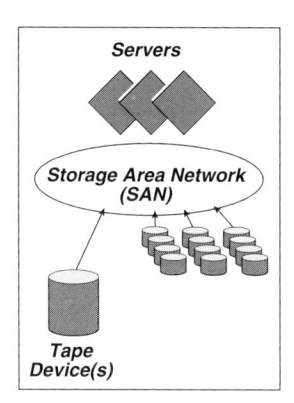

Storage Layer Components (Hardware)

Examples:

- Business continuance hardware (disk and tape)
- Business continuance software (tape backup, mirroring, etc.)
- Host interconnect
- Storage area network (SAN) interconnect
- Storage server

Figure 2.4 The Storage Layer

implementation, addressing scalability and availability issues associated with Web server farms. SANs are a more adaptive approach than traditional disk storage, but have a higher initial cost. Chapter 6 discusses using a SAN as part of an overall pattern design.

The Server Layer

The server layer includes the server hardware and the operating system software that both support applications. Figure 2.5 summarizes the server layer components.

All of these components were marshaled for e-Business purposes, and are equally applicable in the post e-Business world. Notice that this book does not immediately divide server technologies along traditional lines, such as workgroup, midrange, and mainframe platforms. The days of organizing infrastructure around the capabilities of a particular hardware platform are over, since technology evolution is increasingly blurring these differences and hardware is becoming the least-expensive component of application infrastructure. Instead, this book defines server choice in terms of infrastructure patterns, particularly the 1-Tier, 2-Tier, and 3/N-Tier Transact patterns defined in Chapter 3.

This approach is especially crucial for e-Business and beyond, where established enterprise server vendors are challenged by new vendors championing e-Business scenarios. The best approach is a rational one that first leverages your organization's existing infrastructure and uses it in the right places. Using this approach, you can leverage the new server platforms required for specific e-Business applications or services, keep-

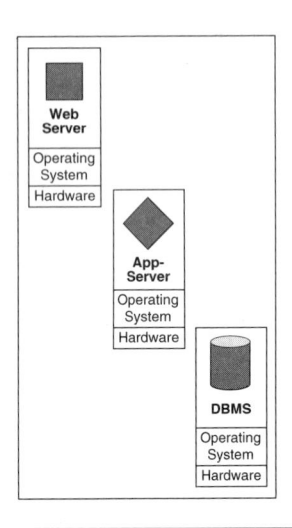

Server Layer Components (Hardware/Software)

Examples:
- Operating system software
- Hardware
- Web server
- Application server
- Database server
- Integration server
- File server/network-attached storage (NAS) ...and other hardware servers

Figure 2.5 The Server Layer

ing in mind future infrastructure convergence and sourcing opportunities that might further restrict platform choices.

Functional Components

The functional part of your platform includes software associated with database systems, integration servers, and application servers. These layers are outlined on the following pages, with more detail in Chapter 7.

The Database Layer

This layer includes all the software components used to deliver database services such as mainstream relational database management products from vendors like Oracle, IBM, and Microsoft, as well as other components such as gateways, middleware, and voice-messaging repositories. Figure 2.6 summarizes the database layer components.

The database market for transactional systems has been relatively stable in recent years. Despite this stability, a proliferation of applications such as data warehousing, knowledge management, and customer care have moved the focus beyond individual transactions and across the enterprise. These applications, in turn, have increased the demand for integrated access to previously independent data stores such as relational databases, object databases, e-mail, and spreadsheets. Specialized data

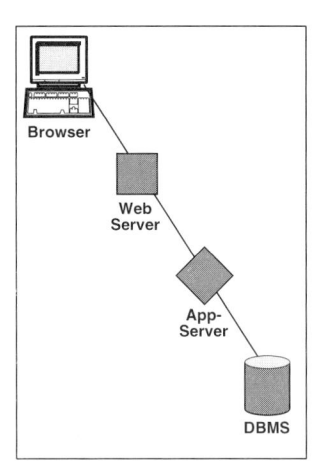

Database Layer Components (Software)

Examples:
- DBMS products (software)
    - Oracle
    - DB2
    - SQL 2000
- Database gateways
- Data access middleware
- Voice messaging store

Figure 2.6 The Database Layer

stores will continue to support unique applications (e.g., data warehousing) by enhancing performance and supporting a variety of data types.

From a component standpoint, most organizations approach the database layer by choosing a particular DBMS server platform and sticking to it. However, some users cannot make so simple a choice, either because individual applications demand particular products, or because technology enhancements or pricing changes introduce new options.

As e-Business and traditional environments converge, your choices might be more controllable, because e-Business software vendors typically provide only limited support for legacy platforms, with most applications limiting database support to the major vendors. Nevertheless, using a pattern-based analysis, as described in this book, can provide a clearer range of options and associated use cases.

For example, since many database-driven Web sites need a read-only database (the Web Publish pattern), some organizations use a different solution for Web publishing than for read/write transactional applications (the 3/N-Tier Transact pattern). The Web Publish choice can be optimized for scale-out design, with many copies of the underlying data, rather than for transactional integrity. Memory-resident solutions might be more useful in e-Business cases requiring smaller but more frequently accessed read-only databases, such as simple catalogs and lookup tables. Chapter 4 of this book provides examples of how to refine these two major e-Business patterns.

The Integration Layer

This layer contains all components that provide integration services between back-end applications and Web servers, application servers, or database servers. Components typically include adapter toolkits, application adapters, integration servers, EDI gateways, file exchange servers, and more. The integration function could be internally focused, such as Enterprise Application Integration (EAI), or externally focused, such as inter-enterprise integration (IEI). Figure 2.7 summarizes the integration layer components.

Integration servers provide a way to move beyond e-Business by integrating e-Business applications with enterprise and legacy systems at the application layer. Application servers are used to build applications, and integration servers are used to integrate applications once they are built. These two types of products are the main drivers in a rapidly converging middleware market. And both are crucial to maintaining a robust, flexible infrastructure.

Good infrastructure planners use application server infrastructure for building application functionality, but separate integration server infrastructure to integrate these applications. While generally appropriate for most integration problems, this approach doesn't work for everything. The need for state-handling and transaction-handling features on application servers will cause the application server and integration server platforms to converge eventually. Ironically, the evolution of Web services indicates that this convergence may actually become virtual at times. Applications will call on Web services that could be anywhere,

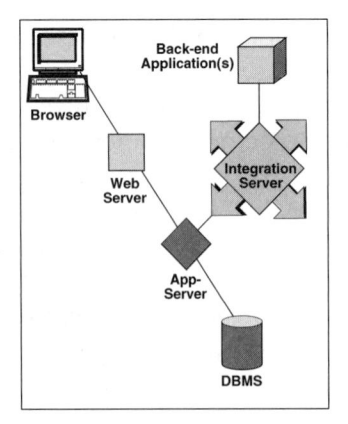

Integration Layer Components

Examples:
- Enterprise application integration (EAI) server
- Inter-enterprise integration (IEI) server
- Application adapter/adapter toolkit
- Integration transport software
- Process modeler/execution engine
- Computer telephony integration (CTI) server
- EDI gateway
- File exchange server
- Integration transport server
- Middleware encryption software
- Process modeler/execution engine

Figure 2.7 The Integration Layer

with the only requirement being that the services comply with Universal Description, Discovery and Integration (UDDI), XML, Simple Object Access Protocol (SOAP), and related standards.

The Application Server Layer

The application server layer contains the software that supports business logic. Examples are 3/N-Tier applications involving J2EE/EJB-based products such as IBM WebSphere and BEA WebLogic, along with Microsoft Windows 2000/.NET Server and related Microsoft products. Figure 2.8 summarizes the application server layer components.

As opposed to the server operating system software discussed earlier, the application server layer contains software that offers higher-level application development and service functionality. Keep in mind that this layer does not contain the applications themselves. Instead, it provides front-line components upon which the applications are directly built.

The rapid ascendance of e-Business, along with the realization that business logic must reside on the server, not the client, propelled the application server to center stage. When this market was in its early growth stage and crowded with products, business units often selected incompatible products for different projects. Today, organizations must choose between products based on Microsoft's COM+/DNA/.NET or Sun's J2EE as their enterprise application or integration architecture.

Given current trends, most larger organizations will have both application and integration servers and will need strategies for maintaining

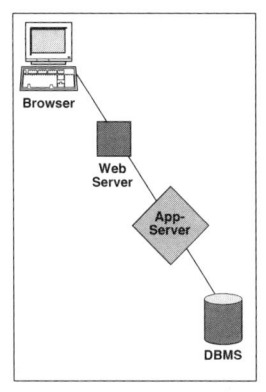

Application Server Layer Components (Software)

Examples:

Java (J2EE) Application Servers:
- IBM WebSphere
- BEA WebLogic
- iPlanet (SunOne)

.Net Application Server:
- Microsoft Windows 2000/.NET Server
- Microsoft Visual Studio.NET
- Microsoft BizTalk Server

Infrastructure planning and deployment tools

Figure 2.8 The Application Server Layer

the least variety possible. This model forms the core of the discussion on the 3/N-Tier Transact pattern outlined in Chapter 3 and the e-Business pattern design covered in Chapter 7 of this book.

Interface Components

The interface components of your platform include application programming interfaces (APIs) and presentation layers. These layers are outlined on the following pages and explored in depth in Chapter 8.

The Presentation Layer

The presentation layer offers a variety of hardware and software tools. This layer includes interface devices for desktop or mobile environments, ranging from PCs running Windows applications or Web browsers to mobile phones, PDAs, browsers, and telephones. Presentation server components are also in this layer, including terminal servers, streaming media servers, interactive TV, e-mail servers, and Web servers. This layer can support presentation methods such as interactive voice response (IVR), wireless application protocol (WAP), and computer telephony integration (CTI)—each with its own hardware and software options. Figure 2.9 summarizes the presentation layer components.

As e-Business and traditional enterprise initiatives converge, new use cases are accelerating presentation layer variety, since users increasingly need to access information and applications in many different ways. Component selection involves picking the right presentation model for

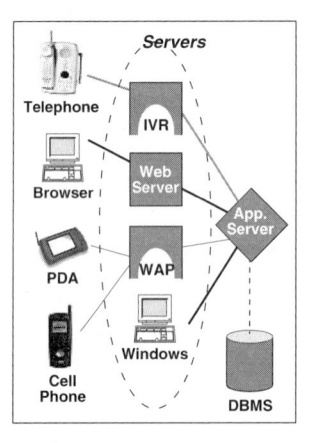

Presentation Layer Components (Software/Hardware)

Examples:
- Web server
- Wireless Application Protocol (WAP) server
- Integrated voice response (IVR)
- Voice/telephone
- Terminal server
- Streaming server
- Interactive TV
- E-mail MTA
- Telephone
- Desktop/notebook hardware
- Personal digital assistant (PDA)
- Embedded services (e.g., in vehicle systems, intelligent appliances)

Figure 2.9 The Presentation Layer

the right application. To provide agility, your infrastructure might need to support, or integrate with, a number of different presentation models. Today's applications must support tomorrow's presentation devices.

This situation means you must be prepared to support multiple points of interaction (POI) for customers, partners, employees, and suppliers. Content can be transmitted through a Web browser, PDA, short message service, cell phone, or one of the many Internet devices rapidly arriving on the market. Tomorrow's applications will need more than one user interface for essentially the same information.

For this reason, one of your key goals in the post e-Business era should be to integrate systems and present a consistent user experience across increasingly varied points of interaction. Tying application logic only to a Web interface defeats this goal. You might have encountered this problem before with Windows-centric 2-Tier client-server designs, which made it very expensive to move to a Web interface.

A new infrastructure approach should change the behavior of application developers so that multiple points of interaction are designed in. Organizations must cleanly separate presentation logic from application logic to promote proper 3/N-Tier design principles.

The Application Programming Interface (API) Layer

One of the key principles of adaptive infrastructure is the idea of breaking out APIs as a distinctly separate layer in the infrastructure stack. Creating a separate layer for APIs makes it easier to separate applications from the infrastructure, which is essential to avoid stovepipes and create a shared, reusable infrastructure. Figure 2.10 summarizes the API layer components.

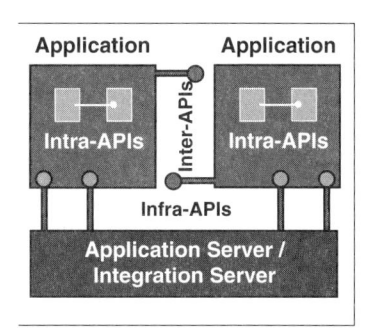

API Layer Components (Software)

Intra-API—exposes business logic used within an application
   Examples: COM IDL, EJB IDL

Inter-API—exposes business logic used between applications
   Examples: Rational Rose

Infra-API—exposes infrastructure services to application and infrastructure planners
   Examples: J2EE, .NET, LDAP

Figure 2.10 The API Layer

In the past, programmers wrote applications from the business logic all the way down to the operating system. Currently, however, most application developers are insulated from the operating system by at least one layer of "packaged" infrastructure tools such as CICS, Tuxedo, Forte, PowerBuilder, J2EE/EJB, or COM+/.NET. However, the application developer must still fill in the large gap between the packaged infrastructure and the business logic at the core of the application. In addition, the application developer must become adept at tuning and debugging the infrastructure itself.

Much of the work involved in creating an adaptive infrastructure occurs at the API level. To be successful, you must create a separation in the job functions of infrastructure developers and application developers by recognizing that APIs fall into three distinct categories:

- Infra-APIs include low-level technology services, such as security, naming, or object invocation, that application developers and infrastructure developers use to create business logic.

- Intra-APIs help business logic communicate within individual applications, and they are typically not exposed to other applications. For this reason, Intra-APIs are created and managed only by the application's developers.

- Inter-APIs help business logic communicate between applications. They expose the application business logic to be used by other applications. Since this logic affects other applications, Inter-APIs should be defined and managed by infrastructure developers.

Application and infrastructure developers must create a formal policy and framework for creating, cataloging, and storing APIs. Infrastructure developers must combine the application requirements and the principals generated by the architectural group to design efficient, secure, and manageable interfaces.

Other Components?

Other infrastructure components that don't fit neatly into the preceding categories should be mapped as a separate component layer if they are:

- Reused often
- Politically correct, i.e., adding them causes no problems in IT

You might need to incorporate more components and create more layers over time as innovation continues. For example, in Figure 2.11, management tools exist for each layer's components, but overall management can be a separate service.

As application tools continue moving into the infrastructure, anticipate changes in layer structure. For example, the application server layer defined earlier in this chapter includes only user application services such as transaction servers. As more collaboration servers and analytic servers start executing business logic in a way that is reused across multiple applications, you will want to add these components to the application server layer, as well. Web services promise to take this case to the extreme, with hundreds of services joining the infrastructure.

Other Layers?

As you add other common sets of components to your complete infrastructure model, you should create a separate layer and include them in your component portfolio if any of the following applies:

- They are often referred to as a group (such as security or management).
- Including them will not overly complicate politics in IT.
- Including them helps simplify infrastructure complexity, with no more than 10 layers.
- The components will not form a service themselves.

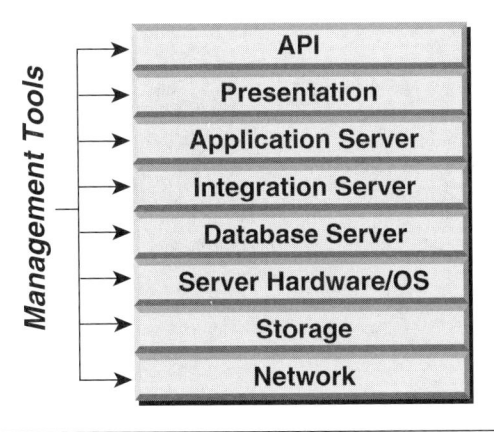

Figure 2.11 Adding New Components

For example, security can be used as a shared layer by isolation, identity, and permissions infrastructure, as discussed in Chapter 5. Figure 2.12 illustrates the concept of adding a security layer to the overall infrastructure stack.

Instead of just creating layers, however, think about creating services: physically reusable instances of product combinations to be used by multiple applications. Components from multiple layers can be used for a service, even if they do not normally fit together in a layer. For example, don't put security databases or directories in the new security layer, especially if they might be used for more than security purposes.

Developing Adaptive Services

While the definition of layers and components is a significant first step in infrastructure planning, it still isn't the entire solution. A large part of adaptive infrastructure strategy hinges on the way that you define *services*. Having reusable services that applications can share efficiently is a key element that will make your infrastructure more adaptive and agile. As you design patterns (end-to-end blueprints), you will also be defining shared infrastructure services that make it easier and cheaper to design, develop, and deploy applications. With so much new development having been conducted in the e-Business arena, and the likelihood that much of it will continue in the post e-Business era, you have a unique opportunity to fit in a few services for best reuse and simplicity.

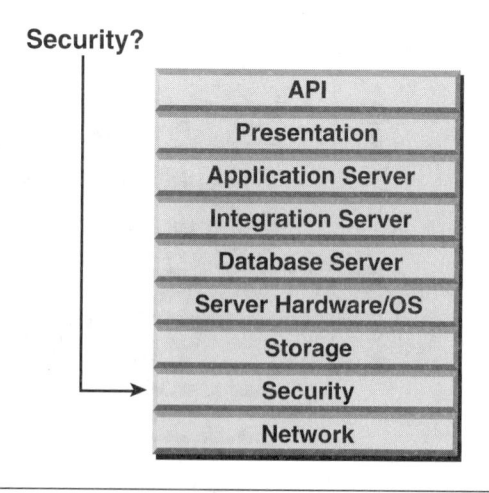

Security?

| API |
| Presentation |
| Application Server |
| Integration Server |
| Database Server |
| Server Hardware/OS |
| Storage |
| Security |
| Network |

Figure 2.12 Adding a Security Layer

Understanding the Concept

To better understand the concept of adaptive services, think back to the definition of infrastructure first outlined in Chapter 1 and illustrated again in Figure 2.13. The traditional view of infrastructure is that it is something purely physical, such as the roads and bridges that support our transportation system, or the cable, hubs, and routers that support our networks.

Instead of thinking in terms of physical hardware, you should realize that some of the most crucial components of infrastructure might actually be considered *services*, similar to water, electricity, gas, and phone. Even though multiple houses in a subdivision might share utilities through the physical infrastructure, the idea of services implies more than just a technology component. It also implies a set of processes and people that provide additional support, such as the phone company, the light company, and the gas company.

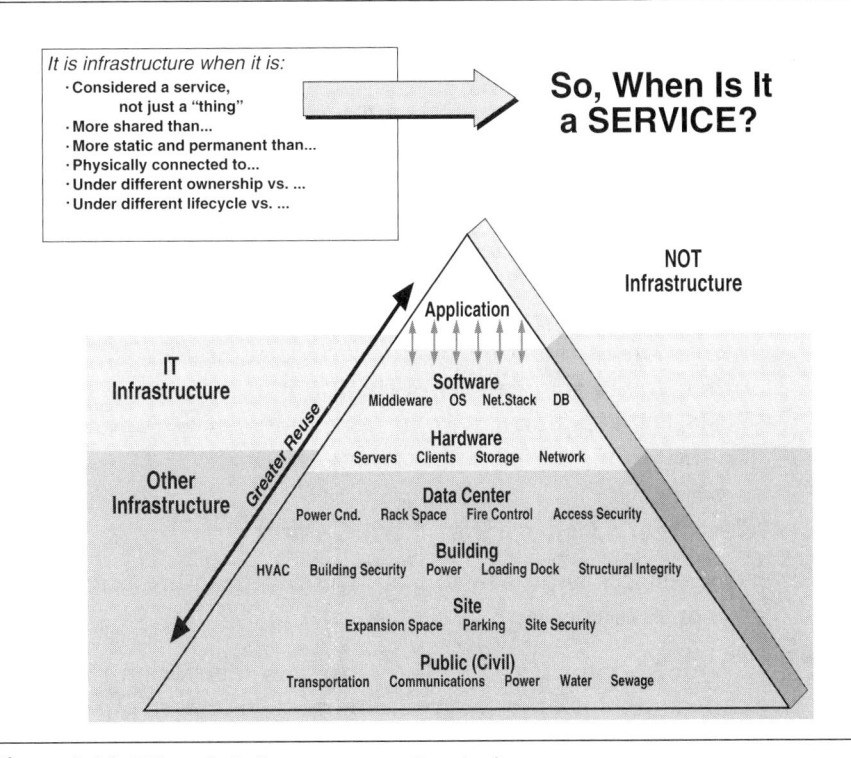

Figure 2.13 When Is Infrastructure a Service?

Applying the Model

The same kind of service model applies to adaptive infrastructure services in your IT department. To be successful, adaptive infrastructure services must provide:

- Sharing. An adaptive infrastructure service is one that is shared by multiple applications. If it's not shared, it can still be infrastruture, but it won't really be a service.
- Stability. An adaptive infrastructure service should be more stable, more permanent, and less likely to change than the applications it supports.
- Separate ownership and lifecycle. An adaptive infrastructure service is distinct from the structure it supports in terms of its ownership. In this case, the application developers don't own the service. The infrastructure developers own it and are responsible for the lifecycle of creating it, improving it, and marketing it to applications teams in order to make sure that new applications use it. As a service matures, operations support plays a bigger role.

Remember that a service is not just a physical object but also a collection of processes and people that make the components work well, day in and day out. As a result, services should have long-term funding models that go beyond the basic up-front installation costs, often employing usage-based pricing models to hide the up-front investment costs.

Adaptive infrastructure services differ from traditional infrastructure services in important ways. First, they allow you to change the implementation of one side of the service interface, without affecting the other side in any way, other than to improve service levels or decrease costs. Second, an adaptive infrastructure service is much more likely to be shared by multiple applications.

Benefits of Adaptive Infrastructure Services

The services approach to adaptive infrastructure brings with it a number of key benefits.

Reduced complexity. The more you transform to a service-based architecture, the fewer raw components you need to organize or build from scratch to deliver applications. Soon, all you need to do is link services together. Thus, you might actually build an N-Tier application from something like six services, instead of 40 components. That kind of modularity automatically brings with it efficiencies and incredible cost savings.

Performance improvements. Defining infrastructure as a set of services helps control the type of service levels you are providing to the rest of the organization. If it is designed correctly, you can gradually improve performance for your customers by making sure that service levels are always more than adequate to ensure applications run well.

Increased agility. Through more effective use of the API layer, specifically Infra-APIs that connect to shared infrastructure and Inter-APIs that connect applications, you can decouple important services from the application, freeing each application from the burden of supporting the service itself. Using this method makes it much quicker and easier to design, develop, and deploy mission-critical applications. Instead of having each application perform its own user authentication, for example, that function can be provided by an Identity Infrastructure service, as described in Chapter 5.

Different organizations have different approaches for defining adaptive services. This book provides definitions and examples of services that large organizations are using successfully for e-Business, because it is very likely that services forged will continue to be highly useful in a world where e-Business and traditional business increasingly converge. However, no one can provide an absolute definition of what infrastructure is or what shared infrastructure services are. In fact, almost anything can be a service, including many non-automated operations, which involve no physical infrastructure at all, but only business processes performed by people.

Physical strata components in the network, storage, and server layers are more obviously infrastructure and the decision on sharing these should go along with the software decisions. With this concept in mind, you can start taking a look at what's involved in developing adaptive infrastructure services.

Shifting Services to the Infrastructure

The most important work involved in developing an adaptive infrastructure is to make sure that key services with a potential for sharing are shifted out of the application layer and into the infrastructure layer, where they can be more efficiently shared and reused. This method requires a thorough analysis to determine which software is considered the *infrastructure* and which software is considered the *application*.

As key services are identified and moved into the infrastructure layer, they must fit the definition of infrastructure provided above in terms of permanence, ownership, and lifecycle, or else they will be unsuccessful in their role as shared infrastructure services. If successful, they will become more adaptive, manageable, and reusable, saving your organization considerable amounts of money and time and creating agility in the process.

Of all the tasks involved in developing an adaptive infrastructure, however, this challenge is the biggest one you will face. The reason lies in the whole issue of ownership and lifecycle: the way that adaptive infrastructure services shift responsibility out of the application domain and into the infrastructure domain.

Figure 2.14 shows that you can't just shift the physical technology or code. You must also shift the responsibility for designing it, building it, employing it, maintaining it, and upgrading it. Everything, including technology, people, and profits, must come over the line. You must also plan to market these services to application teams. Otherwise, you face a strong possibility of the services going unused and the application teams creating their own variants. Making this shift happen will require political as well as promotional skills, as discussed in Chapter 4.

Decoupling the Lifecycles

One of the greatest advantages of adaptive infrastructure is its ability to change a service without having to change all the applications that depend on it. Conversely, your inability to get this part of the model right can be the greatest inhibitor to adaptive infrastructure, causing the

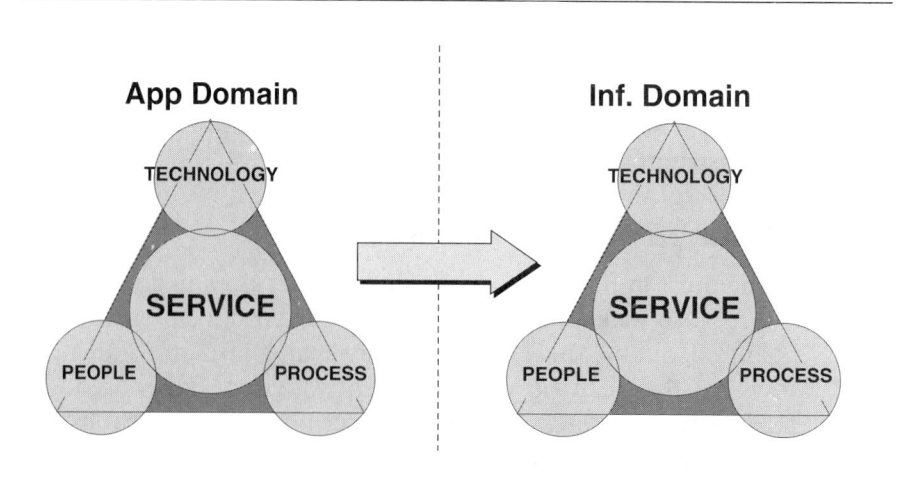

Figure 2.14 Shifting Service into the Infrastructure

application and service functionality to get intertwined, so that changes in service functions have unforeseen repercussions in the applications themselves.

In theory, you should be able to change your databases, servers, or the network without ever affecting the applications that depend on them. Theory and practice are often different, however. In practice, you might not be able to change database management systems without moving to a new application version. Moreover, instead of managing design and installation of new components, the job of infrastructure designers will be to manage capacity on existing services.

To get the desired level of independence requires a high degree of *decoupling* between the lifecycles of both the service and the application. This decoupling must occur at all stages in the lifecycles, including design, build, deploy, and upgrade.

A Decoupled Web Services Architecture

The decoupled approach can be seen in the recent proliferation of Web services architectures. Here is how the interface embedded in the consuming application adheres to the low coupling requirements of an ideal adaptive infrastructure service:

- Minimal. The interface hard-codes Simple Object Access Protocol (SOAP) over HTTP. This method involves very simple protocols, with minimal noncomplex coding requirements.

- Standard/Stable. HTTP provides a standard and very stable interface. XML will be a widespread standard, while SOAP is also a standard and increasingly stable interface. Universal Description, Discovery, and Integration (UDDI) publish/find/bind will be an increasingly stable option.

- Bootstrap Capability. UDDI's find/bind mechanism and the Web Services Description Language (WSDL) could be used to bootstrap a more complex interface than SOAP for the actual interaction with the service.

When decoupling a service from related applications, make sure you decouple the right pieces, specifically service elements that can be shared by the widest possible audience. When you look at all the pieces of an application, you must ask yourself: Which part is the application and which part is the infrastructure?

The idea of sharing and reusability is critical when developing adaptive infrastructure services. If you remove an infrastructure service from an application, but only that one application ever uses the service, then what have you gained? Not much. The idea is to pull out common elements that many applications need to use. This approach can mean the difference between a stovepipe infrastructure, with one hardware server per application, and a more shared adaptive infrastructure service, where multiple applications or application components can share servers.

The elegance of your solution depends on how well you can operate the infrastructure below the service interface. If you can't upgrade it transparently and incrementally, you will have problems. However, it also depends on how you design the interfaces between the application and the service provider. Luckily, the TCP/IP stack, which is the interface between applications and the network, has been fairly stable over the past decade and can serve as a model for solving this problem.

Examining the Network Model

Let us clarify the fundamental difference between what application developers often call component or object-oriented architecture and this book's definition of a service-oriented architecture. Our philosophy is that the interface to a service and the implementation of a service *must be physically separated by a network*.

Although traditional object-oriented and component architectures have always stressed the importance of logical separation between interface and implementation, these architectures had intrinsic flaws. For example, in a traditional object-oriented architecture, many component objects were physically incorporated into the application itself. If someone wanted to change a component, it required rebuilding, recompiling, or relinking the application. The amount of work involved effectively prevented the component from ever being changed.

Dynamic link libraries (DLLs) lessened the rebuilding issue to some degree, but since the DLL was still physically incorporated in the computer containing the application, any changes to DLLs must be implemented on each device individually.

An adaptive services architecture effectively separates control between the use of a service and the implementation of a system by separating the two over some kind of network. This arrangement allows the *service provider* to be physically decoupled from the *service consumer* so that the service provider rarely needs to come on-site to change any aspect of the service. This arrangement is essentially a prerequisite for Web services.

To make this arrangement work best, the service interface (the physical component that connects the consumer and provider) should be kept as simple as possible. For example, a wireless connection for television or phone is the simplest. The adapter and transceiver are on the premises, but no wiring connects them. All you need is electricity or batteries for a cell phone. It has no plug for the service anymore, unlike landlines and cable TV service, which you must plug in physically.

Consider a more IT-centric example: a managed network service provider installing its own router on the premises. The managed service provider doesn't let customers modify their on-premises equipment. In fact, tampering with the equipment typically voids the service contract. Sometimes, such on-premises equipment is locked in a closet or box that only the provider can access. Even so, a clear interface or demarcation line, such as an Ethernet port or serial cable, allows customer equipment to plug into the service.

This same model also applies to adaptive infrastructure services. For these services to work well, the service interface on the consumer side should be as minimal, as standard (not customized), and as stable as possible. Any change to the interface should not require rebuilding or retesting the applications in which the interface is embedded. In a sense, the embedded, hard-coded part of the interface should be a bootstrap interface. It should have just enough intelligence to plug into a network, access a "full interface" service, perhaps download a more robust interface, and go from there. Everything possible about the interface should be as dynamic and run-time configurable as possible.

Decoupling is aided by the API layers identified earlier in this chapter. Infra-APIs and Inter-APIs are specifically developed and maintained by the infrastructure team for use by application developers. The third type of API (Intra-API) is used only within applications by the application developers themselves. Figure 2.15 shows how the API layer architecture works in practice.

ASA API Layer Architecture

Figure 2.15 API Layer Architecture

Service Interfaces and Service Level Agreements

Once you decouple services from the application and create APIs, what remains in the application is really a *service interface*, as shown in Figure 2.16.

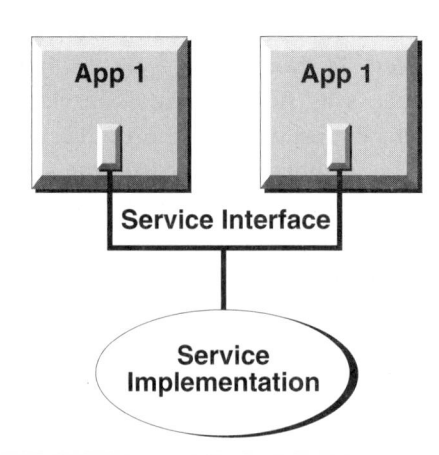

Figure 2.16 The Service Interface

This interface is more than just an API issue; it is also a contractual issue. Service interfaces involve political, power, and control boundaries. All of the issues surrounding the delegation of authority manifest themselves when a service interface is created or modified. Questions arise as to who owns this particular function, and who is responsible for it.

Creating a service interface, however, gives you better control over the *service levels* that you can deliver to the organization. Defining service levels on a per-project basis will help make sure that your infrastructure can provide the quality, speed, and scalability demanded by the business for each application deployed. Likewise, they will help you better understand and communicate the limits of your infrastructure so that application developers, other IT personnel, and even business people are less likely to deploy applications that will overload the system.

The emerging model for this relationship is a service contract between the consumers and providers of adaptive infrastructure services that specifies certain "service level attributes" governing the speed or capacity of the service. One part of the contract spells out the functions and information provided under the contract (the process model), while the other part of the contract spells out the performance terms promised under the contract (the service levels).

Establishing a service contract also helps you establish the owner. Even though a service might be needed, it is never going to work without an owner to provide budget funding and support at some level. You can't just propagate a paper standard and hope everyone follows it. It needs to be centralized by ownership. A more detailed discussion of people and funding issues is included in Chapter 4.

Where to Create Service Boundaries

The essence of infrastructure adaptiveness is to foresee those parts of applications that will need to change independently. For best results, look for high rates of change in:

- Component technologies (e.g., server and storage hardware)
- Supply process and suppliers
- Network and middleware
- Policy and implementation
- Service name and location

Knowing what to externalize or separate from applications is the fundamental skill required for adaptive infrastructure. Business, application development, and infrastructure planning teams must all work toward adaptiveness, and they all must agree on what processes, people, and technologies are involved. Interfaces should be loosely coupled. Proper decoupling among layers enables not only changeability, but also scalability.

For example, in Figure 2.17 and Figure 2.18, moving Step 302 out of the application and into the infrastructure requires a service interface to replace the deleted step. The application developer responsible for the implementation of Step 302 is now simply responsible for invoking the interface to the service, which must still be embedded in the application. For adaptive infrastructure services to work, you must minimize the amount of embedded interface code and maximize the use of stable standards.

Keeping it Real

When defining services, you can conceivably have an infinite number of services with an infinite number of APIs to be consumed. That kind of situation clearly cannot be supported. So keeping the number of sevices (and APIs) as low as possible makes a huge difference to your organization.

The best service design narrows the list of service options to a few major choices. For example, you might ask yourself: "What are the five things I absolutely have to provide?" Focus on the upper and lower ends of those requirements, and then determine what can be accomplished realistically in the near term, medium term, and long term. Designing a service that is too difficult to build or run is not worth the trouble. Start with something that can work, get it working and used, and then

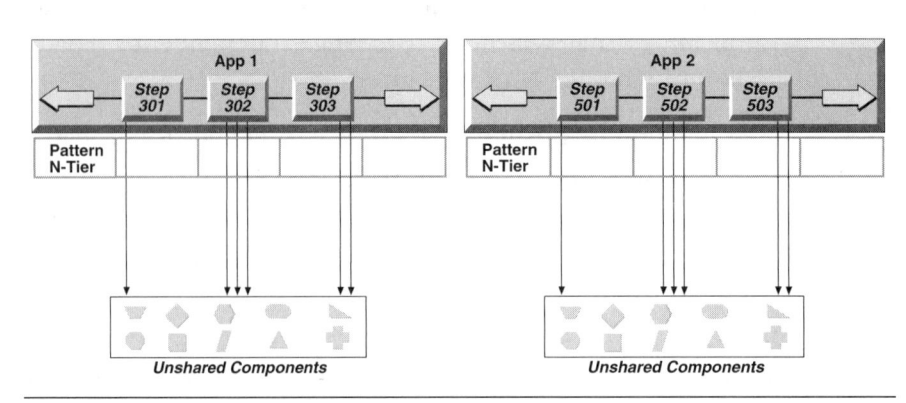

Figure 2.17 Defining Service Boundaries (Before)

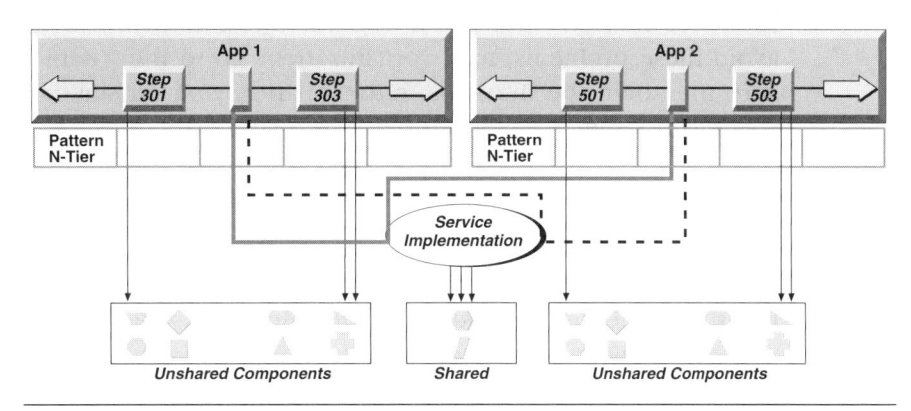

Figure 2.18 Defining Service Boundaries (After)

expand from that base. The services that work best are those that repeatedly provide real value to customers.

Another pitfall to avoid is using too many different interface standards. For example, suppose you have an application that uses hard-coded SQL calls to a particular database. What happens if the client decides they no longer want customer information directly in the database, but want it controlled by another application? This decision means one of two things. You either have to write a SQL gateway for the application, and then retarget and retest the SQL database calls, or you have to recode the application extensively.

Whenever possible, use a single interface mechanism to reach any kind of service process or data. Build a general service interface up front that masks whatever you are ultimately reaching out to, whether it's a database, an application, or a Web service.

As you move from a hard-coded service model such as static SQL calls toward a looser coupling, you will see a reduced impact when you make changes to applications. By defining service boundaries, you avoid having to retest and recompile the application every time you make a change. All you have to do is restart the application. In some cases, you can even have zero downtime for consumers; for instance, if you are just changing the implementation of a Web service.

If it's done correctly, you can completely decouple changes in a service implementation from other changes to the application. However, one thing that you don't want to change is the interface specification itself, whether on the consumer side or the provider side. Changing the specification might require recoding and recompiling the application.

Therefore, it is important to be sure that you are choosing interface standards that are very stable and are not going to change much. To avoid these problems, many organizations go to the trouble of making sure they own the interface, rather than relying on standard interface specifications, at least for internal cases.

Design Guidelines

Now that you understand the concepts and techniques behind adaptive infrastructure services, the question naturally arises: "Where do I begin?" The following guidelines will help you get started finding logical service opportunities and turning them into real services that will move you closer to the goal of adaptive infrastructure:

- Snapshot of the current state. Conduct an inventory to portfolio existing services and determine where some services might prove useful.
- Create interfaces. Put into place interfaces, including both APIs and people-process workflow handoffs, that better insulate the consumers of the service from implementation changes on the service provider side of the interface.
- Define service levels. Upgrade and expand the service provider side of the interface to improve service levels.

You must do a thorough job of assessing the current application inventory to get a good feel for the API issues. You need to understand which standards are available and which calls are being made, as well. You should also have a good idea of what kind of integration is required and which services are fragmented.

For example, you could choose between hundreds of different methods for conducting file transfers. If you find yourself in this position, you should seriously consider creating a transactional integration service that handles bulk inter-process communication, not just single transactions. Your inventory of integration applications should tell you how much of an opportunity you have for improvement. You might end up with a very clear map with a few well-defined interactions, or with a map that is extremely complex, which has no unifying threads at all.

In addition to defining functional interfaces, you should also capture the use cases. How reliable is the current file transfer protocol (FTP) service? How quickly can I change or add a new application into the FTP flow? What is the latency between generating a request and getting a response? Capture this information, because you can use it to design, package, and sell the new unified transactional integration service to skeptical business managers.

How to Apply Services to New Applications

Once you create a service, some art is still involved in applying the new service to new applications.

First, you must redefine patterns to use services where applicable. Even if some implementations of a pattern won't use the service, making a connection between patterns and services at least gives people an idea what patterns could potentially use the service. For example, an Identity Infrastructure is a good way to provide a single sign-on for Web applications. Therefore, you might specify that all applications in the Web Publish pattern use this service, but make it optional for other patterns to use the same service. Limiting use to one pattern can help application developers get accustomed to the new service, thus increasing the chances they might use it voluntarily on other patterns.

Figure 2.19 shows how an identity infrastructure service might be applied. Applying a service at the pattern level makes it available to all applications using that pattern.

Over time, some application patterns will evolve into complete end-to-end service architectures. As this happens, services will increas-

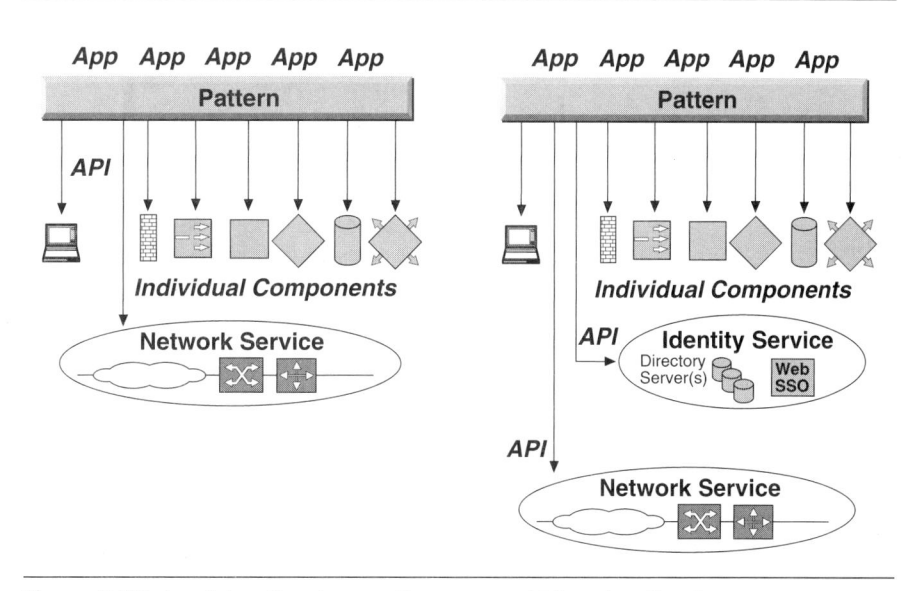

Figure 2.19 Applying Services to Patterns and New Applications

ingly be used in the assimilation process and become like a component in application pattern inventory. When this happens, assimilating a new application will increasingly become a process of mapping onto a set of services via interfaces with service levels.

The most evolved case of a pattern using services is the Web Publish pattern shown in Figure 2.20. This pattern uses Identity and Isolation services as discussed more fully in Chapter 5. This pattern is almost entirely composed of just a few major services or provided by a single Web hosting service.

With this approach to services, a whole pattern can be outsourced easily. For example, once you provide HTML application code and data, Web hosting service providers can do the rest. Rough market conditions in the early 2000s helped force a consolidation of Web service providers that was necessary to create a long-term market for these services. Ironically, these services will be provided by broader-based service organizations that were formed after the merger and acquisition of Web service providers by traditional outsourcers and telecom service providers.

The Web hosting service model can teach you a lot about how to operate and charge for the same kinds of services inside your business. If you run a Web hosting service internally, you can adopt many of the same operational and pricing practices as Internet service providers and alter them as necessary. Later, if asked to benchmark your service against outside vendors, you'll find it easier to differentiate your service

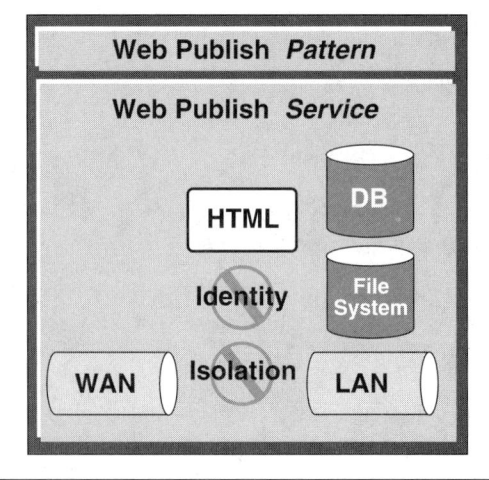

Figure 2.20 When a Whole Pattern Becomes a Single Service

offering or to compete with outside vendors, because you will have already done the market research. While having to compete with outside vendors sounds challenging, it will be an increasing requirement as business demands for efficiency and cost-effectiveness increase.

Over time, a service-focused approach will help make application development and infrastructure planning easier. When fully realized, a services approach should make it as easy as inserting the appropriate code and data into existing services, and then turning on a switch to make it all run.

Summary

This chapter helped you start thinking about ways to organize infrastructure components. Once you organize components into layers, you will have a portfolio that you can immediately start showing to the business or to application developers.

As new technologies arise, this new component structure will help you organize your thinking about it to the point where you can easily identify the proper roles and infrastructure "fit" for new components. As part of the categorization process, you might identify which expert is responsible for the new technology or who would be assigned to conduct additional research and analysis tasks.

Using this method is logical and matches the way the real world actually works. Most people, building any kind of architecture, do technology analysis quite well. They often realize, however, that analysis is not enough. You must also convert technology choices into real running solutions and create adaptive infrastructure services as necessary to improve the reuse of such technologies.

In general, to best define an adaptive infrastructure service, you should:

- Use the network as a guide in service design, application, and pricing.
- Be prepared to deal with the shift in power over the service from the application realm to the infrastructure realm.
- Keep an accurate inventory of service users to gauge impact of service changes.
- Strive for loose coupling between applications and infrastructure.
- Look to outsourcers for models and service suppliers.

- Remember that, just like outsourcers, any internal service provider must set aside an allowance for marketing the service.

Now that you understand how to think about technology in terms of component layers and services, you need to understand better how these get used in particular application cases, which is where the concept of patterns becomes useful. Chapter 3 will introduce the concept of patterns, and Chapters 5-8 will show how to refine pattern designs that emerged from e-Business and will continue to be critical beyond e-Business.

Chapter 3

Identifying and Using Patterns

The fundamental concepts presented so far are quite useful from the standpoint of organizing infrastructure. But they don't help much when someone wants a new Web, wireless, or other type of application deployed and needs a full range of cost estimates and delivery dates.

Instead of cobbling together a hasty response, an adaptive infrastructure strategy gives you the ability to reply quickly and accurately with a set of proven options. Using a blueprint that you have already tested, you can reply in a matter of hours with detailed plans, architecture diagrams, costs, and schedules.

The key to this tour de force is the idea of "patterns," which are complete, predesigned, end-to-end solution blueprints that can be quickly molded to fit the latest business requirements. By identifying and creating a series of reusable infrastructure patterns, you will be prepared to handle most of the application requests that come your way.

Your adaptive infrastructure strategy starts paying off when you can identify basic infrastructure patterns and see how easily they can be adapted to describe the existing applications within your organization. This chapter summarizes the nine major patterns typically found in the IT world, and then devotes extra scrutiny to the two patterns most common to e-Business: Web Publish and 3/N-Tier Transact. These patterns were highlighted not only for their role in e-Business, but for their staying power as the world moves beyond e-Business. You can use the pattern definitions and concepts described in this chapter to simplify your own infrastructure planning and make application development easier.

What Are Patterns?

Technology and business evolution can wreak havoc on your infrastructure in many ways. It can happen when you try to consolidate incompatible hardware and software infrastructures after a merger or acquisition. Or when you try to create an enterprisewide intranet to enhance workplace collaboration. Globalization efforts can easily descend into chaos. And each new application that you deploy can bring with it new infrastructure challenges or just further add to the chaos.

Yet it doesn't have to be this way. If your infrastructure is planned and maintained properly, new applications can be incorporated rapidly and efficiently.

This outcome is made possible through the identification and use of patterns. As outlined in Figure 3.1, the goal of a pattern-based architecture is to create infrastructure that is reusable across multiple applications. Instead of having stovepipes, in which each application has its own unique infrastructure requirements, you can have a shared infra-

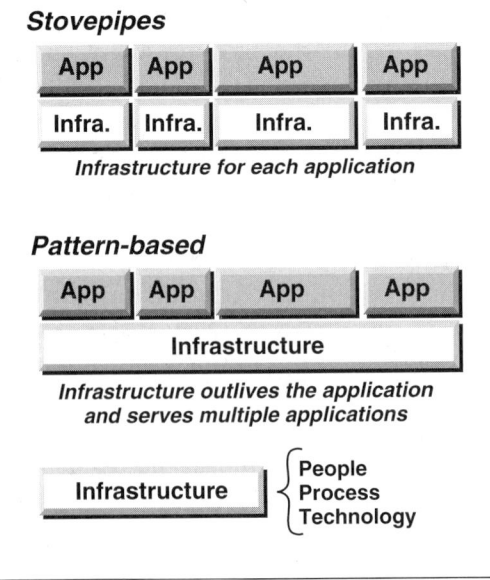

Figure 3.1 Goals of a Pattern-based Architecture

structure that is truly independent of individual applications and that outlives the applications.

As mentioned before, the best model for this paradigm is the network layer, which once was tied intimately to application architectures. With the rise of TCP/IP as a universal protocol, the network layer is now independent of applications and most applications operate across a TCP/IP network without modification.

The infrastructure necessary for a given application is determined by who uses it and how they use it. Since users interact with applications in only a small number of ways, and applications interact with other applications in a similarly small number of ways, it is not difficult to describe an application by the types of interactions it employs, and thus its infrastructure requirements. The adaptive infrastructure patterns outlined in this chapter have evolved to reduce many possible infrastructure options to a small number of descriptive archetypes, so they could be used to plan for simplified and reusable infrastructure configurations.

Designing for the Future

In a way, good infrastructure design works the same way a real estate developer creates a master-planned community. Though thousands of houses are to be built, all are based on a set of perhaps 10 basic home designs. And while each design can be customized, the builders already know these 10 designs and have worked with them often. Most houses won't need massive amounts of customization anyway.

Meanwhile, having 10 predefined home styles keeps home buyers from spending the extra time or money to have an architect design each of their homes from scratch. The ideal is to have a primary contractor build the whole subdivision quickly and cheaply, yet have him do it well.

Will there be compromises on each house? Yes, of course. But more houses will be built faster, with higher quality, at a more reasonable cost than custom-built houses, since not everyone can afford a unique and elegant mansion.

The same rationale applies to adaptive infrastructure. In the place of builders, substitute application and infrastructure developers who will be reusing the same patterns repeatedly. When you want to add a new Web application, for instance, your developers should recognize that it shares a pattern of interaction and use with other applications in the infrastructure. This approach means that less time and money is wasted creating new, and often redundant, infrastructure implementations.

Reusability is the hallmark of an adaptive infrastructure. Recognizing patterns in your infrastructure allows you to reuse existing technology, IT processes, and skills. It also lowers the risks associated with integrating an increasingly complex number of individual components into actual systems that support real applications. The infrastructure will be well understood already in terms of how all those components work together.

Patterns should be considered a reuse of design blueprints rather than a reuse of built systems or implemented infrastructure. The latter is what services do, as explained previously in Chapter 2. However, because they are application-centric, patterns help make services even more reusable.

Asking Who, Where, and What?

How are patterns determined? The details of Infrastructure Pattern Matching (IPM) will be covered in more detail in Chapter 4. But basically, you can start by asking the following key questions:

- Who are the users?
- Where are they located?
- What kind of work do they need to accomplish?

In many cases, patterns can be differentiated simply by asking "what?" For example, the requirements of a transactional Web-based e-Commerce system are different from a static Web site used to publish corporate documents. On the other hand, many transactional applications can run on all three of the Transact patterns.

In some cases, "where?" and "who?" are more appropriate questions to ask. In many e-Business contexts, the answer to "where?" was often that the users were "in the cloud" or "anywhere," which means that applications are accessed via intranet or Internet connections. Internet-based applications often require different planning than traditional LAN- or WAN-based applications. You no longer control the entire network from application server to user interface. e-Business planners had to take this lack of control into account, and so must their successors, who must apply this concept not only to the Web, but to pervasive devices such as mobile phones, PDAs, game consoles, intelligent appliances, wearable computers, and in-vehicle systems such as OnStar.

You can also use specific "how?" and "what?" questions to differentiate patterns. For example, do you want to be able to add support for multiple points-of-interaction (POIs) such as Web, Interactive Voice

Response units (IVRs), PDAs, or mobile phones? One type of pattern might allow this easily, and another might not. So the question boils down to "What does the business need to deliver on the promise of its brand?" If your company values flexibility and adaptiveness, you should implement the appropriate pattern infrastructure that provides it.

Another "how" question is how much growth can a pattern design accommodate? Will this approach serve future needs? Can the blueprint itself be used repeatedly, even if scale requirements change? Can the pattern implementation be upgraded easily as the scale of the application changes, such as when new advertising brings an onslaught of users to a Web site? The scalability of a pattern could be the deciding factor when choosing between it and another pattern that could perform the same basic task.

In an e-Business context, for example, Web Publish is the pattern most often used. But 3/N-Tier Transact is the up-and-coming new approach for emerging commerce applications. Many existing e-Business transactional systems are 2-Tier Web-only infrastructure designs that will be harder to scale and leverage over time.

The different versions of patterns described in this chapter are derived from research done on the history and installed base of different application types. Typical deciding factors when choosing between patterns might include service level requirements, quality of service needs, installed base realities, or cost restraints. The deciding factors might not directly involve technology issues, such as whether an application should use a certain brand of server. Patterns should change the nature of the conversation you have with business managers and application developers so that it is more service level–oriented and less technology-oriented.

How Detailed Should It Get?

While you can think of patterns as a blueprint for IT architecture, the standards that you develop must also have concrete depth and immediately usable detail. In fact, the detail level is often what differentiates one organization's 3/N-Tier Transact pattern from another's.

When defining a pattern, you should specify not only the architecture, but also the technologies and products used. For example, a particular pattern might use a specific database product or a certain vendor's network load balancer.

Configuration details can even be standardized for other, more mature patterns that are commonly and widely implemented. Newer, less-

> ### Are Patterns Just for New Infrastructure?
>
> Patterns can help you manage the complexity of existing infrastructure, rather than simply describing blueprints for the future. Learning what patterns you already use, but perhaps didn't recognize as such, helps you discover experiences that could prove useful in continuing your existing patterns or in adopting new or different ones.
>
> Perhaps you don't have a large e-Business infrastructure yet. But if you do, you should take into account things you're already doing well as you refine your infrastructure designs and upgrade your patterns beyond e-Business. Once such an evaluation is made, you can focus on the investments needed to update your existing infrastructure.
>
> The future should be based to some extent on the past. Innovation doesn't have to mean completely changing everything you do, every time you do it. However, you need to maintain a balance: giving appropriate consideration to new ways of doing things, instead of just defaulting to the way things have always been done.
>
> Before planning for future development, first inventory your existing infrastructure to determine what patterns you already have and whether they are viable, require modification, or need a complete overhaul. If a pattern needs changing, determine whether existing applications should be upgraded or whether you will adopt new applications that operate in a different, more advanced way.

mature patterns might lack detailed configuration standards at first. Even product choices might need to be revisited for the first few implementations. But, as they are implemented more often, the standards should fall into place.

The relationship between pattern maturity and level of detail is shown more clearly in Figure 3.2. Pattern architecture tends to fall into place fairly quickly. But only later, after several iterations, are standards set for technology, products, and configurations.

Developing patterns within a typical organization is not an entirely unfamiliar exercise. Most organizations already have existing infrastructure that could encompass a number of the patterns outlined here. But

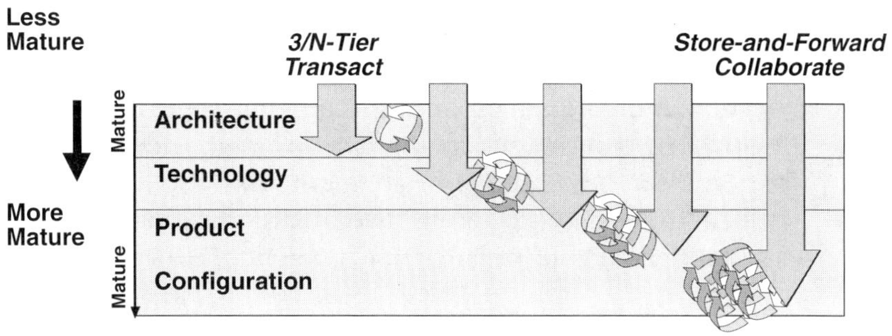

Figure 3.2 Pattern Maturity Differences

what is often lacking is infrastructure standardized at a high level—not for just one layer or component, but for all—and in a way that is application-centric, yet with an end-to-end perspective. Once patterns are defined this way, they help you make better decisions.

In fact, few organizations will need to develop all of the patterns outlined in this chapter. Once you've designed a useful set of patterns, adding or aggregating infrastructure to support a new pattern requires a strong business case. You shouldn't end up with new patterns each time an application is added or each time a minor component change is required. There must be some stability to your standards, or they become unmanageable.

Understanding the Major Patterns

IT research over the past decade has yielded considerable information about how organizations use infrastructure. Most applications fit into a basic set of nine infrastructure patterns, which in turn fall into three major application categories:

- Transact. This category includes applications that store business data for long periods, such as online customer orders and other transactions, usually working with one record, or possibly a few records, at a time.

- Publish. This category includes applications with read-only data, such as online marketing information published in Web pages.

- Collaborate. This category includes applications that allow users to share information contained in files and documents, such as a word-processing document shared by a development team or an e-mail-driven customer support system.

The patterns detailed on the following pages provide a good model for patterns you might already have or might need in the future. These patterns can be modified or augmented as applications demand and as current infrastructure allows. Eventually, these patterns must also be refined to match your organization's practice, experience, and goals.

Transact Patterns

Applications in this category let users make durable changes to the state of the business, or to business processes. This category includes applications that update a centralized database, make remote modifications to a portal profile, or control large-scale enterprise resource planning (ERP) systems. The category includes several types of Transact patterns, as explained on the following pages.

1-Tier Transact

This pattern includes batch processing or online transaction processing (OLTP) applications without logical abstraction between the presentation, application, and data logic. Although the application itself is fully centralized, users could be widely distributed over wide area networks. Figure 3.3 summarizes the 1-Tier Transact pattern.

Most mainframe systems run 1-Tier Transact applications, with data, business, and presentation logic all contained in a single application. These applications use network-based terminal emulation to display data on remote desktop devices such as terminals or PCs running terminal emulation software.

Also called the "host pattern," 1-Tier Transact includes systems such as CICS and IMS, as well as batch applications and applications based on flat-file databases. Typically, host applications run under IBM's OS/390 operating system, but some companies support this pattern using Microsoft Windows 2000/.NET Server, AS/400, UNIX, or specialized high-end systems, such as IBM's TPF. The 1-Tier transact environment allows massive servers to be constructed.

The 1-Tier transact pattern typically targets internal employees, primarily in campus and branch locations and has, in fact, been optimized in this environment for more than 20 years. While much data and business logic is already on mainframes, many organizations no longer

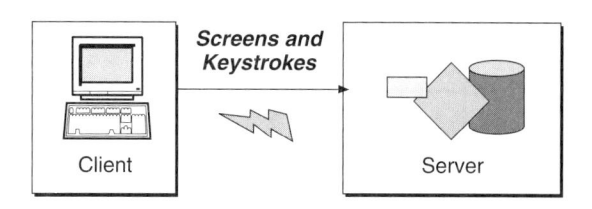

```
                    Screens and
                    Keystrokes

        [Client]         ⚡         [Server]


▲ Description                    ▲ Popularity
  ▸ Presentation and data access logic    ▸ The majority of mainframe applications
    is inseparable from business logic      are based on this pattern

▲ Service Level Matches          ▲ Practices
  + Scalability                    + Wrapper (maybe migrate)

  + Availability                   − This pattern is not a best practice

  − Everything else              ▲ Futures
                                   ▸ Although applications based on this
▲ Commom Examples                    pattern will exist for the foreseeable
  ▸ CICS                             future, no new applications should be
  ▸ IMS                              based on this pattern
  ▸ Flat-file-based applications
  ▸ Batch applications
```

Figure 3.3 The 1-Tier Transact Pattern

design applications to run exclusively there. Instead, they use client/server and Web applications to access as much mainframe data as possible. This situation, in turn, has created a need for transactional integration services to handle the data transfer process.

2-Tier Transact

This pattern involves a "smart PC" on the desktop communicating directly with a back-end database server or Web server. This category includes most traditional client/server applications popular in the early 1990s. Common examples include Visual Basic and PowerBuilder applications that access a database server. In the Web world, examples include applications created using Microsoft active server pages (ASP), Java server pages (JSP), or tools such as ColdFusion or Haht Software for quick Web-page-to-database Structured Query Langague (SQL) calls. Figure 3.4 summarizes the 2-Tier Transact pattern.

This pattern is the quickest and cheapest Transact pattern from a development standpoint, but it lacks reusability and scalability. These drawbacks make 2-Tier Transact unsuitable beyond the workgroup level or for many e-Business scenarios.

62 ■ Chapter 3: Identifying and Using Patterns

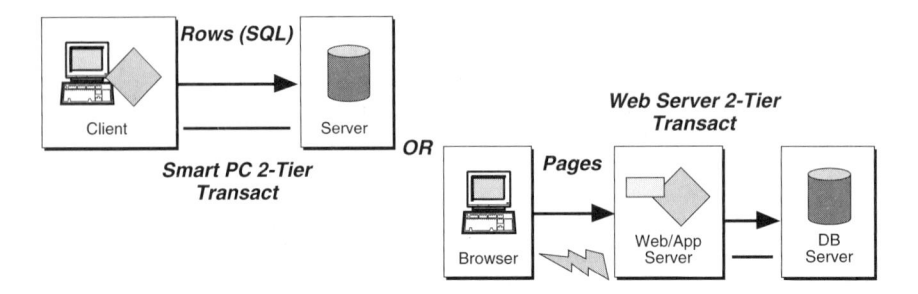

[Diagram: Smart PC 2-Tier Transact — Client sends Rows (SQL) to Server. OR Web Server 2-Tier Transact — Browser sends Pages to Web/App Server to DB Server.]

▲ Description
- Presentation is inseparable from business logic, but data access is partitioned to an RDBMS

▲ Service Level Matches
+ Speed of initial development
− Scalability
− Changing presentation logic
− Deployability (Smart PC only)

▲ Common Examples
- "Smart PC" Visual Basic or Powerbuilder applications
- Most Active Server Page (.asp) or Java Server Page (.jsp) applications

▲ Popularity
- The most popular transactional pattern

▲ Practices
+ Limiting use of the Client/Server version to small-scale applications
+ Using Terminal Server to move app to server
− Use of the Web version for large-scale applications

▲ Futures
- Prototyping and piloting will continue to use this pattern
- Smart PC version wanes
- ISVs slowly migrate from this pattern to N-Tier Transact

Figure 3.4 The 2-Tier Transact Pattern

A traditional (non-Web) 2-Tier Transact pattern is best suited for implementation on a LAN or in a campus environment. Unfortunately, SQL code and database access middleware perform poorly over high-latency, low-bandwidth WAN connections, causing user response time to slow considerably. Performance problems are particularly evident in traditional 2-Tier applications, but problems also can be found in Java applets that perform SQL/JDBC calls directly from the desktop client.

While most 2-Tier Transact applications create smart PCs, it is also possible to have a thin-client 2-Tier Transact pattern that is either Web-based or terminal server-based. Even though it looks like a 3/N-Tier system, the fact that the presentation logic and the business logic are not just co-located but also inextricably intertwined makes even this thin-client flavor a logical 2-Tier design, and thus a 2-Tier Transact pattern.

An easy way to distinguish between 2-Tier and 3-Tier applications is to ask the developers how easy it is to create a different front-end presentation. In the past, many people thought that moving Windows applications to the Web would make it easy to redesign the presentation layer. However, it is not easy to change many Web-only applications to support multiple points of interaction.

Web-only design also limits scalability, since upgrading the pattern requires bigger servers to run both presentation and application services. As a result, Web-only design can cost more than 3/N-Tier designs, which more efficiently leverage commodity-level servers. Finally, Web presentation limits reusability from an application integration perspective, since you have no Intra-APIs to leverage, just a screen to scrape. Using the Web application's business logic remotely from another application is very complex and expensive to engineer.

3/N-Tier Transact

This pattern uses a thin client carrying presentation-only logic to communicate with a client-neutral, server-based application. The server-based application, in turn, communicates with a back-end database server. Common examples include Peoplesoft v8 and SAP R/3, especially version 4.6 or later. Figure 3.5 summarizes the basic features of this pattern.

Since this pattern is one of the most widely used in both e-Business and the rest of business, it is covered in more detail later in this chapter. Chapter 4 also shows an example of a refined design for this pattern.

Publish Patterns

Publish patterns involve applications that provide read-only data access. In effect, these applications let the user download, view, listen to, or analyze data without changing it. Good examples include reporting and analysis tools, Web brochure-ware, and streaming audio/video. This category includes several types of Publish patterns, as explained on the following pages.

Client/Server Publish

This pattern is defined by the use of a smart PC, such as a sophisticated business intelligence client, with associated session-oriented protocols such as SQLNet inserted between the client and the back-end database. This pattern is best used for implementing sophisticated data analysis capabilities for a small, well-defined user base. Figure 3.6 summarizes the Client/Server Publish pattern.

This pattern is different from the other Publish patterns in terms of the amount of processing that is performed after a query is made to a

64 ■ Chapter 3: Identifying and Using Patterns

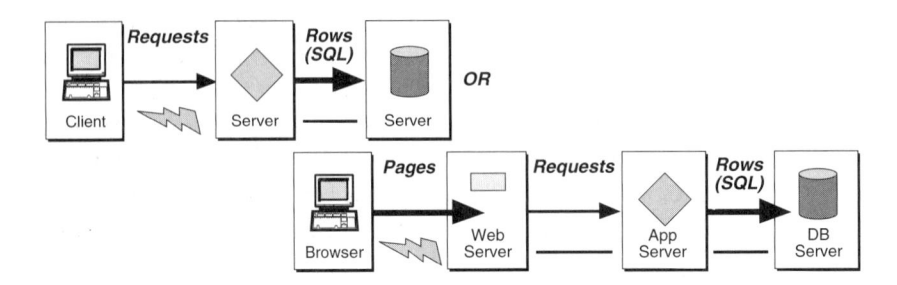

▲ **Description**
  ▶ Presentation, data access, and business logic are all partitioned

▲ **Service Level Matches**
  + Scalability
  + Changing presentation logic
  + Integrating new sources/consumers into the application
  − Speed of initial deployment

▲ **Common Examples**
  ▶ SAP R/3
  ▶ Peoplesoft 8

▲ **Popularity**
  ▶ Most popular with "architects"

▲ **Practices**
  + Designing scalable 3-Tier apps that work well across WANs
  + Designing N-Tier applications to integrate with other applications
  − Limiting support to a single point of interaction

▲ **Futures**
  ▶ Evolution of N-Tier to an Adaptive Services Architecture
  ▶ ISVs slowly migrate to this pattern
  ▶ Better app development tools supporting this pattern

Figure 3.5 The 3/N-Tier Transact Pattern

database. Applications that fit this pattern include online analytical processing (OLAP) tools and reporting-intensive applications, which require a smart PC for post-query processing support. Common examples include products from Brio, Business Objects, Cognos, Microstrategy, and SAS Institute.

The Client/Server Publish pattern is the most popular Publish pattern inside the enterprise, but it is rarely used for e-Business applications. Historically, much of the knowledge about this pattern comes from the data-warehousing world. What data-warehousing applications have clearly shown is the importance of providing access to data in a much simpler, timelier way.

The Client/Server Publish pattern, along with an associated data-warehousing analytic integration service, is the one that deals best with the complexities of moving and interpreting large amounts of data, at a

```
                    Rows (SQL)
     [Client] ←——————————— [Data Server]
```

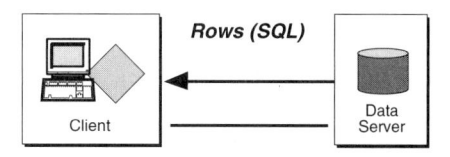

▲ **Description**
  ▸ Client-based ad hoc query, OLAP, or reporting application that accesses a database over a network

▲ **Service Level Matches**
  + Speed of initial development
  − Scalability
  − Deployability

▲ **Common Examples**
  ▸ Business Objects
  ▸ Cognos PowerPlay

▲ **Popularity**
  ▸ Most popular Publish pattern inside enterprise

▲ **Practices**
  + Limiting use of this pattern to LAN networks
  + Creating a unified analytic integration service via DW/ODS
  + Using publish-specific tools rather than VB or PB
  − Allowing direct access to transactional data

▲ **Futures**
  ▸ Client-based slicing and dicing of data will remain popular, especially for disconnected users
  ▸ Convergence of Web and Client/Server publish with the ability to move transparently between them

Figure 3.6 The Client/Server Publish Pattern

relatively low cost. One of the keys to this pattern is to define a consistent process for information movement, including answers to the following questions:

- How should information be extracted from transactional systems, with minimal impact on transactions in progress?
- How should information from various sources be transformed, made consistent, and loaded into a data store?
- How should information be broken down into subsets targeting particular analysts (i.e., data marts)?
- How should the data marts be made available to those analysts?
- When are data marts appropriate versus enabling an analyst to perform analyses on the core data warehouse directly?

Web Publish

Currently, this Publish pattern is the most popular one for applications reaching beyond the enterprise boundaries. Common examples include brochure-style Web sites, express delivery package tracking, and Web-

66 ■ Chapter 3: Identifying and Using Patterns

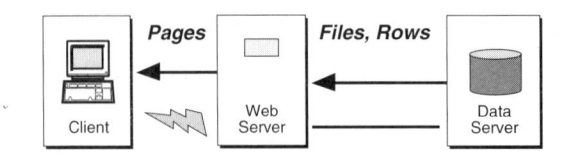

▲ **Description**
  ▸ Accessing, reading, or querying information via browser-based HTML/HTTP

▲ **Service Level Matches**
  + Speed of initial development
  − Changing presentation logic

▲ **Common Examples**
  ▸ FedEx package tracking Web app
  ▸ "Brochure-ware" sites
  ▸ Web-based bill presentment

▲ **Popularity**
  ▸ Most popular publish pattern beyond enterprise boundaries

▲ **Practices**
  + Scaling out stateless Web farms
  − Limiting support to a single point of interaction

▲ **Futures**
  ▸ N-Tier publishing based on XSLT, XML, and XQL
  ▸ Convergence of Web and Client/Server publish with the ability to move transparently between them

Figure 3.7 The Web Publish Pattern

based account review or bill presentation applications. Figure 3.7 summarizes the features of the Web Publish pattern.

Since this pattern was one of the most widely used in e-Business, and will continue to be important as we move beyond e-Business, it is covered in more detail later in this chapter. Chapter 4 also shows an example of a refined design for this pattern.

Stream Publish

This pattern is used for real-time publishing of streaming content such as audio, video, and text, to multimedia players operating on the client side, such as Windows Media Player and RealPlayer. Figure 3.8 summarizes the Stream Publish pattern.

Although the Web Publish pattern enables playback of multimedia files, this type of streaming is more akin to a traditional file download, because the user must wait for the entire file to download before playback can begin. In Stream Publish, the file starts playing in near real-time, even while parts of it are still being downloaded. The latency requirements of real-time multimedia delivery are different enough that streaming requires its own pattern.

Common examples of stream publish include Internet radio stations and film clip Web sites. Streaming media is a centerpiece of most con-

Figure 3.8 The Stream Publish Pattern

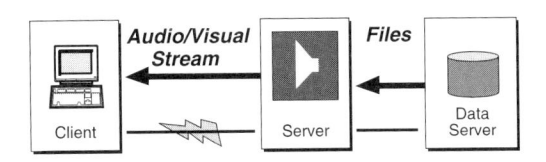

▲ **Description**
  ▶ Accessing, reading, or querying information via browser-based HTML/HTTP

▲ **Service Level Matches**
  + Speed of initial development
  − Changing presentation logic

▲ **Common Examples**
  ▶ FedEx package tracking Web app
  ▶ "Brochure-ware" sites
  ▶ Web-based bill presentment

▲ **Popularity**
  ▶ Most popular publish pattern beyond enterprise boundaries

▲ **Practices**
  + Scaling out stateless Web farms
  − Limiting support to a single point of interaction

▲ **Futures**
  ▶ N-Tier publishing based on XSLT, XML, and XQL
  ▶ Convergence of Web and Client/Server publish with the ability to move transparently between them

sumer entertainment Web sites, and it has become an increasingly valuable feature of many other kinds of Web sites since it enhances the "stickiness" of the site.

The most common tools for stream publishing are proprietary vendor solutions that require matching servers and multimedia plug-ins. Stream Publish components deliver the multimedia content only, and they are not normally used to deliver the static pages or applications of a Web site. For this reason, multimedia Web sites typically require the Stream Publish and Web Publish patterns to be used together. Over time, these solutions will become more standardized.

Most companies break out Stream Publish as a separate pattern for one main reason: It requires a direct focus on improving network design and distributed storage techniques. Breaking out streaming also allows you to focus on realistic service level decisions for business stakeholders who believe that adding fancy content to an e-Business Web site will somehow please their customers.

Even if your Web site is not currently outsourced, it might be a good idea to outsource the streaming component or the publish-focused infrastructure to service providers, such as Web hosting companies and content delivery network (CDN) providers, who have much more scalable network designs and connectivity. This consideration becomes even more important if you're supporting video and not just audio streaming.

Collaborate Patterns

The Collaborate patterns can involve peer-to-peer communication, document sharing, message exchange, or just a standard telephone call to someone. This category includes several types of Collaborate patterns, as explained on the following pages.

Real-Time Collaborate

Applications in this pattern use streaming audio, video, graphics, or text to share information between users. Communication can flow through a server for improved scalability and interactivity, or directly from peer-to-peer. Common examples include Microsoft NetMeeting, Voice Over Internet (VoIP), instant messaging, and videoconferencing (Web-based or otherwise). Figure 3.9 summarizes the basic features of this pattern.

This pattern is similar to the Stream Publish pattern because both involve real-time transmission of audio or video. However, real-time collaboration warrants its own separate pattern as the collaboration here is bidirectional, as opposed to the one-way flow of the Stream Publish pattern.

Every organization has built or sourced at least one real-time collaborate infrastructure: the voice network. The PBXs, phones, and wires used to carry traffic can all be considered a Real-Time Collaborate system, and a very mature one at that. Most other examples of Collaborate infrastructure depend on how data networks are configured. They either use dedicated networks, such as the dedicated lines often used for video conferencing kiosks or campuswide videoconferencing, or they ride over the TCP/IP network shared by many other applications.

When these applications ride on existing shared networks, cost savings are apparent, and the services are more easily provided. Since the data network already connects the business, a new one need not be built. Unfortunately, these same Real-Time Collaborate applications have special network requirements, including low latency and low jitter, which many current data networks cannot provide without significant new investment. Also, these applications can have a potentially negative impact on other patterns that were running fine on the same network until the Real-Time Collaborate application appeared.

Understanding the Major Patterns 69

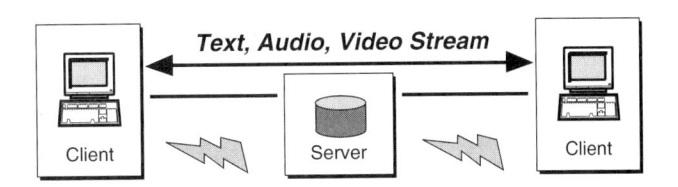

▲ **Description**
- Streaming audio/video/graphics/text from client-to-client using real-time streaming protocols, either through a server or peer-to-peer

▲ **Service Level Matches**
- \+ Usability
- − Affordability
- − Scalability
- − Availability

▲ **Common Examples**
- NetMeeting
- Voice
- Instant Messaging
- Videoconferencing over the Internet

▲ **Popularity**
- In its infancy

▲ **Practice Maturity**
- \+ Homogeneous instant Messaging
- \+ NetMeeting on intranets
- − VoIP
- − Videoconferencing over the Internet

▲ **Futures**
- QoS support within Intranets and then Internet makes this pattern more available and affordable

Figure 3.9 The Real-Time Collaborate Pattern

Store-and-Forward Collaborate

This pattern involves the basic transfer, replication, and storage of files or documents. Common examples include e-mail attachments, distributed file systems, and print queues. Most organizations also put desktop support and software distribution into this pattern, since the same people who support the network operating system (NOS) often support desktops as well. Figure 3.10 summarizes the basic features of this pattern.

With the exception of traditional voice telephony systems in the previous pattern, Store-and-Forward is the most mature and popular Collaborate pattern. Many organizations have become very standardized in the products they use, including network operating systems, mail servers, desktop configurations, and connectivity. They've even become standardized in minor configuration details, such as specifying that shared documents go on the "F: drive."

Applications in this pattern are often deployed on every desktop in the organization, so that they become ubiquitous. Microsoft Office applications such as Word and Excel are obvious examples.

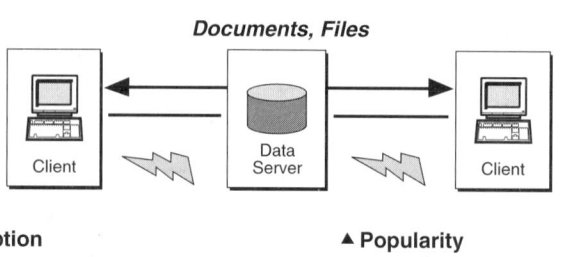

- ▲ Description
  - ▸ Basic transfer, replication, and storage of files or documents
- ▲ Service Level Matches
  - + Scalability
  - + Affordability
  - − Deployability
- ▲ Common Examples
  - ▸ E-mail
  - ▸ Distributed file system
  - ▸ Print queues
- ▲ Popularity
  - ▸ Most popular Collaborate pattern
- ▲ Practices
  - + E-mail interoperability
  - + File and print consolidation
- ▲ Futures
  - ▸ Directory services decoupled from NOS
  - ▸ File systems decoupled from OS (e.g., network-attached printers)

Figure 3.10 The Store-and-Forward Collaborate Pattern

For e-Business cases, this pattern focuses on SMTP gateway solutions and e-mail applications, including the e-mail response systems that many organizations are now offering as part of their online customer interaction centers. The planning for all these e-mail enabled applications can be grouped by this pattern.

Structured Collaborate

This pattern includes any application that provides shared access and coordinates changes to a document, file, or other data structure. Common examples include Lotus Notes groupware, workflow applications (except simple e-mail), document management applications, software development environments, and shared groupware calendars. Figure 3.11 summarizes the basic features of this pattern.

The Structured Collaborate pattern, also known as workflow or document management, provides many important integrity-checking features that are missing from the Store-and-Forward Collaborate pattern, including version control, check-in/check-out, and data validation. For this reason, it is more scalable for business use cases requiring these capabilities. But it also requires a longer implementation cycle and is considerably more expensive.

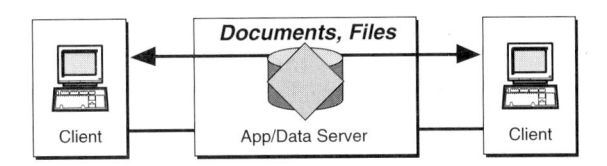

▲ **Description**
  ▶ Shared access and automated coordinated change to a document, file, or other data structure that is the focus of group collaboration

▲ **Service Level Matches**
  – Scalability
  – Integratability

▲ **Common Examples**
  ▶ Notes "workflow" apps (other than e-mail)
  ▶ Document management
  ▶ Shared calendars

▲ **Popularity**
  ▶ Often not recognized as a distinct from Store & Forward or 2-Tier Transact

▲ **Practices**
  + Check in/out document management
  – Large document collaboration over Internet

▲ **Futures**
  ▶ Convergence of this pattern and 3/N-Tier transact
  ▶ Becoming more transactional and 3/N-Tier evolving toward workflow and long-lived transactions

Figure 3.11 The Structured Collaborate Pattern

Key Patterns for e-Business

Of all the patterns discussed on the previous pages, the Web Publish and 3/N-Tier Transact patterns stand out as the two most critical patterns to plan and execute well from an e-Business standpoint. Furthermore, these patterns will continue to be important as the world moves beyond e-Business, since many of the benefits and analyses associated with e-Businesses will continue converging with the business mainstream. The benefits and best practices of each pattern are discussed in more detail below.

Web Publish Pattern

This pattern is defined by the use of a Web browser and Hypertext Transfer Protocol (HTTP) to provide read-only access to structured documents that contain Hypertext Markup Language (HTML) and, increasingly, Extensible Markup Language (XML). As such, it is more flexible than the Client/Server Publish pattern in supporting large, less well-defined user groups, but it is limited in the sophistication of read-only interactivity and analysis it can support. The basic configuration is shown in Figure 3.12.

Notice that this pattern includes Web sites that *interact* with a database, allowing users to view the data but not to *transact* with it by changing the data. A user might enter a tracking number to track a package on a shipper's Web site, but this information doesn't change the database. Instead, the system uses it for query purposes only.

Likewise, the same model applies to a sales manager performing analysis on sales data. The manager can pick from a list of territories, specify date ranges, and then submit the query. Since the query doesn't update the database, it's still a read-only operation.

User behavior statistics captured from Web sites can be stored long term, even for publishing applications, but this is a special case that fits into this otherwise read-only pattern.

Benefits

Due to the maturity of this pattern, many solid tools are available for developing read-only Web publishing applications. Deployment is similarly well understood, resulting in a very rapid initial development phase and a wide availability of Web hosting service providers. However, it remains difficult to change the presentation logic from Web to non-Web presentations without completely rebuilding the application.

Scalability is simple to achieve with scale-out (as opposed to scale-up) designs using stateless farm architecture with network load balancers and masses of cheap Web servers and file system or database servers. (See the section on "Scale-Out Design" in Chapter 6.) Moreover, unlike 3/N-Tier Transact, even the file system or database server itself can be replicated to scale. Assuming the data doesn't change often, this replication is easy to support.

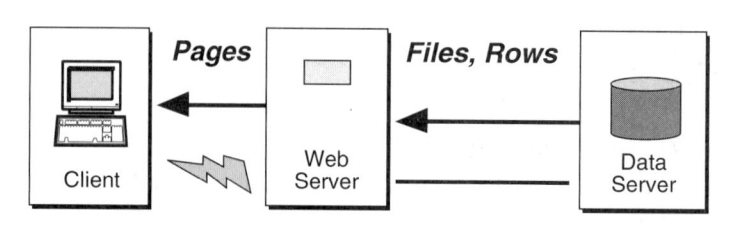

Figure 3.12 Web Publish Configuration

Cheaper hardware and software is supported, since the scale-out design means you can choose database systems that need not be best at online transaction processing (OLTP)—and therefore not as expensive. Moreover, you can choose less expensive Intel-based servers and have more of them to scale. At some point, data center rack space might become critical, but the point still holds. For this pattern, you should not be buying large expensive servers.

New, Internet-centric solutions that provide acceleration or performance enhancement often work well in this pattern to help satisfy scalability requirements. Many of these solutions were initially created for e-Business rather than internal needs, including:

- Network load balancers and multi-site balancing
- Secure sockets library (SSL) offloading for encrypted content
- Caching for databases and memory, reverse caching in the data center, client caching, intermediate ISP caches
- Content delivery network (CDN) services such as Akamai
- Traffic or rate shaping

IT organizations can offer this pattern to customers as centralized and shared infrastructure, in the process converting most of this pattern into a service. Later chapters of this book will show how to refine this pattern's design by taking each of these components and determining specific requirements and functionality that provide an advantage in e-Business.

Weaknesses

Despite best efforts, it is difficult to manage scale or load on e-Business Web sites that fit this pattern. Many clients plan for 4x or 10x site capacity, and they are still surprised when the application overflows its capacity. The collapse of many dot-coms and a general slowdown in Web growth percentages has reduced this risk, but the threat of being "too successful" remains.

Publishing to multiple points of interaction, not just Web, is still a work in progress. Web-only approaches are still common, with completely separate portals for voice or PDA interfaces. Over time, XML-based multi-POI publishing portals will help address this issue.

Best Practices

So, what should you do?

- Focus on availability first, then throughput and response time.
- Design-in at least a two-way redundant solution, even for internal needs.
- Use content delivery network (CDN) services for static content targeting very large audiences.
- Scale-out by using load balancers to duplicate and replicate Web and data servers.
- Support multiple POIs, or at least plan on this in the future.
- Manage, limit, or disallow direct access to transactional data.
- Create a unified analytical integration service using data warehousing and online data stores (ODS).
- Don't use expensive online transaction processing (OLTP) databases.
- Leverage cheaper hardware and software in general for data storage components.
- Don't neglect security issues, particularly data defacement or tampering. Even read-only data can be changed by the malicious, and denial of service attacks can prevent user access.
- Shore up relationships with corporate marketing so you are not surprised by long-planned marketing campaigns that drive 10x–100x spikes in e-Business Web site load overnight.
- Examine Web hosting service providers for designs and sourcing, or just examples of services to offer to your own organization internally.
- Design for outsourcing, even if you never do.
- If an e-Business site is mission-critical, install response time and load monitoring services to keep track of load better and plan accordingly.
- Take a service-centric approach. You can achieve significant real infrastructure reuse widely within this pattern, not just blueprint-level value.

Many Web sites today use a combination of Publish and Transact patterns. However, infrastructure planners should separate these distinct functions to get a better picture of the infrastructure that is needed for each activity. Clearly, you will find some opportunities for reuse, but initial planning efforts should split up the functions of the application to clearly understand the fundamental building blocks of each pattern.

The read-only nature of the Publish patterns in general and the Web-centric nature of this pattern make wide-scale replication viable. For large, externally focused implementations, it often makes sense to outsource this pattern for hosting so that speed of deployment is maximized. Service providers can also help address network latency issues by caching content in multiple places, so that it is logically close to as many users as possible.

Looking Forward

The pressure to accommodate multiple points of interaction will drive this pattern toward N-tier publishing based on XML and the style sheets and query language associated with it, including Extensible Stylesheet Language Transformations (XSLT) and XML Query Language (XQL). These new technologies will allow you to present Web content in a variety of formats, thus broadening the market for Web Publish applications.

3/N-Tier Transact Pattern

Compared to other Transact patterns, this pattern is highly adaptive and popular with infrastructure architects who focus on long-term trends. It is also often used as the model for transactional e-Business systems.

This pattern can fit many transactional applications and is excellent for geographically distributed operations. Locating shared server resources in centralized data centers provides high-quality support at the lowest cost. For all these reasons, this pattern is well suited both to e-Business use and to support of the broader converged vision beyond e-Business. Figure 3.13 shows two typical configurations for 3/N-Tier Transact.

3/N-Tier Transact can support multiple business functions and is the best pattern for supporting highly complex, transaction-intensive, or large-scale transaction volumes. However, the 3/N-Tier Transact pattern requires significant customization at the application and tool level, which translates into a considerable investment of time and resources.

The extra "N" tier results when certain functions are moved to separate servers. With a Web server, the presentation is generated on a separate Web server tier, yet still rendered by the user's Web browser. Since this configuration is truly an N-tier rather than just a traditional 3-Tier design, this book labels the pattern as 3/N-Tier Transact.

Within this pattern, data can be located close to the application process, either on a back-end database server or on an application server,

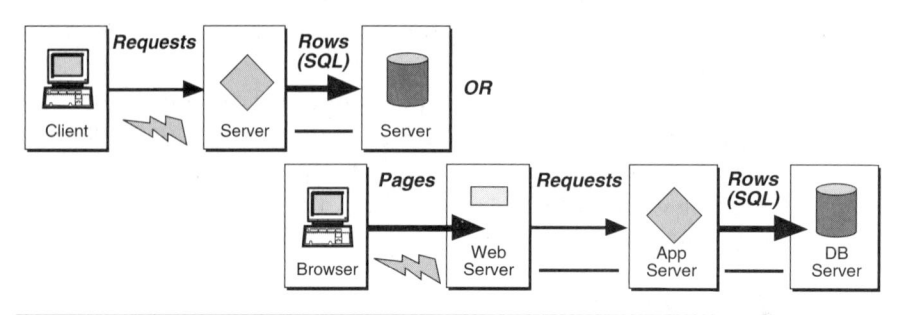

Figure 3.13 3/N-Tier Transact Configurations

instead of running all the way out to the user. This practice minimizes network traffic between users and application servers, which is critical in cases where the Internet is concerned. Enterprise software packages such as Peoplesoft v8 and SAP R/3 have made this pattern mainstream.

This pattern is the most scalable and flexible of all the Transact patterns. Due to its WAN-friendliness, users can be highly decentralized, while the complex parts of the application and infrastructure remain entirely centralized. When implemented correctly, this pattern results in clearly defined interfaces, making it the most flexible to integrate with other applications or points of interaction.

The 3/N-Tier Transact pattern, with back-end database, client, and any number of application servers, offers the greatest distribution of processing functionality in a transactional environment. Typically, application functionality is deployed on multiple individual servers, while database functionality is allocated according to the degree of data synchronization required across supported application modules.

Thin clients prevail in this pattern, and shared business logic can be supported from multiple points of interaction (POIs). This technique allows the same checking account balance routine to be used from both a Web browser and an Interactive Voice Response (IVR) system. Upgrading the code is much simpler, since you have only one instance to change, not one instance per POI.

The foremost strength of the 3/N-Tier Transact pattern is its adaptability, particularly for applications where scalability, support for multiple POIs, reusability, and speed are important. Developers of customer applications must understand and accommodate the practical aspects of locating and distributing data. Meanwhile, most application package vendors are following SAP's lead and instituting the 3/N-Tier Transact model for their applications.

Benefits

The following are specific benefits of the 3/N-Tier Transact pattern, especially when compared to 2-Tier Transact:

- Scalability. Distributing the processing load on multiple server tiers provides significant scalability, particularly in offloading the DBMS server. From a reliability perspective, 3/N-Tier requires considerably more design effort, but it limits dependencies. If any component of the system changes, the whole system need not be replaced. (See the related section on "Scale-Out Design" in Chapter 6.) Proper 3/N-Tier design partitions business logic, presentation logic, and integration logic so that if any one of the three dimensions changes, you can plug in alternative technology to replace it without affecting the other dimensions.

- Security. Quite often, 3/N-Tier designs include Web Single Sign-On (Web SSO) products to provide multi-tier security with role-based resource authorization. These new directory-centric products are becoming easier to use, and they avoid the need for multiple authentication procedures in each application. Moreover, the proper partitioning of business logic enables you to split up the 3/N-Tier applications so only the presentation portion resides in the demilitarized zone (DMZ), while the application code and data reside in the trusted network. For details on security and identity infrastructure, see Chapter 5.

- Presentation. With the 3/N-Tier Transact pattern, if development is done correctly, all user interfaces leverage the same application logic. Communicating with multiple user interfaces—such as the ability to check order status from a call-center PC, Web browser, telephone, or two-way pager—doesn't require "check order" application logic on each user interface platform. Instead, the logic is implemented centrally, which means it is physically located on an application server. Then "check order" user interfaces are implemented for each client platform.

- APIs. The ability to use application APIs independently of the application's presentation is another key advantage of this pattern. 3/N-Tier reduces the cost of enterprise application integration (EAI) because sharing APIs between applications reduces the time and expense required to integrate the applications. Since business initiatives such as supply chain management (SCM) and customer relationship management (CRM) largely depend on cross-business EAI, the ability to rapidly integrate and deintegrate applications becomes critical to overall business success.

Weaknesses

Known weaknesses of the 3/N-Tier Transact pattern are:

- Needs customization. All this flexibility and power comes at a price. The 3/N-Tier Transact pattern requires significant customization at the application and tool levels, which consumes considerable time and resources both for application and infrastructure development.

- Too long to implement. Development slows down due to lack of capability or integration at the toolkit level and the tendency to use expensive third-party integrators. Support and management offerings in this area are also lacking. The paucity of non-vendor-oriented skills heightens support and management concerns.

- Misunderstood. Good design is difficult to achieve with these complex systems. Many organizations are trying to use 3/N-Tier architecture, but their programmers routinely use large Web-server-based servlets with traditional 2-Tier code mapping to connect Web interface code directly to Java Database Connectivity (JDBC) or Open Database Connectivity (ODBC) database calls. Since it is not really 3/N-Tier, this coding approach does not provide all the advantages of that design.

- Expensive. Systems integrators maintain that integration and implementation expenses will exceed hardware and software costs by a 4-to-1 ratio. According to users, the ratio is sometimes as high as 8-to-1, or even 12-to-1, due to the significant resources and customized tools that are sometimes required.

Best Practices

For best results with 3/N-Tier, you should:

- Develop transactional integration services to match 3/N-Tier applications.
- Work closely with application developers in the early stages, as they build or buy tools.

- Use scale-out stateless farm architecture (explained in Chapter 6).
- Leverage experience from existing OLTP database management system (DBMS) and server OS/hardware platforms, even if other server tier platforms are different.
- Do not replicate OLTP data as a technique to increase scale. The exceptions to this normally golden rule are database products, such as Oracle's Real Application Cluster (RAC), that bring a significantly higher level of sophistication to replication.
- Take advantage of pattern benefits.
- Develop a test lab, including equipment and procedures for investigating the infrastructure impact of various patterns and services.

Looking Forward

The 3/N-Tier Transact pattern will continue to be the preferred choice for transactional applications. Organizations will get more accustomed to this pattern, while traditional software vendors will increasingly embrace it. Much volatility and complexity still exist in this area, however, so standardizing your own version of this pattern and sticking with it should improve your success with applications of this class. Chapter 4 presents an example of a refined 3/N-Tier Transact pattern design.

What Patterns Do You Need?

You can adapt and use patterns described earlier in this chapter as necessary for your particular organization's requirements. When developing your own portfolio of patterns, you should consider a number of issues discussed on the following pages.

First look at your business processes, your applications, and your existing infrastructure solutions, and start analyzing where the major patterns lie. As part of this exercise, ask yourself these two questions:

- Do I use this pattern a lot?
- Does this pattern cover the applications that are most critical to my business?

Any patterns for which you can answer yes to these two questions should be automatically entered into your list of required patterns.

Some patterns won't be required at all. If you don't have mainframes, 1-Tier Transact probably isn't a concern. You might not use Structured

Collaborate yet, but you should be prepared to deal with it in the next few years. If you find some very unique infrastructure, but it only applies to a small workgroup or to one simple application and you don't anticipate it becoming a highly leveraged solution, don't bother making it a full pattern.

Use the 80/20 rule, which states that 80% of the challenge is usually addressed by 20% of the solution set. Include the smallest number of patterns that provide the maximum value toward infrastructure planning. The patterns you adopt represent all the technologies at which you plan to excel, so limiting them to the smallest number possible helps reduce the complexity of your situation. When finished with your pattern analysis, you might settle on five patterns or less.

Focus on planning those patterns that will have significant impact on future application delivery. Spend less time on patterns that are more mature, such as Store-and-Forward Collaborate, or that should only be kept running without significant new investment, such as 1-Tier Transact.

When a pattern is so mature that the primary goal is to squeeze the last drop of return on investment (ROI) out of the instance, the real ownership and leadership for change will be driven by operations. Less mature patterns will require more planning and design to drive toward maturity and to handle many new application requirements, though operations must still be involved.

Subdividing Patterns

A large percentage of your business applications could fall into a single pattern. For this reason, you might want to further refine these patterns into sub-patterns, or separate pattern instances, if the infrastructure needs are significantly different.

Before breaking apart a pattern, consider the following issues:

- Is the infrastructure different enough to be worth planning it separately? Will it remain different for at least two years?

- Is the infrastructure highly disruptive to the business as a whole or to other sets of applications? For instance, real-time video applications that slow down all other applications in the business must be controlled or even eradicated as a class, not one at time.

- Do you have two parallel product choices that are both commonly used, yet require somewhat different infrastructures? For instance, an N-Tier architecture implemented with Microsoft DCOM/.NET versus Java 2 Enterprise (J2EE)? You might consider treating these as separate sub-patterns, or as instances of a single pattern. Defining two solid instances and making them easily repeatable is still much better than having 10 different choices.

- Do you have two instances of a pattern that represent different service level requirements, such as enterprise 3/N-Tier versus 3/N-Tier for one business unit?

Each organization must base its patterns on its own knowledge and experience. Patterns then become totally adaptable to your own unique business requirements.

Should Patterns for e-Business Be Different?

Should your organization consider developing a separate group of patterns solely for the purpose of designing and maintaining e-Business applications? In general, the answer is no, because e-Business and the rest of business are converging. Instead, driving leverage is the key point.

In the past, many organizations have created a separate e-Business infrastructure with completely different architectures, technologies, products, and configurations than internal enterprise cases. Now, some organizations are trying to take innovative e-Business infrastructure techniques and apply them to non-e-Business scenarios.

While it was considered common wisdom in the past to have separate pattern designs for e-Business, it is now a better goal to design all application infrastructure, particularly for Web Publish and 3/N-Tier Transact, as though the application might be supporting all user types, including partners, employees, customers/consumers, and suppliers. Once this is done, applying the pattern only to internal applications could be as simple as dropping a few components and services from the design, such as the firewall component.

For e-Business patterns, remember that you don't control the entire infrastructure that the applications run on, particularly the end user desktop and the Internet itself. Those elements that you *can* control must be well structured to make up for the other elements that are difficult to control.

e-Business innovations have provided some solutions that make control easier, with ubiquitous Web technologies such as HTTP, HTML, TCP/IP, and more. But the rest of the infrastructure must leverage these technologies as well as possible. Chapter 6 of this book will discuss how patterns, components, and services can leverage these technologies directly, in particular through network load balancing and caching.

Regardless, you should design separate patterns for e-Business only if you think you'll do things so much differently in the external environment than in the internal environment that it makes sense to keep track of things separately. If you end up creating a separate set of patterns and infrastructure, at least try to keep the number of e-Business pattern cases small, and link them as much as possible to internal patterns. Then you might have a chance to leverage their similarities later, at least at the staffing level.

Applying Multiple Patterns

While many applications can be described by a single pattern, it's also possible that large-scale applications will require two or more patterns to describe them fully. From an IT perspective, you shouldn't feel obligated to run every part of an application on a single infrastructure or pattern. Using patterns helps identify when the staging of a single application across multiple infrastructures can help maximize efficiency and minimize redundancy.

For example, think of an application that is primarily a Web Publish pattern, such as a Web portal. Consider putting a business process on a separate infrastructure when it is write-oriented, such as logging on to the portal or updating a profile. Thus, you might have one infrastructure (Web Publish) to support access to the read-only part of the portal and another infrastructure (3/N-Tier Transact) for portal profile updates.

The process of matching new applications to existing infrastructure is covered more extensively under "Infrastructure Pattern Matching" in Chapter 4.

Summary

Creating and developing a basic set of infrastructure patterns will help your organization actually plan or manage a more adaptive infrastructure. Infrastructure patterns deal with business change from the bottom up.

Instead of trying to deal with all possible infrastructure variability, the patterns place some boundaries on that variability and give infrastructure developers a framework with which to approach the business. You can take hundreds of different application demands and structure them into a handful of common cases (often less than 10). Then you can direct planning skill, effort, and time to this smaller set of general goals.

Actual implementations will modify pattern standards to some degree. In general, however, you can advance the goal of standardization by using pattern blueprints to govern design and implementation activities for each individual application. These benefits are not just for the enterprise; they apply equally well to e-Business design cases, only more so!

If your organization maintains an enterprise architecture development function, the basic set of infrastructure patterns also serves as a reference point for architects and infrastructure developers or planners. The patterns that you choose for your enterprise describe the work to be done in constructing an infrastructure and the systems that need to be created.

On a more tangible level, a good set of infrastructure patterns will help you be more proactive in addressing business requirements, by engaging the business earlier in the change process. The patterns can help leverage your experience in planning, building, and running real applications on real infrastructure across a larger set of increasingly demanding business conditions and new applications.

You might have many of these patterns identified already. Your organization might not need to implement every pattern listed in this chapter, or you might choose to create new ones. A new business proposal could result in a debate over patterns, but once the concept of patterns is in place, this debate can be lively and beneficial, not fruitless and circular.

Infrastructure patterns are a key component of the adaptive infrastructure approach, as they are used for Infrastructure Pattern Matching, Predictive Cost Modeling, and other techniques outlined in Chapter 4. They should prove useful in structuring the understanding of other IT groups when doing infrastructure planning. If application development, architects, operations, and other groups all understand the basic patterns, your discussions with them will benefit from a commonly understood terminology. Patterns are uniquely suited to simplify the traditional dialogue around the plethora of components that have been difficult to map to applications, e-Business, or enterprise.

Finally, patterns should also be used as reference points within an overall IT-to-business discussion, where infrastructure development should be addressed. Decisions related to infrastructure development will be some of the most important that occur within IT over the next few years.

Chapter 4

Infrastructure Planning and Design

By now you've heard plenty about adaptive infrastructure concepts. You understand components, platforms, patterns, and services. You've laid the technical foundation for success in preparing for and adapting to high-speed change in both e-Business and the converged world that comes next.

Now you need to think in a different context. It's great to understand the fundamentals of adaptive infrastructure, but how do you apply these concepts to infrastructure planning within your organization?

This chapter provides extensive details on how to refine pattern designs for each of the major e-Business infrastructure components and services that will continue to be critical beyond e-Business. It explains why process matters and examines strategic and tactical concerns related to the infrastructure lifecycle. In particular, this chapter addresses:

- The business/IT project lifecycle
- The roles and responsibilities required for infrastructure planning
- The overall infrastructure planning process
- The per-project infrastructure planning process
- How to package infrastructure plans for funding
- How to refine pattern designs

This chapter concludes by showing examples of refined pattern designs for the two most common e-Business patterns: Web Publish and 3/N-Tier Transact.

The Business/IT Project Lifecycle

Infrastructure planning must address legitimate business concerns. An infrastructure strategy has little chance of success unless it is closely meshed with business strategy.

Strategy integration assumes that business decision makers assess application benefits and IT decision makers assess capabilities and costs. Once these responsibilities are clearly defined, you can make significant headway toward common goals by pursuing the steps that are summarized in Figure 4.1 and detailed on the following pages.

Step 1: Setting Strategy

The first step in the e-Business project lifecycle is for the business to develop its own strategies. A common issue is how involved IT should be in this process. Usually, the Chief Information Officer (CIO) or the Chief Technology Officer (CTO) is best qualified to evaluate the strengths and limitations of technologies available to help the business meet its goals. Thus, the proper role of IT is to educate the business about the promises and pitfalls of technological solutions, *not* to set business policy. Cer-

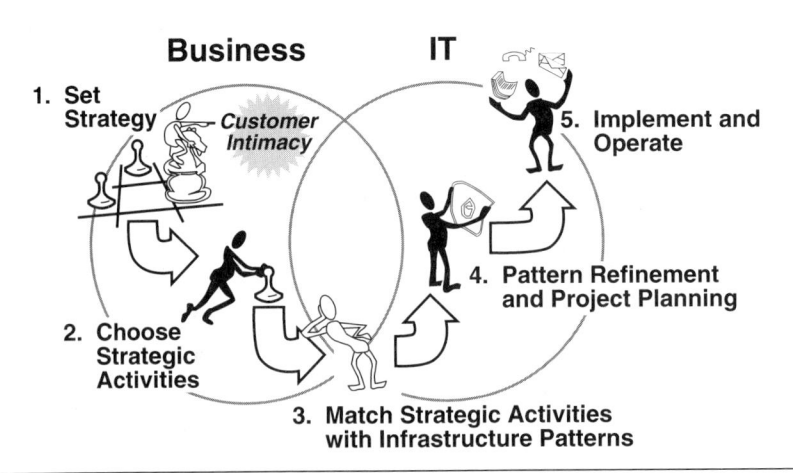

Figure 4.1 The Business/IT Project Lifecycle

tainly, IT can help brainstorm future scenarios and determine feasibility. But the actual setting of strategy is not an IT role unless IT has become the business, which is still pretty rare.

Step 2: Choosing Strategic Activities

An appropriate role for IT is advising business managers of the costs and time lines for various projects designed to accomplish strategic goals. To be most helpful, IT must provide solid input that can be used by the business in the decision-making process.

Business decision makers often confuse *strategic activities* with *strategy*, resulting in goals that are too nebulous. This trap was particularly prevalent when executives went around adding "e" to everything, as in, "We will become an e-company," or "We will become e-Business enabled and more customer-intimate." Even today, the same issue remains: Given such vague goals, how can IT decide what to do?

In such cases, the business has not identified strategic activities to accomplish its strategy. IT groups receiving such vague strategy statements must return to the business for more detailed guidance on appropriate strategic activities, or with workable projects for the business to consider that might help achieve strategic goals. But IT must let, or even force, the business to select and prioritize the projects.

To be most effective, you must be able to present clear options to the business managers and articulate the trade-offs. If business managers present you with a project that must be completed in six months, the project has already failed. You should be involved in meetings where project time lines are decided. To recover, you must be quick to present various options for meeting the deadline while effectively communicating the trade-offs and costs associated with each option, such as lack of future adaptability or reusability. Then let the business managers decide whether meeting the deadline is worth the trade-offs.

Step 3: Matching Activities to Patterns

Once strategic activities are chosen, use gap analysis to identify infrastructure patterns and components needed to support these activities. Highly adaptive organizations know how to change the infrastructure requirements of planned applications so that they mesh more closely with existing infrastructure and skill sets. This kind of adaptability results in improved reusability, speed, and cost efficiency on an enterprise scale.

Infrastructure managers can be more adaptive by getting involved as new applications are being designed or selected. Infrastructure developers can use tools such as Infrastructure Pattern Matching and Predictive Cost Modeling to identify and communicate the extra cost of nonreusable or inefficient applications early in the project lifecycle. This information allows planners to mold application specifications to more closely match infrastructure goals and best practices, as well as business objectives.

Some infrastructure managers complain that they are not invited to planning meetings, so they don't have the opportunity to influence solutions. However, these infrastructure managers can't contribute to the planning process if they haven't spent enough time developing mature patterns, services, and cost models that enable them to assess new projects quickly and suggest reasonable options. Doing this sort of work in advance makes it easier to provide fast, early cost estimates and deployment time lines, which are quite valuable in the business planning process.

Once infrastructure managers have demonstrated proficiency with this type of analysis, business units will invite their involvement. Infrastructure managers will be able to steer business managers toward more suitable application infrastructure decisions that more closely match core IT competencies and existing infrastructure.

Step 4: Refining Patterns and Project Plans

Infrastructure development priorities must match business priorities and leverage points. Rarely will a larger application or significant business project fit into one pattern. More commonly, a set of patterns with services and other components must be linked together into an e-Business chain, to achieve the more complex design required for e-Business projects or even broader initiatives that follow when organizations integrate traditional business and e-Business. Pattern refinement is addressed in more detail later in this chapter, and in the later half of the book.

Step 5: Implementing and Operating

Once you define strategic activities and infrastructure requirements, the rest of the project is a matter of implementing and maintaining the application. Infrastructure subassemblies should be built with evolution and manageability in mind. Periodic "feedback" sessions with business should guide efforts to refine IT implementation plans.

The Importance of People Skills

No process can happen without people, at least not in infrastructure planning. So who are these people and where do they come from? Even more challenging is this question: How can current team members find time for infrastructure planning processes such as the ones defined above?

The first step is to get the process defined. Don't assemble a team and fail to assign roles. Organize the team only after clearly identifying which processes really work inside your organization. Then determine which centers of excellence should exist and reorganize staff to ensure even more excellence and efficiency. Meanwhile, get team members from different organizational entities to work together without making them all report to the same group.

This method is a virtual team, or matrix, approach. One key strategy is to have at least one full-time person assigned to lead key processes. Depending on the size of the organization and volume of work, you might need more than one person. These full-time infrastructure planners assemble teams to complete the work, inserting appropriate experts in specific technology areas as needed.

Infrastructure planners also document the infrastructure plans and handle other tasks between team meetings. It's important that infrastructure planning resources be dedicated. They should *not* be on a pager or have too many other responsibilities. Otherwise, they will not have time for important infrastructure planning processes and the work will never be finished.

Eventually, infrastructure planners should report to management separately from application development and operations, precisely because their job is to make sure work gets passed efficiently between the two groups—that applications are deployed and operated successfully through better planning. Not having to report to either group helps infrastructure planners make more independent decisions to best connect the two major IT constituencies.

Similarly, infrastructure planners work best when they are separated from traditional architecture concerns and are more in touch with day-to-day infrastructure deployment and operational planning. This separation helps ensure that the plans they develop will be realistic. Figure 1.7 depicts the delicately balanced role that infrastructure planners play in the space between administrative, operational, and architectural responsibilities.

To cope with future challenges, infrastructure planners need strong skills in networking, security, and middleware. These skills are critical compared to more traditional skills in servers or other physical infrastructure strata components.

To build an infrastructure planning team, hire people who have a larger view of infrastructure and are not going to concentrate on simply holding up their particular technical area's goals. In contrast, a few traditional architects do this very well, but they must be willing to plan for implementation and compromise long-term architectural goals to get something done in the short term as well.

Assessing the Skills Required

People issues are especially important when it comes to the convergence of traditional business and e-Business. Important goals first need to be translated into infrastructure requirements. For example, if you want to improve customer retention by coordinating multiple points of interaction (call center, Web, and e-mail response), you should translate this goal into infrastructure requirements, such as improving the level of consistency across multiple points of interactivity and the speed with which a change in one interaction mechanism is updated to others.

Previous sections of this book discussed Infrastructure Pattern Matching methods for translating business drivers into infrastructure patterns and using the adaptive infrastructure platform structure as a checklist to identify and select critical components. At some point, however, infrastructure requirements become people requirements.

For example, if the business driver is speed to market, you should buy existing applications instead of doing significant development work in-house. You might also need to hire outsourcers or system integrators to help develop the project. What impact will this approach have on your staffing requirements? Application development skills might be less important than outsourcer and project management skills.

Similarly, a goal of increased market share might call for bleeding-edge multimedia site design, supported by new technology skills and new operational techniques. Increased customer service levels might require strategic activities, such as integrating multiple points of interaction (POI). Beyond the technical skills required to integrate multiple POI, organizations will require someone with excellent relationship management skills to closely coordinate the activities of the formerly autonomous call center and the Web development team, or between the marketing department and the Web operations team.

A number of e-Business initiatives focus on supply chain management solutions, which help reduce business costs via electronic interaction with partners in the supply chain. The need to integrate with multiple partners requires an employee skilled in managing partner relationships.

Just as business requirements drive infrastructure requirements, they also indirectly or directly drive staffing requirements. Business planners must translate business and infrastructure drivers into skills requirements, even at a very early stage, then inventory their own organizations to see if the requisite skill sets are available.

In many cases, these initiatives will create new roles within IT that are less technical and more business related, although applicants still must have strong technical knowledge. In many cases, IT will be required to recruit business people adept at soft skills such as relationship management and project planning.

The critical issue in this planning stage is that you develop a list of skill requirements and then map those to existing skill sets—not the other way around.

Increased Pressure to Deliver

The speed of business change is clearly the biggest difference for e-Business projects as opposed to traditional IT projects. The fact that the business cycle is now shrinking from years to months increases the pressure on development and implementation teams. e-Business teams must include people who enjoy working under this kind of pressure.

However, externalizing services creates even more pressure on IT staff. Once applications are customer-facing, they become the de facto image of an organization. Slow, unreliable, inefficient, and antiquated applications make your company look the same way in customers' eyes, whether the customer is looking at a Web site or navigating through an IVR system. Consequently, this situation increases the pressure to provide high availability and high-performance infrastructure, even if it is infrastructure that your organization no longer controls.

Excellence is mandatory in customer-facing applications and the people behind these applications must be excellent, too. But new skills and process will be required to maintain 99.999% availability.

Delivering applications to multiple POI increases the importance of integrating data and supporting diverse user interfaces. New roles must be created to ensure the appropriate level of consistency across interfaces for applications being developed by different departments.

As business and e-Business converge, infrastructure developers must create standard application programming interfaces (APIs), procedures, and templates to be reused consistently by multiple development teams. Speed must be replaced with reusability as a core goal.

Consistency requirements also drive organizational coordination. Multiple disciplines, such as marketing, legal, human resources, and sales, must cooperate to produce a successful implementation. Internal relationships are critical, especially those that involve building and coordinating applications across business boundaries.

Many of the internal challenges are even more critical for external applications involving partners or alliances. You might solve these problems more effectively on the external side, simply because you *must.* The business is visibly pushing and helping; use that leadership support to take new approaches.

Indeed, relationship building is the key skill for effective business. Meeting shortened development lifecycles demands coordination across internal disciplines, cooperation with partners, and effective outsourcing. These efforts require more effective relationship skills than IT has required in the past.

New Types of Relationships

Organizations must stop categorizing relationships as "inside" versus "outside" and stop looking at vendors as the only form of partnership. The combination of traditional business and e-Business demands a new spectrum of relationships, including joint ventures, independent agents, and partners, as well as careful selection of vendors, service providers, and outsourcers. Each of these relationships has an infrastructure component, and each must be managed.

These demands exacerbate problems with internal constituencies, including human resources, legal, marketing, public relations, accounting, and the line of business itself. For example, hiring and retaining skilled IT people is still a problem, though not as bad as it once was. It is important to have an excellent working relationship with human resources to coordinate an effective strategy, and to educate human resources on the unique care and feeding requirements of IT staff.

The legal department is another good example. In the past, IT has not generally needed legal advice. However, e-Business introduced new legal issues, and the legal landscape continues to shift rapidly. Software patents that affect the way companies can do business are introduced daily. Privacy issues are escalating, especially for international organizations. Which government's laws govern global e-Business, or orders telephoned into a call center? What state or national laws are changing? How do they affect existing Web-based applications and future strategic activities? These issues must be addressed at the strategic level, as projects progress, and even as rules change, affecting existing applications. Organizations must establish an effective legal oversight and early warning mechanism for efforts in this new world.

As the above examples illustrate, it is imperative that organizations establish effective relationships, define processes involving internal and external partners, and clearly establish responsibility to manage these relationships.

Figure 4.2 shows the increased complexity of the relationships required to develop effective next-generation business processes. The concentric ellipses represent different degrees of autonomy within an organization, fanning out from internal IT and the relationships that IT must develop and maintain. This list does not by any means show the number or scope of all possible relationships.

Organizations must develop their own diagram and evaluate the key people who manage these relationships, as well as the processes and mechanisms they have in place to develop and enhance the value of the relationship. The new relationship is defined by the elegance of your process plus the human beings actually doing the work.

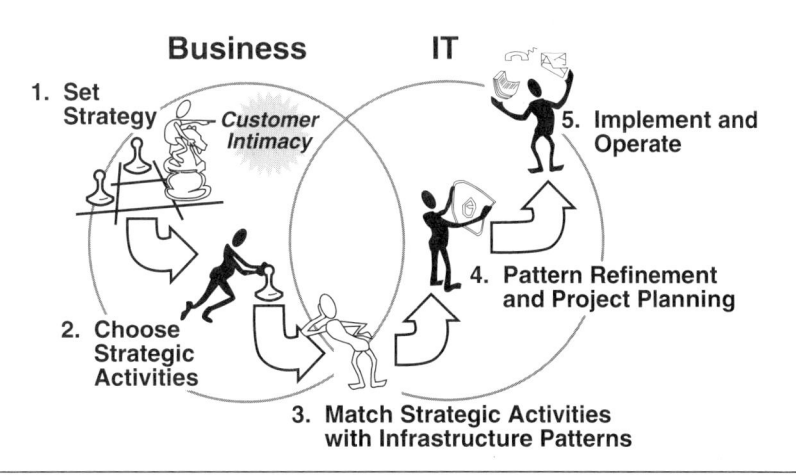

Figure 4.2 Important Internal and External Relationships

Developing Relationship-based Management

Going beyond good relationships, you need a key role and skills to make relationships work. A relationship-based management structure should include new roles, responsibilities, and defined processes to help manage relationships. Organizations must apply to all these other relationships the same formal methods used to manage outsourcer relationships, such as partnerships, internal cooperation, and community development.

Organizations should implement relationship-based team structures, skills, and management processes. Relationship-based management (RBM) involves working with third parties to accomplish change and improve performance.

Three key success criteria for implementing RBM are:

- Solid, well-defined contracts that retain intent
- Correct relationship management focus and skills
- Clear, balanced metrics that are continuously improving

The mission of the RBM team is to maximize:

- Success of the partner/outsourcer relationship
- Business relevance of partnered/outsourced services
- Customer satisfaction on both sides of business relationship

To implement a relationship management structure, organizations must employ new skill sets and teams. Table 4.1 illustrates the hierarchy of new skills required, beyond the fundamental finance management and project planning kills. The critical role in the new RBM structure is a

Table 4.1 Key RBM Skills

Fundamentals	People Skills
Contract and finance management	Personnel management
Technology, market, and business awareness	Team building and goal setting
Project planning and management	Motivation
Relationship advocacy	Relationship
Expectation setting and management	Skills
Negotiation and communication	

relationship manager. This individual (or individuals, in larger relationships) has profit-and-loss responsibility, authority of approval regarding contract revisions, and accountability for the overall relationship. The relationship manager requires full executive sponsorship.

The relationship manager must have previous executive-level experience, with the following specific skill sets:

- Familiarity with the purpose of the outsourcing relationship, its history, and the structure of the agreement
- Understanding of general business strategy and direction
- Self-motivation and the ability to command respect within the organization
- Knowledge of user requirements
- Strong communications and marketing skills
- Familiarity with technology issues and challenges
- Strong negotiating and problem-solving skills
- Team-building and motivational skills

New Business Roles

Leading-edge organizations are inventing new positions and helping traditional roles evolve. Brand managers take on new responsibilities, such as ensuring consistency of the look-and-feel across different POI. In most organizations, these new roles evolve at the new speed of business. Organizations must be flexible and open up new roles as the paths of business and e-Business converge.

Not all organizations will need all of these new roles, nor is this list exhaustive. The critical point is that organizations must be flexible and understand that to be effective they have to create new roles and modify existing roles. Table 4.2 shows a number of examples.

Human resources must establish an effective process to define new roles and establish an effective compensation package.

Effective Recruiting

The next obvious questions are how do you find the bodies to fill these roles, and how do you establish effective compensation and motivation packages that will retain existing employees?

Table 4.2 New Roles for e-Business

Role	Description
Relationship manager	Works with business partners and vendors at business and technical levels to promote a smooth working relationship.
Vendor and sourcing manager	Maintains relationships with vendors and outsourcers.
Internal partner manager	Maintains relationships with internal corporate resource groups.
Chief security officer	Coordinates security activities across lines of business; determines policies and sets security standards at the highest level across the organization. This position is more independent than traditional security roles in IT. This person reports directly to the CIO or separately to the CEO.
Chief technical officer (CTO)	Works with IT and business to evaluate impact of new technology and to show where new technology or sourcing options should be applied. This person must have one foot in the technology world and the other in the business world, and be able to clearly communicate in both languages. This person must communicate at the highest level to help articulate the business value of technology.
Chief customer officer	Owns the extremely valuable corporate asset known as customer relationships. Helps establish and manage the customer relationship management (CRM) strategy, associated tactics and operational policies; and establishes guidelines for cross-functional integration of the customer view. This person reports to the CEO, representing the interests of the customer.

For many companies, compensation is reaching 40 percent of their IT budgets, not including outsourcing, contract, or consultant labor cost. IT managers must be proactive in addressing human capital management issues.

Retention and turnover are major problem areas for most IT groups. On average, IT departments experience a 15 percent annual turnover, highlighting the greater need for focused retention and training efforts.

The estimated cost of turnover is 1.5 to 2 times the annual salary of the lost employee, as placement fees hover at 20 to 30 percent, with sign-on and special bonuses adding to the costs. In addition, there could be relocation costs and other perks or incentives.

Human resources must establish an effective process to define new roles and establish an attractive compensation package. Finding, training, and deploying IT staff require creative, responsive recruitment policies. Some enterprise human resources departments are out of touch with the recruitment challenges within IT. More adaptive corporations are creating the role of IT recruitment specialist to develop new strategies for recruiting and retaining IT staff.

Even in people-rich environments, critical skill sets could be scarce. IT must work closely with human resources to enable innovative recruitment and training processes. For successful sourcing strategies, look to the following potential employment sources.

Dot-com fallout. Dissatisfied or laid-off employees from dot-com companies increasingly understand the benefits of working for large, stable companies with plenty of resources. Many experienced IT staff are also disillusioned when their stock options lose value. Watching the stock market valuations of related companies can help tap into this potential talent source.

International experts. Many IT recruiters look outside the U.S. for help. Hiring internationally requires knowledge of immigration laws or retaining experienced immigration consultants. Organizations that look overseas for talent might have to adapt the work environment to accommodate staffers with limited English skills, sensitizing coworkers and making sure foreign workers can still become part of the team.

Retraining talent. Former Y2K experts can lead other projects and programs. Organizations should look for promising individuals who are interested in a career change. New programming concepts can be taught, but loyalty, intelligence, diligence, and commitment cannot.

Strategic use of consultants. Free agents can be effective resources, freeing staff from more mundane tasks to assume more value-added endeavors, thus aiding retention.

Retaining Employees

Although compensation plays a large role in employee satisfaction, it isn't the only factor. IT managers must actively manage employee commitment. High-tech employees expect above-average compensation, but they are also attracted to an environment in which they are valued and appreciated for technical and business skills, and where they have a chance to work on interesting projects.

Organizations that encourage skills development and career planning tend to keep employees longer. Other tactics, such as non-cash incentives that focus on quality of life, are helpful to improve long-term retention. However, standard retention strategies such as paid tuition, flextime, day care, and a relaxed work environment are no longer significant differentiators in a total compensation package.

Organizations must vary the incentives offered to appeal to the desired people, jobs, and skill sets.

Understanding Infrastructure Planning

Once you comprehend the business/IT project lifecycle, it helps to understand a bit more clearly what is involved in infrastructure planning. Two approaches to infrastructure planning are:

- Tactical, or "per-project" planning, is performed for every new application development or infrastructure-driven project. This type of planning is normally associated with the business/IT project lifecycle.

- Strategic, or "periodic" planning, is performed annually. It sets the standards and strategies across projects, evaluating and adjusting priorities as appropriate.

The diagram in Figure 4.3 helps clarify infrastructure planning, illustrating a high-level view of a process model adapted specifically to infrastructure planning.

This model, based on the well-known Integrated Test and Operations System (ITOS) methodology, shows that infrastructure planning has various related inputs, tools, outputs, and services. Traditional concerns, such as architecture domains or application development, are indicated as processes outside of, but interfacing with, infrastructure planning. The inputs and outputs show what is needed to do the work and what is being produced that will contribute to the next step in the process. The steps in Figure 4.3 are *outside* the infrastructure planning process. Figure 4.4 shows the steps *inside* the process.

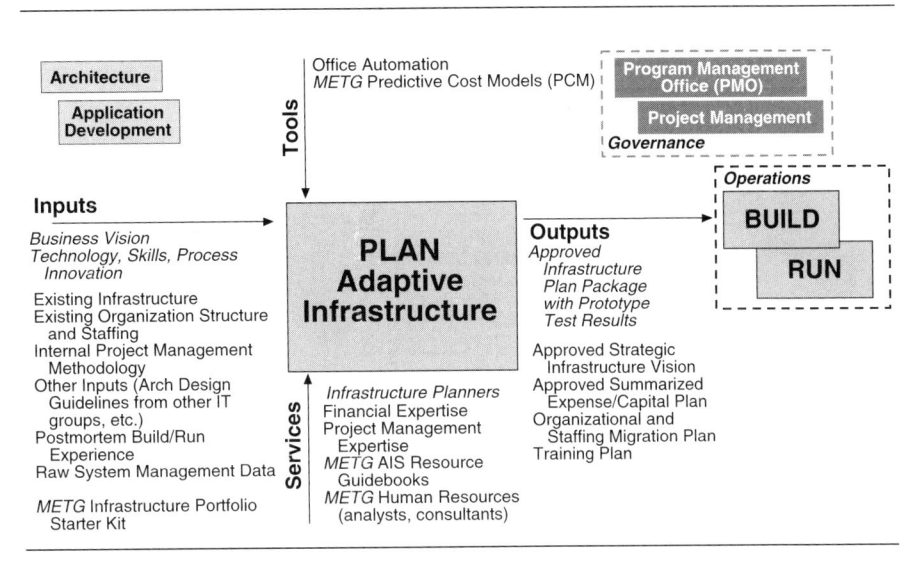

Figure 4.3 Infrastructure Planning Model

This diagram shows the two major aspects of infrastructure planning discussed earlier:

- Periodic/strategic processes are represented by the block labeled "Manage Infrastructure Strategies and Standards."

- Per-project/tactical processes are represented by the blocks labeled "Assimilate Infrastructure Change."

The diagram also shows other activities related to infrastructure planning. For instance, before starting the planning process, you might generate game plans and assess new or unfamiliar infrastructure through proof-of-concept testing. These steps should be taken independently of the main strategic and tactical planning activities. As an outcome of the process, you might use integration and stress tests to prototype and verify projected service levels on actual infrastructure. Additional work could be required for planning or recommending organizational improvements.

Output from these processes is reviewed by governance bodies such as technology steering committees, program management offices, and budget committees. Most organizations have some sort of governance oversight for major project stages. For example, before plans go into prototyping, governance should approve new budget expenditures.

The next section of this book examines in detail the steps involved in per-project planning and in refining infrastructure pattern designs. Later

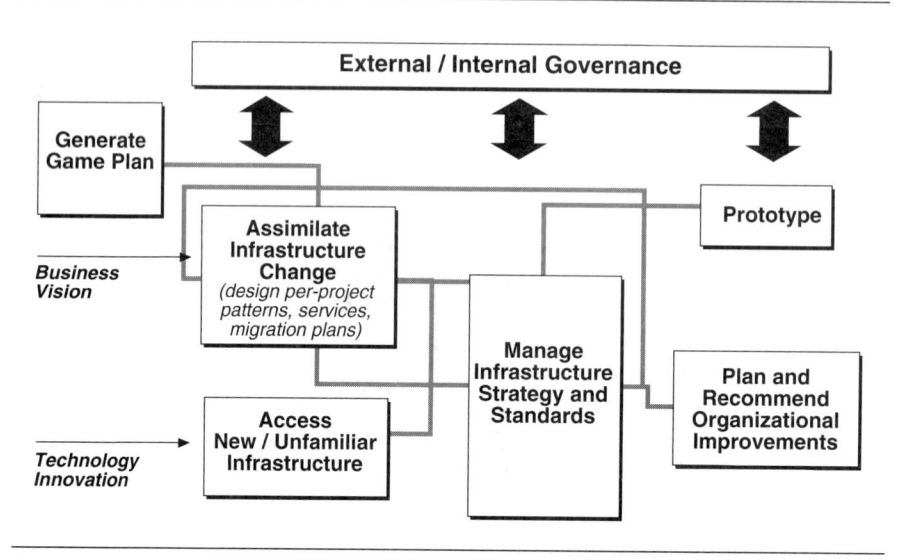

Figure 4.4 Major Steps in the Infrastructure Planning Model

chapters will examine detail design considerations for each of the major layers in the adaptive infrastructure platform.

Details of Project Planning

Per-project planning involves developing plans for supporting each project that the business requires. As shown in Figure 4.5, per-project

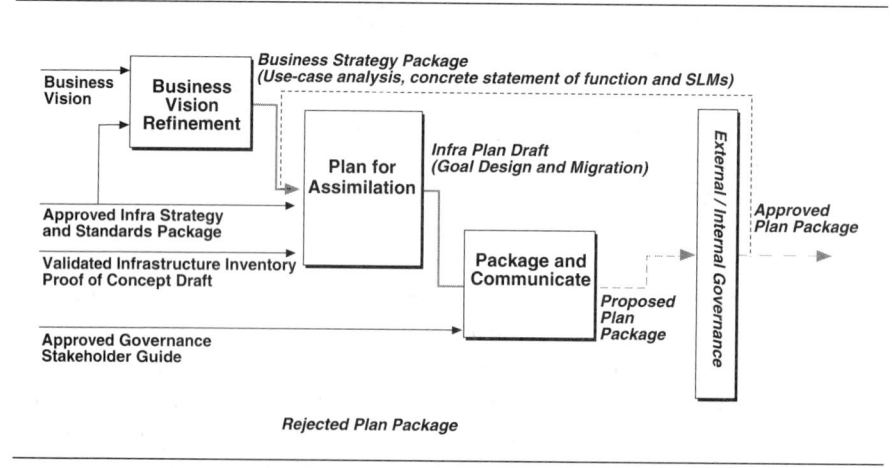

Figure 4.5 Per-Project Planning Activities

planning includes specific activities you must conduct for each project that requires infrastructure support.

Three major activities occur in the project planning stage:

Business Vision Refinement. You must understand the customer's vision to be able to plan properly. As part of this activity, you must collect business vision information that you can use in other process steps. A good approach is to leverage application developers' use-case analysis reports. Detailed statements of user behavior are easier to map to infrastructure patterns than are vague formulations such as "business-to-business." The output of this activity should include a use-case analysis, a concrete statement of functionality, and service level metrics.

Assimilation Planning. Figure 4.6 shows the steps involved in assimilation planning. Assuming you have an inventory of current infrastructure, define a goal and plan migration toward that goal. The final task, assembling the infrastructure plan draft, helps verify that the migration plan and the initial goal plan are unified and communicated effectively.

Once you define design goals, you can develop a preliminary migration plan and assemble a draft of the infrastructure plan. Here, you must understand the use cases and describe in detail how you will address them. Full refinement of your design should wait until you communicate with the customer and obtain budget approval.

Package and Communicate. This activity is required to secure management approval. Your packaged project plans must be based on realistic

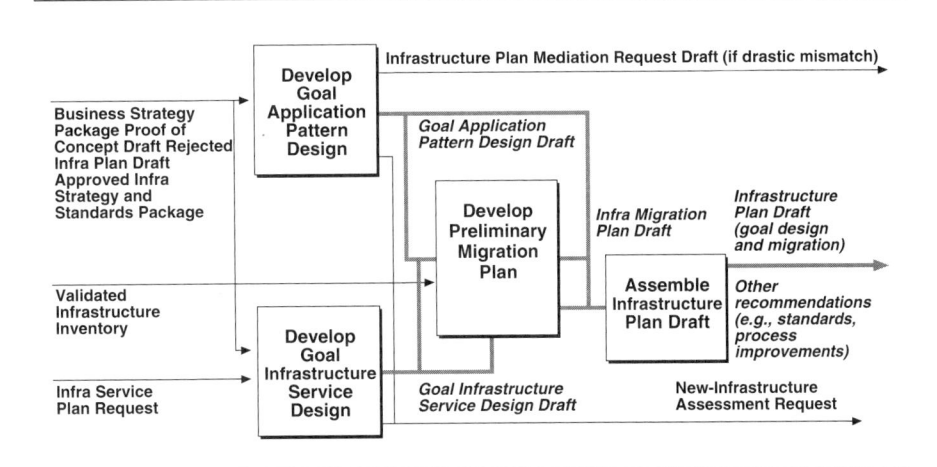

Figure 4.6 Planning for Assimilation

vision requirements. The packaging process can include such activities as finding champions and funding for the project, preparing presentations, and calling meetings to explain your plan to key participants.

A formal communication plan helps structure your thinking about which constituencies must be addressed, including those who approve the budget and those who might influence budget approvers. Once you develop a successful approach, continue to use it for later projects.

Packaging Infrastructure

Obtaining startup funds for e-Business or for converged business projects is not usually a problem. Most of these projects are a highly visible priority for the organization, although it can be a challenge to garner sufficient funding for infrastructure such as networks, storage, and servers as opposed to user interface tools and applications. The application development stage of these projects is generally more visible to the project stakeholders than the infrastructure that the application must run on.

Infrastructure developers must relate the infrastructure to the application so that business leaders and project stakeholders understand how the failure or inadequacies of the infrastructure will affect the specific application.

A more significant challenge is to obtain funding for the ongoing maintenance of the application. This potential funding disconnect was exacerbated by the fact that many e-Business projects were built with immature tools, yet the application must be highly available (7 days a week, 24 hours a day, with no planned downtime).

Projects are often infused with an exciting energy in the initial development stage. People work longer hours to get the project going. However, it is unrealistic to plan on the same level of effort once the project is in production. Budgeting must take into account more realistic work hours and the need for additional staff to take up the slack when the hectic pace subsides and staff returns to normal working hours.

Infrastructure planners shouldn't lump all infrastructure into one monolithic budget and expect to get funding. Planners must, as much as possible, tie discrete chunks of the budget to specific applications or services that are tangible to the business. Infrastructure funding must be married to business value. Infrastructure planners have four basic options for packaging infrastructure, as shown in Figure 4.7.

Behind-the-wall assets. This portion of the infrastructure is universally used so that it cannot be tied to any particular application; it is the

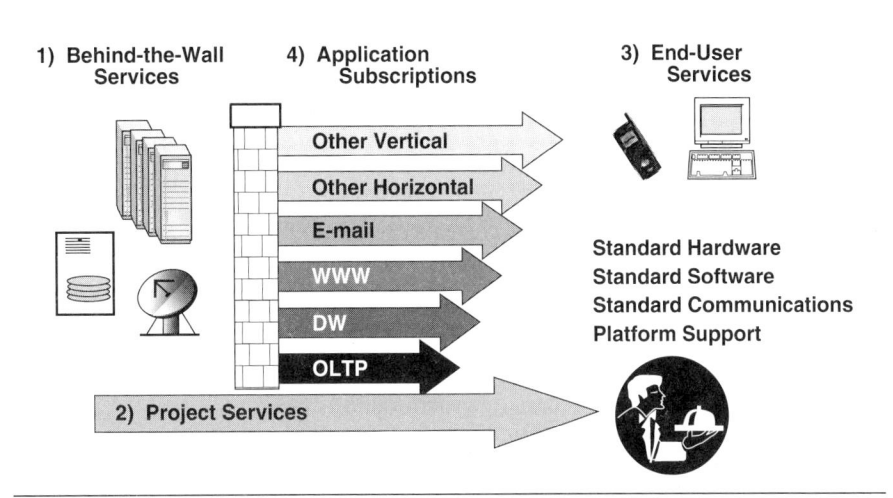

Figure 4.7 Packaging Infrastructure

infrastructure required to keep the business running. While it's a good idea to dedicate as much of the budget to services the business can understand, a set of core components will always need to be funded regardless. Unfortunately, many organizations stop the budgeting process before such funding is committed.

Desktop services. This portion of the budget represents the incremental cost of employees. Some organizations subdivide this budget category to offer different services for different employee types. Others standardize on one or two platforms to simplify management. Usually this budget component consists of the PC and the collaborative applications, such as Microsoft Office. It can also include portions of the campus network infrastructure, such as LAN ports, as well as desktop and LAN support costs.

Application subscriptions. This method takes into account the cost of delivering applications to users, regardless of whether they are employees or customers. If the user is anonymous, as in many e-Business applications, the user base could be defined as the number of concurrent users the infrastructure is expected to support. This approach is similar to the application service provider (ASP) model. For application subscriptions and desktop services, it is important to offer a range of prices that depend on the total number of users. If a group of desktop users suddenly relocates to another site, it is not realistic to expect the same price for the remaining users. The incremental price per user must increase to account for the relative increase in the fixed cost component. Similarly, business should not expect an infrastructure that is designed to support 100 users to scale to support 1,000 users without significant investments in new infrastructure. The price increment helps remind business managers of infrastructure realities.

Project services. Generally, project funding refers to the funding required to get a project operational. These costs are usually associated with the development portion of an application project or with onetime infrastructure investments. Once the project is operational, the subscription service kicks in.

Packaging simplifies negotiation with the business by tying costs to services that the business values, and using those services to help guide how infrastructure is apportioned. When you are developing pricing models for discrete services, don't present a budget that is too granular. Regardless of pricing technique, you should proactively obtain proposals from outsourcers and ASPs for the same services to justify budget levels and to get ideas on how to structure packages.

Wherever possible, use package pricing to drive behavior and to achieve infrastructure goals. For example, you should charge more for nonstandard desktops or 2-Tier applications. Offer clear choices tied to application or service functionality, and let the business make the trade-off decisions.

The emphasis should be on delivery of a package of "services and products" to the business, not technologies. It is imperative that you sell the *benefits* of the package to the business in a way that relates to their goals, not technology *features*.

Designing Patterns

Designing patterns involves two activities:

- Apply business vision and strategy to develop a preliminary set of pattern choices.
- Then create from them a more refined set of pattern designs, either for the first time (to jump-start or to fully define the standard pattern) or to adapt the standard pattern to the particular per-project details.

Pattern design consists of five major steps, as shown in Figure 4.8 and outlined on the following pages.

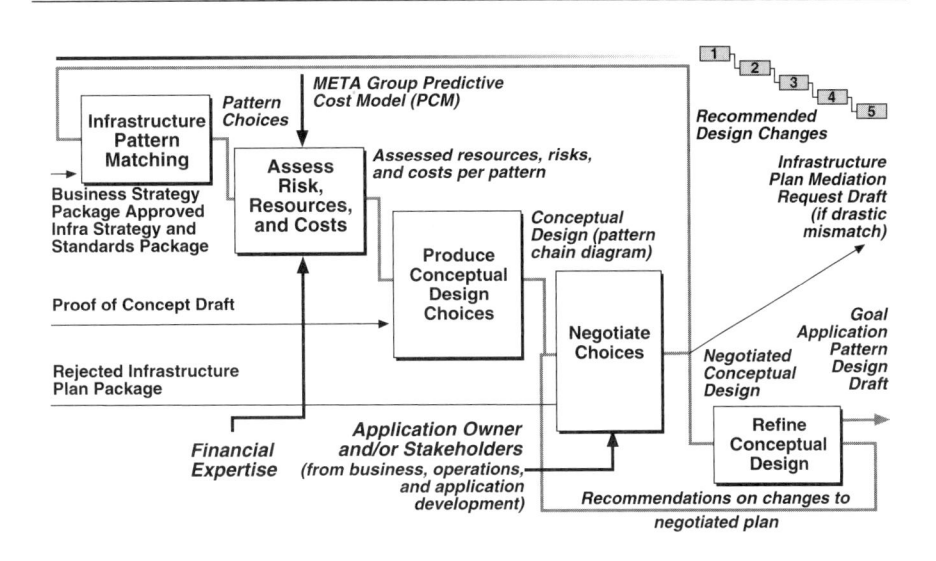

Figure 4.8 Designing Patterns

Step 1: Infrastructure Pattern Matching

Infrastructure pattern matching (IPM) is used during project planning to determine which patterns best fit given business requirements.

Typically, infrastructure professionals jump into detailed design and implementation as quickly as possible. It's familiar, it's interesting, and it's what they are paid to do. As the design gets more technical, it is more difficult to engage the business. Design problems are encountered and trade-offs must be made; yet the business usually is incapable of participating in discussions at the technical level.

IPM helps keep the discussion at an appropriate level to get infrastructure planning started and yet keep the business engaged in the process. Using IPM, infrastructure developers, working with the business, can highlight business-critical design trade-offs and adjust infrastructure investment priorities. IPM revolves around three questions:

- Who is the user? Users might include employees, customers, or business partners.
- Where is the user located? Locations might include headquarters, branch offices, remote individuals, or anywhere on the Internet.
- What work is the user performing? Answers to this question map to the various pattern categories. In other words, the user might need to Transact, Publish, or Collaborate.

As shown in Figure 4.9, these business-friendly questions can uncover the information necessary to predict what infrastructure is required for new business initiatives very early in their lifecycle—even before a product is selected by the IT applications development group.

The infrastructure patterns outlined in Chapter 3 provide established sets of infrastructure that can be described or differentiated by who the users are, where the users are, and what they're doing. For example, the three pattern categories are a simple set of "what" answers to use. Simple answers to simple questions help you identify the right pattern(s) for the initiative or application program.

Table 4.3 shows an example of Infrastructure Pattern Matching. Notice that the table shows the entire list of available patterns, and allows you to quickly map user requirements to the appropriate pattern(s).

Step 2: Assess Risk, Resources, and Costs

After determining the patterns required for a business initiative or application, the next step is to define detailed service level requirements and to generate initial cost, resource, and risk assessments for the project. These factors give the business early guidance in deciding what infrastructure will be required.

Predictive cost modeling (PCM) techniques help put a price tag on infrastructure development projects by helping identify what resources are required and what those resources will cost. PCM takes into account

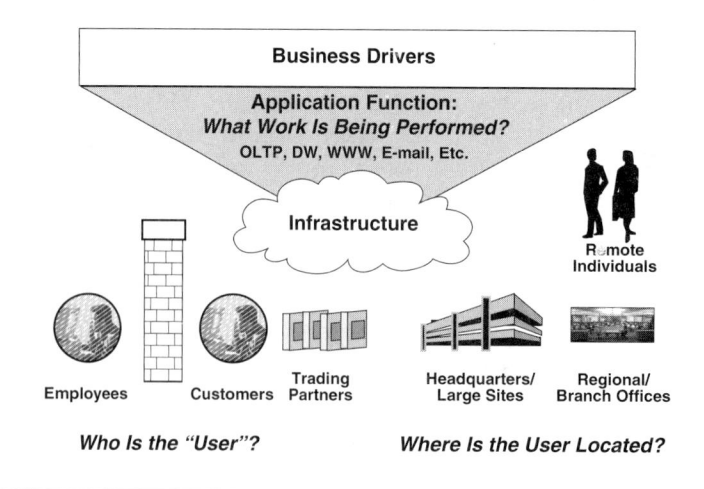

Figure 4.9 Designing Patterns

Table 4.3 An Example of Infrastructure Pattern Matching

INFRASTRUCTURE PATTERN MATCHING (IPM)

Pattern		IPM Primary	IPM Secondary	IPM Tertiary	Use Case
Publish	Web Publish	Document	Read-Only	None	Advertising, Online catalog
	Client/Server Publish	Record	Read-Only	None	n/a
	Stream Publish	Stream	Read-Only (one-way flow)	None	n/a
Collaborate	Real-time Collaborate	Stream	Read-Only (two-way flow)	None	n/a
	Store-and-Forward Collaborate	Document	Read/Write (sequentially)	Coordination: Manual	Push Notification
	Structured Collaborate	Document	Read/Write (sequentially)	Coordination: Automated	n/a
Transact	1-Tier Transact	Record	Read/Write (simultaneously)	Partitioning: Monolithic (Host)	n/a
	2-Tier Transact	Record	Read/Write (simultaneously)	Partitioning: Data only (2-Tier)	n/a
	3/N-Tier Transact	Record	Read/Write (simultaneously)	Partitioning: Data and presentation (3/N-Tier)	Ordering, Registration

the infrastructure complexity involved in supporting an application or business function.

This technique is different from most current total cost of ownership (TCO) models, which aren't structured to analyze new applications. The rapid proliferation of business application choices has expanded infrastructure complexity and cut the life span of TCO models to about 6 to 12 months.

Making assumptions about future applications using dated cost models, especially while application development cycles continue to shrink, institutionalizes existing thinking, good or bad. Such assumptions lead to a repetition of mistakes when assembling applications and their requisite infrastructure. Most TCO models are resource-based, accounting for the number of servers to be used, the number of database licenses, and so on. These types of measurements offer little that you can use in negotiation with business users, since you have no easy way to tie the application benefits and complexity to resource costs.

PCM, on the other hand, is an easy-to-use, coarsely grained model that will help you select the most cost-effective infrastructure option within a number of days, while still accounting for TCO.

PCM moves IPM from simply matching a pattern to providing detail on risks, bills-of-materials, and costs. To reach this next level of infrastructure definition, you need more than three questions to pick which pattern is required. You need a structured, repeatable questionnaire.

Three components are used in PCM:

- Cost drivers. Drivers are characteristics of a business initiative or application that affect complexity. For example, how many users are expected? What response time is required, and what availability is required?
- Cost buckets. Buckets help PCM define costs for each item that consumes resources and costs money, such as a server or a person.
- Linking. PCM establishes a link between the complexity of the cost drivers and its effect on any possible resources.

For example, there are 28 cost drivers within the 3/N-Tier Transact pattern. Cost drivers can be discovered by asking a series of simple questions, such as:

- How is data being shared?
- What is the transaction load?
- What is the security requirement?
- What is the business volatility?

These questions are interview tools that infrastructure developers can use to gather information from application developers, business users, or the operations group. The multiple-choice answers to these questions more closely target the appropriate technology to the application being developed.

Even if you don't use a PCM tool and use infrastructure pattern matching instead, you must do similar work to define costs, resources, and risks. Then you must work to keep these definitions directly tied to business requirements for the project so that those costs can be easily mapped back to what the business wanted during negotiation.

Step 3: Communicate Conceptual Design Choices

The next step is to create a simple diagram of pattern choices that shows what the infrastructure might look like, for the benefit of any interested parties, including business managers, application developers, operations people, architects. Figure 4.10 shows an example of what such a diagram might look like.

You need not develop huge Visio diagrams with all the details. Detailed diagrams will come later. This initial diagram must be simple enough for business people to understand immediately. More detail will be developed during the "Refine Design" step, later in the planning process (Step 5).

Omission of the simple design step leads to later misunderstandings that could have been avoided or cleared up with earlier documentation of goals and designs. Take the time to generate simple yet appropriate diagrams before starting negotiations with business stakeholders on costs versus design trade-offs. You'll have something to show, but you will *not* have spent too much time refining the details, because things will likely change again during negotiation. The goal is to complete the negotiation phase in a timely manner.

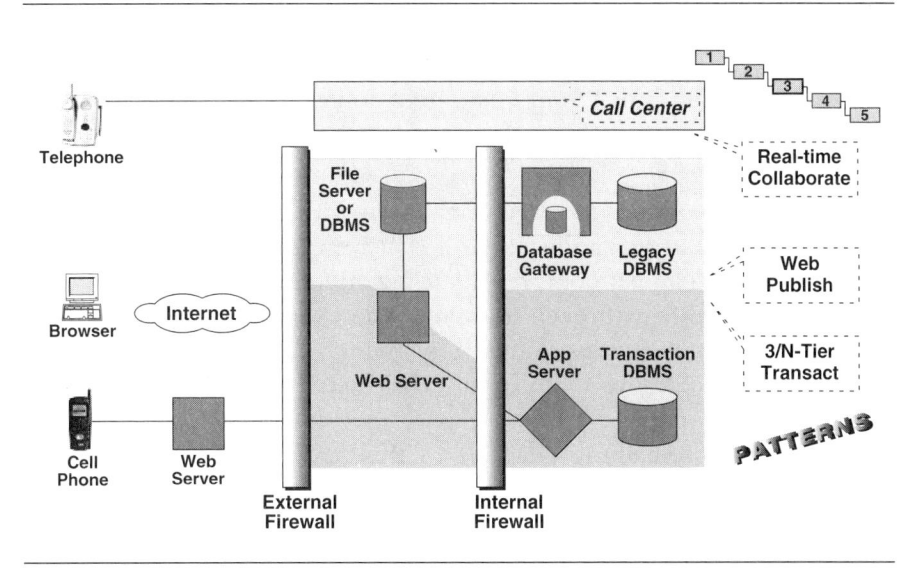

Figure 4.10 A Simple Conceptual Design

Step 4: Negotiate with the Business

Early and direct negotiation during the design process keeps business stakeholders engaged and happy. During negotiation, you should:

- Provide options for stakeholders to consider. Do not let business people dictate technology. Provide them with a set of options that represent the range of choices within the patterns you support.
- Distinguish options by service levels. If business managers ask for excessive service levels, don't say no. Find out what they care about and what service levels they might pay for.
- Provide complete costs and an idea of affordability. Complete costs include costs across the entire infrastructure lifecycle of plan, build, deploy, and run. Any cost assessment should also take into account the *adaptive cost,* which is the cost to change over time.
- Show full value. Communicate the complete cost and benefits, speaking in business rather than technical terms, so that business stakeholders see the full value of what you are proposing. Initial presentations can use informal, face-to-face meetings that secure buy-in with the immediate group. Later, you can formally package and communicate these ideas for final approval by a wider audience.

During the negotiation phase, use communication plan templates as guides for making informal value propositions. As convincing arguments are developed in this direct negotiation session, capture these for later use when preparing the full communication package. Likewise, note things that your customers don't buy into—and avoid them later.

Step 5: Refine Conceptual Design

The last step is to refine the design with complete design blueprints that reuse patterns and standards that were developed by other processes.

You can get good results using an iterative design process, increasing the depth with each iteration. The example below goes through a recommended series of iterations, which you can collapse into fewer iterations for more mature patterns. Figure 4.11 gives a basic overview of this process.

The remaining chapters of this book apply this process to the two adaptive infrastructure patterns that are most important in the emerging IT world: Web Publish and 3/N-Tier Transact.

First iteration: Focus on architecture. When refining the pattern design, first determine architecture designs that will fit. Leverage any

```
┌─────────────────┐
│  Architecture   │
├─────────────────┤
│   Technology    │
├─────────────────┤
│    Product      │
├─────────────────┤
│  Configuration  │
└─────────────────┘
```

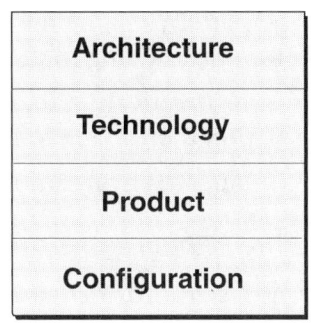

Figure 4.11 Refining Components of an Infrastructure Design

work that was done by architects in the organization, including documented principles. For example, the architecture of scale-out and stateless farm designs will greatly influence the details of both Web Publish and 3/N-Tier Transact pattern designs. If you select a pattern that will work now rather than in a few years (so a project can get built now), document the deviation from the goal's principles and the reasons for the deviation.

Second iteration: Focus on technology decisions. Use the component model of platform layers along with services to create refined pattern designs. Sometimes the solution requires nonstandard technologies, and these should also become corporate standards, even if they are not industry or open standards.

Third iteration: Focus on products. Which products meet the architecture and technology requirements? Corporate pattern standards must include product choices. If they do not, the implementation groups will be left to make decisions that generate greater variety in deployment. This proliferation of solutions would not occur if your pattern standards already describe the actual products required.

Fourth iteration: Focus on configuration issues. This factor mostly applies to more mature patterns, where enough successful implementations have occurred to determine the correct configuration details. In a mature pattern, such as Store-and-Forward Collaborate, configuration details such as file service home directory drive mappings, and other relevant information should be standardized and implemented uniformly across the organization.

When refining the design, you should:

- Agree on the pattern's higher-level design (architecture and technology) before proceeding to the lower level (product details).
- Design patterns iteratively, rather than over-optimizing components in isolation then trying to integrate them.
- Compare to standards by iteration and by component.

Example of Refined Pattern Designs

A refined pattern design provides more graphical detail about the proposed design than the earlier conceptual design used for negotiation. The same graphics and tables can be used, but they should be expanded to include all required components. Then a more complete physical design must be generated, showing appropriate redundancy levels of links and devices, along with details on configuration issues such as server and network link sizing. This physical design becomes a deliverable to the build and/or run group.

Figure 4.12 and Figure 4.13 present examples of refined designs for the 3/N-Tier Transact pattern and the Web Publish pattern.

Summary

Repeatable and periodic processes are required to design infrastructure efficiently. A portfolio approach helps ensure that standards developed in the periodic process are used during the detailed per-project planning process. Without process, even good decisions cannot become repeatable within your organization.

Correct execution of per-project processes is critical. This chapter explained per-project planning techniques in some detail, describing how to gain a clear business vision, assimilate business and other internal visions to plan goal states and migration plans, then package and communicate the basic concepts for presentation to the appropriate stakeholders. The remaining chapters of this book show you how to take the "Refine Conceptual Design" step of the pattern design process, describing the detailed architecture and technology requirements, especially as they apply to the Web Publish and 3/N-Tier Transact patterns.

Summary **113**

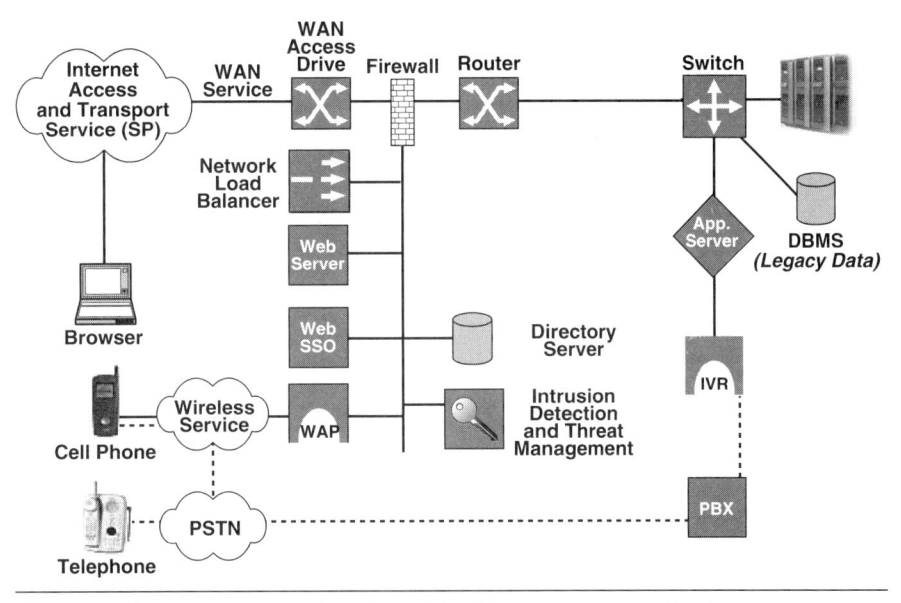

Figure 4.12 Example of Refined 3/N-Tier Transact Pattern Design

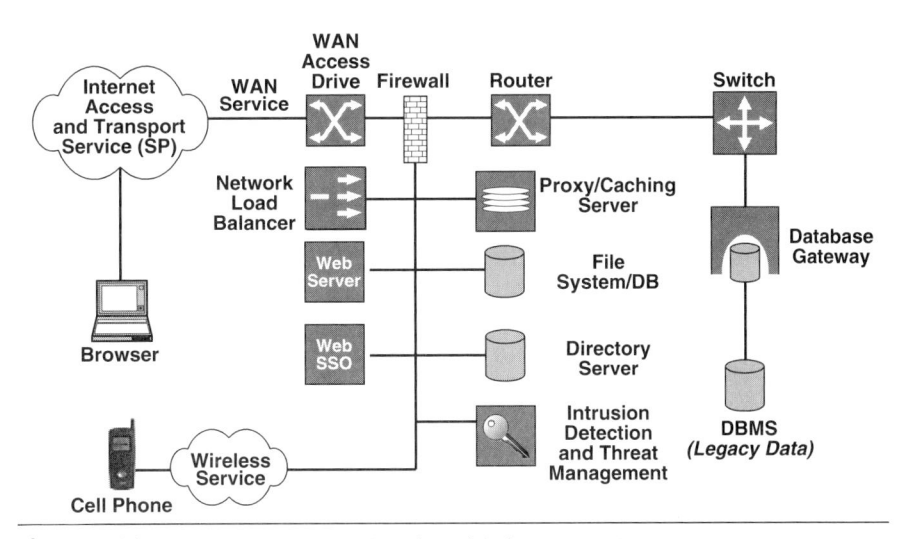

Figure 4.13 Example of Refined Web Publish Pattern Design

Chapter 5

Security Services

So far you have seen the big picture of adaptive infrastructure, including its related components, services, and patterns. You have also seen the techniques used to analyze and refine these patterns. The remaining chapters of this book explore the logic of pattern refinement at a more detailed level, explaining how to build different pattern architectures that assimilate various components of the adaptive infrastructure model.

For e-Business and beyond, the first category to consider is security services, which include both an isolation infrastructure service and an identity infrastructure service.

- An *isolation* infrastructure service focuses on protecting your perimeter and information traversing trust boundaries, including components such as firewalls, the demilitarized zone (DMZ), intrusion detection, threat management, and encryption.
- An *identify* infrastructure service focuses on user authentication and authorization, including Single Sign-On, directory services, public-key infrastructure (PKI), and more.

Remember that adaptive services are the best way to provide complete packaged sets of reusable infrastructure to the business. Although e-Business drivers pushed the need for the services "over the top," these same services are critical in a world where e-Business and traditional business converge. Later chapters will examine the key physical, functional, and interface components of e-Business infrastructure, which you should consider merging into your overall infrastructure.

Isolation Infrastructure Service

Isolation infrastructure is the set of security components that protect internal infrastructure from external attacks. In a more general sense, isolation infrastructure can be applied to any trust boundary between internal sites, business units, key processes, or the outside world. Since the goal of e-Business infrastructure is to connect to the outside world through the Internet, isolation means keeping bad things from happening, such as hacking, and allowing good things to happen, such as business, revenue, and profit.

Building a complete isolation infrastructure service requires many components, including firewalls, intrusion detection and threat management systems, and virtual private network (VPN) solutions. For the Web Publish and 3/N-Tier Transact patterns, VPN solutions are less common than firewalls, intrusion detection, and threat management. Therefore, this book focuses more on the latter components and how they fit together to provide an appropriate DMZ architecture. The discussion starts with the firewall, describes the full details of DMZ design, and finally lists other required or optional components.

Understanding Firewalls

A firewall is a boundary device located immediately behind the Internet router, or behind any router that connects to a less trusted network. The router controls the flow of packets or sessions to and from the Internet based on factors such as the source, destination, protocol, port, time of day, and activity. The main function of the firewall is to protect resources from unauthorized or malicious access, while still allowing appropriate traffic to flow through with minimal interference. Figure 5.1 shows the general configuration of these components.

Firewall Types

Firewalls generally use two fundamental approaches to analyzing Internet traffic.

Application Proxy Firewalls. These components act as an intermediary much like the typical proxy server discussed in the caching server

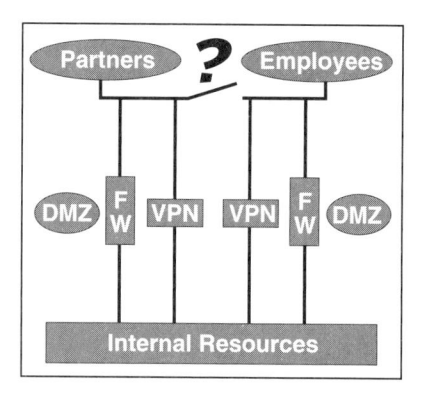

Figure 5.1 Understanding Firewalls

section of Chapter 6. The firewall relays client session requests to trusted resources. Because these firewalls operate at the application layer, they provide some degree of session reassembly, which means you can filter based on high-level details such as context or commands. This level of security degrades performance, however, because the firewall must reassemble and inspect every packet. Additionally, this type of firewall is less flexible because new proxies must be developed for every new protocol or application.

Stateful Packet Filtering Firewalls. These components control access by inspecting packet headers and tracking the state of all connections. This structure trades some security in exchange for better overall performance. However, the actual level of security ultimately depends on the quality and types of security checks written into the firewall code. While application proxies include more thorough checking, these checks are not done automatically or in all cases. In specific instances, a set of stateful checks can approach the same degree of security provided by a specific application proxy installation. You should also realize that the degree of checking can vary on a protocol-by-protocol basis.

Of these two firewall types, most security-conscious organizations favor application proxy despite its relatively poor performance. However, the differences are now blurring because hybrid products are emerging. A recent surge in the use of stateful firewalls has earned some products their security stripes, such as Check Point FireWall-1 and Cisco PIX, while vendors of application proxy products, such as Symantec, Raptor, and Network Associates, are adding stateful inspection-like capabilities to boost performance. Stateful filtering vendors have also added application proxies to improve security for specific protocols.

To deal with these variations, look for experience as a primary gauge of security strength. Then gain more assurance by conducting detailed technical/comparative reviews for the protocols most important to your organization, or those considered most suspect from a security perspective.

Appliances versus Software Firewalls

Another feature to look for is whether the firewall is a stand-alone device, also known as an appliance, or whether it is software-based, running on a common server platform. Table 5.1 compares the security, performance, and manageability of the two approaches.

Once you understand the architectural differences, and as vendors continue to blur them, you should consider additional criteria, such as ease of use, technical support, reliability, scalability, and comprehensiveness of security/firewall portfolio.

Decisions cannot be made solely on the desire for solid security. They must be balanced by related business issues, such as costs and the corporate security philosophy, and risk management in particular. The momentum behind firewall appliances will continue, with firewalls becoming the dominant form factor for perimeter defense and choke point implementations. However, software firewalls will play a growing role in

Table 5.1 Comparison of Appliance-based versus Software-based Firewalls

Aspect	Appliance	Software-based
Security	Provide greater security, because the operating system has been minimized and hardened by the firewall manufacturer	Often rely on the user to harden and maintain the OS
Performance	Improved by dedicated hardware and minimized instruction sets	Offers the flexibility of upgrading the underlying platform as needed
Management/ Troubleshooting	Easier due to pre-integration of software/hardware and use of a stripped-down, hardened OS	Benefits from OS-level logs; vendor diagnostic tools are substantially more important

end-node implementations such as personal firewalls. Distributed firewall architectures will be important in dealing with both internal threats and those coming from outside due to the proliferation of multiple points of interaction (POI) and external applications. The result will be a stronger demand for a new generation of robust, scalable management products that are integrated with other security functions, such as intrusion detection and antivirus.

The current trend is toward appliances, for good reason. Implementation, maintenance, and security are generally easier and better for firewall appliances due to pre-integration of software and hardware, and the use of a stripped-down, hardened OS. Appliances have an estimated 30 to 40 percent reduction in the total cost of ownership (TCO) when compared to software firewalls. With a range of sizes and price points, they are increasingly appropriate for branch offices due to their Plug and Play nature and improved remote management. Many companies are also converting from software to appliances at head office and hub locations.

The best approach for software firewalls is to select a mature operating system that is stable and thoroughly tested. More important, select the one for which your organization has the strongest skills. For appliances, notice how individual vendors approach the question of a "hardened OS." Vendor responses are typically vague, but you should determine whether the OS has simply been stripped of unnecessary services or whether something further has been done to actually harden it. Also, verify the vendor's process and history with regard to security updates. A lack of security updates should be viewed as a bad sign.

Other Considerations

Other firewall considerations include these four issues:

- Deployment. Company expansion and globalization introduces the need for more connections to the Internet. However, the best practice is to carefully limit these additions. Ideally, a central team conducts a detailed review that considers business cases, costs, logistics of management and support, security implications, stability and permanence of the proposed site, latency, and bottlenecks if forced to use the nearest alternative site.
- Internal Threat Management. Beyond perimeter control, most organizations realize that they must do more to counteract statistically significant internal threats. Surprisingly, most analyses conclude that internal users are responsible for more than 50 percent

of all attacks. An effective first step is to treat internal users more like external users by more tightly regulating access control and authorization. This effort is made easier in part by using distributed firewalls, such as firewalls located at the network interface card. The personal firewall, another type of distributed firewall, will grow in popularity as workforce mobilization leads to increasing numbers of laptops and handheld devices connecting directly to the Internet.

- Configuration. The primary configuration choice is whether to block all traffic by default and then allow only specific types (default-deny), or to allow all traffic by default and then block only specific types (default-allow). From a security perspective, default-deny is the obvious choice, particularly because new technologies make it more difficult to selectively block items and effectively implement a default-allow approach. If default-allow is the chosen policy, you should consider blocking risky services.

- Maintenance. Since firewalls are such critical security components, it is essential to keep up with code patches and release levels. Unfortunately, the practice of verifying firewall configurations is inconsistent. This check should be done periodically and after any configuration or code changes, ideally using a mix of commercial scanners and freeware tools such as nmap. You should strongly consider using constant verification in the form of a properly configured intrusion detection system residing immediately downstream from the most critical firewall interfaces.

Architecting the Demilitarized Zone (DMZ)

The demilitarized zone (DMZ) is a common way of providing network security by creating a semi-protected network segment just outside the main corporate network where resources such as Web servers are made accessible to external users (see Figure 5.2). The premise behind a DMZ is relatively straightforward. The DMZ provides a semiprotected buffer zone to facilitate communication with the Internet without directly linking the Internet to your organization's private network.

Firewalls provide protection at the DMZ's external and internal boundaries, or between the Internet and intranet. The firewall provides protection using services such as access control, protocol filtering, and user authentication, all of which can be consolidated into an identity infrastructure service as discussed later in this chapter. Typically, when handling inbound traffic from the Internet or other distrusted networks, the firewall takes into consideration whether the traffic is bound for resources inside the DMZ or beyond it. For instance, the firewall exercises some degree of control and filtering if the traffic is destined for resources just inside the DMZ, but much tighter controls on traffic destined for the internal corporate network.

The critical nature and growing volume of e-Business traffic is making it increasingly important that DMZs be designed for high levels of performance, reliability, scalability, and manageability—while addressing traditional security concerns. Furthermore, the term DMZ has expanded to describe not just the semi-protected buffer zone itself (the *traditional DMZ*), but other components such as routers and switches that comprise the overall external access infrastructure (the *extended DMZ*). This book uses the term "isolation infrastructure service" to describe these commonly deployed, reusable infrastructure components.

As a result of these changes, most IT organizations must evolve DMZ designs continuously to keep pace with changing business objectives. Simple, single-firewall designs are already giving way to designs incorporating backup components and multiple firewalls of different types.

In the next few years, scalability, reliability, and performance demands will require increased use of server and firewall load balancing, supply-side caching, and cryptographic acceleration. Meanwhile, manageability issues will be addressed by adopting functional and physical decomposition techniques as well as robust, integrated, security-networking management platforms. Over time, most organizations will employ geographical load-balancing techniques between distributed replicas of their extended DMZs and associated application or data sets.

Design Alternatives

Figure 5.2 shows several ways to use firewalls within a DMZ.

Note In Figure 5.2, the term "Web Server" refers to the standard 2-Tier Transact pattern combination of Web and application server.

No Firewall (not pictured). This method is not recommended because you have little control over denial-of-service attacks and site defacement by hackers. The only control is provided by router features or other high-level data and system protections. However, you can use this method on personal Web sites and simple marketing sites if you do not

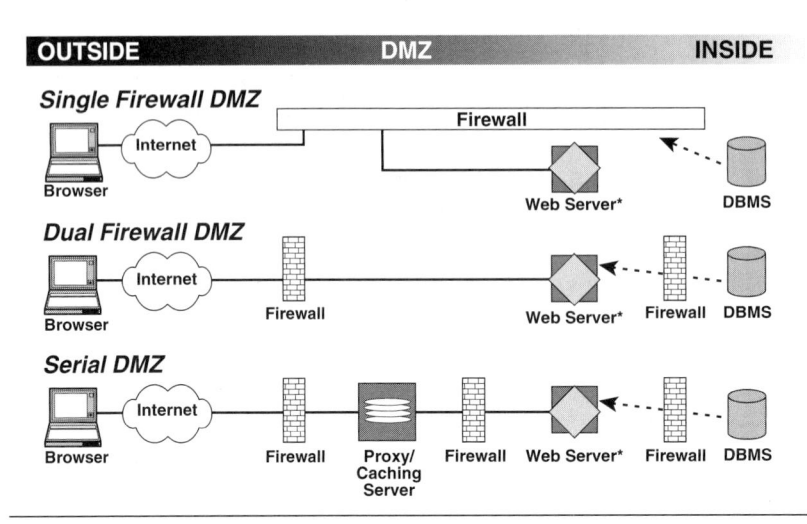

Figure 5.2 Architecting Externalization: The DMZ

have internal resources or other reasons to protect your data. Even so, this configuration is not recommended for serious corporate users.

Single Firewall. This configuration features a firewall structure with three legs: outside, DMZ, and inside. The installation is basic, but this method requires you to put all your eggs in one basket. From a physical standpoint, the days of a three-legged, single-firewall solution are over for all but the smallest organizations.

Dual Firewall. This method uses two firewalls with an independent DMZ network between them. The firewalls have a common configuration, offering a clear distinction between points of policy enforcement. This configuration not only boosts performance, but it improves security if the two firewalls are from different manufacturers or—better yet—if you use two different types, such as stateful packet filtering for the outer unit and application proxy for the inner unit. Both the Web Publish and the 3/N-Tier Transact patterns can easily leverage this approach. For Web Publish, you can put all the pattern servers in the DMZ, at least for cases where the read-only data is less mission-critical. For 3/N-Tier Transact, you can locate the Web servers in the DMZ but leave application and database servers on the internal side. This configuration satisfies a number of the DMZ best practices outlined later in this section.

Serial Firewall or "DMZ Sandwich." This approach has at least three firewalls with two or more independent DMZ networks between them. As sites become more complex, a new approach is emerging that involves adding a separate partition for proxy caching or authentication control in a separate zone. This approach works particularly well for 2-Tier Transact pattern configurations. Like the dual firewall, this configuration not only boosts performance, but it improves security when the firewalls are from different manufacturers or use different security paradigms.

DMZ Redundancy. Configurations with hot-standby firewalls are relatively common, but firewall clusters, which offer fault-tolerance and load balancing simultaneously, will certainly displace them now that appropriate technology has become available.

For extended DMZs, you can use numerous techniques and mechanisms to boost performance, scalability, and reliability. For the most basic configuration, provide hot-standby units for each component in a single access path from the Internet to internal resources. However, as with fault-tolerant firewall solutions, many companies favor cross-linked, dual-path configurations incorporating load balancing, due to their ability to also boost performance and scalability (see Figure 5.3). The dual-path trade-off has significantly higher costs along with increased management complexity.

Other techniques and mechanisms that can boost performance, scalability, and reliability include server and firewall load balancing, hardware-based cryptographic accelerators, and supply-side caching. However, be

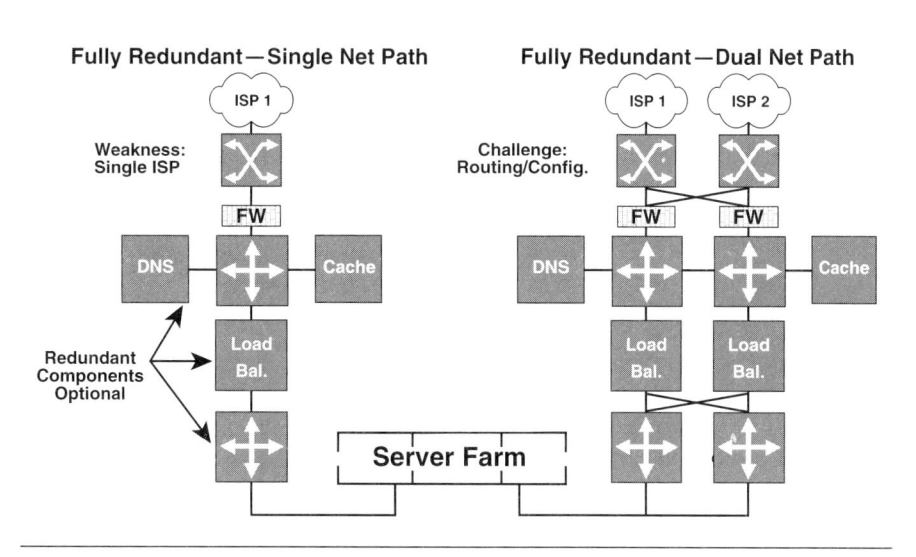

Figure 5.3 Redundant DMZ Design Alternatives

careful not to create a self-defeating situation when implementing multiple mechanisms simultaneously. For example, don't reduce the effectiveness of load balancers by locating them logically in front of decryption devices.

Undoubtedly, all these enhancements add complexity, which must be countered by advanced management capabilities. Over time, leading internetworking, security, and management vendors will release robust, integrated applications to manage all components of an extended DMZ, including distributed and multi-site scenarios.

Parallel DMZs. Functional and physical decomposition of a DMZ can minimize management and troubleshooting complexities, as shown in Figure 5.4.

Creating separate and parallel paths, or portions of paths, can accommodate components that support different business objectives. For example, you could create separate paths for inbound, remote-access VPN traffic, outbound Web traffic, and business-partner extranet traffic.

Multi-Site DMZs

The most sophisticated DMZ designs completely replicate single- or dual-path infrastructures to multiple geographically distributed sites, as shown in Figure 5.5.

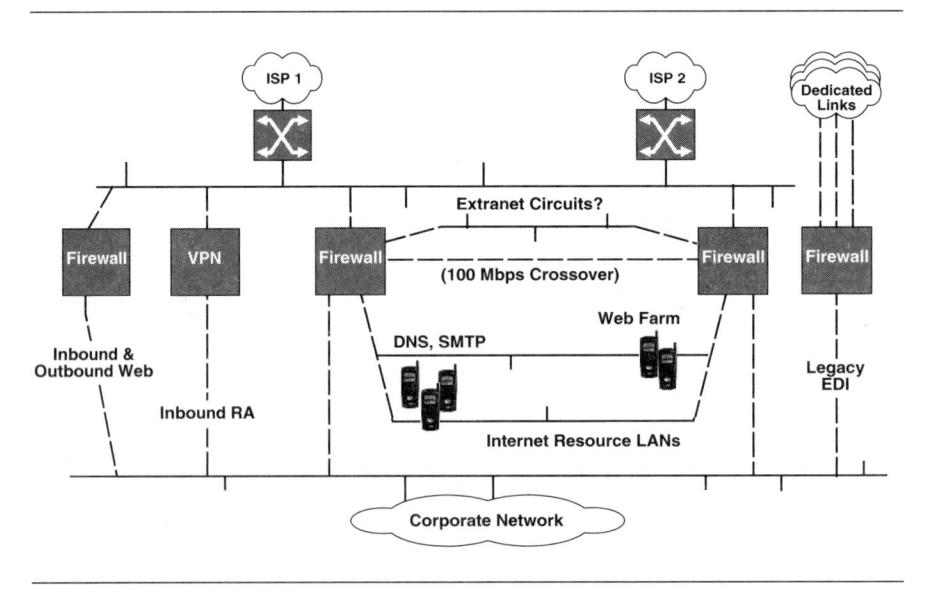

Figure 5.4 Parallel DMZs

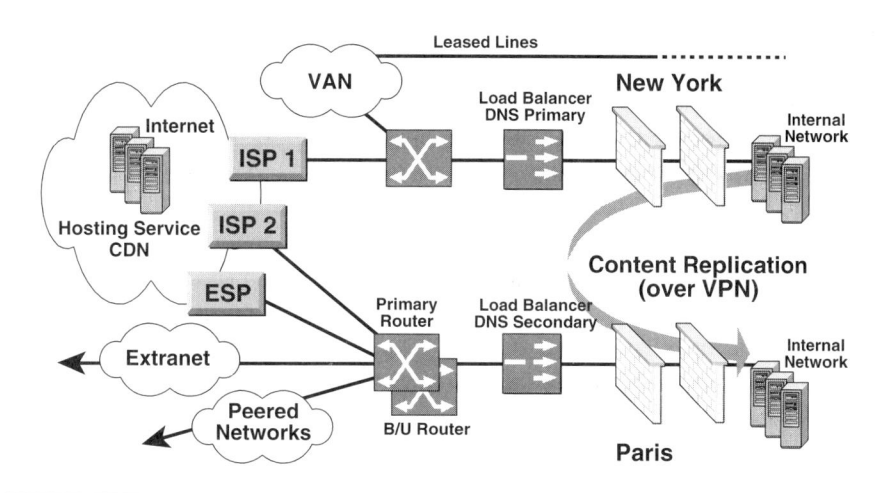

Figure 5.5 Multi-site DMZs

Not only does this method enhance overall reliability and scalability, but when properly configured, it also improves the performance of individual user sessions and minimizes latency by routing user sessions to the nearest set of resources.

Typically, companies implement multi-site DMZ architectures to achieve better scalability and fault-tolerance. If the main goal is high availability, consider creating two sites using network load balancers (NLBs) to provide global load balancing across both sites. (See Chapter 6 for details.) If scaling is important, sites can be located in key geographic regions, such as the U.S. and Europe. Language support and even localized domain names, such as domain.com, domain.fr, and domain.au, should not be the rationale for multi-site architectures. However, in some cases, legal and tax issues can force you to locate site infrastructure within national boundaries.

Due to the extensive resource commitments and high-complexity levels of multi-site DMZ configurations, most organizations will not reach this level of DMZ design for several years. Some applications, such as those with complex or poor state management, are not designed to operate from different data centers. Always test applications extensively to verify they can perform in multi-site architectures before investing in this type of solution. If you have transactional applications, such as 3/N-Tier patterns, you must also address data synchronization issues before expanding beyond a single data center.

Examples of DMZ Designs by Pattern

The following examples show various DMZ scenarios based on different types of adaptive infrastructure patterns.

2-Tier Transact. A 2-Tier Transact pattern application is a combination of an HTML-only Web/application server and an HTTP listener/gateway such as Microsoft IIS with HTTP/ISAPI. This configuration offers a mixture of Web-specific presentation services with the opportunity to incorporate business logic directly instead of calling a separate application server. Since business logic is exposed in this configuration, a server is inherently unsafe in the outer layers of the DMZ. Consequently, best-practice installations often include a separate proxy server inside the DMZ to make the business logic less accessible.

3/N-Tier Transact. Another common approach is to designate two DMZs for public Web servers and private application servers, as shown in Figure 5.6. Using a 3/N-Tier Transact pattern design would work well in this model, including appropriate routers, firewalls, Web and proxy servers, application servers, internal databases, and enterprise application integration (EAI) servers.

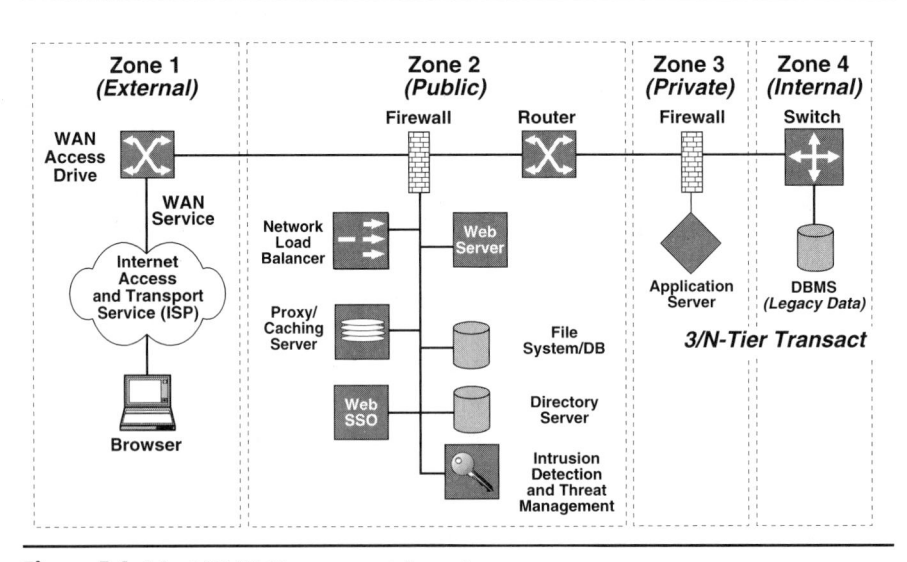

Figure 5.6 Ideal DMZ Component Locations

Figure 5.6 summarizes the best practice DMZ locations for these infrastructure components. Most components are the same for both patterns, but the ones unique to 3/N-Tier Transact are highlighted separately.

DMZ Best Practices

Observe the following best practices when designing the DMZ or applications that will be located inside the DMZ.

- Make simplicity a key design goal. For new applications located inside the DMZ, make sure all processes are straightforward and very repeatable. Taking this step leads to greater confidence that all appropriate safeguards are in place. In contrast, if every new application implementation requires fundamental changes, system configuration can get so complex that mistakes are bound to happen, leaving vulnerabilities open.

- Certify all systems to be placed in the DMZ against a DMZ security checklist. Such a checklist might include items such as availability of a secure management mechanism, inclusion in change control processes or periodic vulnerability assessment processes, installation of the latest OS patches, and configuration in accordance with platform-specific hardening procedures.

- Don't allow one protocol to be tunneled within another when crossing the internal firewall, unless you have specific security team approval.

- Encourage the practice of requiring a change in protocol for traffic crossing the DMZ. For instance, you might use one communication protocol for inbound requests terminated inside the DMZ, and a separate one for the requests traveling through the DMZ to back-end resources. As an example, applications using the 3/N-Tier Transact pattern could stop incoming HTTP protocols at the DMZ-located Web servers. Then, a separate Web-to-application-server protocol could be passed through the inner DMZ boundary. Another example is allowing HTTP requests to enter the DMZ, with SQL/ODBC calls used for internal communication. However, this 2-Tier Transact pattern configuration is not considered the best practice for other security reasons described above.

- Use reverse proxies to provide security for front-end, legacy 2-Tier applications that can be vulnerable if located in the DMZ. Refer to the 2-Tier Transact example earlier in this section for more detail.

- Practice "defense in-depth," creating multiple layers (or tiers) of protected zones with more sensitive resources buried deep behind increasingly rigorous filters. Defense in-depth will certainly make the solution more resistant to security breaches, while enabling less sensitive resources to be accessed more readily. One common tiering technique is to separate the authentication, proxying, and filtering components from the Internet-accessible Web servers, which reside at a deeper tier in the infrastructure.

- Don't let network traffic access the DMZ unless it requires access to services, content, or applications stored there.

- Weigh the total cost of security—which includes hardware, staff, and performance—against the value of the information it protects.

- Be aware that an HTTP wrapper can contain all kinds of protocols. Closing all ports except port 80 does not guarantee security.

- Serve public data from outside the DMZ using secure database management systems (DBMS), file servers, and regularly refreshed caches. Serve this data only when it is very replaceable, such as with file download sites.

- Make sure that servers in the DMZ perform user authentication before allowing access to applications on the inside network.

- Always use secure access mechanisms to monitor and configure servers in the DMZ.

- Be aware that appliances currently require less maintenance and have fewer known holes. However, this advantage won't last. Their greater value over time will be ease of maintenance and cost.

Intrusion Detection and Threat Management

Intrusion detection systems (IDS) are an accepted part of many Global 2000 security strategies and are important components of an isolation infrastructure. These systems alert you to suspicious events that could affect data security, such as administrative changes or if event patterns fit well-known attack profiles. Table 5.2 shows the major types of attacks to expect.

Indeed, many organizations without security monitoring capabilities go weeks or months before detecting an attack. In those cases, the perpetrators have time to entrench themselves deeper into the network and cover their tracks. Driven by externalized applications and third-party access requirements, more Global 2000 organizations are improv-

Table 5.2 Types of Attacks

Attack Type	Description
Insertion	A form of attack based on the fact that an IDS can accept packets that an end station rejects, due to lack of time synchronization, differences in TCP/IP stack implementations, and so on. Data can be inserted into the IDS, disrupting its pattern-matching capabilities and masking an attack on an end station.
Evasion	The counterpoint to insertion, this type of attack is based on a network IDS rejecting packets that are still completely processed by the end station due to its looser set of processing criteria. Crucial information that contains the key pieces of an attack slips by the IDS, but is fully reconstituted on the end station.
Denial of Service (DOS)	The IDS itself is susceptible to these attacks, which are based on starvation of resources. This attack can be particularly severe, since the passive network IDS will "fail open," leaving the resources it was protecting open to subsequent attack. Unfortunately, staging such an attack is relatively easy. Flooding a system with bogus traffic can saturate the IDS CPU through excessive pattern matching, its memory through maintenance of excessive state information, or its disk capacity through excessive logging activity. Even more insidious, however, is a pass-through DOS attack. This event can occur when an IDS is configured to react to attacks by resetting a TCP/IP session or blocking a router port. The attacker tricks it into doing so by instigating a false-positive reaction.

ing information security, forming dedicated security groups, revisiting security architectures, and implementing security infrastructure. An IDS provides a critical automation element for the security monitoring and operational audit process.

Traditionally, IDS vendors have used two approaches: network-based and host-based.

Network-based IDS has enjoyed some commercial success as large organizations rush to monitor security-related events as they occur, such as hacker intrusions and administrative changes. Typically, these systems use network sniffer models, inspecting packets for attack patterns. Switched networks present a challenge to network-based IDSs in that you can't see all segments simultaneously. Many vendors are forming partnerships with switch vendors and inserting agent code into the switch to resolve this problem.

However, increasing use of encryption will present a larger problem to the sniffer model, and will likely break it. Sniffers cannot inspect encrypted traffic to determine if suspicious activity is taking place. Most network-based IDS vendors are transitioning their architectures to a network-node-based model, where an agent sits on a host, inspecting network packets as accepted by the system, and importantly, doing it post-decryption.

Host-based IDS has typically lagged in both adoption and maturity, with initial products proving difficult to deploy and destabilizing to the computing environment they protect. Both political and technological difficulties are involved. In many organizations, different groups own different components of the infrastructure, so it is sometimes difficult to require installation of an agent on all servers. Also, host-based IDS installation is more invasive than network-based because the agents are actually installed on systems rather than sitting passively on the network. As a result, immature code can destabilize the system, as many early host-based tools did.

You can segment host-based tools by when they examine events. Some tools are more useful after the fact, for forensic investigation. These tools take a snapshot of a server's configuration, alert you when it has changed, and highlight changes. Other tools provide near-time analysis and detection—watching events as they are put into event logs. An emerging group of vendors has begun placing an inspection component directly in front of the operating system kernel, trying to capture events even before they start. This technique has the potential to halt dangerous events or attacks before they take place. This approach, while attractive, remains immature, so you should expect limited applicability of it in the near future.

Due to its real-time inspection capabilities, a network IDS is better at preventing attacks, whereas a host-based IDS is better at verifying attack occurrence and collecting forensic information about the attacker and his or her methods.

Network-based IDSs have been more successful due to their ease of deployment. However, parity and integration between the two types of systems are being driven by growing maturity in host-based products and by architectural changes in network-based tools brought on by changing network traffic dynamics, such as switching and encryption.

While global integration promises abound, real integration of IDS paradigms, such as a shared data model and code base, will occur through network IDS transitioning to network-node-based IDS. Integration will occur at the console level and at the agent level. However, correlation of events across both domains and other data sources will lag significantly. Further market developments include integrated threat management consoles.

As packet-based network IDS migrates from a centralized sniffer model to a host-based agent model, differences between host- and network-based intrusion detection become harder to distinguish. Both will use host-based agents, making integration more feasible. With this shift, integrated agents will appear more frequently as a requirement on end-user requests for proposal.

Limitations of Network IDS

Current network IDS limitations suggest how these tools should be used now, as well as how they will evolve in coming years:

Performance. Network IDS can handle line rates up to 10 Mbps, but detection or response capabilities degrade beyond 30-to-40 percent usage of 100-MB links, which can be common in a DMZ. With larger buffers providing only marginal improvements, vendors might eventually develop hardware-based solutions, such as PCI cards. A temporary solution is for the IDS to reduce the number of attack types being profiled, using a vulnerability assessment tool to scan the system and identify attacks against which a given environment is already protected.

Accuracy and Thoroughness. In this context, accuracy means not mistaking valid traffic for attacks (false positive). Thoroughness means not mistaking real attacks for valid traffic (false negative). Unfortunately, a network IDS has limited effectiveness in both areas because data retrieved promiscuously from the wire is inadequate. What's missing is an intimate knowledge of how each end station treats an incoming packet stream, as well as time synchronization with each end station. This situation makes all network IDSs susceptible to insertion, evasion, and denial-of-service attacks as defined in the list of attack types (Table 5.2). Correcting these deficiencies requires TCP/IP stack-specific and OS-specific products based at each end station. Experts do not expect the availability of these kinds of products until 2005. In the interim, you must manually discover IDS/end station inconsistencies and create or load corresponding attack signatures into the IDS.

Encryption. Encryption technologies pose a potentially significant problem for the network IDS, which relies not only on packet header information, but also on payload information. Impact varies by organization, based on the adoption rate of various forms of encryption, and impact should be a determining factor when purchasing the network IDS. The most common form of encryption for site-to-site communication (such as firewall-to-firewall), is of little concern because it merely dictates that the IDS be located logically behind the device providing decryption services. However, the use of encryption from desktop to server relocates decryption services to the OS, in turn forcing similar architectural changes on network IDSs.

Ease of Use. The usability issue has many facets, but a particular one is the need to maintain yet another directory of policy information. Experts say this need will be resolved in the medium-to-long term, as vendors provide integration with other tools in their security portfolio, such as firewalls and authentication tools. Security implementations, in general, are time-consuming, and implementation and operation of a network IDS is no exception.

The largest ease-of-use issue could be the handling of attack notifications. For example, an overwhelming number of notifications could require a unit-by-unit tuning exercise. Even then, you must decide how to address the remaining notifications, with each one requiring laborious follow-on data collection and root-cause analysis. Expert analysis and correlation capabilities, which could relieve this situation, are several years away.

Other ease-of-use issues relate to:

- Integration with Simple Network Management Protocol (SNMP) management platforms
- Simultaneously managing multiple detection and response engines
- Creating ways to define new types of attacks, or obtaining updates from the vendor and propagating them

Switching. Network IDS vendors believe their devices are needed on every network segment, particularly as a way of protecting against the 50 percent of attacks that come from internal sources. However, the implementation of switching technologies in campus networks makes this situation untenable. The rate of implementation should figure into network IDS purchasing decisions. This situation requires that network intrusion detection capabilities ultimately be packaged in a form suitable for deployment on end stations, which would also make it suitable for deployment in other networked components, such as routers, firewalls, and switches.

Threat Management

The possibility of being hacked is one of the greatest security concerns for organizations, particularly when externalizing networks. Threat management is a comprehensive strategy that addresses this concern. It includes elements of intrusion detection and vulnerability assessment across both network and system domains.

Scanning and intrusion detection are essential components of threat management. Therefore, you should focus on the order and extent of implementation. However, developing a more detailed strategy—a prerequisite to success, given the excessive information output of these products—depends heavily on the availability of money, personnel, and expertise.

Integrated threat management (ITM) consoles initially will use a common interface to present information from various sources, such as host IDS, network-based IDS, firewall/proxy server logs, policy audit tools, and scanners. The ability to correlate this data will remain elusive, however, except in the case of managed security services (MSSs), where service provider leverage can justify building deeper rule bases for correlation. To demonstrate the value of their services, MSS providers will offer reports, status pages, and Web-based consoles that can be used to understand vulnerabilities and threats, as well as report on service levels.

The value of ITM to Global 2000 organizations is threefold:

Policy Compliance. With console monitoring of all key operational audit functions, it will be possible to overlay security policies, understand compliance problems from an enterprise perspective, and take action to correct them.

Improved Threat Detection. ITM will help organizations understand suspicious activity, such as attacks or breaches, from multiple perspectives. This feature is especially useful when currently deployed network-based tools miss encrypted or heavy traffic, or when host-based tools are not deployed on a particular system.

Security Metrics. After making information security a priority, many organizations want to understand how much of a difference that decision is making and whether they are actually more secure. The evolution of ITM will parallel enterprise systems management (ESM), as ITM consoles will allow reporting of security metrics and service-level management. Status pages for executives could show red-light/green-light and "top-ten lists" of exceptions reporting on policy compliance and security effectiveness. Initial ITM tools communicate largely through proprietary protocols, but some use Simple Network Management Protocol (SNMP). Although many security issues can be circumvented with proper deployment, such as putting ITM agents inside the firewall, users should analyze communication methods and vulnerabilities associated with security tool deployment.

The ability to detect network intrusion is a necessary component of emerging threat management systems. Use your knowledge of the shortcomings of network intrusion detection systems to guide selective deployment, to improve solution efficacy, and to manage corporate expectations. Intrusion detection systems can help large organizations understand security events when and after they occur. While architectural challenges and changes abound, look for tactical benefits now and drive toward integrated products, as host-based and network-based product differences are reconciled.

From a practical standpoint, you can effectively implement only so much threat management technology in a year. For example, it might be possible for two to three full-time equivalents (FTEs) to deploy 30 network detection devices and associated management consoles in a year. Therefore, while a larger package can be purchased, negotiate yearly payments based on anticipated implementation plans and treat maintenance fees similarly. To this end, you should conduct a pilot implementation, perhaps covering 10 percent of an organization's anticipated needs, as a way to gauge resource requirements and reasonable implementation goals. Then you can use this experience to negotiate a multiphase, enterprisewide deal.

SSL and Encryption Hardware

Secure Sockets Layer (SSL) is the standard protocol for securely transmitting documents over the Internet. It both encrypts data and validates the Web server to users, ensuring that users are not exchanging sensitive data with imposters. In conjunction with public key encryption (PKI), you can use SSL for client authentication as discussed in the PKI section later in this chapter. However, widespread deployments are difficult at this time because of PKI immaturity.

All the major browsers support SSL, providing significant cost and deployment advantages to the protocol, because no additional client software exists to distribute and manage. However, SSL offers little control over security policy management. One policy applies to all users. SSL has no user-based access control, and it has minimal use in non-HTTP applications. Furthermore, SSL cannot distribute authentication or encryption information to other servers in a multi-tiered application. Still, the wide-scale deployment of business-to-business (B2B) extranets will only accelerate SSL use.

SSL encryption processing is extremely CPU-intensive. Key signing and encryption activity also degrade Web server performance considerably. Research indicates the number of simultaneous SSL connections a server can support using secure HTTP (HTTPS) is only one to ten percent of the number of simultaneous connections it can support with a clear, unencrypted HTTP text workload.

You can overcome this security burden by adding more servers, but doing so is expensive. SSL acceleration devices enable Web servers to process more SSL transactions by offloading the intensive floating-point math required for key signing. SSL accelerators are a cost-effective way for secure applications to increase performance by up to 25 percent and increase scalability with up to 30 times more HTTPS connections per second.

SSL acceleration devices are measured by the number of new SSL sessions per second that the device can accommodate, known as transactions per second (TPS). In this context, the term "transactions" refers to key signing, not Web server transactions. You must size the SSL accelerator to accommodate the peak incremental load of new and renegotiated SSL sessions expected. In practical applications, traffic will be mixed between new sessions and existing sessions, so the total number of supported user sessions will be considerably higher than the total TPS, depending on site traffic patterns.

SSL Accelerator Configurations

As shown in Figure 5.7, you have three potential locations in the network path where you can implement SSL acceleration:

- In the personal computer interface (PCI) card for each Web server
- In a standalone device upstream from the servers
- In a network load balancer (NLB)

Each location has its limitations, and you should evaluate current and future site requirements before selecting an SSL acceleration solution. Regardless, to minimize performance drag, Web application designers

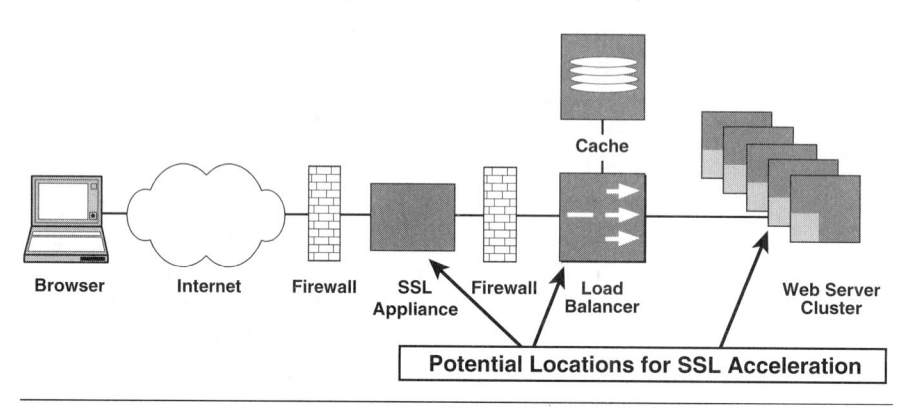

Figure 5.7 Potential Locations for SSL Acceleration

should use SSL encryption only for interactions where sensitive data is exchanged. Each of the accelerator configuration options is discussed in more detail below.

SSL Acceleration Cards in Web Servers. The simplest, most inexpensive way to accelerate site performance is to install PCI cards that relieve the Web server CPU of encryption duties. This solution can scale linearly because each server performs its own key signing and encryption; it has no single point of failure. PCI cards are available up to 600 TPS. Although users can add more cards to further boost performance, bus and memory bandwidth constraints limit the incremental contribution of each additional card. PCI cards are relatively inexpensive and support a wider range of encryption protocols than current upstream devices, including SSL, SSH, TLS, IPSec, SET, Swan, and IKE. Unfortunately, these cards do nothing to simplify certificate management (one per Web server, not per site). And, since SSL traffic remains encrypted until it reaches the server, they don't improve performance of devices upstream from the Web server, such as proxy servers, firewalls, bandwidth managers, caches, and load balancers.

SSL Acceleration in Dedicated Intermediate Devices. The alternative to server-based SSL acceleration is to move the key-signing duties into a central device responsible for all traffic. Centralizing SSL acceleration also simplifies server certificate management and reduces server certificate costs, since only one certificate is required per domain name, not one per server. Moreover, if the system decrypts inbound requests early in the network path, other components upstream from the Web server can provide valuable services. In this architecture, the SSL accelerator works like a VPN device that terminates IPSec traffic at the edge of the local area network. Decrypting traffic before it reaches its final destination might make security-conscious organizations nervous, but if decryption occurs in the same physical location as the Web server—meaning the same rack—the incremental threat of interception is negligible.

You can place standalone SSL acceleration appliances anywhere in the network path upstream from the servers. Using a stand-alone appliance offers the advantages of upstream decryption, while not limiting load balancing product selection.

SSL Acceleration in Network Load Balancers (NLBs). Networkload balancing vendors now offer integrated SSL acceleration cards built into the load-balancing products. Integrating SSL into load balancers provides simpler network management in that fewer devices must be managed. It also enables the load balancer to perform valuable Layer 7 functions in the OSI stack. For instance, the load balancer could use information within the encrypted packets, such as cookies, file names, or extensions, to make intelligent load balancing decisions or to intercept application errors.

Without SSL decryption, load balancers must maintain persistent sessions between clients and a particular server, negating the effectiveness of load balancing. Scaling beyond the normal threshold of 600 TPS involves running SSL traffic across multiple load balancers in parallel. This option can be expensive, although vendors are increasing scalability rapidly. Despite the advantages of integrated SSL acceleration, however, you should evaluate NLB products primarily on their load balancing characteristics and view SSL acceleration as a valuable feature.

When installing SSL acceleration in the network path, either on a standalone device or on the NLB, make sure that you can "failover" to an appropriate backup device, to eliminate single points of failure for SSL traffic. If you configure backup devices to operate in an active/active mode to manage traffic simultaneously, you must have unique certificates on each device. Hot or cold standby devices can use duplicate copied certificates.

Pattern Analysis: SSL Acceleration Component

The need for SSL acceleration depends on the nature of the site, the traffic, and the data, as well as user requirements. Many financial brokerage sites encrypt almost all of their content in SSL. However, some bulky content associated with the Web Publish pattern, such as stock price graphs, is not usually encrypted, since it is not unique or private. In contrast, critical data associated with the 3/N-Tier Transact pattern, such as credit card numbers for purchases, should always be encrypted.

Storing user data online is not the same as encrypting its delivery. When hackers steal credit card numbers, they typically steal an entire database from a disk. SSL does not protect data that is stored on a disk, so it is only a partial component of a security policy. Making SSL security truly scale might require offloading from Web servers. Therefore, depending on requirements, SSL acceleration might be required for some Web Publish patterns and almost all 3/N-Tier Transact patterns.

Refining Pattern Designs for Isolation Infrastructure

Table 5.3 summarizes the list of potential components in an isolation infrastructure service and shows how important each component is for the Web Publish and 3/N-Tier Transact patterns.

To select the appropriate firewall solutions, you must examine deployment factors, internal threat management capabilities, configuration issues, and maintenance requirements. You can use best practices in DMZ design to boost security, performance, scalability, and reliability through techniques such as load balancing, cryptographic acceleration, and supply-side caching. DMZ designs will evolve continuously over the next few years to keep pace with changing business objectives.

Intrusion detection systems (IDS) provide a crucial automation element for security monitoring and operational auditing processes. These systems can be network-based, host-based, or they can rely on agent

Table 5.3 Isolation Infrastructure Service Pattern Summary Chart

Layer or Service Component	Web Publish	3/N-Tier
Isolation Infrastructure Service:	2	1
Firewall	1	1
Intrusion Detection/Threat Management	2	1
SSL and Encryption HW	3	2
VPN Device and Service	4	4

Key
1 = Critical, All Cases
2 = Highly Recommended, Most Cases
3 = Optional, Some Cases
4 = Optional, Fewer Cases

integration. Future IDS products will provide integrated threat management consoles, which will include important scanning, intrusion detection, and data correlation features.

Secure sockets layer (SSL) is a powerful and inexpensive technique for transmitting secure, encrypted data over the Internet. Evaluate current and future site requirements before selecting an SSL acceleration solution for the 3/N-Tier Transact or Web Publish patterns.

Identity Infrastructure Service

For a full discussion of security services, it is important to consider isolation technologies and strategies, as well as issues related to authentication and permissions management. This section discusses various approaches to user authentication that are commonly used in e-Business and beyond, plus the use of a directory service component to store all user information within an identity infrastructure.

The real value of an identity infrastructure service is that it gives you a single way to approach user authentication and an authorization approach that can be reused for a variety of applications. Although a directory service alone can provide user data, it does not provide an easy way for applications to leverage the service—even if all that's needed is user name and password information. By adding Web Single Sign-On (Web SSO) solutions, all Web-based applications can leverage user name and password credentials automatically without being reprogrammed to specifically support the Lightweight Directory Access Protocol (LDAP). Web SSO software also provides a simple, effective, and centralized way to manage permissions with multivendor Web server products on a Web site.

Thus, the solution used by many organizations combines Web SSO with an LDAP directory to service Web applications, particularly in situations where external users, such as customers or business partners, are accessing internal systems or Web sites. Figure 5.8 shows all the potential components of an Identity Infrastructure service.

Web SSO: Simple Web-Centric Authentication

Web-centric and e-Business-focused applications often require users to be authenticated before accessing content or services. The easiest and most cost-effective method is simple authentication through a user name and password sign-on, with secure encryption provided using SSL. In scenarios where the cost of a private key infrastructure (PKI) cannot

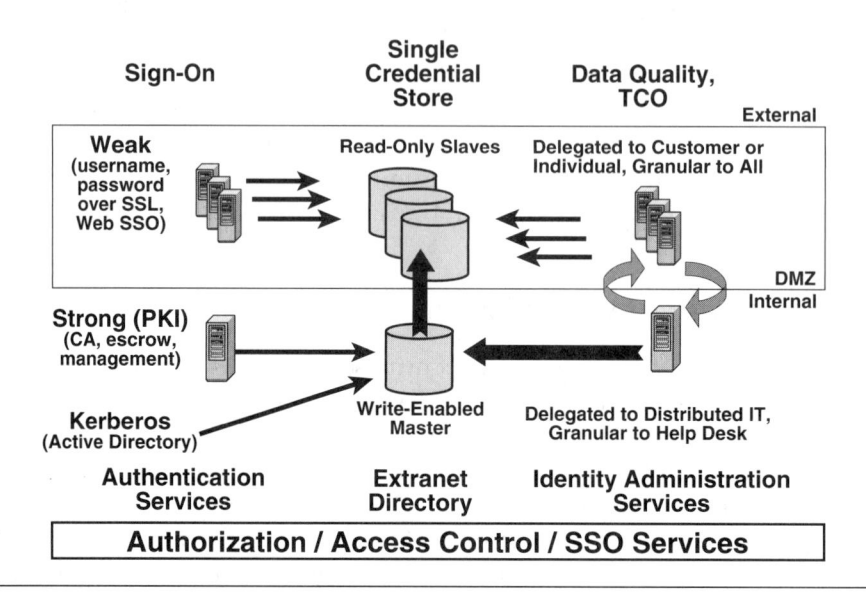

Figure 5.8 Components of an Identity Infrastructure

yet be justified, this approach has proven successful and should suffice for many applications in the foreseeable future.

PKI implementations are the preferred strategic direction, due to their strong authentication and scalability, but many users find the initial startup costs prohibitive and other current technology and product limitations problematic, particularly for large-scale applications. Refer to the PKI section in this chapter for more details. In addition, many scenarios do not yet require this level of authentication because the risk is less substantial. Figure 5.9 shows how to configure simple authentication state management for Web applications.

Using simple authentication credentials such as a user name and password is efficient and effective. However, using a single credential for a variety of applications requires the ability for all applications to honor the same Single Sign-On (SSO). Web-centric applications offer a unique opportunity to solve some classic SSO problems.

One problem with Web-based authentication is that the Web protocol (HTTP) does not allow users to maintain a long-term session on a Web server. Even HTTP 1.1, with its pipelining of requests across a single TCP session, does not guarantee sessions across separate page requests. Moreover, the increased use of network load balancing (NLB) products moves user interaction across an array of Web servers, defeating any single Web server–based mechanism for managing the user authentication

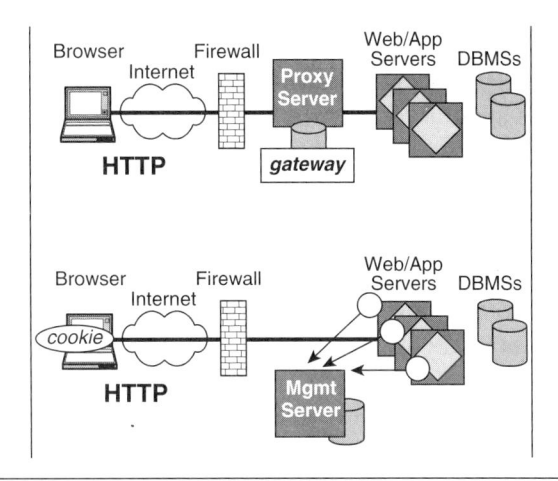

Figure 5.9 Simple Authentication State Management for Web Applications

state. In the absence of other application-specific state management methods, such as those used in online shopping carts, each user would have to reenter a user name and password on each new Web server encountered.

An LDAP directory can provide single credential storage, and you can point all Web applications to it. But this technique still doesn't keep the user from having to present credentials over and over again to each new Web server that needs authentication. So, while all Web servers at a particular site could check user name and password credentials in a single shared directory service, this technique doesn't provide a viable Single Sign-On solution.

Users quickly grow frustrated with a system that requires them to reenter a user name and password repeatedly, even if it's the same one each time. As more business initiatives attempt to make applications as user-friendly as possible, true SSO will become more important than ever for internal enterprise applications.

Web SSO products allow the Web server to determine the state of authentication before prompting the user for credentials. Application developers do not even need to use proprietary authentication APIs, although such application-integrated approaches are possible and might be necessary for more complicated applications.

Most Web SSO products take advantage of standard Web server mechanisms. They intercept the normal call that the Web server makes for user authentication and replace it with their own. The first time a user logs on, the Web SSO product stores the authentication state so that it can be safely reused when other Web servers require it. Thus, each individual Web server can determine, by looking at the user authentication, whether the user has already signed on—and avoid asking the user for a sign-on again.

To perform this nifty trick, Web SSO products use mechanisms that range from client-based cookies to centralized gateways.

Cookie-based authentication. Several products create time-stamped and encrypted cookies on the client. As the user browses the Web and encounters a new Web server, agent code on the Web server intercepts the normal credential challenge routine to check first if an appropriate cookie exists. The cookie check then substantiates that the user has already been authenticated. While this solution is scalable with no single point of failure and supports various Web server products, some corporations and users do not allow cookies as a matter of policy.

Gateways. Other products authenticate users using an intermediate gateway proxy server as shown in Figure 5.10. While scalability is more of a concern with this approach, multiple gateway support improves the situation somewhat.

Some products offer both gateway and cookie approaches. Most organizations use the cookie approach, particularly due to vendor relationships. But certain verticals, such as the financial market, commonly use gateway solutions.

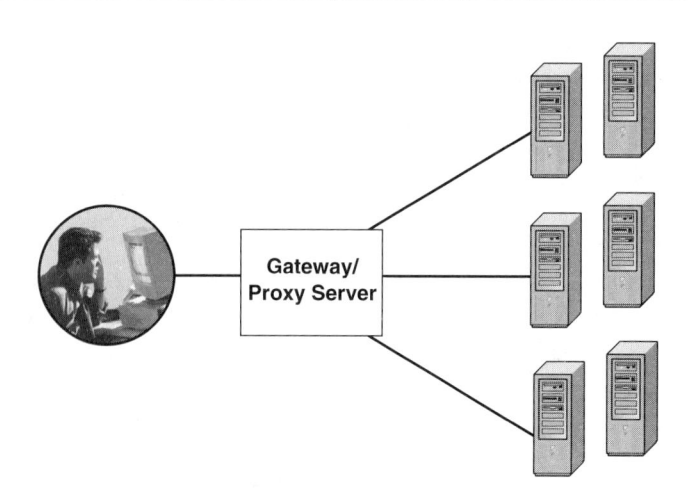

Figure 5.10 Gateway Approach to Web SSO

Web SSO products also help with authorization or permissions management for Web-centric applications. These products use a single permissions database to match user identities already authenticated for a variety of back-end Web servers—whether they are based on Windows 2000/.NET Server, UNIX, or other directory permissions and access control systems. These products actually replace the existing permissions systems and centralize their processing and management across the back-end resources. This configuration can make running a larger Web site with lots of content much easier, particularly if control over Web server choices is weaker.

Web SSO is increasingly focused on access control and authorization for Web servers, managing the permissions of the Web server file system and other accessible services. However, PKI-based authentication solutions will likely overtake Web SSO. Still, Web SSO remains a viable solution to the e-Business authentication management problem, without strong authentication but with suitable, cost-effective user authentication and authentication state management.

Centralized and Automated Administration

Administration of user information is a challenge with any centralized service, particularly for an identity infrastructure service. Most Web SSO, directory, and portal vendors offer simple self-administration solutions so users can administrate their own data directly. But this method is not always appropriate. Sensitive data such as permissions, social security numbers, and management controls should not be handled by individual users but by centralized IT professionals. Some use cases require multiple people to approve data changes.

Web SSO vendors are moving to automated user administration. As shown in Figure 5.11, many large organizations struggle with the user enrollment and administration process, both within the enterprise and increasingly outside it as well. Problem areas include: chaotic request handling, poor service levels, lack of security, unclear roles and approval processes, poor scalability and efficiency, and poor audit ability.

Some IT organizations have tried user administration tools to help resolve the problems, but most tools solve only bits of the problem, such as covering only a few platforms or delegating administration.

However, some previously disparate administration functions are now coming together, including:

- Administration infrastructure (user store/metadirectory, agentry, and rules)

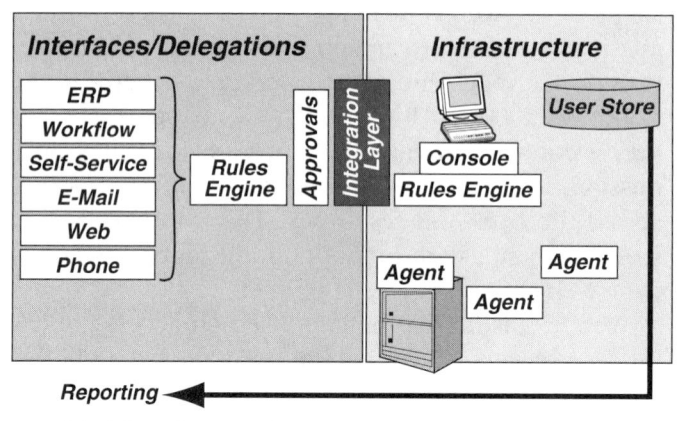

Figure 5.11 Automated Security Administration

- Administration workflow (self-service, delegated interfaces, and application interfaces)

While Web SSO products offer better solutions to centralized management problems, pay careful attention during project planning to whether the vendor's management interface must be extended. All products offer control over attributes, so that only the authorized users can see or change their own list of attributes. Many products offer simpler delegation features, so a centralized group can structure who can manage groups of users. But few products have branched out into automated administration, including workflow, to further enhance administration efficiency.

Some products offer a form of administration-based integration, supporting a single point of administration (SPA) function across multiple directory or other user account information stores. These products often are not full metadirectory solutions. Instead, they address only changes made through a centralized administration system. Such systems often do not reconcile changes made independently.

Web SSO vendors will continue to refine interfaces and push function and delegation granularity into their administration offerings. Interface refinement will include improving off-the-shelf graphical user interfaces (GUIs), developing secure self-service, and incorporating more complex trust models.

Future Web SSO Differentiators

While basic functionality is becoming a commodity, some additional components will differentiate one product from another in the Web SSO market. These features include breadth of application support, delegated administration, session sharing, and fined-grained authorization. As support for common Web servers increases, so will the requirements for supporting Web application servers and Web versions of packaged applications.

Delegated administration is currently the most important criterion in 30 percent of Web SSO purchases. Critical for large-scale deployments, delegated administration enables organizations to assign user administration tasks to different people—such as help-desk workers or a business partner's trusted administrator. Some organizations ultimately delegate administration to the end user, with "self-service" systems that allow users to handle many common administrative functions for their own accounts, including account changes, creation requests, and password resets. Many requests for proposals (RFPs) now have self-service as a requirement.

Session sharing is an important capability that allows multiple companies to create a trusted session network. In this type of network, users can log onto one partner's site, then seamlessly access another partner's site without logging in again. However, the second partner knows exactly who the user is, which company he came from, and more.

Session sharing has the greatest potential appeal of all advanced functions, which explains the excitement surrounding Security Assertion Markup Language (SAML).

A few specialty vendors have tried to deliver fine-grained authorization down to the object, field, or transaction level. But very few Global 2000 companies will be able to centralize fine-grained authorization, driving any remaining independent players into existing Web SSO vendors. Many Global 2000 organizations will purchase Web SSO packages claiming fine-grained authorization based on the recommendations of their architecture team, but organizational, technical, and vendor lock-in issues can cause failures in many cases.

Web SSO: Looking Forward

Web SSO products provide a valuable yet admittedly interim solution for Web application authentication, particularly for consumer-centric e-Commerce. Users examining Web authorization/Web SSO should continue to evaluate top-tier vendors, but they should expect upheaval due to mergers and acquisitions. Delegated administration and self-service will be important differentiators in the short term, with session sharing becoming important longer-term. While large deal sizes and deep discounts appeal to Global 2000 organizations, they should buy only what they need for the short term, as ongoing price pressures will make buying too far in advance financially unsound.

Bundling directory service and Web SSO solutions into a single identity infrastructure service offering provides a single application leveraged solution. With this very e-Business-focused approach, reuse happens more quickly than with enterprise applications, which are not all Web-based. An equivalent but distinct solution is more common for internal Web or intranet solutions as well, often based on different information stores and products. Over time, this critical identity infrastructure service will add centralized authorization control that coordinates with various authentication solutions, such as passwords, PKI, Kerberos, and tokens.

Public Key Infrastructure (PKI)

Public key infrastructure (PKI) is often referred to as the key solution to security services for e-Business. While PKI theory is good, the practice needs lots of work. Figure 5.12 provides a basic diagram of how PKI fits into the overall infrastructure.

PKI relies on encrypted identity information stored as a key in a digital certificate. The encryption algorithm used with PKI is not a single key (symmetric approach) but a key pair (asymmetric approach). One key of the pair is private, to be guarded very carefully; the other key is public, to be shared.

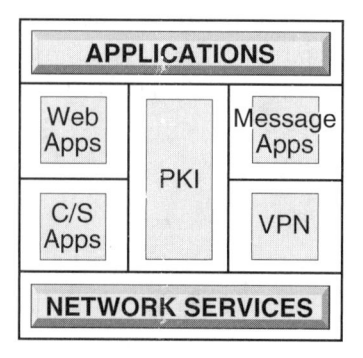

Figure 5.12 PKI Infrastructure Configuration

A PKI includes more than just the key pair, however. PKI includes the set of management functions that allows the digital certificate to be issued, managed, and revoked in conjunction with a trusted certificate authority (CA).

A fully functioning PKI must perform key history management, archiving old encryption keys and linking them to old documents or messages. Keys are changed periodically for security reasons, much the same way passwords are changed, and the key history management function ensures that you can always view old information—no matter what key was used to encrypt it.

A true PKI can handle the complex problem of certificate revocation as well as certificate and key rollover, which is the issuing of new certificates or keys to users. These management functions must be transparent to the user because of the complexity of the processes they entail. If ordinary users had to perform these processes, the system most likely would fail.

The following features distinguish a true PKI from a simple issuer of certificates:

- Certificate revocation
- Key backup and recovery
- Key history management
- Dual key pair support

You can use these criteria to evaluate any PKI product. Much has been written about PKI and the encryption algorithms on which it is based. This book doesn't dwell on details of the algorithms themselves. Instead, it focuses on the use of the technology. While some aspects of PKI form an important part of current e-Business and internal infrastructure, many of its potential uses are not yet feasible for larger-scale Web sites due to immaturity in products and even in technology standards.

Using PKI and SSL for Encryption and Authentication

Secure socket layer (SSL) is one aspect of PKI technology that is used widely today. SSL requires a Web server to have a public key, which can be checked to see if it is current, preferably a certified one held by a trusted third party or CA service provider such as VeriSign. Most users never check, but it's at least possible to verify that the Web server to which you are currently connected really is the site for that company. This kind of site authentication (as opposed to user authentication) might not seem important, but as e-Business evolves and as hackers discover more ways to masquerade as legitimate sites, this situation becomes critical.

Even more critical is the SSL encryption of the traffic a Web server generates to send to an end user's browser. For some sites, such as financial and purchasing companies, this problem becomes so critical that the sheer volume of data to be encrypted and decrypted must be dealt with using specialized infrastructures. Refer to the "SSL and Encryption Hardware" section earlier in this chapter for information about SSL acceleration solutions.

Unfortunately, because of cost and support issues involved with complicated technology, many other possible uses of PKI technology are more difficult to achieve realistically. The next few sections detail PKI-based services and capabilities, particularly to show where PKI still needs some work, where specialized uses can make a difference, and where current non-PKI practice must be aware of future PKI-centric issues.

Using PKI for User Authentication

User authentication is certainly one way to use PKI, but you should be aware of significant caveats. Many PKI trailblazers have found deploying these technologies to be both expensive and highly complex. Therefore, many users have opted for simpler approaches. Historically, most organizations have erred on the side of learning to live with multiple passwords and user IDs internally. When the Web came along, many users turned to Web Single Sign-On (as discussed earlier in this chapter) instead of full PKI deployments.

Using PKI for user authentication starts with digital certificates, which have emerged as the leading technology for strong end-user authentication. These certificates are also used for Single Sign-On (SSO), to replace the multiple user IDs and passwords end users currently endure. At the same time, the back-end infrastructure for PKI can leverage a common directory for applications and network services, acting as a shared repository for these digital certificates and other user data. Thus, a solution with PKI and directory service components can provide an identity infrastructure.

Several CA product and service offerings allow organizations to distribute their own end-user certificates for internal use. For external use, it is more common to distribute certificates using third-party CA service providers such as GTE and VeriSign.

For e-Business needs, only the external case usually applies. That is, a customer might need to verify a certificate on a Web site and prove that it was legitimately obtained from the service provider. Issuing your own certificates, even if they provide strong encryption and user authentication, doesn't give users enough assurance that your site is legitimate.

Using PKI for Digital Signatures

In contrast to simple user authentication, where PKI might not be necessary, the high monetary value of some business-to-business (B2B) transactions demands that businesses strongly encrypt and authenticate multiple security functions. This requirement is one reason that some companies use *digital signatures*. A digital signature refers to the use of PKI technology to create the electronic analog of a physical signature: a binding of user-specific information to a transaction or document.

The value of a digital signature depends on the security of the private key each user receives. Digital signatures provide a service known as *non-repudiation*, which means that participants cannot later deny making transactions to which they agreed, nor can they change the terms of the transaction at a later date. Their signature on a document proves that they made the transaction. Assuming no one else has that user's private key, no one else could have signed it.

SSL alone lets you encrypt the content of a transaction during transit. But it doesn't provide a way for the transaction to be approved or examined at a later date. No signature or audit record exists. Granted, a secure pipe provides a lot of comfort. But through PKI and signing of the transaction itself, rather than just securing the transmission, businesses can uphold non-repudiation by checking digitally signed records.

As noted previously, users don't often check or validate certificates. Moreover, the actual technology and standards for validity checking are just now solidifying. Organizations often achieve this validation through real-time queries that determine certificate status using Online Certification Status Protocol (OCSP), which is supported either directly by VeriSign or through vendors that provide OCSP support, such as CertCo or ValiCert.

Over time, more applications will allow the creation and audited storage of time-stamped digitally signed records (or digital receipts, if linked to a payment). Certificate holders will have a dispute resolution process that allows them to examine the secure record store, as needed. However, organizations must be careful to make sure new features won't hamper interoperability and reusability. For example, one service offering from a major CA included assumptions about additional certificate content that precluded the use of any other certificate type. This sort of implementation prevents interoperability, thus it hampers reusability.

Instead, look for PKI implementations that can be integrated with existing technology and previously issued certificates. Even when a "standard" PKI is used, it could prove to be less reusable than expected.

Using PKI for Permissions Management

Authorization or permissions management is a critical security service currently unavailable as a centralized infrastructure. While *authentication* refers to verifying user identity, *authorization* refers to the rules of what users are allowed to do, once their identity has been verified.

You can distribute authorization rights through attribute certificates, similar to the way that identity certificates carry identity information. However, the challenges facing PKI encumber the deployment of attribute certificates even more. Applications have no standard way to interpret certificate-based authorization information. And the management challenges are daunting, given that attribute certificates change much more often than identity certificates.

Problems with PKI

The bumpy transition from architecture and technology standards into actual product implementations has seriously hampered effective use of PKI. Immature standards and technologies are largely to blame. No single product or service solves all the issues with making PKI successful. PKI has a significant set of real limitations that must be addressed before it will be easy to use and ubiquitous.

Application Integration Challenges. As of this writing, few applications could make use of certificates in a meaningful way. While applications such as e-mail and Web browsers have included basic certificate support for years, significant improvements still need to be made in terms of usability and links to back-end certificate revocation infrastructure. While some protocols, such as IPSec and S/MIME, make use of certificates, they still lack the ability to digitally sign a transaction online. Therefore, some of the true business efficiencies that public-key certificates promise can't be achieved yet.

Historically, PKI vendors have provided toolkits, many of them proprietary, assuming that PKI was important enough that users would perform integration. To speed adoption of PKI and shed proprietary stigmas, PKI vendors made their toolkits open. Increasingly, IT organizations are using the various public key cryptography standards and PKI Certificate Management Protocol standards to improve interoperability. Some products are relatively easy to use, with fewer controls to reduce confusion and prevent users from implementing an insecure solution. Others are highly customizable, yet more difficult to use for all but highly experienced security developers.

Alternatively, modules are available that preintegrate some applications with PKI from all players. These offerings from non-core PKI vendors are fundamentally different because they are based on security middleware. This middleware is designed to create a bridge between applications and PKI, but it doesn't eliminate the need for application integration. Furthermore, since parts of the middleware are centralized and application-aware, these products provide an opportunity to define and enforce application-level policies, such as encryption and digital signing of all e-mail sent to certain user groups.

Some IT organizations, however, have focused on browser-based PKI initiatives, making the pervasive Web browser the primary client software of interest. In this environment, neither toolkits nor modules are useful. Instead, organizations use applets to bolster SSL—for example, by providing digital signing capabilities. This method allows functional interfaces in a browser to access Web-based PKI applications that often use server-stored certificates and private keys to provide mobility.

Mobility and Reuse Challenges. Another problem with PKI is that private key reuse from one Web interface to another is not yet easy. Because digital certificates are primarily stored with password-protection within browsers or on hard drives, use across multiple PCs requires that you either store digital certificates on a diskette and reinstall them at each PC, or download the digital certificates and private keys from a secure, central database.

The use of server-stored certificates and private keys violates the premise of "one user, one key." This premise is the basis for non-repudiation. Extensive cryptographic protocols and advanced auditing procedures are required to deal with this problem.

While smart cards and readers will become more common over time, they still lack effectiveness. Early offerings by major vendors only demonstrated how far these technologies still have to go before they become viable. While met with enthusiasm, the strong online authentication requirements of some early cards and readers made them too difficult to support. In addition, buying services were difficult to integrate with participating Web sites. Until smart cards and readers become more widespread, centralized private key storage is a flawed tactical (short-term) solution with strong authentication and encryption a must for key downloads.

User Authentication Challenges. While PKI promises the ability to perform user authentication, in fact this goal is very difficult to achieve. In most models, the system stores certificates and private keys in the browser, and only occasionally protects them with a password. Hackers can easily compromise this storage approach, thus making strong user authentication impossible. While a certificate provides incremental improvement over password-only schemes, true strong authentication requires a two-factor method: a combination of something you know and something you have. In the world of PKI, this combination translates into a certificate stored on a smart card and a private key protected by a personal identification number (PIN).

Scalability Challenges. The problem of realistic proportions only compounds PKI's problems. In e-Business, user volumes in the millions are significantly higher than volumes inside a single business. Supporting millions of users might be the goal of a Web site, but PKI technology hasn't been used in these proportions yet. Significant run-time issues at this scale include supportability and key management, which includes revoking, renewing, escrowing, and more. There is little precedent for these issues in current real-world e-Business cases.

Trust Challenges. Politics and economics will always intrude in PKI processes. For example, whose certificate will a given business decide to use and whose certificate will they trust? In some cases, you might not trust a given entity with your personal information. Even more important, you might not trust the procedures or integrity of a given company enough to put any faith in a certificate that the entity issues. In contrast to the American Express use of smart cards, for example, Microsoft's Passport service does not use PKI for user authentication. This service transmits a user name and password over SSL, but it still suffers from realistic concerns about third-party ownership of user information. For this reason companies like Microsoft are trying to work with third parties that are more likely to be trusted.

Business models are only now being developed for shared PKIs and cross-certification. Experimentation will take time. Companies are still trying to figure out how to handle the business issues associated with wider data sharing. It is not yet clear who will run the authority that issues certificates, used by consumers and businesses, as they interact with each other. Trusted third parties are emerging to fill this gap by acting as intermediaries between users, but development is still slow.

This situation often makes PKI too costly to implement, whether due to the outright purchase costs, though these factors are decreasing, or more likely because of back-end and user retraining support costs. The benefits, other than SSL, are still unclear for many e-Business cases. However, PKI still can be a valid choice in some cases.

PKI: Looking Forward

Organizations with aggressive e-Business goals should investigate PKI further and start building solutions, especially if the monetary value of their individual transactions is so high that losing one transaction could lead to significant loss. Most Web sites do not need sophisticated PKI features, so PKI is often used only for secure sessions (SSL) and not user authentication (Web SSO) or other services.

Effective security measures, such as PKI-based non-repudiation and verification, should be a prerequisite to help safely unleash the revenue opportunities of B2B exchanges and markets. In contrast, widespread deployment of PKI for user authentication or other digital certificate-based services awaits solutions to proprietary APIs, certificate revocation list (CRL), and mobility limitations. Therefore, in the short to medium term, PKI has more value for safely securing B2B transactions than for simpler user authentication.

Nevertheless, PKI technology will be the basis for long-term solutions to the problems of access control, non-repudiation, and authentication. You should experiment with this technology on small-scale deployments until more complete robust solutions are ready.

In some industries, regulations sometimes mandate the use of PKI or other strong encryption technologies. Make sure that your organization satisfies B2B security requirements with fully functional PKI solutions. In doing so, be careful to implement a PKI that not only supports B2B initiatives, but is also reusable for other applications. Unfortunately, it could be a long time before you see a single PKI solution that works worldwide—or even nationwide—across many businesses and for all users.

Directory Server

A directory server is another major component of an Identity Infrastructure. Directory servers provide centralized storage of:

- Shared user data, such as authentication credentials, personalization attributes, groups, and distribution lists
- Machine data, such as configuration and policy information
- Application data, such as configuration data

The directory server is a database optimized for read functions with a hierarchical structure, called the directory tree. Directory server technology is increasingly being focused into shared and read-only identity infrastructure applications.

In the short term, many organizations are moving ahead with plans to build a shared directory and security infrastructure for e-Business or extranet applications. The acceleration of rushed, high-profile, extranet-centric, directory projects has forced many organizations to develop a two-pronged directory strategy focused on:

- Enterprise directory services, tied in with a network operating system (NOS) strategy for internal users
- Extranet or Web application–centric directory services

Extranet directories support the needs of new Internet, extranet, and e-Commerce applications. At the same time, these solutions can be used for Web application–centric directories internally, though these projects typically are less common and not as well-funded. Directory servers support a different set of user accounts that are not necessarily employees, but business partners, consumers, and other customers. Best-of-breed directory products provide single-server scalability for highly centralized applications, with capacities ranging from 100,000 to more than one million entries and more than 1,000 requests per second.

Extranet Directory Services and Solutions

While X.500 vendors had early success for high-volume white-page intranet implementations, they were overcome in the late 1990s by Netscape Directory Server's momentum in the extranet and Web application arenas. As a result, leading products are now mainly based on the Lightweight Directory Access Protocol (LDAP), not full X.500.

LDAP defines a standard interface between applications and the directory. It is also the standard protocol for communication between directory user agents (DUAs) and directory service agents (DSAs), which work as clients and servers in the LDAP environment.

A server-based application, including components such as Web SSO and Web servers, can be a client of an LDAP directory. LDAP provides a single standard protocol and API for directory services, which even Web SSO applications use. Extranet applications should be designed to use this interface and protocol to provide adaptability to future directory server products.

Storage for authentication credentials and other user identity information remains the key offering of extranet directories. Users should include either Web SSO or PKI integration requirements in shared directory and security infrastructure projects to ensure compatibility and develop internal expertise. Avoid outsourcing extranet directories, even if the outsourcer is completely extranet-targeted. Most large organizations won't delegate control over the list of customers or employees because that control is still too mission-critical to share with third parties.

Beyond platform issues, extranet directory solutions need better administration solutions that allow delegated administration, particularly for new applications being administered outside the IT group, or even outside the enterprise. Aside from the market-leading products, additional third-party directory management applications will adapt directory administration to individualized business and application requirements. Metadirectory tools will assist extranet-centric customer relationship management projects, consolidating customer information into a single view. All of these events will likely dovetail with Web SSO vendor efforts to offer a more controllable centralized user identity management solution. But clearly, this situation is a short-term challenge to all implementations of identity infrastructure services.

Identity Integration Metadirectories

Integration solutions called metadirectories can handle cases where the same credentials must be mirrored in two or more separate identity infrastructures. Many e-Business identity infrastructures do not need this added capability, except for a onetime download of customer data from internal DBMS sources to get started. However, some attributes in an identity infrastructure's directory store might need synchronization with legacy customer data systems. For example, address changes might need to be synchronized so that both the billing system and the online portal are consistent.

This situation, however, is part of the larger issue of legacy system integration that should be addressed with enterprise application integration (EAI) or other transactional integration solutions, as addressed later in this book. Metadirectory solutions, as well as some competing administration utilities, are focused on only user identity stores and attributes. These solutions work best when a few disparate identity infrastructures or directory stores must be synchronized.

This solution might involve synchronizing with a business partner, though this isn't a common approach yet. There are many technical difficulties, such as a lack of standard schema, that might cause problems for e-Business integration, such as product incompatibility, secure transmission worries, and so on. But the politics and culture of data ownership across business boundaries remain major issues.

Metadirectory use is less common for individual internal Web sites, since internal directory solutions hold employee data only and not much customer data, and they do not need to be synchronized. Some metadirectory offerings do not offer real-time dynamic synchronization. In the absence of these services, employees accessing an e-Business Web site must log in with separate distinct credentials or you can use a Web SSO product to check both the secondary user credential store and the primary customer LDAP directory for a match.

In the future, integrated directory services for internal and external applications will provide an important way to manage business services across traditional business processes and e-Business. Meanwhile, you can simplify directory infrastructure planning by separating it into two directory service initiatives: one for the enterprise (distributed) and another for extranet (centralized, Web-oriented). Because no single product currently handles both initiatives well, you should make directory service product selections separately for each category.

Building a Complete Identity Infrastructure

So far, you've seen the individual components of an Identity Infrastructure service. But the best way to integrate these critical components into an infrastructure strategy is to assemble the complete set of components as a packaged service. The goal is not just to centralize the storage of credentials, but also to provide the easiest approach to reusability. Figure 5.13 shows the components needed for a complete identity infrastructure.

This section explains how to build a complete identity infrastructure view, borrowing from discussions of individual components in previous sections. This section also explains how to create a permissions infrastructure as a longer-term separate function from identity management.

As your company increasingly uses directory services for various authentication requirements, you must coordinate user security credentials and attribute management to mold a complete identity infrastructure. Although many e-Business initiatives use and add various components at different stages of maturity, a complete identity infrastructure should include planning and building a single set of critical integrated functions, including the following:

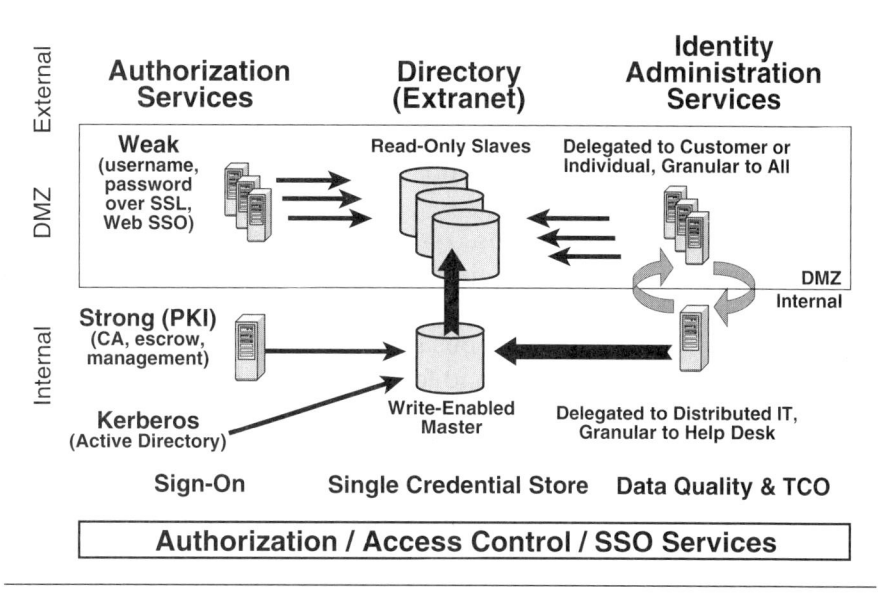

Figure 5.13 Building a Complete Identity Infrastructure

- Directory. Shared user authentication credentials and attribute store
- Authentication. From simple user name and password (including Web SSO features) to stronger methods, including PKI
- Delegated administration. Enabling the IT group to distribute administration tasks to business units or business partners
- Data quality management. Enabling individual user attention to data accuracy, coordinated across attribute ownership or control

A distinct permission infrastructure complements the identity infrastructure. Identity infrastructure is part of an IT security architecture that acts as a gatekeeper at the enterprise boundary, prior to a user gaining application access. Permission infrastructure resolves what a user might do after authentication, based on defined roles or other attributes. Permission infrastructure components include the following:

- Exit-processing routines that route subsystem calls (Web servers, etc.)
- APIs that route application-level calls
- Proxies that trap application actions
- A policy engine that processes authorization checks

- Legacy integration components
- Non-technology components that control role definition and structure

Identity infrastructure and permission infrastructure are evolving to provide a more scalable, secure, and reusable infrastructure for application access.

The primary purpose of directories is still to store people information, which is used to authenticate and authorize user access to applications. This role is particularly true in identity and permission infrastructures. Early e-Business adopters used an LDAP extranet directory for B2B and B2C, and for a few applications, they chose a NOS-centric and LDAP-based enterprise directory to consolidate internal directory needs and centralize identity infrastructure management.

The next business wave will probably move from a centralized extranet directory infrastructure to a distributed one, pressuring vendors to standardize replication and synchronization capabilities. Key standardization techniques will include LDAP enhancements, use of Extensible Markup Language (XML), and metadirectories. Enterprise metadirectory needs will increase, fueled by Web-enabled enterprise resource planning (ERP), integration of portal services with legacy systems, and voice/data convergence. Nevertheless, a single directory for both external and internal environments will remain elusive due to the fact that data store requirements and management will continue to be different for B2B and B2C versus internal requirements.

Authentication engines within the identity infrastructure can serve as gatekeepers, blocking users who shouldn't have access and guaranteeing the identity of those allowed in. Some first-line authentication engines currently use LDAP directories as data stores. Web SSO applications provide weak authentication through user IDs and passwords but are positioned to support stronger authentication using biometrics, tokens, and PKI as lower costs and improved standards become a reality. The latest NOS environments, such as Microsoft's Active Directory Services (ADS), provide strong authentication capabilities, but poor and incomplete features have hampered enterprise implementations.

The permission infrastructure provides post-authentication within the protected network. It maps role identifiers to actual permissions and provides services for system and application components to validate security conditions for requested actions. Web authorization engines combine two elements:

- Standard exit processors for major Web servers, to check page and field access
- Custom application calls, to invoke a centralized policy engine and pass user authentication information to the engine so the correct user gets access

The existence of user authentication data creates a SSO environment where multiple Web servers can act as one.

Although one vendor product can deliver both identity and permission infrastructures, these infrastructures differ fundamentally both in terms of features and processes. Although strong arguments for a centralized identity infrastructure exist, permission infrastructure will be distributed into the application and handled by the application owner.

All complex, scalable, Web-based application development will include permission infrastructure engines to provide local coarse or granular authorization capability. NOS environments will create much of the permissions infrastructure for newer enterprise application environments as well, but legacy application integration in this environment will remain cost-prohibitive. Therefore, while an identity infrastructure is currently valuable for Web and, particularly, e-Business cases, the permissions infrastructure will evolve much more slowly as a centralized infrastructure service.

Even as user attribute information increases in complexity and value, organizations implementing identity and permission infrastructures are finding that integrated data, received from sources such as Human Resources, e-mail, and telecommunications, is often incorrect. For e-Business environments, customer profiles must be managed as well, on a greater scale in B2C environments than in enterprise accounts. Organizations need automated approaches that extend data management to the individual user through self-service, with IT groups and business management authorizing many of the changes. Leading Web SSO vendors are expanding this capability within the products, but effective integration of delegated and single-point administration, self-service, and robust change automation will not occur right away.

Directory Service Markup Language (DSML)

Due to the major directory vendor support of LDAP and the scalability of current server architectures, businesses now routinely use directories to authenticate e-Business trading partners. However, LDAP support is not enough. Although this protocol handles queries and modifications well, it isn't very sophisticated. For example, LDAP cannot discern what kind of directory entries exist, how they are named, or what attributes they possess. LDAP also does not include object-level access control. Although current directory vendors provide a proprietary way of implementing this control, if organizations have multiple platforms, multiple directories exist as well.

Organizations building an identity infrastructure for business exchanges and electronic marketplaces must quickly find a platform-independent method to provide applications with access to these directories. The Directory Service Markup Language (DSML) could be the answer.

DSML represents the use of XML technology applied to outstanding directory issues, particularly those surrounding server-to-server communications and interoperability. This promising standard aims to help organizations faced with difficult and complex e-Business integration issues, especially those involving user authentication across multiple organizations. Many key vendors have already adopted the published interoperability specifications. This group includes not only the major directory players, but also directory service providers, such as Netegrity, Critical Path, Oblix, and Radiant Logic.

Identity Infrastructure Deployment Strategies

An identity infrastructure serves a dual purpose: providing for e-Business and streamlining internal infrastructure operations. IT organizations must quickly identify, prioritize, and implement the initiatives necessary to build the enterprise and e-Business identity infrastructure.

External Priorities. As a first priority, many organizations have a unique but limited window of opportunity to build an identity infrastructure for e-Business and get it right. Doing it right involves the careful selection of directory services, authentication and authorization capabilities, delegated administration services, and methods of ensuring the quality of directory data. The primary purposes of the extranet identity infrastructure are to:

- Provide a repository for business partner and customer directory information
- Provide a common infrastructure layer for authenticating and authorizing users of Web-enabled applications across security infrastructures, such as firewalls and DMZs

- Provide services to manage the directories themselves
- Ensure the accuracy of the directory data, particularly when internal directory data must be extracted and replicated to create or feed the extranet directory

A second key priority is creating an external identity infrastructure service that is highly adaptive. Authentication and authorization solutions must be able to evolve efficiently into more robust security mechanisms, incorporating such technologies as PKI without significant effort or modification. Directory schema must be designed and documented flexibly and simply to incorporate a changing set of business partners and customers, as well as absorb merger, acquisition, and divestiture activities. Applications must be chosen and/or written based on their ability to integrate with the Web SSO solution. Even projects involving corporate intranets must be able to reuse large portions of the external infrastructure.

Internal Priorities. Organizations often make a decision regarding identity infrastructure without realizing it when they upgrade the corporate network operating system (NOS). Regardless of the NOS they choose, this decision is a key component of the enterprise strategy. The NOS directory serves as a foundation for an enterprise identity infrastructure, but deployment is actually part of a series of strategic initiatives aimed at reducing the number of directories in the organization. NOS upgrades and reductions in the number of overlapping e-mail applications should be part of the first initiative. However, undertaking such an effort requires a detailed inventory of existing directory services within the enterprise, an effort that is consistently underestimated. The second reduction phase involves consolidating remaining directories, particularly stored people information, such as human resources data and authentication tables for applications access. Phase three involves synchronizing critical data within the remaining directories where applicable. This synchronization could require significant management tools and some organizations might even dictate the use of metadirectory services.

Refining Pattern Designs in Identity Infrastructure

Table 5.4 summarizes the list of potential components in an identity infrastructure service and shows which components work best with the Web Publish and 3/N-Tier Transact patterns.

Table 5.4 Identity Infrastructure Service Pattern Summary Chart

Layer or Service Component	Web Publish	3/N-Tier
Identity Infrastructure Service	2	2
Public Key Infrastructure	4	4
Web SSO	2	2
Directory Server	2	2

Key
1 = Critical, All Cases
2 = Highly Recommended, Most Cases
3 = Optional, Some Cases
4 = Optional, Fewer Cases

Directory, Web SSO, and related identity infrastructure product vendors will enhance product features to deal with expanding permission infrastructure requirements over the next two years. These products will provide broader role-based authorization capabilities and application integration functions, and they establish permission infrastructure as an essential infrastructure component that is separate from, but complementary to, identity infrastructure.

Both internal and external identity infrastructure are enhanced with stronger authentication mechanisms such as PKI and biometrics, plus better management, administration, and control capabilities. Identity infrastructure insulates application transition from simple to strong PKI authentication until technology and the market matures. Nevertheless, PKI technology will be the basis of a long-term access control, non-repudiation, and authentication solution.

Over the next few years, multiple directory environments will become a reality for IT organizations and a driver for expanded metadirectory functionality. However, flexible, standards-based metadirectory services that cost less than $1 million will continue to elude enterprises for some time. Until then, you should focus on single-directory vendors for e-Business identity infrastructure. At the very least, you should make sure that part of the infrastructure works—no matter what the internal strategy suggests.

Summary

Security services are an important new layer that you can add to your Adaptive Infrastructure Platform, as originally discussed in Chapter 2 (see Figure 2.12 for details). Two security services in particular can help you score relatively "easy wins" in the effort to build a more adaptive and reusable infrastructure.

- An isolation infrastructure service provides a solid bulwark of firewall and DMZ to make all internal applications and data more secure, but especially those applications that communicate using the Internet. This service is critical for all applications using the 3-N/Tier Transact pattern, and is highly recommended for applications in the Web Publish pattern.

- An identify infrastructure service provides a useful Single Sign-On method for all of your Web-based applications. Instead of having each individual application handle user authentication separately, you can create a single authentication service that is reusable for multiple applications.

Both of these services provide a good starting point for your efforts. With these in mind, the next chapter starts delving into each of the more traditional layers in the Adaptive Infrastructure Platform, starting with the physical components first, including the network, storage, and server layers.

Chapter 6

Physical Components

This chapter discusses the physical parts of an adaptive infrastructure, which include the network, storage, and servers. Particular components in each layer are of special importance to both e-Business and general infrastructure planners:

- In the network layer, components such as network load balancers, caching servers, and content delivery networks help enhance the performance of the e-Business and converged infrastructure.

- In the storage layer, components such as storage area networks (SANs) and network-attached storage (NAS) will play an increasingly important role in both traditional business and e-Business.

- In the server layer, platform consolidation and the ability to "scale-out" will make your e-Business pattern design more cost-effective.

This chapter presents a discussion of key components within each of these layers. Later chapters will examine the key functional, interface, and management components of an adaptive infrastructure. For a complete list of infrastructure components, including those used in both enterprise and e-Business computing, see Appendix A.

Network Layer

Networking components are an essential part of e-Business or any innovative enterprise application. The performance of the network is crucial to the ability to deliver speedy data access to end users and applications no matter where they are located: on the local area network (LAN), wide area network (WAN), or in some remote corner of the globe.

This section examines important component technologies and other factors you should consider when planning network services and infrastructure. In particular, it pays special attention to scalability, performance issues, and decision factors involved in using external network service providers.

Overview of Networking Technologies

The network layer supports communication among devices and users in a secure and manageable way. To be complete, any infrastructure design must address networking issues.

Figure 6.1 shows infrastructure components included in the network layer that deserve special attention.

Examples of the network layer software and hardware components include LAN or WAN hardware such as cabling, switches, routers, proxy/caching servers, and content delivery systems.

Transmission Control Protocol/Internet Protocol (TCP/IP) is the standard technology used to integrate these components, as well as for integration with other layers. TCP/IP is central to internal enterprise and

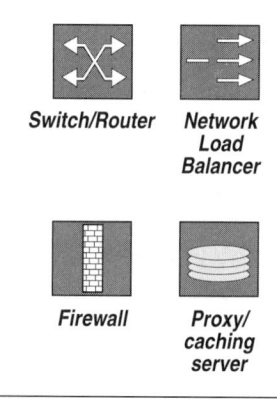

Figure 6.1 Network Layer Software and Hardware Components

e-Business needs because it is a reliable, standardized protocol for delivering data and applications across all types of networks, including the Internet. Over the last decade, IP has become the de facto standard for business-to-business communication and data sharing. The majority of business applications require IP support. Any application that uses one of the major databases, such as IBM, Microsoft, or Oracle, must run on a network that supports IP. Furthermore, many applications require it, including Internet, virtual private network (VPN), intranet, and extranet applications.

Below TCP/IP are many networking components that must be part of the plan, including hardware, services, and technologies such as fiber, copper, Ethernet, frame relay, and leased lines. TCP/IP provides a simple yet critical transparency layer between this lower-level complexity and upper-layer usage. The network is usually offered as a service to applications, which makes it something more than just a set of components. In this sense, it includes staffing and process details, culminating in network service level agreements.

Scale-Out Design for Performance and Availability

A major concern of infrastructure planners is addressing the tremendous growth in size and importance of network infrastructure. Over the past decade, the growth of LANs and WANs has given way to a huge wave of Internet traffic, which is being overtaken by the impending broadband future. To cope with this rapid growth and conduct business with any kind of agility, IT organizations need to continually address a wide range of networking issues.

Many e-Business designs must handle high-volume network conditions while maintaining acceptable service levels, particularly performance and reliability. IT organizations can meet this challenge by building in extra capacity, but important questions arise: How big should this component be? How much headroom should be included? What else can be done, besides buying huge amounts of capacity and availability for all components?

The answers lie in an incremental approach to performance and scale. For performance, don't buy too much too soon, yet plan to implement new capacity quickly and gracefully. For availability, don't buy high-availability features on all components, but create a high-availability strategy that matches the whole pattern. At times, this high-availability strategy means duplicating low cost, commodity components instead of spending money on single instances of expensive, "scale-up" solutions.

Low-Cost Scalability

In the case of Web-based interactions, scalability is simple to achieve with scale-out, rather than scale-up, designs using a stateless farm architecture containing network load balancers, masses of inexpensive Web servers, and file system or database servers. Unlike the 3/N-Tier Transact pattern, the read-only Web Publish pattern applications easily can scale by replicating file systems and database servers. Assuming the data doesn't change often, this pattern is easy to support.

Using a scale-out design for the Web Publish pattern means that the database systems you select need not be the best at online transaction processing (OLTP), and therefore both your hardware and software costs can be less expensive. You can choose less expensive commodity servers and add more of them to scale. At some point, data center rack space becomes an issue, but the point for this pattern remains: You should purchase lots of commodity hardware instead of expensive equipment.

In these scenarios, many new Internet-centric acceleration or performance-enhancement solutions work well. These solutions include:

- Network load balancers and multi-site balancing solutions
- Secure Sockets Library (SSL) offloading for encrypted content
- Compression
- Caching for databases and memory, reverse caching in the data center, client caching, and intermediate ISP caches
- Content delivery network (CDN) services such as Akamai
- Traffic or rate shaping

Redundancy and Failover

High availability is generally ensured by adding redundant components throughout the network path in a load-balanced, load-share, or active/standby configuration. *Load balancing* ensures that each device takes an equal share of the load, while *load sharing* merely splits traffic without regard to the load on the devices. In an active/standby, or hot standby scenario, active devices automatically failover to standby devices. Regardless of the approach, it is important that application-level session information, such as a shopping cart, is transferred upon failover in a manner that is transparent to the user.

The level of resources allocated to the redundancy of a given component depends on the average mean time to failure and criticality of the component. Focus your attention on devices that have lower mean time to failure, such as load balancers, servers, and firewalls, and move toward more robust devices, such as switches and routers. Mission-critical hosting infrastructures should be completely duplicated at alternate sites with separate Internet connections for effective disaster recovery.

To provide linear scalability and highly resilient systems, you should group Web and application servers into farms (see Figure 6.2) with mirrored applications and content across all servers. This configuration provides extensive failover backup. Web servers typically are farmed using network load balancers. Application servers are more likely to use native stateful load-balancing features to provide failover. In some cases, a network load balancer is also used with non-HTTP protocols.

Providing failover for database systems is more complex due to the unique nature of data content. Farmed databases are appropriate for the read-only content found in Web Publish pattern applications. Transactional systems, however, usually require read/write capabilities, making data synchronization problematic in farmed situations due to network latencies and other system issues. Most organizations provide failover in data systems by using a mirrored Redundant Array of Independent Disks (RAID), which are storage systems that contain constantly updated copies of the primary data. Partitioning data and storing each partition on

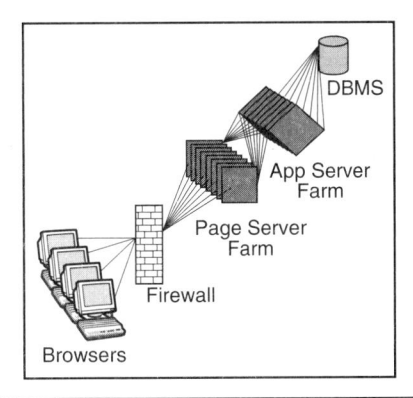

Figure 6.2 Stateless Farm Architecture

independent storage devices provides linear scalability and a higher degree of availability, so that not all data is offline at the same time.

For very large transactional cases, true database or server clustering could be a workable solution; so could federated database solutions that split transaction content into predefined sections, alphabetically or using other schemes. Another method involves fully maximizing performance and availability solutions for the database platform by purchasing high-end servers rather than commodity servers. The OLTP database component of 3/N-Tier Transact pattern applications might be the one place where a more traditional scale-up design should be employed. But even this approach should be done in the context of the larger scale-out design for the rest of the system.

System Partitioning

In addition to failover capability, e-Business patterns must run independently so that the failure of the back-end transaction system in a 3/N-Tier Transact pattern application does not affect the Web Publish pattern functionality. Effective data and system partitioning allows independent activities to continue even if data subsets are lost.

When designing highly available sites, be sure to institute effective processes such as change control, testing, upgrade fall back, and business resumption planning. Each of these activities must be formalized and practiced to avoid process-related outages. Backup/recovery of information contributes to business continuity. However, application uptime is dramatically affected by networking, application architecture, application integration, online storage, and server clustering. Thinking in terms of a comprehensive end-to-end pattern makes operational processes more effective and complete.

Ensuring performance and high availability requires a thorough examination of all potential points of bottleneck or failure for a given pattern, then allocating resources to provide capacity and failover protection. Device redundancy alone is not sufficient; instead, you should concentrate on application failover. Pay attention to processes and provide detailed business resumption plans for all potential points of failure.

The next few sections will examine some of the individual components mentioned above for a scale-out architecture, including network load balancers, caching, and content delivery networks.

Network Load Balancer

The network load balancer is one key component used for e-Business scalability that you don't typically find in the traditional enterprise designer's toolkit. Since e-Business applications are generally Web-based, they can benefit from the services of a network load balancer.

A network load balancer leverages the stateless nature of the HTTP protocol to route traffic to any appropriate server behind it. This technique is transparent to many applications. However, some applications require specialized services because they store their state on a Web server. For example, if a network load balancer routes traffic to another Web server in the middle of a shopping transaction, the user's shopping cart contents could be lost.

Sharing file systems across Web servers is a partial fix, but the best solution is to store the state in a back-end OLTP system, where it is stored as long as necessary. An alternative for less critical, more session-oriented data is to store the state in client-based cookies or URL headers. This technique has security and reusability complications, however. If users return to a shopping cart from a different browser or after closing a session, they are unlikely to find the cart or contents still available.

Many corporations have implemented Web-server farms with simple DNS round-robin load balancing to scale Web applications. However, simple DNS policies are not sophisticated enough to avoid unhealthy servers in a cluster, resulting in unacceptable service levels.

To further eliminate single points of failure and to reduce distance-induced network latency, enterprises now use pairs of server load-balancing products and balance across multiple geographically dispersed data centers, particularly for higher-volume public Web sites. Network load balancers intelligently manage traffic across a cluster of servers that support HTTP and other protocols, and they distribute the processing load based on various policies, including round robin, least connections, and CPU load.

Network load balancers do not all use the same approach to providing these additional services. Vendors use three primary architectural approaches:

- Software deployed on servers in the cluster
- Network appliances
- Switches

Figure 6.3 provides a diagram of the various configurations.

Network load balancer vendors will continue adding deeper and broader feature sets as core features, as reliability, performance, and cluster management become commodities. Indeed, most recent product

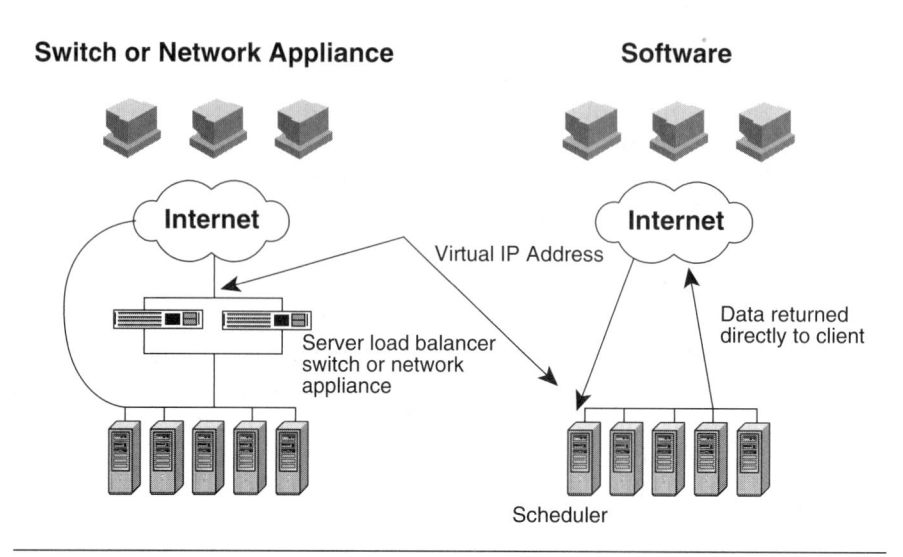

Figure 6.3 Network Load-balancing Approaches

improvements focus on application-specific features, SSL traffic acceleration, and site resource management tools.

Larger sites, or those with significant e-Business traffic volume, tend to use intermediate appliances or switches, which allow for more heterogeneous server clusters with a mix of operating systems. Appliances and switches are more flexible and easier to install, since no device software resides on the Web server. Appliances are the most flexible and provide a greater range of features, while switch-based products provide the greater capacity and throughput required for very large sites and service provider infrastructure.

Core Advantages

The three core advantages of using a network load balancer solution are:

1. Increased redundancy for failover and redirection around unhealthy servers, to more easily support unscheduled maintenance without service interruption.

2. Better price performance through more efficient use of existing CPU power, allowing more servers with less brawn to service users rather than requiring CPU upgrades on specific boxes to handle scale.

3. Management ease, such as support for scheduled maintenance tasks, adding or removing servers from clusters, and advanced reporting.

Network load balancers are most often deployed at the presentation tier in Web Publish and 3/N-Tier Transact pattern applications. Complete redundancy calls for parallel network infrastructures from the WAN to the database, and should include global load balancers across multiple geographically separate data centers to avoid catastrophic outages, as discussed later in this section.

Although it is not a best practice, some e-Commerce applications establish and maintain a stateful session between the client and a particular server. Methods to identify a client for a persistent connection include SSL session ID, IP address, or cookies stored on the client browser. SSL session ID and cookies are more granular methods used when the client originates from an ISP with multiple proxy servers. An IP address identifier won't work when multiple users communicate through the same proxy server IP address, which is very common in large organizations that have a "Class 10" addressing scheme (IP addresses beginning with 10.x.x.x). Before selecting a product, carefully consider the source of your e-Commerce customers to determine the most appropriate method of tracking persistent connections.

The network load balancer's persistence mechanism is really just a tactical solution. Whenever possible, Web applications should be designed to work in farms, without relying on the load balancer to maintain persistent connections. You should also use an OLTP database as a more supportable central repository to hold state information, if possible. For sites with secure transactions using SSL encryption, place SSL acceleration devices upstream from the Web server, either in the network load balancer or before it, to allow the network load balancer to perform Layer 7 activities and to eliminate the need for persistent connections to a Web server.

Distributed Load Balancing for Multiple Sites

Load-balancing vendors offer distributed or global load balancers that redirect clients to the most appropriate data center. These solutions use algorithms and policy mechanisms to determine the best site for a particular client request to be handled. Algorithms include proximity, response time, packet loss, local server load, local server health, and content requested. For high-performance needs, you might need more advanced metrics, such as router hops, network latency, packet loss, time of day, Border Gateway Protocol (BGP) statistics, and round-trip time. Hosting service providers offer multi-site hosting packages for customers using these products.

Before investing in this type of solution, you should test applications extensively to verify that they will perform in multi-site scenarios. Some applications, such as those with poor state management, are not designed to operate from distributed data centers.

In the case of 3-N/Tier Transact applications, you must also address data synchronization issues before expanding beyond a single data center. Web Publish applications with minimal dynamic data generally work well in a distributed environment, but you can get better performance by using content delivery networks to distribute content closer to users. Multi-homing a single data center, with redundant ISP access and dual network paths to the server farm, can improve availability of applications that do not perform well in a distributed architecture.

One way that global load balancers distribute client requests is by examining site/application health and load thresholds. The global load balancer often collects this data via proprietary protocols. As a result, global load balancers are more effective when paired with local server-centric network load balancers from the same vendor.

When selecting local network load balancers, evaluate how the vendor handles both distributed and local load balancing. Some vendors support the ability to communicate metrics through XML, but it could be several years before you see seamless communication between network and global load balancer solutions from different vendors.

Vendors of global load balancers offer a variety of competitive site selection metrics and various levels of flexibility, which be used in a customized load-balancing algorithm with these metrics. Try to go beyond the checklist approach when evaluating these products and examine how the site selection metrics are derived, since vendor approaches for obtaining performance and proximity metrics vary widely. Initial deployments can use coarse metrics, such as continental location and server health. Then you can gradually add more metrics while continuously monitoring the server performance to validate the effectiveness of each new metric.

Performance vs. Reliability

The primary reason for creating redundant data centers domestically is to improve availability. However, many global organizations try to improve performance by distributing data centers closer to their audience, limiting distance-induced latency.

To pick the best solution, think of the reason that you want to establish multiple data centers. If high availability is your primary goal, first try using single-site high-availability options, such as disk mirroring, local load balancing, high-availability servers, redundant components, and multi-homing, before planning to adopt a multi-site architecture. To boost performance across continents, use products with appropriate performance metrics and redirection mechanisms that go beyond DNS redirection. Also, weigh investments in global load balancers against those for content delivery networks.

Using Load Balancers in Pattern Design

Solutions that enhance Web-server scalability and performance can dramatically improve a customer's Web experience. The use of network load balancing is a crucial design best practice for Web Publish and 3/N-Tier Transact patterns. Implement server-centric network load balancers to improve the reliability, manageability, and performance of their Web-server farms, but remember that network load balancers are only one tool in an end-to-end solution.

Network load balancers, content delivery networks, caching, and SSL acceleration are increasingly bundled into a "Web edge" service for HTML acceleration and assurance. These services are increasingly being offered in a single appliance box configuration, particularly SSL acceleration. See the following component discussions for more details on each of these.

Caching Server

Caching servers can reduce Web traffic by 30 to 60 percent on the Internet or intranets. This traffic reduction can help delay expensive access upgrades and alleviate congested pipes. Caching servers are an essential component for mission-critical applications and remote access to corporate information, as well as overall Web surfing. Research indicates that about 75 percent of Global 2000 enterprises use caching to improve network performance.

Caching Server Deployment

Caching servers can be deployed in a variety of locations. The effect on Web-site performance depends on the location of the cache, how it's used, and the nature of the application.

- The most common deployment is a proxy cache, which acts as a gateway for all Web-surfing requests from inside the trusted network. Located close to the user, proxy caches intercept outbound HTTP messages and request Web content on behalf of active users. They also store the content for later reuse. Subsequent requests for the same content are serviced from the cache, eliminating expensive trips across the WAN infrastructure.
- Forward caches are the opposite of proxy caches, since they are located closer to the content than to the user. Forward caches intercept incoming HTTP requests and serve cached content, avoiding expensive trips deeper into the data center that overburden Web servers. In both cases, the purpose is to serve content faster and to eliminate requests traversing the same infrastructure twice.

Figure 6.4 provides a diagram of caching servers. The following sections discuss the features and benefits of each cache type in greater detail.

Caching Server Form Factors

Besides the common usage scenarios discussed above, caching servers are also distinguished by two form factors:

- Software that can be loaded on general-purpose hardware
- Black-box "appliances" using a specialized OS software/hardware combination

Caching software helps you to leverage existing hardware or commodity hardware purchased off-the-shelf. The software approach makes it

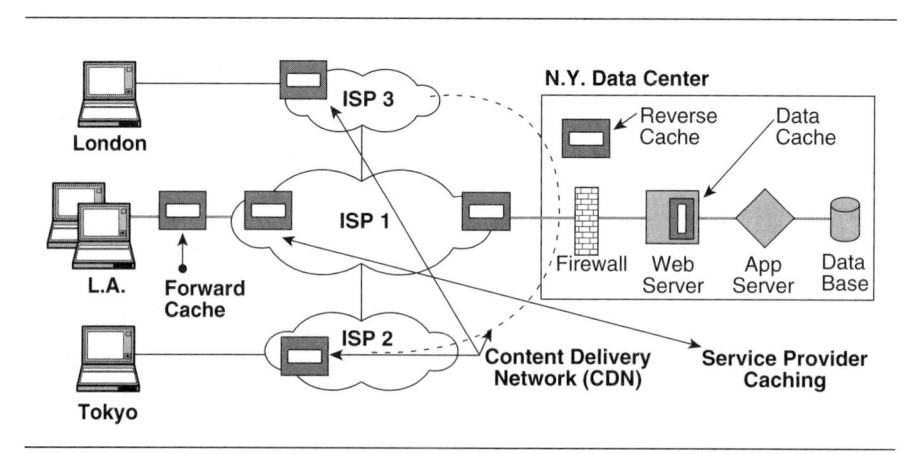

Figure 6.4 Caching Locations

easier to bundle relevant applications, such as firewalls, DNS, and filtering, on a single platform for quick branch-office deployments.

On the other hand, dedicated appliances offer significant performance advantages, as well as easier installation and maintenance. The specialized nature of the appliance provides better security because the underlying OS typically has no well-known security holes. And it provides better fault tolerance since the OS is often mirrored across multiple disks.

For larger enterprises, the most important product evaluation criteria are fault tolerance, manageability, compatibility with third-party management tools, auto-propagation of configurations, and LDAP compatibility. Performance indicators such as maximum throughput, connections per second, and hit ratio do not particularly differentiate forward cache products. Instead, when comparing products, focus on price/performance metrics such as throughput combined with connections per second.

Forward Caching

The major benefits of forward-deployed caches include:

- Cost savings by delaying expensive WAN and firewall capacity upgrades, particularly for your own ISP link
- Better performance of existing HTTP traffic, since caches can serve 30 to 60 percent of HTTP page requests
- Better bandwidth use across existing infrastructure, alleviating traffic jams at firewalls and other potential bottlenecks
- Improved ability to enforce Web usage policy through usage monitoring and control

Forward caches can be installed in either of two modes. In proxy mode, the device makes HTTP requests on behalf of the client and stores the results. In transparent mode, they are installed with switches and routers redirecting the HTTP requests and responses to the cache.

Reverse Caching

Some Web pages contain up to 70 or 80 distinct object files. Although portions of pages are dynamically generated, many of the page object files are rich graphics or static text. Serving this data from a reverse cache deployed directly in front of the Web server (see Figure 6.4) can accelerate delivery of these elements and reduce the load on more expensive Web servers, enabling them to service more dynamic

> ### A Caching Glossary
>
> **proxy server** An intermediary or gateway that fetches data from the Internet for users in a private trusted network. A proxy server improves security by masking the IP address of resources inside the private trusted network; it also minimizes WAN traffic and latency by storing information. The cache then provides the requested information the next time it is requested, instead of the traffic having to traverse the WAN link.
>
> **cache** A device that stores frequently accessed content locally for quick access by users without traversing the WAN. Also referred to as a forward cache.
>
> **proxy cache** Performs both proxy and cache functions.
>
> **forward caching** Any deployment of a cache or proxy cache on a LAN that stores information locally, instead of having clients access the same information repeatedly over a WAN link.
>
> **reverse caching** The storing of frequently requested local content for quick access by external users, alleviating the need for external requests to access the internal network. It is generally used in Web-site hosting implementations to serve graphic and other static content, reducing the load on internal Web servers and firewalls.
>
> **reverse proxy** A device that sits in the DMZ and makes dynamic content requests on behalf of incoming clients, providing an added security layer and masking internal server IP addresses.

requests. This caching can result in overall faster page views for less cost. In addition, when deployed outside the site firewalls (DMZs), caches can alleviate traffic bottlenecks at firewalls, delaying the need for expensive and complicated firewall clustering efforts.

Despite these advantages, sites with heavy text or media files can benefit more from specialized FTP or media servers. Furthermore, large fast-growing sites with frequently changing content should consider deploying Web-server farms in a scale-out design rather than caches. Also, users should reconsider reverse caching if customers are globally dispersed and distance-induced latency is the key issue. This latency is better addressed through forward caching or a content delivery network.

Typical reverse caches are deployed transparently on a load-balancing switch that operates at layers 4 and 7 of the OSI stack. These switches also manage cache clustering. A number of large Web sites are putting the cache outside the demilitarized zone (DMZ) while constantly updating the content to keep it fresh. The decision to put the cache outside or inside the DMZ depends on the tolerance for loss of the cached content, as well as the device type. It's not a good idea to put general-purpose hardware caches outside the firewall.

In reverse cache installations, performance is most important. The cache must scale to handle the expected page views per second, and it must be able to return the expected file load to clients comfortably. Sites with large data files or streaming media still require significant transmission rates and storage. Indeed, sites with substantial streaming media plans should closely evaluate vendors' streaming protocol strategy.

While all caches work on HTTP and FTP traffic, not all caches can cache heavy protocols such as multimedia audio and video streams. The number of page elements that can be serviced from the cache is more predictable in a reverse cache installation, so disk space is more predictable. However, disk redundancy and fault tolerance are more significant issues.

Manageability remains a significant factor in reverse caches. Organizations will want to manage caches remotely, especially if the caches are located in outsourced data centers. Site statistic collection and reporting remain important, as does third-party integration for site monitoring. Organizations that co-locate their sites at hosting provider data centers should also consider performance density, or performance per rack space, in total cost of ownership calculations. Vendor support offerings are always a consideration, including warranty replacement policy, on-site support costs, and so forth.

Reverse Proxies

Reverse proxies are often confused with reverse caches. Reverse proxies are placed in the Web site DMZ to pass along incoming requests to applications sitting on servers behind a second firewall, inside the trusted network (see Figure 6.5). Reverse proxies are often used to secure 2-Tier Transact applications that would have been vulnerable if placed entirely inside the DMZ. Since requests are funneled through the reverse proxy, the source and type of request can be tightly controlled,

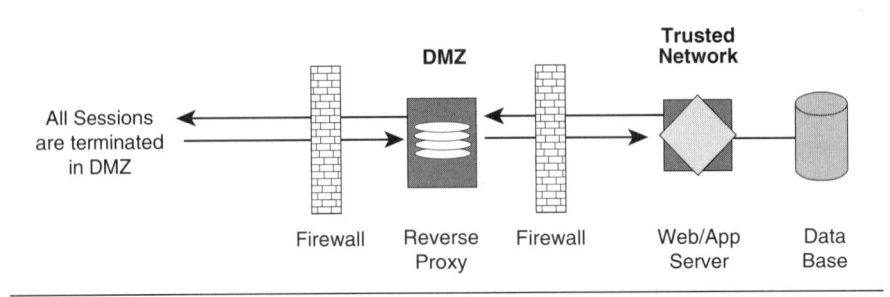

Figure 6.5 Reverse Proxy

minimizing the risk of hacking. Although reverse proxies can also provide caching functions, the real benefit is added security. Web SSO and application proxy firewall products are rapidly replacing reverse proxies, as discussed in Chapter 5 of this book.

Dynamic Caching

Web-site architects increasingly employ Active or Java Server Pages to dynamically generate Web pages on the fly, simplifying site management and personalizing content. These database-driven technologies drive significant transactional loads to assemble each page for thousands of simultaneous clients. Traditional static caches provide little benefit to these types of Web sites. Until recently, site architects used the brute-force approach of adding computing power to scale. Now, an emerging class of caching software substantially reduces the number of redundant page generations, accelerating site performance up to 10×, providing surge protection, and reducing infrastructure requirements.

Sites that have a reasonably limited number of nonuser-unique page objects are the best candidates for dynamic caches. Static sites are still better served by traditional caches, though future product improvements will make this distinction less important. Most dynamic caches are completely transparent to the site design. However, caching pages with user-unique links require slight modification to the page markup, and one vendor requires script modification.

Future versions of this software will have multiple distributed dynamic caches that help alleviate distance-induced latency and could, in some cases, replace distributed data and its inherent synchronization problems.

Effect of Caching on Web-Site Performance

Web designers should make sure their pages are cache-friendly to improve performance. Figure 6.6 shows the factors that affect Web-page performance.

Web-site owners have little control over forward caches, since these don't favor your traffic over anyone else's, and thus can't be used as a tool to differentiate your Web site's performance. However, a Web-site owner can use a cache in reverse mode to accelerate the Web servers behind it. This acceleration is accomplished by answering repeat requests for the same heavier objects without burdening the Web server or application server.

Reverse caches can reduce the server processing time required to assemble a page for delivery to an end user. Indeed, new "dynamic caches" have emerged that help assemble dynamic Web content pulled from a database for each visitor. However, as shown in Figure 6.6, server processing time is typically only five percent of the total time required to deliver a Web page to a customer.

Reverse caching does not accelerate the delivery of pages over the congested Internet, which is 80 percent of the problem. To address Internet latency, you would have to use forward caches located out on the Internet. While ISPs sometimes do provide these caches, they use them primarily to reduce their own bandwidth costs and might not accelerate your content. Individual browsers also have local caches, but such caches only accelerate content once it is in the cache; that is, once someone has viewed it and he or she clicks the Back button.

Furthermore, these two types of anonymous caches accelerate all Web sites equally, minimizing your ability to differentiate your own site's

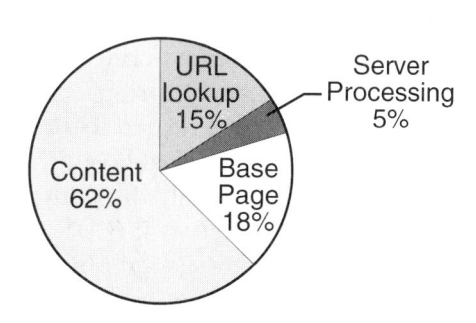

Figure 6.6 Factors Affecting Web Performance

performance. For latency-specific performance problems, you might consider a content delivery network, as discussed later in this chapter.

Using Caching Servers in Pattern Design

Although caches are well positioned to compensate for traffic surges by offloading static requests from Web servers, the cache must have sufficient capacity to handle the surge. Site infrastructure must be carefully designed to deal with legitimate traffic surges and denial-of-service attacks.

With regard to the two e-Business patterns discussed in this book, reverse caching is the only approach that can help accelerate content. However, if you are designing a pattern from scratch, this approach is not optimal.

- The Web Publish pattern needs no caching if you deploy a full stateless farm and scale-out architecture. Reverse caching can be added later if it is more cost-effective than adding Web servers.

- The 3/N-Tier Transact pattern usually doesn't need content acceleration of this sort, since the content usually isn't large and is more likely to be unique and encrypted. However, if a reverse cache is already being used for Web Publish, some 3/N-Tier Transact applications could also benefit marginally. In fact, both patterns could use the Internet latency performance enhancements that content delivery networks (CDNs) offer more than any caching that the Web-site owner can deploy.

Content Delivery Network (CDN)

A stable Web presence is essential to Global 2000 enterprises, yet the Internet's disjointed structure lacks centralized administration. This situation makes ensuring customer service difficult. To effectively improve overall site performance and distribute processing and network loads, Web infrastructure designers turned to alternative delivery mechanisms as a way to supplement traditional hosting services.

High-volume sites with widely distributed users can benefit from the use of a content delivery network (CDN). This method serves content by caching it in local servers, geographically distributed throughout the user environment, and serving content to each user from the closest "edge of the Internet."

CDN Configurations

Two typical configurations for content delivery networks are:

- Network-based overlays. These overlays are terrestrial- or satellite-based services provided by vendors who build network capacity on top of the Internet through private links between major backbone providers, or paid transit agreements for traffic-traversing ISP partner networks.

- Server-based overlay networks. Network providers place caches and other content servers on key ISP backbones around the Internet.

Server-based overlay networks offer the broadest applicability, with high overall customer satisfaction. The principal benefits include better performance to remote clients, reduced load on the Web host, and more efficient network use. By pushing caching closer to the user, content is served up without traversing the Internet. This process improves user response time, possibly making your site's services seem much faster to users compared to other providers. This competitive edge in performance might be worth the price, but the service is not inexpensive. Figure 6.7 shows how content delivery networks overlay multiple ISP networks using caching servers.

The major server-based content delivery networks augment traditional forms of Web delivery by pushing content out to distributed servers that are close to the user from a network perspective. In a variation on this model, new services are emerging that are built upon a smaller number of high-capacity nodes with fiber connectivity to major backbones.

Each of these models takes the same broad approach: HTML pages, images, and streaming content are served from the most optimal server

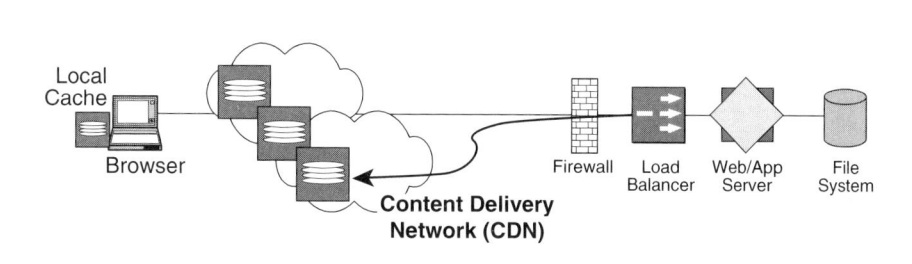

Figure 6.7 Content Delivery Network

in the overlay network. A centrally managed, though physically distributed director (operated by the service provider), guides requests to the most appropriate server, as determined by current network performance, server availability/load, geography, and other factors.

Unlike network-based overlay services, most CDN providers do not offer transport networks. Instead, they place servers on the backbones of major ISPs in target regions. Because no single service provider can be expected to service a large percentage of requests over its own network, a well-architected, network-independent server overlay provides better performance than a single-network approach. This overlay approach further avoids problems associated with any single provider's backbone, such as administrative errors and chain-reaction router or switch software failures.

Network-based overlays, in contrast, attempt to avoid Internet congestion by building private transport and switching capacity between major ISPs, using fiber interconnects, satellite delivery, or paid transit agreements across ISPs. These service providers make extremely high investments in facilities, and they cannot respond to dramatic shifts in Internet backbone usage as quickly as the server-based overlay providers. Satellite-based services are further limited because they lack a back-channel transmission capability and must send return traffic over conventional links. However, in extremely remote locations where terrestrial links are severely constrained, satellite-based solutions can be quite effective.

Organizations targeting specific geographies should carefully select a CDN partner on the basis of corporate viability and the strength of the ISP hosting arrangements in the countries they serve. Customers should select CDNs with partner ISPs offering the largest backbones in a given region; it is not sufficient for servers to be hosted at second-tier partners with limited connectivity in the region. The number, type, and size of servers in a given region should also be considered.

CDN services eliminate many single points of failure in their own networks. However, best practices dictate that customers should continue to maintain a traditional approach as a hedge against networkwide CDN failures. Customers of providers that require users to point URLs directly to the CDN should maintain alternative markup mechanisms, such as standby content reverting the company's domain name. In contrast, providers who use DNS-level redirection require less substantial changes within the content. For example, www1.mycompany.com returns as a URL from www.CDNprovider.com through DNS manipulation. As a result of this technique, the customer can more easily switch content away from the CDN, if needed.

Although content can be hand-coded to point HTML references to the CDN network, this labor-intensive markup process is more effectively automated. Coding chores can be made much less onerous by redirecting content to the CDN on-the-fly using Web application server extensions, content management products, or network infrastructure. You can also use server-side software to provide this function. An automated approach provides quicker activation of the CDN service, helping to optimize use and reduce expenses.

Best Uses for CDNs

CDN services should be implemented only in the appropriate infrastructure pattern (Web Publish). Inappropriate use of these services can lead to excessive costs without associated benefits. In particular, transactions requiring direct interfaces to back-end application/database servers might not be supported over CDN. While CDNs can be used to lighten the load on the central Web server and the network feeding it, CDNs do not eliminate the need for traditional back-end failover and fault-tolerance capabilities. Just as with conventional hosting, critical originating content servers must be protected with local or distributed server load-balancing services as appropriate.

CDNs support more application intelligence at the edge of the network and push beyond simple static object acceleration. The use of a special markup language called Edge Side Includes (ESI) helps CDN servers assemble pages dynamically. As these functions make intensive use of server resources, advanced CDN services can reduce the cost of centralized hosting by reducing the need for high-end servers at the origin site.

Beware of content delivery services with a narrow span, especially those that are limited to the Web hosting provider's backbone. To compete in the future, CDNs must extend beyond basic content delivery of static images and audio/video streams to host local databases and application logic via mechanisms such as ESI. Supplementary services, such as geographic location, wholesale hierarchical caching, and performance measurement services will be available as options.

Understanding CDN Costs and Pricing

Understanding traffic patterns will help control CDN costs. CDN cost models are based on traffic through the overlay, a model similar to the usage-based pricing used by many Web hosting providers. As with all usage-based Web hosting models, customers struggle to predict the traffic-based costs that will be associated with any new initiative.

CDN cost models are based on bandwidth used or total amount of content delivered by region. Some CDNs make region-specific pricing adjustments based on the origin and destination of the traffic. Bandwidth-based charges penalize sites prone to extended "flash crowds" (bursts extended over a full day), while the payload-based approach hurts widely dispersed usage. None of the offerings put caps on charges, requiring the customer to understand and project traffic patterns, which few customers can consistently predict in the initial stages of a project.

Using CDN in Pattern Design

Content delivery networks can dramatically improve the Web-based customer experience, particularly for international Web Publish implementations. As with caching, CDNs do not necessarily improve 3/N-Tier Transact applications, but have been used to make simple repeated objects such as corporate logos appear more quickly on unique, mostly text pages that are associated with transactional applications. Future adoption of Edge Side Includes (ESI) will increase a CDN's ability to support dynamic page assembly. Consider deploying server-based CDNs to support critical services and international penetration only if the application of these techniques can justify the monthly costs. The effective use of CDNs requires careful attention to traffic patterns to control high usage costs.

In addition, to get the best use of CDNs as well as other caching solutions, organizations should follow the Web design guidelines in the associated sidebar titled "Infrastructure Concerns for Web-Page Designers."

Internet Access and Transport Services

Internet connectivity is increasingly a central networking component. As businesses find new ways to use the Internet, Internet Service Providers (ISPs) are expanding services to differentiate themselves and meet demand. Meanwhile, IT budget pressures are forcing companies to develop more economical ways to address network demand, while improving the quality of application and network service.

The ISP purchasing decision is more complex than simply buying a leased line, where it is easy to compare price and bandwidth. When purchasing Internet services, assess the quality of the backbone and its relationship to other networks and geographies. To use an analogy,

Infrastructure Concerns for Web-Page Designers

While Web-page design is certainly an application design issue, some aspects are important to infrastructure design, as well. When dealing with limited bandwidth and high latencies, it is important to minimize the download burden of page elements, especially image file sizes. Gratuitous use of heavy images can slow response time and negatively affect the user experience.

Caches and CDNs can't be used to accelerate unique or encrypted content. For a Web site to benefit from caches, and particularly from CDNs, designers should use the following rules to make content as cacheable as it can be, improving site performance in the process.

1. One best practice is to actually have two different versions of your site. One version is designed for users on high-speed, low-latency connections with a larger, more complex mix of images and content. The other version is designed for users on low-speed, high-latency connections and uses a simpler content mix.

2. Use thumbnail sketches that are clickable to their full size, rather than larger images. For biggest impact on loading time, crop the graphic, reduce its resolution, and increase compression.

3. Do not scan images at more than 600 dpi. A resolution of 72 dpi is ideal to achieve drastically smaller file size and speed download time.

4. If you have a series of images side by side, combine them into a single graphic. The single image will load more quickly than separate ones.

5. Reduce the number of colors, especially within the same bit plane. The fewer the colors, the greater the resulting image compression (18 colors make a smaller file than 32). Be careful with dithering, which can create larger files by increasing color range.

Infrastructure Concerns for Web-Page Designers *(continued)*

6. Limit use of graphics for text blocks. Since most browsers have limited fonts, some designers use graphics to display flashier text styles. Limit this use of graphics to small areas, such as headlines. Avoid carrying large blocks of text-as-graphics, which slow page download time.

7. Use GIF or JPEG appropriately. GIF uses fewer colors, but compresses to only a 3:1 ratio, while a JPEG compresses up to 50:1. The downside is that a JPEG loses image quality at the higher compression ratios and might not be as appropriate for straight-line art.

8. Use the GIF interlacing feature, which loads a rough scan of the image quickly, gradually bringing it into focus. This feature allows users to quickly preview images without having to wait. With JPEG, consider use of the specific HTML attribute (LOWSRC) that allows downloading a low-quality, small footprint image first, followed by a high-quality image.

9. Exploit the browser image-caching feature by reusing graphics more often. Because the viewer's computer already has the images, the user experiences no further downloading delays after the first use. This feature meshes with branding strategy, since company logos should always appear the same regardless. Browser image-caching doesn't work unless you *use exactly the same URL path each time.* Don't store copies of the same image in separate locations on the server; caches treat these as different files.

10. Always define the height and width of images using IMG tag attributes. These attributes allow the browsers to fill in the text correctly before loading images, so the user can start reading immediately.

11. Rely on CDNs and caching to distribute rich, static content such as graphics. These techniques place the content closer to the user, alleviating the burden on your ISP link and shortening the download distance and time.

> **Infrastructure Concerns for Web-Page Designers** *(continued)*
>
> 12. Don't use metatags; they are honored only by browser caches. Instead, use HTTP 1.1 and cache control headers.
> 13. Set realistic "expires" headers. To maintain control of pages, place a short time to live on the source page, and then cache all images and text.
> 14. For images, specify the longest possible time to live; if an image changes, change the name of the image file rather than attempting to control it with an "expires" header.
> 15. Don't use SSL for content that doesn't require encryption. Encrypted pages are not cacheable.
> 16. When rearranging files on the server side, move them without copying them. Copying affects the "last modified" date.
> 17. Write cache-aware scripts. If the script outcome is not unique, it can likely be cached.

you're buying much more than a pipe, you're buying access to an entire plumbing system. Thus, service provider selection is becoming increasingly complex.

ISP Selection Criteria

In selecting an ISP for corporate connectivity (including access from the Internet to an internally hosted e-Business Web site), consider the following criteria.

Network Architecture. ISPs that wish to be seriously considered by corporate customers should be prepared to divulge details about network architecture, performance, and reliability. In particular, check to see how providers designed their networks, paying special attention to the following points:

- Number and type of backbone nodes. The more nodes, the greater the network's overall reliability, but a large routed network can have unacceptably high delay. Therefore, most major ISPs migrated to a hybrid switched/routed network, with core ATM switches surrounded by high-speed routers. Core IP router products, which directly support high-speed optical connections, are replacing ATM switches in many carrier cores, effectively replacing ATM with IP Multi-Protocol Label Switching (MPLS) for cost-effective, efficient traffic management at high bandwidths. Most providers continue their inexorable migration to increasingly faster pipes. At the time of this writing, backbone connections are moving to OC-192 (10 Gbps), while minimum acceptable connectivity for a backbone node is OC-3 (155 Mbps), with OC-48 (2.4 Gbps) representing a reasonable middle ground.

- Number and type of peering points. Peering points are places where ISP networks interconnect with each other. Peering points can be public, allowing many ISPs to interconnect, or private, for one-to-one connection between ISPs. Private peering points provide redundancy and fault tolerance, because traffic can be routed across an alternate provider in the event of network failure. Public peering points are subject to congestion, thus degrading performance. Private peering points offer an additional degree of reliability with much higher performance. As a result, more traffic now traverses private peering points than public exchanges. Customers should insist that candidate ISPs divulge the number and capacity of peering points they interconnect with, along with the names of their peering partners. In addition, they should reveal the traffic management metrics used to determine when new peering points would be added. A common rule of thumb is that 30-percent sustained utilization should trigger the ISP to supply additional capacity over peered links.

Expertise. Border Gateway Protocol (BGP) routing expertise is a critical talent that is uniquely required by top-tier ISPs. The lack of such expertise translates into increased outage times and diminished reliability. In this respect, not all ISPs are created equal. Some top-tier providers have many years of experience with BGP routing, while others are relatively new to the game. Weakness in this area can also prevent an ISP from effectively delivering services, such as when they have difficulty architecting multi-homed solutions. Other key areas of expertise are driven by advanced services an ISP might offer, such as security or content caching/delivery.

Related Services. Evaluate a provider's ability to deliver additional e-Business services, including hosting, firewall management and administration, VPNs, and public key and directory services. Several ISPs with top-notch transport capabilities have only recently begun to provide advanced services. (See the section on Extranet Service Providers.) Others have a strong complement of such services. Many Internet services can be purchased as part of a larger master services agreement with a telecommunications company, allowing these purchases to count toward a larger contract offering deeper discounts than if they were purchased individually.

As markets consolidate, ISPs move from providing remote dial access to broadband access and site-to-site VPN services. VPN services will constitute the largest single growth segment for ISPs, as favorable pricing (up to 80 percent less than comparable frame relay service in international markets) and increasing security expertise push more companies to embrace IP VPNs for enterprise WAN requirements. With the advent of network-based VPN delivery using MPLS or IP Security Protocol (IPSec), carriers can deploy VPNs without specialized customer premise equipment. Within a few years, IP VPNs will eclipse frame relay as the preferred branch-office connection method. This evolution will happen sooner in regions where the relative cost of international circuits is higher.

Be careful when evaluating IP VPN services. Most carriers rely on MPLS-based VPNs, which do not encrypt data traffic as IPSec does. The same routers carrying private MPLS VPN traffic can carry Internet traffic, potentially opening up VPN traffic to exploits from the public side. Recent passage of legislation affecting data privacy makes this network security distinction crucial for companies in certain industries, such as health care and financial services. The need for premises-based encryption is expected to rise when VPNs are used to connect sites.

Provider Viability. Massive consolidation and fundamental business shifts continue to take place in the ISP market. Dedicated ISPs are undergoing major retrenchment, while core network spending is rapidly decreasing. These dynamics will drive service bundling and continued market consolidation. By mid-decade, the main ISPs will be large multinational players with integrated voice/data, Web hosting, and multimedia services.

Smaller players will focus on vertical markets or special services. Although the price/performance of these providers will beat those of the major ISPs, the long-term viability of these companies is questionable. Include at least one of these competitive ISPs in an RFP to improve negotiating leverage, but make sure that a strong contingency plan is in place if the player is actually selected.

As consolidation continues, performance issues will arise as provider networks work to integrate disparate equipment and overlapping networks. Service levels are subject to modification as providers' conflicting standards are resolved. Exploit these consolidation periods to obtain better SLAs and price concessions.

Feature/Functionality. Take into account other key service offerings and features, such as the access speeds available, "burstable" bandwidth pricing, multiplexing (the ability to merge multiple circuits for higher bandwidth connections), managed router and BGP management services, and SLAs governing latency and availability.

Companies that do business internationally should obtain Internet access from international players. As an alternative, check your ISP's peering relationships with providers that do offer international coverage. The more private peering relationships the ISP has, the better overall performance will be, because network latency is due more to the number of hops through different network points than the overall backbone size.

ISP Considerations in Pattern Design

ISP selection is a critical decision. Negotiate bundled deals with ISPs to lock in good discounts and integrated services. Make sure to choose a stable carrier and include contract terms that allow immediate contract renegotiation or termination in the event of a merger or acquisition.

An ISP is required for any pattern design that involves connecting internal Web sites to the Internet. Naturally, this requirement applies to the Web Publish and 3/N-Tier Transact patterns. For Web Publish, carefully weigh actual configuration issues, such as the bandwidth of the required ISP connection, against the decision to outsource that pattern to a hosting service. Outsourcing will drastically reduce the bandwidth required for the ISP that connects your organization to the Internet. The 3/N-Tier Transact pattern always requires an ISP link. Even if most Web servers are hosted, transactions usually need to be linked to internal legacy systems or back-end databases. Remember that site acceleration features such as caching, CDN, and compression can lower bandwidth requirements.

Finally, keep in mind that many organizations have separate ISP links with completely separate traffic patterns for various types of e-Business needs. One ISP link is associated with their Web site and is sized to handle customers coming in from the Internet. Another link can handle traffic for internal users accessing the Internet. Both are critical. For example, an outgoing link could be required to participate in a trading site that has significant impact on corporate earnings. However, the budget for each link can be quite different. The department that pays for Web-site bandwidth might complain if employee Internet traffic slows down customer use of the corporate Web site. Most large organizations physically separate these links or employ some form of traffic management to control this problem.

Extranet Service Providers (ESPs)

Organizations deploying business-to-business (B2B) initiatives are often frustrated by the lack of providers offering a full suite of extranet services. These companies are searching for providers to offer a combination of IP transport, application hosting, security/directory services, and community management. Community management includes vetting new members, adding them to the B2B network and applications, removing members, and coordinating integration activities.

Many providers offer a subset of such services, but none are equally strong in all areas. ISPs offer comprehensive IP transport services, but deliver only limited application hosting and service level guarantees. Traditional outsourcing and systems integration companies provide strong application hosting, but offer less than robust network connectivity. Over time, extranet service providers (ESPs) will emerge to provide sophisticated community management and billing services (including per-transaction billing) to vertical markets such as financial services, pharmaceuticals, and manufacturing.

Basic Services Required for Extranets

To provide a full range of extranet services, a provider should be able to deliver on the following four main components.

IP Transport. ESPs must be able to provide dedicated and dial-up IP connectivity, including VPN services, with appropriate encryption and tunneling. These IP transport services should include superior quality of service capabilities (QoS). In particular, they should meet stringent requirements for availability, transmission speed, latency, and eventually jitter. Because users must be able to interconnect with business partners using alternate IP transport providers, interconnectivity with other ESPs and retention of QoS across service boundaries is also critical.

Application Hosting. ESPs should excel at hosting and managing shared applications, and they should be able to deliver on SLAs covering server, network, and application performance and availability. ESPs should be able to locate application servers logically within optimum reach of all business partners. This service requires multiple global data centers and high-bandwidth connections to public and private peering points.

Security and Directory Services. Various services are lumped under the umbrella of security, including:

- Firewall and VPN device management and administration. B2B communities must be protected from any one member's security issues, driving the need for firewall management, particularly for VPN and extranet firewalls.

- PKI services. A public key infrastructure (PKI) is essential for providing effective user and device authentication on extranets, but it is a daunting challenge to administer PKI for a B2B community, rather than a single organization. Many customers need service providers to handle PKI management and administration. Given the caveats noted in Chapter 5 on PKI, any identity infrastructure approach could be useful, such as Web SSO instead of PKI. However, PKI for digitally signing messages is the best option for extranets.

- Non-repudiation. A critical requirement for B2B communities is that one member cannot claim they didn't receive something when in fact they did, which is why ESPs must support non-repudiation. This requirement is usually a follow-on feature of PKI deployments.

- Permissions management. Constructing security policy for a community is complex enough. Many organizations prefer to off-load the task of translating that policy into the appropriate rights and permissions, as well as enforcing those permissions.

- Directories. ESPs need a comprehensive extranet directory offering to deliver on security and management services. ISPs tend to offer effective managed firewall services. However, few providers offer PKI and permissions management, whether based on directories or not. A full identity infrastructure service approach is rarely available from such providers.

Management, Provisioning, and Billing. Above all, many organizations do not want to bear responsibility for extranet performance and community management. ESPs should be prepared to deliver a comprehensive solution, including maintenance, monitoring, troubleshooting, and performance analysis for network, server, storage, and extranet applications.

Transaction-based billing is another important issue. Most organizations are willing to pay limited up-front costs, with costs increasing with the volume of extranet business. Therefore, ESPs should develop transaction-based pricing tools. Although risky, this approach drives the market by lowering the entry barrier to acceptable levels. Transaction-based pricing models will emerge following the rollout of extranet infrastructure offerings.

As mentioned, many current service providers offer only pieces of the total ESP puzzle. Several providers focusing on specific vertical industries are further along in their evolution. General-purpose ESP offerings are emerging from traditional value-added network vendors, Web hosting companies, software vendors, and network aggregators.

ESP Considerations in Pattern Design

ESPs are hosting service providers that go beyond traditional network connectivity and data center management solutions. This job is complex and few of today's providers deliver on these promises. Until realistic providers emerge, users will have to fend for themselves, integrating solutions on their own. This situation alone will inhibit stronger B2B interactions between companies.

In fact, ESPs are not required for Web Publish and 3/N-Tier Transact patterns, since these patterns don't require the kind of server-to-server integration found in B2B. Web Publish and 3/N-Tier Transact patterns are required for B2B solutions that allow external business partners access to your Web site. Other uses of these two patterns are focused on business-to-consumer (B2C) or business-to-employee (B2E) solutions. Regardless, these two patterns do not require ESPs, which is a good thing, given the limited choices available. If you require outsourcing for these patterns, consider the hosting service providers discussed next.

Hosting Services

Sourcing Web hosting services is a critical infrastructure decision that will considerably affect performance, availability, and cost. While transactional patterns are often "insourced" for security and performance reasons, publishing is often best outsourced with a hosting provider. Numerous requirements drive the need to outsource services for Web hosting and management, including affordability, time to market, and the need for high-speed connectivity. Many companies take a phased approach, outsourcing initially to achieve a quick, cost-effective Web presence, then they base later decisions on long-term cost and performance issues. Conversely, many companies will host their own Web sites if they are architecturally complex or the incremental cost for providing Web services within their own data centers is low.

Typically, evaluations of hosting infrastructure largely focus on hardware and software platform support. The ability to locate the server close to Internet exchange points has a drastic impact on hosting performance. This search is more easily done by ISPs who are backed by the infrastructure and resources of a major telecom provider. A recent study found that upstream network connectivity problems were among the top three causes of Internet application downtime, listed after administrative errors and application failures. Thus, choosing an ISP with the best connectivity to major backbones enhances application availability and performance.

Why Location Matters on the Internet

Hosting service providers can put your content closer to your users than you can, and they can provide more alternate paths to your applications during periods of Internet congestion. Notice that your content can be located many hops from the place where users actually get on the Internet, as shown in Figure 6.8.

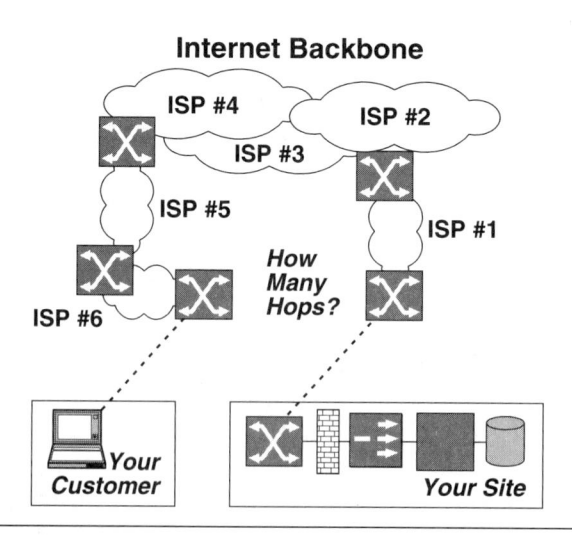

Figure 6.8 Counting Hops on the Internet

The better Web hosting service providers already have links to many ISPs where users actually access the Internet. You could not build such connectivity without huge expense. Instead, you should leverage an ISP that provides this kind of "inside the Internet" hosting service (see Figure 6.9).

Hosting service location matters most for large-scale e-Business systems where large amounts of Web Publish traffic must be delivered to users quickly and reliably. If your needs are smaller, a hosting service might be useful more for traditional outsourcing reasons, such as handling situations where internal expertise or startup funding is lacking and speed is essential.

Hosting Provider Selection Criteria

Like any network provider with Internet links, hosting service providers should be evaluated on network-specific criteria. The same ISP selection criteria discussed earlier also apply to hosting providers as well. Additional criteria associated with hosting providers include:

System Management Offerings and Expertise. Simple co-location service provides only rack space and network connectivity, not management of whatever devices you might put in the rack. Other offerings add

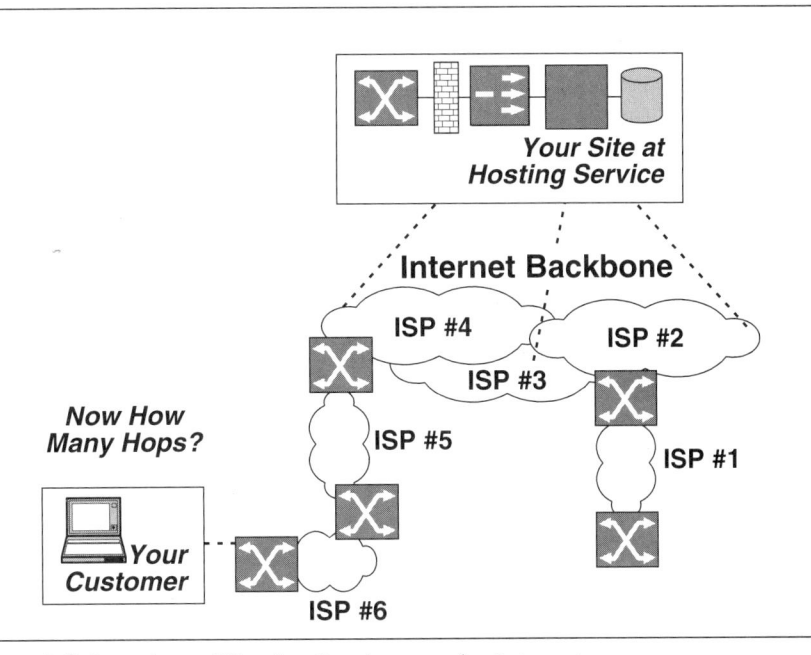

Figure 6.9 Location of Hosting Services on the Internet

more data center services, such as managing the physical server hardware and OS behind the information and applications.

Application Management. Hosting providers typically provide basic management services associated with running Web servers and file systems. More sophisticated offerings include database and content management. At the highest level, hosting providers blur with the application service provider (ASP) marketplace and actually provide application-level management functions.

Caching and Content Delivery. Sophisticated hosting providers include caching or the services of a content delivery network to improve performance and potentially off-load content servers.

Current experience reveals that most hosting providers are still predominantly focused on network and data center infrastructure services. Therefore, you should manage application service contracts or use other third parties. If you need more assistance with the process management components of your Web presence, such as project management and content management, look to full services outsourcing companies, which have more process discipline maturity than typical hosting providers.

Pricing Considerations

Prices vary substantially among infrastructure outsourcers, and buyers of hosting services should expect service bundling, especially for large and complex projects. However, to control ongoing expansion costs, organizations must negotiate a fee schedule with the provider. At a minimum, critical fees will appear in the following broad categories.

Physical Infrastructure. The basic facilities requirements for Web hosting match those for outsourcing standard data center services, such as appropriate power, cooling, seismic protection, physical security, and other environmental factors. Here, the principal cost element is space, and it is typically purchased in racks or half-racks. Many providers offer multi-rack cages of various sizes. Some providers also offer individual shelf-space configurations and might even sell rack space by the individual 1U (1.75-inch of vertical rack space). These fees apply on a per-location basis. U.S. hosting companies frequently charge a premium for hosting from facilities located in Europe or the Asia-Pacific region.

Connectivity. Service providers apportion bandwidth to servers by capping available bandwidth or charging based on usage. Co-location bandwidth is often charged based on bandwidth measurements of megabits per second sampled at various intervals—a method that penalizes sites with sustained peak usage. Dedicated and managed application services are frequently charged on the basis of gigabytes of content delivered, with some allocation of bandwidth built into the per-server fees. Some providers charge different rates based on the country/region to which the content flows.

Servers and Components. Most dedicated hosting providers offer turnkey Web host configurations on various leading OS/server platforms. If you plan to host externally, make sure your OS/hardware server platform choices fit the host company's environment. You might see further charges for "nonstandard" equipment. Fees include the cost of hosts, peripherals, storage, clustered configurations, load balancers, and switches. Additional per-server fees can apply for function-specific hosts such as proxy servers and mail servers.

Hosting providers might charge a substantial set-up fee in addition to a monthly charge for equipment leasing and management services. The total list of options provided by some full-service providers can be overwhelming. For example, one major provider offers more than 700 supplemental service variations.

Management Services. Most providers bundle simple data services into their managed co-location and dedicated services offerings. Optional fees include system and network monitoring and alerting, storage management, and application management services.

Negotiating Service Level Agreements

SLA criteria are used largely as a marketing tool by hosting providers, often based on vague and unmeasurable elements. When evaluating a hosting service provider, discount any claimed benefits that are clearly outside the vendor's control, such as end-to-end guarantees for connectivity spanning other Internet service provider backbones. SLAs should specify detailed escalation procedures by severity level, though only a handful of providers currently specify granular severity levels within their default SLAs. Service quality targets include the mean and maximum response times for customer support, as well as mean and maximum times to repair items dictated in the statement of work. Responsiveness measurements are especially critical with security services.

Key technical targets for service level agreements should include the following.

> **Note** Statistics suggested in the following discussions were taken from best-practice contracts at the time of this writing.

Total System Availability. This metric relates to an overall system view of the site, including network, devices, and servers. Availability targets should be from 99.00 to 99.50 percent for single-site installations, and from 99.80 to 99.99 percent for distributed hosting services. Even if you don't get full services from the hosting provider, you'll want to measure this yourself, as explained in the management layer discussion in Chapter 8.

Network Quality. Local network port availability should be 100 percent, as measured by host servers. Network backbone criteria for single-site installations must rely on service provider measurements. In distributed environments, measurements can be taken between hosting centers from customer devices. Backbone availability should be at least 99.80 percent, with no more than 85 millisecond (ms) round-trip latency within the U.S., 150 ms from the U.S. to Europe, and 200 ms from the U.S. to the Asia-Pacific region.

Server Availability. Single-server installations should offer 99.00 percent uptime, with 99.70 percent availability of clustered or load-balanced servers in a single facility.

Windows for scheduled downtime should be negotiated as part of the service contract. For example, the maintenance window might be 3:00 A.M. to 5:00 A.M., with minimum 48-hour notice. Unscheduled maintenance should always be counted against availability statistics.

Remedies for a service level breach should focus on the vendor/customer relationship instead of financial penalties. Service providers will never agree to be held liable for the collateral financial impact of any outage. Rather, service providers might provide a credit for the actual service cost during the time the service wasn't available. Therefore, focus on how to work with providers to ensure good service through regular meetings and improvement over time. For example, one month's problems should be resolved and not repeated the next month.

Always meet with the vendor account team within one week of a severe outage. This review meeting should include a postmortem analysis of the outage. The analysis should identify the root cause of technical failures and strive to improve notification/escalation procedures for service-quality problems. When two severe outages occur in any rolling 60-day period, conduct a meeting with a high-level vendor representative. With three severe outages in a rolling 60-day period, you should have the option of terminating the contract.

Hosting Provider Considerations and Pattern Designs

The hosting provider market will continue consolidating as ISPs and carriers with nationwide or global reach and traditional outsourcers increasingly win market share from regional and boutique providers. Over the long term, surviving players will have effective network architectures along with strong data centers and improved application management capabilities. For the time being, pay close attention to the financial viability of providers and have a full exit strategy prepared in case the vendor goes out of business.

High-volume sites should use a hosting service provider for the Web Publish and Stream Publish patterns, usually for networking connectivity reasons. Smaller sites wanting to avoid large up-front costs or to gain speed in implementation will also choose an outsourced model for non-networking reasons.

3/N-Tier Transact pattern design should not use a hosting service, unless it is part of an overall decision to outsource much of an organization's information technology. A typical configuration is to locate most of the Web Publish pattern at a hosting service, while leaving much of the 3/N-Tier Transact pattern to be handled in-house.

Alternatively, hosted Web servers could redirect transactional users to Web servers at the internal 3/N-Tier Transact pattern infrastructure. Since the traffic for transactional applications is usually not bandwidth-intensive, your ISP links still won't need to be nearly as big as if both patterns were hosted internally. Moreover, using outsourced hosting services for the Web Publish pattern should mean better performance for end users.

Refining Patterns in the Network Layer

Now that you have reviewed the major components in the network layer, it helps to take another look at pattern design at the layer level, especially as it applies to the Web Publish and 3/N-Tier Transact patterns. While some components differ by pattern, other components remain much the same across these two patterns.

Table 6.1 summarizes the list of potential e-Business components in the network layer and shows which components work best with the Web Publish and 3/N-Tier Transact patterns.

Networking Web Publish and Related Patterns

Web publish applications tend to be the largest bandwidth consumers in e-Business solutions. Bandwidth requirements are on a much larger scale than enterprise cases, sometimes involving millions of users. They are also much harder to predict, in light of phenomena such as flash crowds and runaway marketing campaigns.

Supporting large amounts of streaming video and audio requires even more bandwidth and adds other networking complexity, including quality of service (QoS) and multicasting issues. However, the Stream Publish pattern design should follow the Web Publish design in structure, with greater allowances for bandwidth and a full understanding of the role of quality of service, caching, and content delivery networks.

With this in mind, Web hosting and Web-server component selection are key decision points. Server selection becomes even more complex when using leading personalization applications. These applications of-

Table 6.1 Network Layer Pattern Summary Chart

Layer or Service: Component	Web Publish	3/N-Tier
Network Layer:		
Stateless/Scale-Out	1	1
Network Load Balancer	1	1
Proxy/Caching Server	3	4
Content Delivery Network	3	4
Internet Service Provider (ISP)	1	1
Extranet Service Provider (ESP)	4	4
Hosting Service	2	4

Key
1 = Critical, All Cases
2 = Highly Recommended, Most Cases
3 = Optional, Some Cases
4 = Optional, Fewer Cases

ten require specific combinations of server operating systems and hardware, especially for high-availability solutions.

To leave the option of outsourcing open, your pattern designs should be limited to component combinations commonly supported by outsourcers, particularly for server platforms and Web-server software. Outsourcing parts of the Publish pattern also moves to the outsourcer some of the burden involved in supporting peak traffic loads. Only the subset of traffic associated with patterns such as 3/N-Tier Transact comes back to your site.

From a pattern standpoint, certain investments and technologies prove most significant in the networking layer. The Web Publish pattern, along with others such as Stream Publish and Real Time Collaborate, is most likely to push networking solutions to their limits, particularly for large B2C audiences or customers. The key to using the Web Publish pattern effectively lies in requiring a Web hosting strategy along with careful attention to scale-out design approaches for reliability and performance or scalability.

Networking the 3/N-Tier Transact Pattern

The most important component decisions in the 3/N-Tier Pattern focus on application servers, integration, and databases. However, networking implications of the 3/N-Tier Transact Pattern should be taken into account.

The good news is that 3/N-Tier transactions tend to be relatively light from a network perspective, not consuming much bandwidth or other network resources, particularly when it comes to the traffic between the browser, Web server, and application server. Traffic between the application server and various database or integration servers is potentially another matter.

This latter traffic should ideally remain on a set of high-speed local area connections within a campus. If application server to back-end traffic must traverse a WAN because the servers are in separate facilities, the distances should be kept to a minimum, or you should try some type of message queuing or other buffered middleware. Ideally, the servers should be moved so that they are in the same data center.

The fact that 3/N-Tier Transactional traffic tends to be light doesn't solve all the networking issues. There is always the chance that it can be impeded by other traffic, such as file transfers or streaming audio/video. Ideally, this conflict is handled through quality of service, traffic prioritization algorithms, or increases in bandwidth. Many organizations apply a combination of these techniques to Internet access pipes, making sure that transactional traffic in the access pipe is not impeded. However, these features are not consistently available on the Internet, which highlights the importance of investigating peering arrangements and choosing wisely when it comes to ISPs.

Also, sophisticated sites employ other infrastructure and application design techniques when networks become highly congested. In particular, if traffic loads peak due to a major event such as stock market crashes or civic disasters, many organizations have structured their sites to elegantly shut off capabilities in order of importance. For example, Publish aspects of a site that do not provide immediate revenue are deprioritized compared to the transactions themselves. This activity can be done through network load balancers or server/application design.

Security is another key networking issue that is particularly critical to the 3/N Tier Transaction pattern. Transactions tend to contain information that requires higher levels of security than published materials. For example, transactions often contain credit card numbers and other payment information, which normally justifies the extra effort and expense associated with encryption. For this reason, Publish traffic is not encrypted in many e-Business solutions, but transactions use SSL or more sophisticated encryption technologies.

For the 3/N-Tier Transact pattern, availability, quality of service, and security are the key issues from a networking perspective. The use of network load balancers and SSL acceleration provides reliability, manageability, and improved performance when used with this pattern.

Network Layer Principles

When evaluating architectures and technologies at the network layer, two key principles should guide product and architectural choices.

Use a service provider infrastructure wherever possible. As IT infrastructure reaches increasingly further beyond the business, IT organizations are forced to use external service providers for an increasing part of their networks. The main reason for using a contracted service provider is to get the best performance and geographic reach at the best price. While these services are certainly more tenable than building your own Internet, organizations must insist on enforceable service level agreements (SLAs) as providers struggle to knit together disjoint offerings from partners and acquired companies. Well-negotiated networking services increase overall business performance and flexibility while reducing per-unit operations costs. Consolidation among Internet service providers (ISPs), Web hosting providers, and application service providers will continue as market forces drive integration in search of economies of scale and leverage. Carefully analyze long-term viability issues and design-in exit or replacement strategies for these vendors, as business risk is high with many of them.

Leverage industry standard protocols above the network level to limit interoperability issues. While TCP/IP is a widely used standard, organizations must still focus on other standards and interoperability issues. The difference is that the focus on standards is moving to higher-level protocols. Although each platform vendor uses its own communication approach, most have agreed on a common base of technology to enable higher-level communications. This common base of standards includes Extensible Markup Language (XML); Simple Object Access Protocol (SOAP); Universal Description, Discovery, and Integration (UDDI); and Web Services Description Language (WSDL). This technology stack will expand as these protocols are finalized and workflow protocols are introduced.

This technology mixture is more potent for B2B integration than previous approaches due to its openness, to the likelihood of widespread acceptance, and to the ability to leverage existing Hypertext Transfer Protocol (HTTP) and Simple Mail Transfer Protocol (SMTP) infrastructure. Over time, XML and SOAP will provide a common foundation for cross-platform communication. Clearly, HTTP will be a long-term player on top of TCP/IP, while protocols specific to particular components will become more standardized. Similarly, market simplification is also expected for several major audio/video formats and streaming protocols.

Other e-Business Networking Issues

In the coming years, IT professionals will be charged with finding solutions to several other complex networking issues that straddle e-Business and traditional business.

Call Center Integration/Convergence of Voice and Data. Early implementations of voice/data convergence solutions highlight the need for a high level of service and support, while they underline a shortage of qualified support. Cultural differences between voice and data constituencies often lead to different methods of problem resolution, which further exacerbates the lack of consistency in service level agreements. An infrastructure that supports the highest quality of service (QoS) levels, such as toll-grade quality voice, is essential to the success of convergence efforts. Despite occasional problems, this convergence will become more critical and more attainable in the next few years. Already, traditional, voice-based call centers are converging with other e-Business-centric forms of interaction, such as e-mail handling and Web sites. This convergence has forced businesses to consider a larger scope for customer interaction centers (CICs) beyond simple call centers.

Impact on Existing WAN. This book does not discuss traditional WAN design. However, e-Business infrastructure and application deployments do have an impact on capacity management for existing WAN components. The two areas, though separate, should be planned in concert as much as possible; otherwise, there can be problems. Adding a larger ISP pipe could exacerbate problems in existing internal WAN environments, such as when many internal users download very large files from external Web sites. In the past, traffic from push vendors also affected internal WANs and even the ISP link bandwidth itself. IT must analyze the types of traffic supported in the e-Business environment, such as external users of internal Web sites, internal users of external Web sites, and communication between internal and external systems. This information can be used to plan for capacity and control as necessary. Without this sort of analysis, unseen bottlenecks can occur, such as outbound e-mail traffic stealing bandwidth from paying customers who are trying to access the Web site.

Storage Layer

The storage layer contains the components necessary for an organization to store, back up, and recover business data and systems. In addition to traditional disk and tape units, storage components can include storage area networks (SANs), network attached storage (NAS), and storage management software. Organizations should create a robust storage infrastructure for all applications, with variations based on the business criticality and nature of the applications in question.

Figure 6.10 shows the various hardware components of the storage layer. Storage layer hardware components include business storage hardware (disk and tape) and software (tape backup and mirroring), host interconnects, storage area network (SAN) interconnects, and storage servers.

Storage is one of the fastest growing areas of infrastructure since applications are requiring more storage capacity across the board. However, e-Business is transforming the way organizations approach application architectures and meet ever-changing business requirements. The

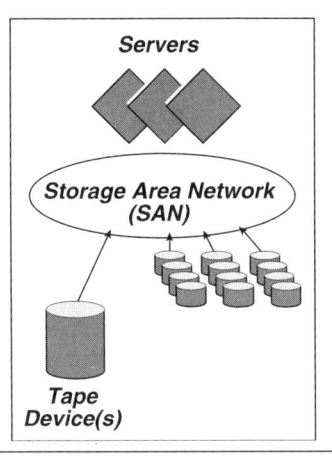

Figure 6.10 Storage Layer Hardware Components

challenge for IT organizations is identifying and implementing a storage solution that will satisfy business requirements and reduce the environment's overall complexity, particularly in the e-Business sphere.

As e-Business and traditional business initiatives evolve, storage infrastructure must evolve. The traditional approach, in which storage units were directly attached to individual servers, is rapidly giving way to use of shared storage in the form of storage area networks (SANs) and network attached storage (NAS). These technologies help address two approaches that are even more sophisticated:

- Enterprise application integration
- Externalization of applications

While the externalization of storage resources is appropriately done through the application architecture, the critical path for business success lies in integration of storage resources as a unified infrastructure, based on storage area network (SAN) principles.

Storage services must be able to satisfy application performance and business continuity requirements. A combination of hardware and software capabilities enable storage systems to recover in the shortest time possible in the event of natural, unplanned, or human-induced failures. Storage infrastructure can be viewed as an insurance policy that varies by industry, company, line of business, and IT organization.

Network Layer Best Practices at a Glance

Follow these guidelines:

- Focus on availability first, then throughput and response time.
- Design a solution with the appropriate level of redundancy for the business value it is providing; that is, invest in the right level of insurance.
- Select an ISP based on its peering arrangements and advanced services rather than price per access pipe alone.
- Examine Web hosting service providers for designs and sourcing, or just as examples of services to offer to your own organization internally.
- Use content delivery network (CDN) services for static content aimed at very large audiences.
- Scale-out (duplicate and replicate) Web and application servers through the application of network load balancers.
- Support multiple points of interaction (POIs), or at least plan for them in the future.
- Manage/limit/disallow direct access to transactional data.
- Don't neglect security issues, especially data defacement or tampering. Even read-only data can be changed by the malicious, or denial-of-service attacks can prevent user access.
- Maintain close communication with corporate marketing so you are not surprised by long-planned marketing campaigns that overnight provide 10x spikes in e-Business Web-site load.
- Design for outsourcing, even if you never do.
- If an e-Business site is mission-critical, install response time and load monitoring services to keep track of load better and plan accordingly.
- Take a service-centric approach. You can achieve significant real infrastructure reuse widely across the network layer.

Storage Area Network Interconnect

From local volumes on each server, storage has evolved to independent storage subsystems that are interconnected by a storage area network (SAN). A SAN is a dedicated network that uses various network protocols such as TCP/IP, SCSI, or Fibre Channel to connect storage subsystems. These subsystems are used by multiple server platforms to improve overall storage capabilities. By isolating storage traffic in separate subsystems, SANs provide known bandwidth that can be available to restore data from a backup at any given time, despite the user/application network workload. The major business requirement driving the adoption of SANs is faster, more predictable data restores.

As shown in Figure 6.11, the SAN is not a single technology, but a set of principles for offloading data storage and backup/recovery traffic from the network. Enterprise SANs span multiple operating systems ranging from today's leading NOS up to the mainframe. This broad implementation requires companies to develop a comprehensive storage infrastructure.

Network Attached Storage Solutions (NAS)

Network attached storage (NAS) can be considered a relative of SAN solutions. Both are attached using file service protocols like Microsoft

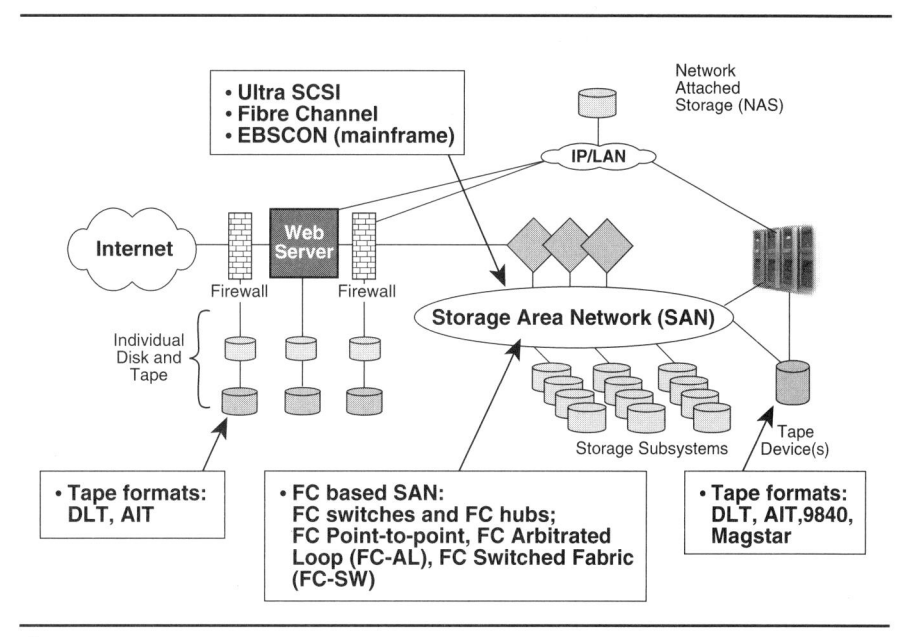

Figure 6.11 Storage Layer Technologies

NT CFS over TCP/IP instead of storage protocols over bus-level networks. Organizations should view the two architectures as complementary, and their staffs must understand the benefits and limitations of each solution to create a comprehensive enterprise storage infrastructure.

While Fibre Channel provides host connectivity from the servers to external Redundant Array of Inexpensive Disks (RAID) controllers, NAS uses a different architecture to solve file-serving requests. Traditional NAS architecture eliminates the general-purpose server. File requests are sent over TCP/IP directly to the NAS subsystem, and the file requests are satisfied within a single storage subsystem.

Comparing SANs and NAS

As shown in Figure 6.12, the primary difference between the SAN and NAS approaches is the network protocol used to request the information from the RAID controller, and the format in which the data is written to the mechanical disk. The NAS approach uses TCP/IP and file systems, while direct or SAN-attached storage uses SCSI or Fibre Channel and writes the information to disk in block formats. Each of these

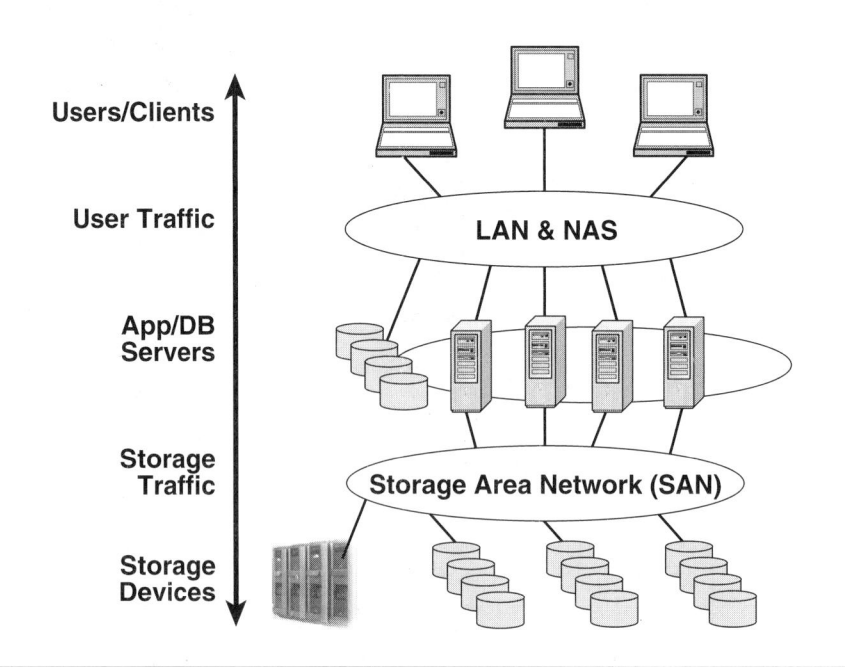

Figure 6.12 SANs and NAS

approaches has trade-offs. Organizations should view them as complementary technologies and examine the possibility of coexistence.

Avoid running databases on NAS solutions; they typically perform better when running on block storage solutions. These solutions should also support modules of application packages such as ERP, CRM, and data warehousing, with some exceptions, such as block-based file systems. When database updates occur in these systems, the only information modified on the physical disks is the information changed by the database.

NAS Drawbacks

When database updates occur in a NAS environment, the entire file is modified on the physical disks, which can add significant overhead and latency to database writes, and ultimately to application response times. NAS solutions can also have a negative impact on administrative tasks such as database performance tuning. In addition, storage management software must be modified to support NAS solutions, and requirements pertaining to scalability, manageability, and business continuity might not be satisfied.

Backup/recovery is another storage management challenge for NAS. Two approaches for backing up NAS are:

- Direct-attached tape drives and automation
- Data backup over an IP network via NDMP or other proprietary solutions

Both of these solutions can affect scaling and recovery time. Direct-attached tape drives cannot scale in numbers. Multiple NAS instances require more human intervention, increasing operational overhead and the possibility of human error.

Operational Issues

From an operational perspective, you have many questions to ask.

- How are the subsystems going to be backed up and recovered?
- What software supports particular hardware?
- What is the backup/recovery data path?
- How are storage availability, capacity, and performance scaled?
- What staff expertise is available?

Answers to some of these questions might dictate a more traditional approach using direct or SAN-attached storage, which in turn would sacrifice some of the benefits of NAS to reduce operational costs.

Backup/Recovery Architectures

To have successful e-Business initiatives, organizations must be able to quickly restore business functions after an outage. Years ago, organizations focused on developing expertise in creating and maintaining disaster recovery plans for mainframe-based applications. Now, servers running Windows 2000/.NET Server or UNIX increasingly run applications and databases that are business-critical, and must be included in backup/recovery architectures. To handle this changing situation, organizations have expanded the portfolio of servers included in disaster recovery and business continuity plans. Best-practice organizations used this opportunity to consolidate the number of backup/recovery solution providers across all platforms.

Over time, backup/recovery architectures will shift to Fibre Channel as the preferred protocol for data movement and support of LAN-free, serverless solutions. Despite ongoing enhancements in this area, Fibre Channel disk storage and backup/recovery infrastructures remain separate, independent channel networks. As a result, you need to assess and implement dual infrastructures. As part of this, you must examine Fibre Channel compatibility in multiple technology domains, including operating systems, tape transports, robotics, Fibre Channel hub/switch configurations, and media management solutions.

Disk-based recovery solutions will increasingly complement traditional tape-based recovery solutions. As capacities increase dramatically and the target time to resume application processing continues to approach zero, tape will be relegated to archiving information older than 24 hours.

Server-to-tape transport connectivity typically is not a cost-effective use of Fibre Channel, leading organizations to use a combination of traditional IP Local Area Networks (LANs) and Fibre Channel/SCSI. However, high-profile, large-capacity servers requiring more than 100GB of storage would justify using Fibre Channel/SCSI for tape transport connectivity. For smaller servers, a dedicated IP LAN transport such as Fast Ethernet or Gigabit Ethernet will satisfy backup/recovery requirements. The key is making sure that network bandwidth is available to meet the restore requirements.

Backup/recovery solutions using Fibre Channel as a network for data transfer will continue to mature. Serverless backup solutions that move data directly from storage subsystems to robotic libraries will emerge soon as robust alternatives for larger application requirements.

Backup/recovery design should focus on recovery time, not just the backup window. Reducing recovery time increasingly drives the use of discs or mainframe-class tape transports. Organizations should standardize backup/recovery hardware to coincide with the standardization occurring in backup/recovery software. Since the lifecycle of robotics hardware is typically four to five years, you must consider depreciation when planning consolidation and standardization.

As part of business continuity planning, IT organizations should consolidate the number of backup/recovery solution providers across platforms. For a business continuity plan to be complete, all servers must be incorporated into backup policies, procedures, and technologies. The combination of premium services, delivered by existing storage, software, hardware, policies, and procedures, will enable organizations to create an agile enterprise storage and business continuity infrastructure.

Storage Options in the Server Layer

Various storage architectures are more applicable for the different server tiers. Table 6.2 shows the available choices.

Storage architectures to be evaluated are:

- Storage internal to a server
- PCI RAID storage, which can also be considered internal storage, but has a slightly higher cost and is more reliable
- External storage, often RAID controller-based, categorized as channel-attached if dedicated to one server or SAN-attached if shared across platforms
- Network attached storage, such as remote NFS or NT file system volumes, often referred to as appliances

The following discussion examines the various storage requirements for a typical 3/N-Tier Transact pattern; yet, similar methodologies can be applied to the other application patterns, as well.

Web Servers. Web servers are typically of a smaller form factor and often rack mounted, with smaller processing requirements and using a scale-out approach for scalability and availability. In addition, Web servers typically contain only the server boot code, while the Web content

Table 6.2 Storage Solutions by Scale-Out Tier

Storage Layer	Server Layer	Hardware Scalability	High Availability	OS 2001	OS 2004
Architectural selection: - Internal - Direct Attached - Network Attached Storage (NAS) - Storage Area Networks (SANs)	Web Server	Scale-out (many systems) Thin rack form factor (1–2U) Small SMP (1–2 CPUs)	Multiple boxes IP load balancing	NT W2K Linux UNIX	W2K Linux Solaris
	App Server	Scale-out (several systems) Rack or standalone form factor Medium SMP (1–8 CPUs)	Same as above plus Application Server Session Management	NT W2K AS UNIX	W2K AS Solaris
	DBMS Server	Scale-up Single instance Large SMP (4–16+ CPUs)	Data storage (mirroring, RAID, replication) OS clustering DBMS clustering Typically 2 nodes (occasionally 4)	UNIX W2K DCE Legacy NT	W2K DCE UNIX Legacy

resides in a database for dynamic content generation or in a file system separate from the Web-server software, as in the Web Publish patterns.

Firewall, domain, directory, and other specialized server functions also fall into this category. Moreover, since Windows 2000/.NET Server and Linux predominate, these operating systems typically have smaller storage capacity requirements due to the work being performed. These servers can often be satisfied cost effectively with internal storage, where availability, scalability, and manageability are less important because the Web server and the storage are "single instance." Attaching enterprise-class storage might not be cost-effective, since it is usually cheaper to deploy multiple instances in conjunction with a network load balancer. NAS could also be appropriate at this tier as a less expensive consolidated storage option to make content and storage requirements easier to manage.

Application Servers. Application servers typically use up to four CPUs, and a scale-out approach. This server tier uses Windows 2000/.NET Server or traditional UNIX versions as the most widely used operating system, with Linux being less common.

Less information is stored at this level when applications are used in conjunction with back-end database servers. Application servers typically contain only the boot code and application code. Internal or workgroup storage might be applicable here, such as PCI RAID controller-based storage. Yet, the increased performance and reliability of enterprise storage often makes application servers a candidate for an enterprise storage approach. When enterprise storage is built on Fibre Channel as the SAN interconnect, it can improve functionality, reliability, and administration.

Storage vendors are developing the capability to externalize OS storage so that a single OS copy can be configured for multiple servers. In a 3/N-Tier Transact pattern, and even more so for a Web Publish pattern, this practice will dramatically reduce the administrative workload required to create identical Web or application servers potentially numbering in the hundreds. Organizations should consider security, management, and maturity issues associated with this approach, as it is not trivial to have multiple servers access a single copy of information within a Fibre Channel network.

Database Servers. This tier often requires a highly scalable and available single-server instance, with clustering for server failover. Organizations use scale-up as opposed to scale-out. This scale-up often requires enterprise-class storage. Storage capacity requirements at this level are dramatically greater than at the application or Web-server levels. It helps to identify where multiple DBMS servers and application servers can coexist on a common SAN that is based on Fibre Channel, as common and consistent storage can be used for entire applications, driving further leverage. This approach benefits application development, testing, and quality assurance environments as well as business continuity plans.

Mainframes. Where possible, mainframes should participate in corporate SAN principles. However, mainframe storage technologies are often unique to the mainframe, which could preclude the use of common tools and solutions across Windows 2000/.NET, UNIX, and OS/390 platforms. Still, many of the same methodologies and operational disciplines can be employed, such as tape media management and automation.

This participation is particularly important because SANs should not be tied to a particular technology but to principles of enterprise-class storage management. Application and storage traffic are managed independently, yet IT organizations recognize the impact of one on another. Some storage hardware vendors can offer disk storage solutions across OS/390 and Windows 2000/.NET Server environments, yet many organizations keep the physical implementations of the subsystems separate. Although connectivity options for sharing physical enclosures exist, organizational and technical issues often make separation a more viable option.

Refining Patterns in the Storage Layer

Table 6.3 summarizes the list of potential components in the storage layer and shows which components work best with the Web Publish and 3/N-Tier Transact patterns.

The storage options discussed earlier apply to the Web Publish pattern, with some exceptions. In the Web Publish pattern, Web servers often have more data associated with them, but such data is read-only. This data can be stored using an onboard disk, separate shared file systems, or through a SAN on separate shared storage systems. As Web Publish evolves, shared file systems or shared SANs should be leveraged for ease of management and content replication.

The storage needs of Web Publish pattern applications, or Web content hosting in the DMZ, can be met by a storage cluster dedicated to Web server farms. This configuration is often used as part of a file system storage consolidation solution. Web Publish needs can also be met by providing each Web server with its own storage, which can be consoli-

Table 6.3 Storage Layer Pattern Summary Chart

Layer or Service: Component	Web Publish	3/N-Tier
Storage Layer:		
Storage Server	2	2
Storage Area Network (SAN)	2	2
File Server and Network Attached Storage (NAS)	2	4

Key
1 = Critical, All Cases
2 = Highly Recommended, Most Cases
3 = Optional, Some Cases
4 = Optional, Fewer Cases

dated with a SAN. Transact patterns, on the other hand, require high-bandwidth connectivity and low seek times to support high throughput.

In general, SANs should be used wherever possible to reduce administrative overhead, to improve availability, and to support storage consolidation initiatives. In addition, centrally managed and automated data archiving is preferable due to large and unpredictable data volumes in e-Business patterns.

When evaluating architectures and technologies for e-Business at the storage layer, use the following key principles to guide your product and architecture choices.

1. Use channel-attached storage or SAN solutions for high-growth applications, such as databases, which require maximum performance and availability. NAS solutions satisfy many file-serving requirements and some very low-end database requirements, but certification, reliability, and performance will be issues for general-purpose DBMS/NAS use in the future. Organizations should consider enterprise storage vendors for most database and mainframe application requirements.

2. Design and procure servers and storage independently.

3. Move away from the traditional disk storage management paradigm, organized by server platform with separate administrators responsible for each. One of the largest benefits of common storage hardware across operating systems is that storage management can be leveraged across specific platforms. This benefit applies equally to e-Business and enterprise systems.

4. Try to consolidate the backup/recovery software, hardware, and infrastructure across heterogeneous environments. Create a team responsible for the enterprise selection and procurement of storage backup/recovery solutions.

5. Storage consolidation depends on geographical access requirements. Not all operating systems can be incorporated within storage standardization efforts. Yet the majority of the benefit comes from the common operations across multiple server/storage subsystems. Storage consolidation is an early step that can be tackled within server consolidation initiatives.

6. Pay careful attention to information recovery capabilities and business continuity requirements. Backup/recovery technologies will see significant improvement during the coming years, as time requirements for application recovery approach zero. While

e-Business might not dictate new technologies, it requires you to select and implement premium backup/recovery resources, such as multiple disk copies. New backup/recovery capabilities are emerging with the adoption of Fibre Channel and dynamic allocation of tape transports. Although individual features and functions are important, standardization of backup/recovery across multiple operating environments helps leverage labor-intensive operations. While not all operating systems should be included, the majority of nonmainframe servers can be included, assuming most high-profile database applications are deployed on top-tier Windows 2000/.NET Server or UNIX platforms.

7. A robust storage infrastructure is extensible to applications within the portfolio. Different storage architectures will be used across an organization because not all application servers are candidates for enterprise-class storage. A separate storage strategy might be required per pattern, given the unique requirements of each application. When evaluating storage solutions, you should evaluate the cost trade-offs, including up-front hardware and software costs and, more important, ongoing administration costs. The business value delivered by particular storage solutions supersedes the cost trade-off.

With a set of servers supported by a single SAN, specific benefits include easier, less expensive incremental upgrades; less overall storage required, since storage capacity is not maintained separately per server; simpler management; and more consistent backup and restore. These benefits in turn lead to lower long-term costs, higher quality, and faster change management.

Server Layer

The server layer includes the server hardware and the operating system software that supports applications. Server platforms play a wide variety of roles, including file servers, network attached storage servers, Web servers, application servers, database servers, and integration servers.

Figure 6.13 shows the hardware and software components of the server layer.

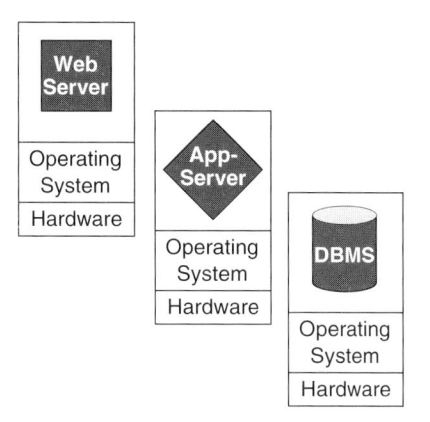

Figure 6.13 Server Layer Hardware and Software Components

Server Evolution

Server technologies continue to evolve rapidly. The traditional focus was to create increasingly scalable and sophisticated platforms through chipset improvements, operating system evolution, and various multiprocessing and clustering approaches. These trends will only continue as chip providers keep pushing the limits of Moore's Law with more powerful bus and multiprocessor technologies, and as clustering becomes more sophisticated and operating systems continue to improve.

However, sophisticated users are reaching a new level of maturity in their server perspective. They are moving beyond traditional fixations on scale-up architecture and proprietary vendor solutions that tightly couple hardware, operating systems, and middleware services.

Best practice organizations have discovered the key to getting the server layer right, which is understanding the type of work that needs to be performed and matching it to the right platform approach. In other words, bigger proprietary platforms are rarely better. Systems based on cost-effective, high-volume components—Intel processors and Microsoft operating systems, for example—address the majority of server requirements remarkably well.

Scale-Up Versus Scale-Out

Even before the e-Business wave, many IT organizations were shifting from a traditional mainframe approach to a server-centric approach that matched server choices to the type of work required, such as file sharing, printing, performing transactions, conducting analysis, supporting e-mail, or some other type of work. During this shift, the underlying concern was always about scalability and the ability of operations departments to deliver appropriate service levels.

The rise of e-Business created a major breakthrough in the server mindset. Many organizations realized that the Web Publish pattern presented a set of challenges different from those posed by traditional transactional systems. With Web Publish, the focus was no longer on maintaining the state of a transaction. Instead, Web Publish required organizations to scale-up their servers so that they could publish content to millions of users through Web browsers using a stateless protocol (HTTP).

Instead of *scaling up*, however, many best-practice organizations realized that they could support huge volumes of Web Publish traffic by *scaling out*: deploying many cost-effective, small servers in conjunction with network load balancers and shared storage solutions. This scale-out approach was not only cost-effective, it also delivered a surprisingly high level of availability. If one of the servers went down, the network load balancer would simply send the next click to the next available server in line.

It is now common for large Web sites to support millions of concurrent users with a combination of load balancers and hundreds of small Web servers. This approach works not only for the regular Web Publish pattern, but also for the Stream Publish pattern with hundreds of servers delivering audio and video streams.

The contrast between scale-out and scale-up is even more apparent in the 3/N-Tier Transact pattern. Most organizations have already applied scale-out concepts to the presentation layer of the 3/N-Tier Transact pattern just as they did for the Web Publish pattern. However, organizations are starting to realize that a scale-out approach can also be applied to the next tier of server in this pattern, the application server.

The application server is a relatively new tier of server. Initially, it emerged as part of enterprise 3/N Tier Transact application packages, such as SAP R/3 and PeopleSoft. These packages were the first to run application logic on a mid-tier server layer, offloading these functions from both the client and the database server. e-Business brought this approach to Web development using platforms such as Microsoft Windows 2000/.NET and J2EE.

As application server designs become more sophisticated, leading organizations are starting to realize that expensive, proprietary platforms are not necessary for application server functions. Rather, a small array of cost-effective, multiprocessing, Intel-based servers handles this chore quite nicely.

The back-end of the 3/N-Tier Transact pattern is the database server, where traditional scale-up approaches apply most directly. However, even this last bastion of "big iron" can be served well through a scale-out approach as products such as Oracle's Real Application Clusters move from a single server instance to a scaled-out set of servers that share one storage instance.

Scaling Out Web Services

Scale-out design especially applies to the emerging field of Web services, which relies on standards such as XML, UDDI, SOAP, and WSDL. The idea is that a presentation or application server can call on a Web service through these standards instead of being tightly linked to the code in question. This development promises to bring an entirely new level of sophistication to scale-out server farms, as presentation and application servers access Web services through a network, without regard to where the services are located.

This trend will drive the creation of even more types of servers focused on various types of work. Today's most common servers include Web servers, application servers, database servers, integration servers, and file/print servers. In the future, the list of server types will expand to include:

- Many more categories of integration servers
- Security servers providing services such as distributed authentication and authorization
- Business process servers providing services such as credit card processing
- Other types of servers providing specific functions that are currently integrated into applications, instead of being shared across applications

Many of these servers will work well using a cost-effective scale-out approach instead of requiring an expensive, complex scale-up solution.

Server Consolidation

Server consolidation is another way to control and leverage a wide range of disparate servers. This approach can generate savings in very targeted and specific ways. Most organizations find themselves somewhere on the server consolidation curve shown in Figure 6.14. The difficult part is deciding how far along the curve you should progress.

Step 1. Server Proliferation. The bottom of the curve starts with a state of random server proliferation. This situation happens when someone buys a server just to handle a single application, particularly at a departmental level. This proliferation results in the kind of usage patterns found at one company where 850 servers were deployed, none with a utilization rate greater than 18 percent. Many of these servers were under office staffers' desks, where they were subject to unplugging or accidental spills.

Step 2. Co-Location. The first move up the curve is co-location: moving servers and associated storage components into a centralized data center. With co-location, however, you still have just as many servers to manage, since centralization does not necessarily equal consolidation. Even so, co-location can result in a fair number of benefits and cost savings. For example, centralization improves manageability while leveraging staff and promoting storage consolidation. This efficiency saves support costs, which is an increasingly large part of total cost of ownership (TCO) for server platforms. But co-location is still just a rudimentary form of consolidation that doesn't work for all applications. Pattern analysis can help you determine which applications will benefit and which won't. For example, applications in the Store-and-Forward Col-

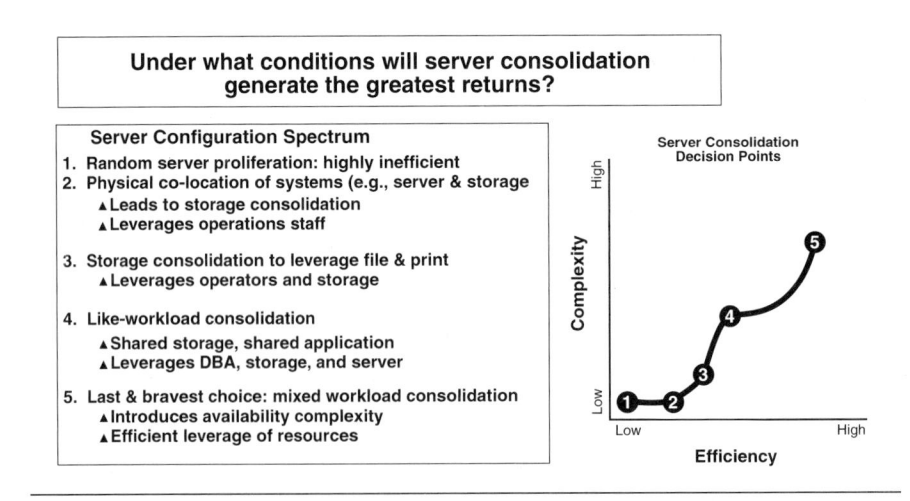

Under what conditions will server consolidation generate the greatest returns?

Server Configuration Spectrum
1. Random server proliferation: highly inefficient
2. Physical co-location of systems (e.g., server & storage)
   ▲ Leads to storage consolidation
   ▲ Leverages operations staff
3. Storage consolidation to leverage file & print
   ▲ Leverages operators and storage
4. Like-workload consolidation
   ▲ Shared storage, shared application
   ▲ Leverages DBA, storage, and server
5. Last & bravest choice: mixed workload consolidation
   ▲ Introduces availability complexity
   ▲ Efficient leverage of resources

Figure 6.14 The Server Consolidation Curve

laborate Pattern, such as file/print sharing and e-mail applications, might not work most efficiently using a co-location strategy.

Step 3. Storage Consolidation. After co-locating the physical server platforms, it is fairly simple to consolidate storage systems. The SAN strategy described in the storage layer section provides more detail on this. Storage is an increasingly large percentage of the overall cost of servers, representing up to 80 percent of the overall hardware cost. However, storage consolidation is not the same as consolidating the server platforms themselves. These first two levels of consolidation, however, are the ones that provide the easiest, most risk-free improvements in cost of ownership. These consolidation strategies should be investigated and accomplished before taking the next steps toward server consolidation.

Step 4. Like-Workload Server Consolidation. Additional efficiencies can be found in the next step on the curve, where you consolidate groups of similar or "like-workload" applications and storage systems that are currently located on distributed servers. The best candidates for this type of consolidation are applications in the Store-and-Forward Collaborate pattern, including e-mail and file/printer sharing. E-mail applications are well suited for this type of consolidation, because one has little concern for such complications as transaction collisions. It is unlikely that a user will log into an e-mail system from two different workstations, so the cost of synchronizing or serializing access to the data is minimal. File and print servers can be consolidated if the users are in the same major location as the servers. However, these applications do not work well over WAN links, so distributed servers are still advised for distributed organizations. A common rule of thumb is that a site with more than 10 to 20 people requires its own local e-mail and file/print server.

With this "like-workload" server consolidation, it is realistic, although not completely easy, to switch loads between servers by reconfiguring users and relocating their data. You can still use multiple servers for these applications if the scale is too high for a particular application to support on a single server platform. You can also proliferate servers, though not as extensively as you could in the past.

To test how server consolidation promotes the idea of a shared infrastructure, first focus on applications such as e-mail. As noted before, infrastructure patterns provide a structured way to determine which applications are most appropriate consolidation targets. Some applications might not perform as well when highly centralized or consolidated, and some might not scale well on a single server platform. You might also find that a server can only handle a certain number of simultaneous users, no matter how much hardware you deploy.

Step 5. Mixed-Workload Server Consolidation. Mixed-workload is the most advanced step in server consolidation. This approach can provide the most efficient use of storage, server, and personnel. However, variability is an important factor. Slight differences in applications lead to huge differences in performance and behavior. Workloads shouldn't be mixed unless the platform can handle it or unless you have done a thorough analysis to be sure that the workload differences are minimal and that dependencies are well understood.

Packing a server full of multiple like-workload applications means that you will spend much time and effort optimizing the last 10 percent of the server's performance. Thus, by extension, you will spend more in support costs, expertise costs, and training costs. Many organizations avoid overloading servers, keeping loads below 80 percent to avoid the cost of upgrading to more expensive hardware platforms, or worse, of adding more management.

The ultimate goal of server layer infrastructure is not to reduce the servers to the lowest possible number. The goal is to save money while preserving or enhancing service, no matter how many servers must be implemented. Consolidating servers into one data center, even if it contains many of them, will lower TCO significantly. In this case, real server consolidation might not really be necessary, as evidenced by the scale-out successes of the Web Publish pattern.

As infrastructures get increasingly complex, a given application will need multiple servers and they need not all be the same server OS/hardware platform. Nevertheless, server platform standardization is required to lower TCO. The strategy must be to minimize the variety of server platform types used for all applications, if not the actual quantity of servers.

Currently, organizations are choosing a scale-out architecture for many aspects of the server layer. Scaling out is often combined with a mixed-mode approach that allows organizations to use different OS platforms on the various layers of infrastructure.

When using a mixed-mode approach with scale-out designs for e-Business scenarios, be very clear that each server platform choice can be used only in the tier for which it was designed, and that this overall design cannot vary. The server platform standards must be set at the pattern level rather than at the server layer level. Using the server layer and service approach creates more commonality across patterns, leaving you with generally fewer server platforms on which to build new applications.

Dealing with legacy platforms is a completely separate issue, of course. But as applications continue to advance, you should emphasize phasing out old patterns.

Refining Patterns in the Server Layer

The server layer is an essential component of both the Web Publish and 3/N-Tier patterns. When refining pattern designs, use the following principles to help guide your product selections in the server layer:

- Wherever applicable, use scale-out designs with large groups of small, inexpensive servers rather than small groups of large servers. This approach to scaling is modular, helping you match investment to demand and respond rapidly to change.

- For systems that face the outside world, aim for the maximum level of robustness possible. Outages on e-Business systems can hurt your brand's reputation. For this reason, you should scrutinize server platform choices and standardize them using a pattern influenced multi-tier structure.

- Partition server resources by server tiers. A mixture of server platform choices can be used for a single application (or as a pattern design standard), but only if the structure of tiers is followed. Don't allow use server types outside of the pattern tier specifications.

- Favor individual boxes over partitions. For e-Business purposes, even single rack units with 1RU can be used in large data centers to simplify the impact of scale-out designs on physical facilities. Partitioning is not advised on Windows 2000/.NET Server or UNIX.

- Beware of cross-layer dependencies created by the operating system (OS). For example, OS/390 implies having DB2 at the data component layer. Such dependencies could compromise discrete component layer boundaries or pattern standards. Allow for this possibility in pattern standards, rather than being surprised by it. In pattern design, you must make decisions across layers rather than just inside them. Otherwise, you will face difficulties trying to match them up later.

- Watch for application-to-server platform dependencies. Applications often have significant infrastructure dependencies, none more historically significant than OS requirements. Although this trend is changing, as applications leverage application server software instead of the OS directly, the problem still occurs. In e-Business, market forces have pushed most applications to support Windows 2000/.NET Server, Solaris, or Linux before all others. This issue alone means that these operating systems will play a prominent role in your e-Business server platform strategy. While you could retain your favorite OLTP database platform based on legacy solutions, most organizations will find themselves putting Web and other servers on one of these three OSs.

- Pay special attention to applications that support multiple platforms, and educate application developers or purchase evaluators on the importance of an application's alignment with infrastructure standards.

Summary

Now you understand the key physical components that contribute to an adaptive infrastructure. This chapter focused on solutions of particular value within three key physical infrastructure layers:

- In the network layer, solutions such as stateless scale-out and network load balancing are absolutely critical if you want to create an adaptive and robust infrastructure for e-Business and IP-based applications. Solutions such as proxy/caching and CDN might also prove useful in some cases.

- In the storage layer, storage servers and storage area networks are highly recommended for all applications. Network attached storage (NAS) is also recommended for Web Publish applications.

- The server layer is an essential component of both the Web Publish and 3/N-Tier patterns. Where applicable, you should use scale-out designs with large groups of small, inexpensive servers rather than small groups of large servers. Beware of cross-layer dependencies created by the operating system (OS), and beware of application-to-server platform dependencies.

Following the precepts outlined in this chapter will help you pick the best solutions for the physical parts of your infrastructure. The next chapter delves into the functional layers of the Adaptive Infrastructure Platform, including the database, integration, and application server layers.

Chapter 7

Functional Components

The next set of components relates to the functional part of an adaptive infrastructure, which includes the database layer, integration layer, and application server layer. Particular components in each layer are of special importance to both e-Business infrastructure and the converged infrastructure that is emerging post e-Business:

- In the *database layer*, scale-out solutions such as clustered databases will help make your applications more efficient.
- In the *integration layer*, the use of message brokers and inter-enterprise integration will shorten deployment time and increase business agility.
- In the *application server layer*, some strategies are especially crucial when developing 3/N-Tier applications.

This chapter presents a complete discussion of key components within each of these layers. Using this information should help you refine your pattern designs so that they include the right mix of functional components. The next chapter examines key infrastructure components in the presentation and management layers. For a complete list of infrastructure components, including those used in both enterprise and e-Business computing, see Appendix A.

Database Layer

The database layer includes all the software components used to deliver database services, including mainstream database products as well as other less visible business components such as gateways, data access middleware, and voice messaging repositories.

Outside of data warehousing, the database market has been relatively stable in recent years with the ascendance of the dominant database vendors. Still, the proliferation of cross-enterprise applications—data warehousing, knowledge management, and customer care—has increased the demand for integrated access to previously independent data stores such as relational database management system (RDBMS), Object Database Management System (ODBMS), e-mail, and spreadsheets. Specialized data stores, which enhance performance and support a variety of data types, will continue to support specialized applications.

Important Design Issues

e-Business drives unprecedented sharing of corporate information between customers and partners. Eighty percent of companies in industries such as IT, telecommunications, retail, and utilities now offer some form of direct online customer interaction. At the same time, their workforce is becoming more mobile, making it more important to access data from remote locations.

Advances in e-Business and e-Commerce technology are causing a rapid increase in transaction velocity. Meanwhile, turbulent market dynamics are forcing IT infrastructure groups to manage rapid change. In this environment, organizations with an adaptive database infrastructure will be well positioned to exploit new opportunities as they arise.

In this rapidly changing environment, several issues demand special attention from infrastructure planners:

Distributed Versus Centralized Architectures. Organizations with a distributed data architecture will find it difficult, if not impossible, to share high-quality information in a timely fashion. Over the next few years, the need for complete and consistent information will drive organizations to identify key data, which is critical for driving leverage across the organization, and centralize it.

Technology evolution will make it easier to centralize and consolidate database infrastructure. Many Global 2000 IT organizations already have server and storage consolidation projects under way. These efforts, combined with database standardization and migration, create the right environment for database consolidation. Over the next two to three years, increasing global network bandwidth and reliability will steadily reduce the need for distributing data for application performance purposes.

Availability. Distributed data architecture involves complex recovery, backup, and restore procedures that threaten reliability. Achieving high availability will require larger SMP platforms for online transaction processing (OLTP) databases, but not for publish databases where you can just have more copies. Other factors contributing to high availability are the appropriate storage infrastructure and effective data backup/recovery tools and policies. For performance reasons, try never to use anything but a high-speed LAN to separate a database from its requesting Web or application server.

Replication. When designing a database, the biggest concern is if it can be replicated for scalability. Transactional read/write databases are far more difficult to replicate due to the fact that the data is constantly changing and requires synchronization; in other words, state must be maintained. Publish pattern read-only databases are far more amenable to replication.

Location. Database location depends on how transactional the application is, and this trait makes it fit well into a pattern-based set of standards. For read-only applications, the database can be moved outside the corporate network to a location inside the DMZ, at the hosting provider's premises, or even at the edges of the network in multiple data centers. For transactional applications, data should be replicated for scaling purposes, so location must be considered more carefully. In addition, transactional data requires heightened security because of its read/write capability. Unauthorized access can do more damage to a transactional database than to read-only information.

Middleware and Gateways. The use of data-access middleware can have a significant impact on the physical location of the database. Data access middleware allows applications and middle-tier application servers to communicate with a database across a network, typically using a protocol such as Open Database Connectivity (ODBC) or Java Database Connectivity (JDBC). Some of these protocols do not work well over the Internet or WAN infrastructure. In addition, not all data access middleware is compatible with all databases. So the selection of this component depends on the selection of the database.

Database gateways are software components that enable applications to access various back-end databases, transforming application calls into native calls for each database supported. In the past, these products were considered necessary when performing data exchanges between two companies with dissimilar database types. They were also used internally when trying to integrate a variety of databases for e-Business or other large applications. Database vendors promoted gateway technology to facilitate data exchange or replication between databases of different formats. The popularity of these devices is waning, however, because the vision remains unfulfilled. Although gateways work for read-only data, few organizations have made them work for transactional data.

Compatibility. Another important issue is the compatibility between application and database servers. Application servers are often designed to work with certain specific databases. However, the move to a more adaptive infrastructure requires you to consolidate databases. Consequently, you should make sure all new application servers and other packaged applications work well with corporate standard databases. Conversely, make sure that any database technologies that you use are widely supported by applications. In other words, pick the database products that are supported by the most applications. Ideally, you can stick to a single one and support that one well.

Security. For the best data security, common sense dictates that every user who accesses a database should be authenticated and limited to seeing only certain database tables, rows, and columns. However, few organizations implement such a granular security policy all the way back through the database in their e-Business architecture, because it limits performance and increases complexity. The main problem with this approach is that it requires a separate database connection for each user. That kind of overhead severely limits database scalability.

For best performance, most e-Business applications currently use pooled database connections. The application opens a number of connections to the database and uses these "always-on" connections for all requests, rather than opening and closing a connection with each request.

To support this method, authentication is managed in the application server layer—most often through role-based authentication, in which users are associated with specific groups that have access rights. Over time, security services such as Web Single Sign-On (Web SSO) will play an increasingly important role in handling permissions management across layers (see Web SSO discussion in Chapter 4).

Auditing Requirements. Auditing is another critical aspect of database security that helps identify improper activity and provides a record that can be used to roll back unauthorized actions. Audit logs are detailed records of data changes that include identify of the person who made each change.

Generally, auditing is accomplished within the application server layer by writing database instructions into a log database and recording the user who made the change. This way, security breaches can be tracked down after the fact for forensic purposes.

Trends in Database Technologies

To develop an adaptive approach to the database layer, you must look carefully at the full range of technologies available. Relational database technology is the dominant technology for both publish and transactional (OLTP) applications, and it remains the most flexible choice. Object-oriented databases are still commonly used for publishing rich multimedia. However, they are not as flexible or mature as relational databases. Data warehouse and data mart solutions are different, but they might not apply as much to e-Business cases, at least not until you let outside users perform analytics on your data. Figure 7.1 shows the relative flexibility versus performance of various database architectures.

One emerging option involves in-memory databases, which are entirely contained in RAM. These databases promise a much better performance than traditional disk-based storage mechanisms, and they could play a significant role in keeping track of application state information, such as transactions in process.

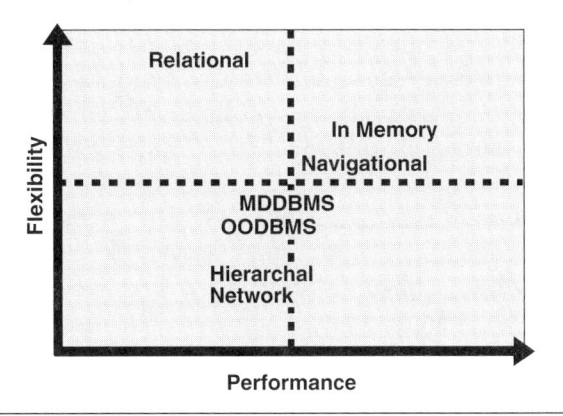

Figure 7.1 Flexibility Versus Performance in Database Technologies

When choosing database technologies, give the strongest consideration to vendors who deliver the most complete toolsets supporting the three largest database vendors: Microsoft, IBM, and Oracle. The toolsets you select should reflect the changing roles of database administrators (DBAs), with integration being a key differentiator.

Over time, DBAs will play a larger, more proactive role in application development and will eventually relinquish their traditional operational duties. To support this new role, companies need to automate or outsource old operational DBA tasks, and provide DBAs with new tools that support tasks such as server-side code debugging, test data creation, load testing, and performance tuning. As they seek to close the loop from logical design to physical implementation, the new breed of DBAs will need testing tools that integrate well with traditional operational tools, such as performance monitoring and schema management. Besides integration, other important factors will be ease of use, ease of installation, and management capabilities.

The next few years will bring highly available architectures to support corporate goals and improve customer/employee interaction while ensuring reliability. Database vendors will provide improved point-in-time recovery options to minimize the need for full restores. Although price/performance has improved, the selection of database technology remains predominantly a business decision, not a technology one.

Figure 7.2 and Table 7.1 depict the basic trade-offs for availability versus the business impact for particular e-Business scenarios. The key is to pick the availability approach right for your business. Furthermore, you must realize that database uptime is not enough. You need end-to-end infrastructure and application availability, so a scale-out architecture becomes essential to solving problems with scaling and availability.

Among other features, database vendors will continue to improve and promote high-availability options such as online utilities, improved replication, and scale-out clusters to meet expected user demand. Meanwhile, IT organizations will struggle to implement and enforce change management processes that lessen the need for planned downtime and the impact that planned changes have on unplanned downtime. Many organizations have fostered an overreliance on redundant infrastructures and change management tools, without devoting proper attention to internal people, processes, and responsibilities.

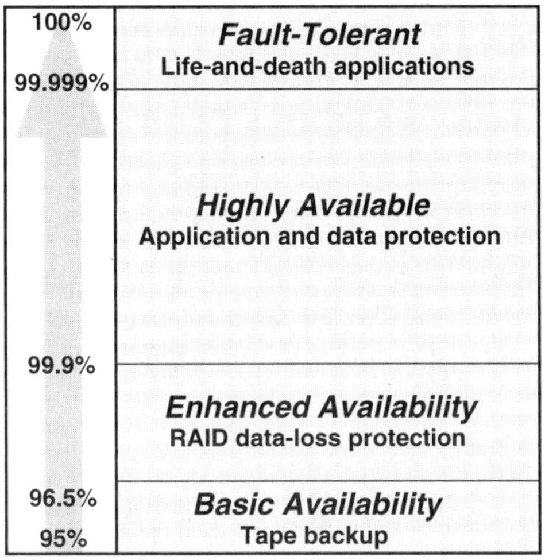

Figure 7.2 Defining High Availability

Scale-Out Solutions and Clustered Database Options

Although routinely used with lightly coupled Web and application servers, the database server is the last tier of an N-tier architecture to defy a scale-out approach. Several standard arguments are typically made in favor of clustered architecture, but to date, it has required a daunting

Table 7.1 The Cost of Downtime

Retailer			Brokerage	
Percentage of Uptime	Annual Downtime Retailer (14×5)	Cost of Downtime Retailer (14×5)	Annual Downtime Brokerage (24×7)	Cost of Downtime Brokerage (24×7)
99.999	2 min.	$1,950	5 min.	$537,000
99.99	22 min.	$19,500	52 min.	$5.584 million
99.9	3.5 hr	$195,000	9 hr.	$58 million
99	36.7 hr.	$1.95 million	88 hr.	$567 million
98	73 hr.	$3.9 million	180 hr.	$1.2 billion
96.5	127 hr.	$6.8 million	307 hr.	$2 billion
95	182 hr.	$9.75 million	450 hr	$3 billion

programming effort by software vendors to deal with issues such as avoiding serialized operations and eliminating internode communication. Improvements in manageability and processor speed have also reduced the market demand for clustered solutions. Over time, however, IT organizations will continue to explore clustered database architectures as a way to reduce infrastructure costs and improve application availability.

Clustered database solutions are fairly common in the decision support world, where data is partitioned across multiple nodes. Products from the leading database vendors all support range, or hash, partitioning, often used in a decision support, read-only environment.

Open Source Databases (OSDBs)

Along with Web servers and operating systems, open source databases (OSDBs) have been described as the "third leg in the stool," one that organizations need to build successful application infrastructures. Yet OSDBs such as MySQL and PostgreSQL face formidable obstacles to commercial acceptance.

In the long term, OSDBs will become a nonfactor in the database market, relegated to noncritical tasks such as clickstream logging and directories. As with the choice of operating system (OS), the choice of database software is often predicated on its intended use, such as transaction processing or decision support. Other factors include scalability, reliability, and third-party vendor application support. Database switching costs are significant, often taking as much as a year and costing $1 million or more, due to the dependence on application code, triggers, and stored procedures—not to mention the need to develop skill sets to support the new database.

In combination, these factors render the option of switching to open source less likely. If anything, OSDBs could be used for inexpensive publish-only databases; however, they will lack the pretrained staff and tools for maintenance that other mainstream products have.

Figure 7.3 shows two types of clustering architectures: shared-nothing and shared-disk.

In a shared-nothing cluster, each node operates independently, with data assigned to a specific node and disk. In this case, applications must be partitioned and internode communication must be kept to a minimum. Failover can take minutes.

In a shared-disk cluster, each node can access all the available data. In this case, applications need not be partitioned. Locking and cache coherency require internode communication, which can reduce speed, but this architecture can handle more users and failover can be completed in seconds.

Some IT organizations have used a shared-nothing approach successfully for querying purposes in large data warehouse infrastructures. This success is due, in part, to the database engine's native support for queries and parallel input/output. The shared-nothing architecture achieves scale by breaking large problems into smaller chunks and sending them off to be processed on individual nodes. Since subsets of data are owned by a single node, internode locking and cache coherency are not issues for predominantly read-only solutions. Also, internode message passing is minimized until results are merged and communicated over the high-speed interconnect.

Even though shared-nothing architecture works well in the customized read-only world of data warehousing, it has failed to catch on in the OLTP market, which is dominated by packaged applications that are

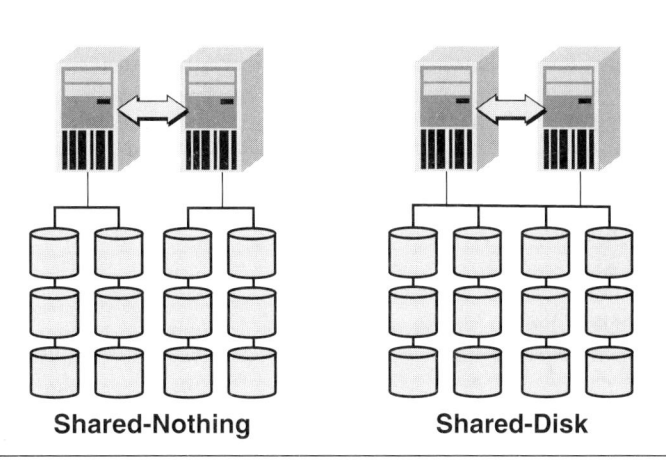

Figure 7.3 Shared-nothing Versus Shared-disk Clusters

challenged by the need to partition efficiently up to thousands of database tables.

The evolution of clustered database infrastructures will be led by cost-conscious IT organizations taking a build-versus-buy approach, using existing or lower-cost hardware to increase processing power, scalability, and availability. Developers will design homegrown applications that use data partitioning to mitigate the need for internode communication. Shared-nothing architectures will be the choice of most developers due to their scalability advantage.

Refining Patterns in the Database Layer

Practical limitations and product choices have led most organizations to use similar database technologies (and products) for e-Business as for internal needs. Since most e-Business applications need read-only data on a scale not seen internally, choosing a publish database becomes a more critical need than just repeating the OLTP choices already made internally. Full pattern scale, however, depends not only on the performance and availability of the database platform, but on the whole scale-out design of which any database (publish or OLTP) will be only a component.

Table 7.2 summarizes the list of potential components in the database layer and shows their relative importance when used with the Web Publish and 3/N-Tier Transact patterns.

For the Web Publish pattern, you should be very clear on the content update requirements and the associated timeliness or latency of the data

Table 7.2 Database Layer Pattern Summary Chart

Layer or Service: Component	Web Publish	3/N-Tier Transact
Database Layer:		
- Database	2	1
- Database Server	2	1
- Data Access Middleware	2	1

Key
1 = Critical, All Cases
2 = Highly Recommended, Most Cases
3 = Optional, Some Cases
4 = Optional, Fewer Cases

replication process. For best results, establish a single data replication solution, typically based on your current data warehousing solutions, to make sure that data is copied appropriately. Use a specific vendor's data replication solution only if that vendor currently supplies all your internal database solutions, and sometimes not even then. You can leverage other third-party solutions or choose a database product that is better at read-only solutions and often less expensive than your choice for OLTP databases. This choice is appropriate if you have a large amount of replicated data, such as product catalogs that can require many parallel copies. Otherwise, you might use the same product as your OLTP solution, just to keep things simpler.

For the 3/N-Tier Transact pattern, use direct integration with internal databases or applications as a strategy to eliminate duplicate storage of write transactions. If no internal integration is required, use your best-understood and best-supported OLTP product.

Database solutions bring up specific DMZ design issues. Never place OLTP databases for 3/N-Tier Transact patterns inside the DMZ. Instead, locate them completely behind the firewall. Web Publish pattern read-only databases can be placed inside the DMZ, but they must be on hardened boxes with strong intrusion detection features. Putting data outside the firewall is not a good idea since there is very little protection.

Guidelines

Remember these principles when working with the database layer:

Create a single source for transactional data. Any transactional activity that changes data should change it in only one place, usually in an OLTP database that supports this type of activity. You might need OLTP data only for e-Business, in which case you should pick from the most common and well-understood solutions.

Be ready to include data from non-e-Business databases. You might want to integrating e-Business applications back into OLTP systems to handle the write portion of the traffic. In this case, use integration solutions to handle write-oriented or read-oriented work. See the "Integration Layer" section in this chapter for more details on how this works. Even in this situation, you can still use a read-only database copy for many requirements, and integrate it only when writing is actually required. Do not choose to first capture incoming writes to an e-Business-only database then try to replicate them to internal database systems. This approach will not scale and will create data integrity problems.

Use replication only for static or non-time-sensitive data. Financial institutions use real-time data replication products, but these solutions are appropriate mainly in read-only, decision-support applications. e-Business has seriously affected the ability of many companies to maintain consistency in their data. Many companies replicate data to give access to external users or to reduce the load on existing OLTP databases. These copies are made periodically (nightly, weekly, or monthly) so the data might not be current when compared to the transactional system. Thus, customers viewing their accounts on the Web might not see transactions such as bill payments that were made more recently than the last data copy. While data replication can improve performance, availability, and security, it costs in terms of data latency. Use this approach as needed to match the business process and data requirements. Make sure users and internal help-desk people are aware of the differences in data timeliness. Avoid using this approach without detailed analysis and scenario planning.

Consider external caching for publish databases. Caching can help improve the performance of a publish-oriented database system. This issue is discussed more thoroughly in the "Caching Server" section of Chapter 6.

Consider niche database products for complex data needs. This recommendation includes the in-memory database products as discussed earlier in this chapter.

Avoid replicating data across business boundaries. The previous warning about copying data unnecessarily also applies when crossing business boundaries. You risk losing control over the data and could have significant trouble using it afterwards. Nevertheless, some business cases demand this sort of replication, so plan carefully to handle bulk data movement cases using transactional integration, making sure to use a single system to manage all data integration across business boundaries. Otherwise, plan only a few such single-purpose replications and manage them carefully.

Database Layer Issues

Consider the following issues when working with the database layer:

Balance the resource friendliness of data replication with data freshness and consistency concerns. As noted above, you can have significant limitations to the freshness of data when copies are used for e-Business cases. Yet this approach is commonly taken to handle scalability and simplify security issues. Follow the guidelines above so that you're clear when data should be replicated. Understand what business rules apply to infrastructure, applications, and support staff such as the help desk or call center, then make sure these rules are properly enforced.

Use integration strategies to deal with cross-enterprise data ownership issues. When sharing data between enterprises, major data ownership issues could arise. The previous discussions of PKI cover the issue of trust, but the remaining business issues cannot be overestimated. Exchanging some types of data will be a great benefit to the business in terms of its supply chains and other B2B activities. In these cases, you should establish clear data format and content strategies and move beyond simple data exchange toward an integration-centric approach that unifies control over inter-business data exchange. See the "Integration Layer" section next for a more complete discussion of this approach.

Integration Layer

The integration layer contains all the components that provide integration services, between back-end applications, Web servers, application servers, or database servers. Components can include adapter toolkits, application adapters, integration servers, EDI gateways, file exchange servers, and more. The integration function can be internally focused, such as enterprise application integration (EAI), or externally focused, such as inter-enterprise integration (IEI).

Integration can occur on several levels:

- *File* or document integration is simple, but has limited functionality and is batch-oriented.
- *Database* integration provides tighter coupling but is more difficult to maintain, especially when integrating more than two systems. Database integration is also batch-oriented.
- Asynchronous *application* level messaging provides the tightest integration, supports synchronous transactions, and is platform-independent.

Since the latter is overwhelmingly the best practice, this section focuses on the architectural and technological choices associated with application-level integration.

The Integration Server (Message Broker)

Integration servers provide a way to integrate e-Business applications with enterprise and legacy systems at the application layer. Application servers are used to build applications and integration servers are used to integrate applications once they are built. These two types of products are the main drivers in a rapidly converging middleware market. And both are crucial to maintaining a robust, flexible infrastructure.

The standard integration server (message broker) architecture consists of five functional technology components, which are shown in Figure 7.4.

Adapter components provide interfaces that applications use to send and receive business events, such as the place, change, or cancel order to/from event.

Transport components move business events around the network.

Formatting components transform business events from one application-specific format to another.

Routing components define which applications receive which events.

Business Process Automation (BPA) components work in a state-handling, run-time environment, generally used to control the execution of long-lived transactions.

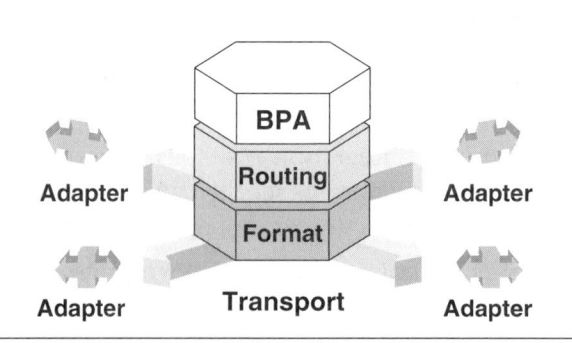

Figure 7.4 Integration Server Components

These components allow applications to communicate with each other without having to know the format, protocol, or location of other applications.

Integration is particularly useful for applications involved in one-to-many or many-to-one business processes, where you need to minimize the impact that changes on one application can have on others. In these situations, integration can reduce the complexity of business process and infrastructure changes, thus reducing time to market.

Components of a Message Broker Infrastructure

No single vendor provides all the pieces of a complete message broker infrastructure, though market consolidation will make products more complete over time. Meanwhile, you can categorize and compare vendors on the strength of the following components.

Message Transport. The message transport moves data from application to broker and vice versa, as well as between partners. While synchronous options exist, such as remote procedure call (RPC) mechanisms, the most effective integration approach uses an asynchronous message transport to decouple the processing and delivery of messages. For example, an online application can generate account updates and communicate them to a back-end database without having to make a synchronous connection to the database—a method called "fire-and-forget." With asynchronous transport, back-end systems using the data can work at their own speeds, including batch mode.

As solutions become more complex, front-end applications cannot wait for back-end applications to process data because doing so can create complex end-to-end dependencies that cannot be supported in larger-scale environments. Most EAI and IEI vendors support message transports at some level, and some promote their own. Business Quality Messaging (BQM) is a term used to describe solutions that deliver fire-and-forget messaging in a reliable manner, so that data cannot be lost.

While messaging might imply a slower transport, this implication holds true if message queues are stored on disk. If messages are stored in memory or if disk input/output (I/O) is highly optimized, queuing can be as fast as synchronous access. More important, while message queuing is slower in relative terms than synchronous transports, in absolute terms—even if messages are persistent—the added overhead is still only a couple of seconds at most.

Formatting Engine. These components transform messages from one format to another and can differ greatly in parsing power. For example, some products can parse recursive message structures from multiple messages into a single message. Typically, vendors include what-you-see-is-what-you-get (WYSIWYG) tools for defining format conversion mappings. A growing number of vendors are supplying predefined sets of message templates for standard message formats, such as Society for Worldwide Interbank Financial Telecommunications (SWIFT), Health Level Seven (HL7), iDoc, and EDI. Over the next few years, XML will play a greater role in defining a canonical, self-describing message format. Meanwhile, users must do the many-to-many process translations themselves.

Aside from parsing power and ease of definition, speed is another important attribute for this component. Formatting engines can handle hundreds or even thousands of messages per second. For some EAI and IEI vendors, this translation is being done by other parts of the infrastructure. However, the best practice is to have a robust formatting engine as part of the core architecture of the integration server.

Routing Engine. These components help apply business logic to events. Also called "rule engines," these products route incoming messages to the appropriate subscribing applications. Power, ease of definition, and speed are key attributes. The rule engine performs complex conditional logic to make sophisticated decisions regarding message routing. All rule engines come with tools that enable descriptive declarations of routing rules, eliminating the need for a conventional procedural language. Of course, routing speed must be on par with formatting speed.

Business Process Automation (BPA). BPA is a necessary component as integration moves from fire-and-forget to more complex and stateful transactions. More control within the integration infrastructure will be required to handle state. The next section describes the various strategies for this emerging feature of integration solutions.

Application Adapter. This component forms the bridge between the integration and application server layers. Most vendors currently focus on rolling out as many adapters as possible. The number of application adapters determines both the horizontal and vertical openness of the message broker framework. Horizontally, it determines how many peer-to-peer connections a message broker can handle. Vertically, it determines how many types of middleware can be layered.

Organizations that have already chosen an enterprise middleware standard should not establish a rival message-broker infrastructure based on a vendor's proprietary transport. Vendors are beginning to position their products as an open middleware stack in which users can swap out various layers.

Product Selection

Avoid building an integration infrastructure that becomes brittle and rigid due to product obsolescence or monolithic implementation. Instead, select EAI vendors with the greatest chance of survival, emphasizing vendor viability over product features. Furthermore, your adapter architectures should shield the application from the integration infrastructure, using intermediate document formats to reduce integration complexity. This approach reduces your dependence on a particular vendor's technology and allows you to modify or replace the EAI infrastructure if necessary.

Overcrowding of the EAI market—at one time, it involved more than 70 competitors—will result in a rapid consolidation. To avoid loss of agility due to product obsolescence, you should focus on three EAI selection criteria: vendor viability, adapter agility, and time to solution.

In a few years, a key IT service level measure will be the time required to add new business partners or business processes. IT organizations that fail to develop a robust and agile EAI infrastructure will have key projects outsourced and lose effective control over their infrastructure. To remain competitive, IT groups must develop an integration center of excellence (COE) to manage, to complement, or to compete with systems integrators.

The Role of the Integration Administrator. Like a network, the value of EAI increases exponentially with the number of integrated applications. To avoid incompatible islands of integration, similar to the networking environment of the 1980s, EAI technology must be treated as an enterprisewide infrastructure—not as an application development toolkit or a tactical departmental solution. IT groups should select one strategic EAI product as the enterprisewide integration backbone and, where necessary, hang tactical EAI products off of that to provide functionality or connectivity not provided by the backbone.

To leverage EAI across the enterprise, leading IT organizations will create a specific integration administrator (IA) team as part of the infrastructure development group. Like systems administrators and DBAs, IA teams provide standard services across all enterprise projects. The IA team becomes responsible for the selection of EAI technology and the creation of an agile EAI infrastructure.

Picking a Vendor. The EAI market is young and highly dynamic, with the top six vendors accounting for only 50 percent of market share. To reduce the probability of obsolescence, IAs should pick a vendor that will be in the top three. Measure potential vendors based on all of the following factors:

- Market share. Estimate the current market share of the product and the recent growth rate, both in dollars and customers.
- Financial strength. Estimate the current and historical market capitalization and net profit of the vendor.
- Reference accounts. Estimate the number, quality, and size of customer reference accounts.
- Road map. Evaluate the business and technical viability of the vendor's two-to-three-year road map.

To minimize the impact of technology becoming obsolete, IAs must develop an agile integration architecture that can cope with technology being replaced over the next few years. Ideally, each layer should have clean interfaces to surrounding layers, enabling IAs to select the best-of-breed formatter, rules engine, transport, or adapter toolkit, and to substitute viable solutions for obsolete layers. EAI vendors have resisted this concept and are developing fully integrated solutions that cannot be interchanged.

Adapter Agility. The agility of the EAI infrastructure is largely a function of the flexibility of the adapter layer. Observe these guidelines to build long-term flexibility into the infrastructure:

- Avoid product architectures that tightly bind the application code to the EAI vendor's code. Instead, create a dynamic architecture that decouples the application development lifecycle from the EAI technology lifecycle through clean, well-defined interfaces.
- Avoid vendor-specific adapter toolkits that bind the application to a specific EAI infrastructure. In particular, make sure the adapter does not require a specific transport layer. Unfortunately, most adapters are tightly bound to a communication protocol.
- Focus on implementing and maintaining well-structured and documented interfaces for applications. To facilitate this, IAs must work to change the application developer's mindset regarding integration.

Time to Solution. An agile EAI infrastructure must minimize the time to solution. IAs should look for rapid-development features in the formatting and routing layers, such as rule-based systems and graphical development environments. Routing and formatting solutions based on procedural coding rapidly become inflexible. The EAI vendor should be rated on the breadth and quality of predefined integration libraries (adapters and formatting) for standard applications. By using vendor-supplied libraries, IAs reduce the time to solution and shift some of the maintenance burden, such as building adapters, to the vendor.

Funding Considerations. The costs of integration can be high. The following list describes general charges for common infrastructure components when this book was first published:

- Message broker

  $25,000 to $50,000 per CPU

- Messaging transport

  Sometimes bundled

  $2,000 per server to $100,000 per server (normally capacity-based pricing)

- Adapters

  Packaged applications $50,000 to $250,000

  In-house applications $10,000 to $50,000

- Business process automation (BPA)

  $35,000 to $70,000 per CPU

An entry-level configuration costing from $300,000 to $700,000 would include broker, transport, and three-to-four adapters with platforms for production, test, and development. Programming or systems integration costs can range from two to five times the software costs, depending on the quality of the application interfaces.

This estimate does not include development costs for complex business process automation. The cost to modify each application is associated with integration, but it is not really part of the transactional integration service. Beyond this initial expense are the costs to change the current service and to actually run it. Integration implemented without productivity tools almost always becomes more expensive and less flexible than integration implemented with them.

Given the high up-front costs, finding the funds for integration can be problematic. While e-Business generally serves as the best reason to start

EAI and IEI, allocating costs to specific drivers can help. For instance, you can allocate all adapter costs to specific application projects so that application requests aren't made without including adapters budgeted for them. Costs for the message broker and communications infrastructure can be allocated based on some agreed-upon cost driver, such as per transaction usage. Some organizations fund integration costs with direct allocations up-front and then assess usage fees on a monthly basis.

Integration and Process Automation

The generic wisdom that you should use application servers to build applications and integration servers to integrate them doesn't apply to certain integration problems.

The belief that message brokers cannot handle integrating complex business processes is also completely misguided.

As integration becomes increasingly critical to a successful business strategy, infrastructure professionals must become adept at identifying the related infrastructure requirements.

When designing an infrastructure to support state handling, infrastructure planners should determine how long the state must be maintained and how often the business logic will change. (See the case studies below.) Application servers generally rely on maintaining sessions to maintain state, which is fine for short-lived transactions, but not feasible for long-lived transactions.

Thus, a traditional application server works well if the state must be maintained over a short period, especially if high throughput is a requirement, such as in a "real-time" inventory check. A process automation server would be a better fit for more "long-lived" processes, such as coordinating the provisioning and billing of a retail bundle of land-line, wireless, and Internet networking services among various back-end provisioning and billing systems.

In either case, the interface should completely decouple any application consuming a service from the place where the logic is implemented, such as on an application server, an integration server, or both. This functional partitioning is the key to business-process agility. In the near future, defining such "application services" using a combination of application server and integration server technologies will be a premium skill set, living at the juncture of application and infrastructure development.

Integration Case Study

The following case study shows an example of an organization that needs to integrate a new Web storefront application and three distinct call centers, each built on different technology, with three distribution centers, each also built on separate technology.

In the original configuration in Figure 7.5, each call center is "hardwired" to only one distribution center.

As a result, the distribution center fulfilling an order is not determined by inventory levels or by the proximity of the distribution center to des-tination addresses. Instead, each order is fulfilled by the distribution center to which the call center is hardwired.

To improve performance, this company added an integration server that tied together applications in the Web storefront, call centers, and distribution centers (see Figure 7.6). The integration server enabled a call center to determine which distribution center should fulfill an order based on the geographic proximity of the distribution center to the order destination.

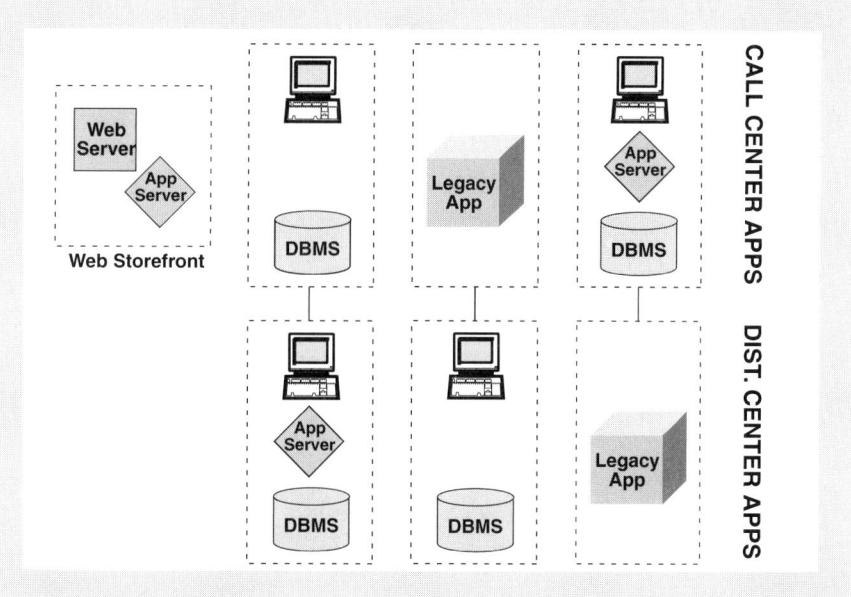

Figure 7.5 Original State of Case Study

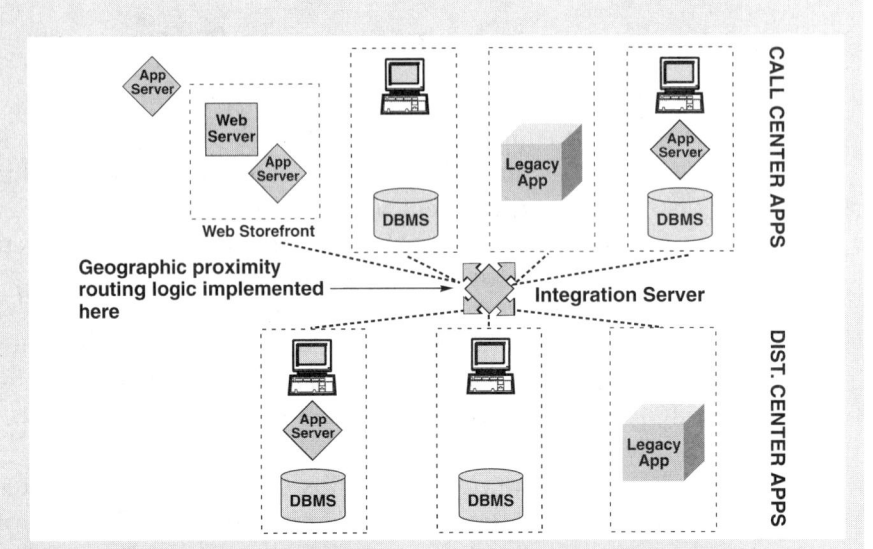

Figure 7.6 Phase I of Case Study

In the second phase of the case study (see Figure 7.7), an application server was introduced with the integration server. This application server contains the logic to check and maintain inventory status in all the distribution centers. By the end of this phase, call centers were able to determine which center should fulfill an order by checking both its geographic proximity to the order destination and its inventory levels.

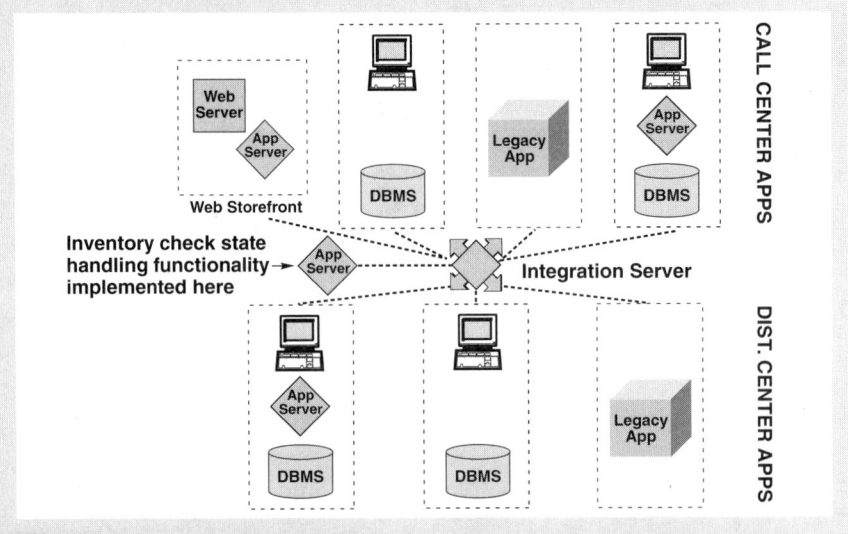

Figure 7.7 Phase II of Case Study

The Inter-Enterprise Integration (IEI) Server

As business partners increasingly share data, they find that inter-enterprise integration (IEI) is easier than other methods, such as point-to-point links between application programming interfaces (APIs) or links to electronic data interchange (EDI) systems.

Overlap Between IEI and EAI

When developing infrastructure for IEI, keep in mind that it is a superset of your internal EAI efforts. Instead of implementing a redundant IEI and EAI infrastructure, you should leverage existing EAI processes and technologies, augmenting them with specialized IEI infrastructure where necessary. Overlap exists in some of the following particular areas.

Message Brokering. Message brokering systems require reliable data-transport mechanisms to establish online cross-application interaction, but they should also include batch-oriented file transfers. This functionality is particularly critical in IEI infrastructures, where infrastructure resource activity (such as execution servers and networks) spans several business boundaries and is more difficult to control and predict.

Security. Security capabilities are certainly important in internal EAI infrastructures, such as when protecting human resources and financial application information from use by other applications. However, these capabilities are even more critical in cross-business environments and should play a decisive role in vendor and product assessments. Some message broker vendors provide sound end-to-end security services with their solutions. Be particularly careful to examine their actual capabilities versus their future plans. As with other markets, many vendors are long on marketing plans, but short on immediately available features.

Security solutions should use SSL to secure transmission sessions and should describe required firewall settings to allow transmission across B2B boundaries on both ends. Emerging standards for Web service, particularly the Simple Object Access Protocol (SOAP), should help simplify security planning, because SOAP is delivered over HTTP and can be sent through a firewall without modification. Nevertheless, this capability might actually cause problems, since security administrators will have little visibility or control over this data. Products may leverage Public Key Infrastructure (PKI) technology for server-to-server authentication or message integrity and non-repudiation, as discussed in Chapter 5. Consider message broker solutions with integrated PKI schemes carrying authentication and non-repudiation functions at the application, broker, queue, and user levels.

Encryption. The financial sensitivity and legal implications of cross-business operations often require any exchange of messages between applications to remain confidential. Consequently, message-brokering solutions used for IEI should provide industry-standard encryption facilities, such as RSA. Since encryption places a significant burden on infrastructure capacities, it's important that these solutions allow you to selectively and dynamically activate encryption functions based on the content, source, and destination of messages, as well as on prevailing infrastructure performance metrics.

Management. Message broker solutions typically use graphical user interfaces to provide remote monitoring and administration. These interfaces vary in functionality and sophistication. Real-time, event-based monitoring consoles help administrators track the flow of messages through different layers of the supporting infrastructure. Real-time tracking of these events is necessary to control the service level of the IEI system, including reliability, scalability, transaction execution times, and integrity.

The solution should be able to monitor events at different levels of the system, including the network, queue manager, broker, intermediate database or storage system, application, and end-user levels. For this to happen, you must install probes or agents in areas that are located in and managed by separate organizations. In turn, you will be required to coordinate management issues and procedures between all the participating IT organizations and get permission to install the probes in mission-critical areas of other people's infrastructures. The challenges are technical as well. For instance, the additional demands on network bandwidth and server processing time could prove intolerable in many IEI environments.

To work well, an IEI solution needs to handle the issue of software updates and distribution. Integrating applications across business boundaries requires organizations to install and run common pieces of exchange broker software in separate servers and organizations. The exchange broker must be aware of version changes in the applications it integrates, so that rule and transformation engines can be kept up-to-date as the applications change.

Convergence of EAI and IEI

Until recently, EAI and IEI were considered to be separate concerns, largely because of technological differences. EAI was based on message-oriented middleware concepts, while IEI was based on relatively new technologies such as XML, HTTP, and SOAP, technologies that connected systems across the Internet. As systems have matured, however, IEI and EAI are starting to have a lot more in common.

The most compelling similarities have to do with process automation. Automating B2B interactions and removing humans from the process has created a tremendous need for highly integrated and adaptive process control. Take customer orders, for example. To automate a simple interaction, such as order-taking, might require creating a process that spans multiple back-end systems, with automatic handling of errors and exceptions. The complexity involved has created an expectation that the entire process—not just a part of it—should be described and automated using visual process tools.

The message-processing paradigm also drives this convergence. Although differences between internal and external systems are substantial in terms of system design and administration, in both cases experts think XML-based messaging interfaces will predominate.

A third driver will be the whole push toward XML standardization. Although much has been said about XML, the main issue will be the processes by which the language develops standards schemas. Since current standardization efforts are either anemic or irrelevant, a series of de facto standards will most likely be created by heavyweight players or accepted in common use.

The unpredictability of communication between partners, however, complicates IEI and makes it a problem different from EAI. IEI initiatives are still based on successful integration with existing internal applications. When viewed strategically, however, the IEI infrastructure responsible for directly communicating with partner systems—such as EDI, XML, or third-party gateways—can be viewed as a specialized adapter connected to a generalized EAI integration server.

With this complication in mind, and especially given the weak IEI vendor market, you should not attempt to implement IEI by relying on IEI vendors alone. Instead, carefully segment the problem into two parts:

- Specific IEI challenges best addressed by current IEI vendors
- Generalized EAI challenges best addressed by EAI vendors

This way, you can use IEI vendor strengths—partner management, inter-enterprise event transport, inter-enterprise security, and business logic for specific communities of interest, for example—to augment EAI vendor strengths, such as integration with internal applications, event transformation, and internal process automation.

Solving the problem this way will result in a faster time to market than relying on IEI solutions alone. This approach also promotes reusability, since it separates the integration of internal applications from the IEI infrastructure itself. This point is particularly important because you can't dictate integration infrastructure to business partners. Consequently, you might have to accept the lowest-common-denominator approach to integration infrastructure, both from a logical standpoint—for example, EDI formats or community-of-interest formats—as well as from a physical standpoint—such as SOAP as an IEI transport or XML as an IEI format mechanism.

In the end, what really differentiates IEI from traditional EAI is the requirement to use less-robust but more-standard infrastructure for certain integration requirements, plus the need for the kind of partner management and security infrastructure that often isn't a requirement in EAI. This set of concerns will also be reflected in the vendor market over the next few years. Providing features that mesh with these realities will differentiate IEI vendors from EAI vendors.

The benefits of EAI/IEI integration will manifest themselves in many ways. Combining the two minimizes the technologies, toolsets, and dedicated human resources involved in the integration environment. Having a single set of tools for process automation would be especially useful. In addition, integration makes it easier to automate more processes. For example, in the past, if a process required real-time access to a supplier's inventory, it couldn't be automated or even executed. Combining EAI and IEI suddenly makes this possible.

Over time, the boundary between internal and external integration components will become increasingly blurred. As surviving ASPs create robust integration infrastructures and as other Web-accessible services become available, the definition of an individual application will change to include both insourced and outsourced components. Ultimately, your integration solution shouldn't require you to change tools, technology, or infrastructure to transition from communicating between your own applications to communicating with someone else's. As Web services architectures become more useful, they will extend across enterprise boundaries.

Refining Patterns in the Integration Layer

Table 7.3 shows major components in the integration layer and indicates the relative importance of each component to the Web Publish and 3/N-Tier Transact patterns.

For e-Business, the 3/N-Tier Transact pattern infrastructure requires at least EAI solutions for legacy or internal integration. Integration layer components should be offered to your organization as a formal and distinct Transactional Integration service. (See the book titled *The Adaptive Enterprise* for details.)

Integration servers in particular will be required for internal 3/N-Tier Transact applications, so the integration layer must be designed in conjunction with that pattern. The Web Publish pattern could require a different kind of integration, such as content or analytic integration (data warehousing).

Guidelines

Use the following guidelines when evaluating architectures and technologies for the integration layer.

Build for flexibility. Over the next few years, technologies based on Microsoft .NET, and Java 2 Enterprise Edition (J2EE) will likely mature and enjoy wider support. However,.these standards still have limited

Table 7.3 Integration Layer Pattern Summary Chart

Layer or Service: **Component**	**Web Publish**	**3/N-Tier Transact**
Integration Layer		
Integration Transport	3	2
Integration Server	4	2
Application Adapter	4	2
Inter-Enterprise Integration Server	4	3

Key
1=Critical, All Cases
2=Highly Recommended, Most Cases
3=Optional, Some Cases
4=Optional, Fewer Cases

scope, stability, and viability, which requires you to retain some proprietary and legacy components at various layers, including transport, interaction, integrity, and security.

Support discrete interfaces. The increasing variety of proprietary APIs and document formats will continue to make integration a complex task. Making these pieces work together across stovepiped environments requires extensive use of one-to-one application interface mapping, transformation, and formatting services. XML will play a significant role in helping applications communicate, but you still must support multiple interfaces for at least a few more years. The key to flexible integration is strict separation of presentation layer functions from application code. Application developers will keep trying to embed the presentation layer in the application to increase simplicity and reduce time-to-market. To counteract this tendency, infrastructure developers should clearly define, develop, and document a service-based alternative. For maximum agility, the presentation layer should be handled through techniques such as parameter setting and configuration of formatting libraries, rather than embedding it in the application logic.

Focus on fundamentals. Networks that carry batch transactions must continually support increased volume, throughput, and speed of file transfers between businesses. To meet this challenge, solution vendors will provide more focused alternatives to EAI/IEI solutions for highly batch-transactional infrastructures. The dichotomy between batch and online infrastructures will continue until a transactional infrastructure is designed that enables both. This infrastructure will be capable of transmitting individual transactions in real time and queuing up batches for bulk transmission later on some predetermined schedule, either hourly, daily, or weekly. This approach reduces transaction costs by lowering communication costs and allowing more efficient bulk processing. While some message queuing products have both batch and online modes, the integration service architectures they support cannot do this without extensive modification. When convergence occurs, batch-only approaches will slowly disappear.

Clearly separate integration functions (rules, format, and transport). Well-designed transactional integration infrastructures, particularly B2B server integrations, will allow cross-system data transfers to be partitioned into smaller units. This approach makes it easier to integrate heterogeneous application environments and increases agility by decoupling higher-level business processes from a wide range of lower-level application components—from large-scale enterprise applications (ERP, CRM, SCM) to specialized EJB or .NET components.

Integration Layer Issues

Consider the following issues when working with this layer.

Maintain direct access to legacy data and systems. For transactional needs, many e-Business applications require direct access to internal systems in near-real time. While each application could link separately to these internal systems, doing so leads to the hodge-podge of one-shot integration solutions that currently exist. For e-Business and beyond, it is important to create a single infrastructure that ties all internal operational systems to e-Business applications. A single infrastructure will be difficult and expensive initially, but it becomes increasingly faster and cheaper as more applications leverage the transactional integration service.

Obtain funding carefully. As with all services, funding an integration initiative will be difficult because it replaces something you already have: custom-built or hard-to-manage single-purpose connections. What's more, no single project will be able to cover the bill. With new e-Business initiatives, however, you might have the chance to start from scratch and get an integration service set up right the first time. You can leverage the investment in e-Business infrastructure for future internal needs. What is critical, however, is that you buy only as much integration as you need to avoid the shock of huge total costs. Then augment these services with more as implementations increase.

Ultimately, integration services are about coordinating business processes and making them consistent. Investments in integration are really investments in maintaining the promises your brand makes about consistency. In other words, integration investments should be justified based on fulfilling the promises of your brand, such as treating customers consistently across business units or across sales and services departments.

Pay special attention to managing third-party integration. Not only are IEI solutions different from internal EAI solutions, but they also require you to have more people focused directly on managing integration of systems you don't own. The speed with which you have to add or change connected business partners could increase the need for flexible IEI approaches. This speed ties directly to time-to-market, another investment justification.

Application Server Layer

The application server layer contains the software that implements business logic within applications, as opposed to the presentation or data access logic. Common examples include in-house, 3/N-Tier Transact applications built on Windows 2000/.NET Server, IBM WebSphere, or BEA WebLogic. Unlike the server OS software discussed in Chapter 6, the application server layer contains more prebuilt application service functions.

Understanding Application Servers

Although the application server market is just emerging, the required functionality is well understood. The features of an application server can be grouped into five major functional areas: execution services, integrity services, gateway services, interaction services, and development or interface tools. Figure 7.8 shows the relationship between these components.

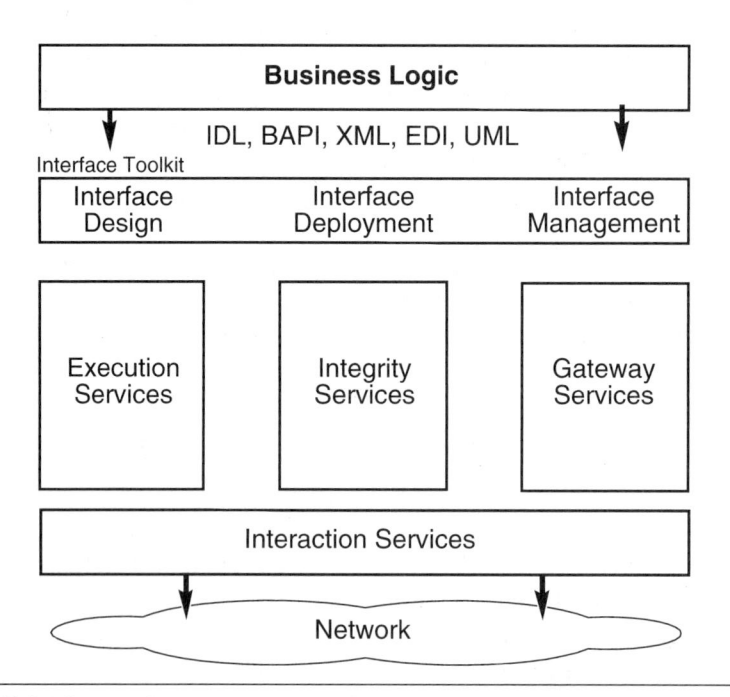

Figure 7.8 The Application Server Architecture

The application server provides a platform upon which applications can be built directly. Most current applications do not use an application server but are built on top of the operating system platform. However, the new N-Tier approach of building application logic on top of a middleware server infrastructure is becoming more common as new applications are built and existing applications are updated.

The rapid ascendance of e-Business, along with the realization that business logic must reside in the server, not the client, has rapidly propelled the application server to center stage. The use of application servers is still in its early stages and accounts for less than 10 percent of new application development and packaged software acquisitions. This situation will change dramatically in a few years, as organizations increasingly adopt component-based development as their default standard and as application software vendors respond to user demands for componentized products. In a few years, applications assembled from built or purchased components, combined with Web-based services and built on compatible component models, will be typical for best-practice IT organizations.

The application server provides a robust, scalable, managed environment for executing processes. For business applications, it provides the same features traditionally provided by the midrange OS, such as process scheduling, memory management, load balancing, high availability, and security. The application server and database manager provide a thick layer on top of the OS, one that augments, extends, and subsumes the services traditionally provided to an application by the OS. From an application perspective, the OS becomes a hidden service layer that supports the application server and database manager by abstracting the hardware.

While the OS remains a necessary service, it becomes less important to the applications. Just as the adoption of relational databases altered the value of midrange operating systems such as VMS and UNIX, so does the adoption of application servers.

The load-balancing and failover features of the application server enable a highly available, highly scalable service to be built using a farm of low-availability, low-performance, and commercial off-the-shelf (COTS) servers. If one of these units fails or goes offline for maintenance, the application server simply moves the executing processes to another system without loss of transactional integrity or the client becoming aware of the change.

Scalability is easy to achieve by simply adding more servers to the farm. Unlike scaling a single image system, the application server can dynamically add or remove additional processing power without bringing down the application. The application server also provides better failover and clustering services than the OS because it has a greater awareness of the application structure and requirements.

Until traditional COTS Reduced Instruction Set Computer (RISC) servers running UNIX become available at the same price and performance ratio, Intel-based systems running Windows 2000/.NET Server are the cost-effective choice for application server platforms. Linux on an Intel-based server could serve this purpose, too. However, organizations are less likely to choose Linux over the widely accepted and well-understood Windows 2000/.NET Server operating system.

Choosing Application Servers

The application server is one of the fastest growing software markets, with dozens of products—each claiming to be the best. Like all rapid-growth markets, boom will lead to bust as vendors are acquired, switch markets, or go out of business. IT organizations must become adept at making strategic platform selections that balance the immediate need of application developers for a feature-rich product with the longer-term need of infrastructure developers for durable and useful platforms. Infrastructure developers must be pragmatic and recognize that some tactical projects are best accomplished with a specific tool. Application developers should take a broader view and realize that many rushed projects become essential to the business and have a much longer life span than anticipated.

Infrastructure and application development groups must set aside their differences and work together on these issues. The best solution is to choose an application server that meets *most* needs, rather than seek a product for its architectural or technical silver bullet. Developing a balanced selection scorecard is a crucial step in this process. This scorecard must include long-term criteria such as product viability and standards support, as well as short-term criteria such as product functionality and empirical validation.

No single application server works perfectly for all application classes. So you should segment your selection requirements by infrastructure pattern. For example, a 1-Tier Transact (host) pattern application server standard might work best for something like CICS, because maturity and in-house experience are important. The 2-Tier Transact standard works best for something like SilverStream, because time to market is essential but scalability is not. The 3/N-Tier Transact standard might work best for something like WebLogic, because transactional processing, high volume, and long-term viability are critical.

Selection criteria for application servers should cover the essential features. Use the 80/20 rule to determine whether the product meets the 80 percent of your needs that are critical. Establish that the product is fit for its intended purpose, rather than attempting to prove some elusive technical superiority. The following sections discuss the various balanced selection criteria.

Product and Vendor Viability

The economics of the software industry give enormous advantage to the perceived early market leaders, which allows them to accelerate away from competitors. The result is two or three viable products and a plethora of dead-end ventures. To avoid ending up with a dead-end platform over the next few years, your selection criteria must establish a short list of the application servers most likely to become market leaders or the immediate market followers. The following are some of the criteria you should use to establish this short list:

- Market share. Estimate the current market share of the product and the recent growth rate, both in dollars and customers.

- Financial strength. Evaluate the current market capitalization and net profit of the vendor.

- Strategic importance. Consider the importance of the product to the vendor's business strategy. If this is the vendor's only product, it will be highly important. If the vendor has a range of products, the importance will depend on the strategic direction of the company.

- Road map. Assess the business and technical viability of the vendor's two- to three-year road map.

Standards

To be truly adaptive, your infrastructure requires well-designed APIs that remain stable over time, that present a high-level abstraction of services, and that hide the details of implementation. The selection criteria should focus on APIs that are exported and used by the application server. Selecting an application server that supports standard APIs provides protection against obsolescence, because the product can more easily be traded out for the eventual market leader. In a rapidly shifting market, buying into a proprietary technology that fails to become a standard can lock your organization into a particular vendor. Infrastructure developers must plan an exit strategy, such as wrapping these technologies and exporting a generic API. Specifically, you should evaluate API standards for Microsoft .NET or Java, since these two are the most widely adopted standards. This evaluation also applies to the integration layer, and not just to application server layer solutions.

Messaging transport. Business Quality Messaging (BQM) is a cornerstone of *n*-tier architecture. The de facto standard is IBM MQSeries, with MSMQ prevailing in the Microsoft world. Application servers that do not support these standards should be eliminated from *n*-tier patterns.

Component architecture. The most widely used component architectures are Microsoft MTS/COM+ and Enterprise JavaBeans (EJB)/CORBA. EJB is unlikely to provide transparent portability between application servers. However, it will be far simpler to migrate between EJB-based architectures than between proprietary architectures or from proprietary architectures to EJB. Choosing an EJB or COM architecture reduces the impact of selecting a dead-end product. Just as important, people with COM or EJB skills are more easily found, or more rapidly cross-trained, than for other component architectures.

Client interfaces. The drive to integrate e-Commerce applications with voice-centered call centers and other points of interaction (POI) requires support for multiple communications channels, such as Web servers and browsers (HTTP), computer telephony integration (CTI), and Wireless Application Protocol (WAP).

Database drivers. The application server must communicate with the most common databases. Support for ODBC or JDBC ensures this communication. However, native drivers often provide more flexibility.

Important Features

When evaluating application servers, you should look for strengths in each of the following five major functional areas: execution services, integrity services, gateway services, integration services, and development tools.

Execution Services. Look for the following capabilities:

- Concurrency. How well does the application server manage cocurrency, thread management, reuse, error recovery, memory management, and garbage collection?

- Load balancing. How well does the application server balance load across clusters? Does it use simple round robin or dynamic load scheduling? Does it provide server affinity for long-lived objects? How is load balancing tuned to suit the application? Does the application server present one image across the cluster? Is load management internal or external to the application server?

- Failover. How well does the application server cluster handle the failure of a node? Is failover transparent to operational staff, or does it require intervention? Is it transparent to the client?

- Error handling. How much error handling does the application server provide?

Integrity Services. Look for the following capabilities:

- Security. In terms of authentication and authorization services, which security APIs are provided: lightweight directory access protocol (LDAP) or public key infrastructure (PKI)?

- Transactional. How does the application server enforce transactional integrity (such as ACID—atomicity, consistency, isolation, and durability)? Is this performed automatically or left to the programmer? Which transactional APIs does the server support?

Gateway Services. Look for the following capabilities:

- Database connectivity. Which database interfaces does the application server provide? Does the application server use native drivers or JDBC/ODBC drivers? Although JDBC/ODBC drivers are now comparable in performance, native drivers might provide more functionality.

- Messaging services. Which messaging services (such as MQSeries, MSMQ, and JMS) does the application server support?

- Client interfaces. How many points of interaction does the application server support? Does it support Web servers or browsers (HTTP), wireless devices (WAP), IVR devices (CTI), standard Win 32 devices, smart cards, or Internet appliances?

- Server connectivity. How does the application server interface with other environments, such as CICS, legacy applications, and other application servers? The introduction of the EAI server has greatly reduced the importance of extensive connectivity features and these attributes can now be considered a low priority.

Integration Services. Look for the following capabilities:

- Connection protocols. Which protocols are used to connect the application server to the client: RPC, IIOP, or RMI?
- Connection styles. Which connection styles does the server provide: conversational, fire-and-forget, or publish/subscribe?

Development Tools. Look for the following capabilities:

- What integrated delivery environment (IDE) can you use with the application server?
- Is it easy to find developers skilled in this IDE?
- How quickly can developers be cross-trained in this IDE? Experts say this will be an area where vendors will attempt to lock users into their products.

Empirical Validation

Using desk-based evaluations to predict the success of a product can be limiting. The balanced selection criteria must show hard evidence that the application server will meet the organizational requirements and that it is truly fit for this purpose. As Year 2000 issues demonstrated, architectural decisions can linger well beyond the life span imagined by designers. Developing a selection scorecard that balances immediate development requirements against long-term viability decreases the probability of selecting a dead-end application server platform. Here are some factors to consider:

- Reference sites. Interview reference sites that have similar requirements to see how well the product actually fits the requirements.
- Scalability. What tangible evidence demonstrates that the product will scale to meet the needs of foreseeable projects, in terms of transaction rate and the number of concurrent clients?
- Vendor performance. How well can the vendor provide support services?
- Component sources. Who can supply off-the-shelf components to run on this application server? Is your only choice the application server vendor, or does a range of independent software vendors supply them?

- People. How easily can skilled people be recruited? How quickly can people be trained?

.NET versus J2EE

When the application server market was in its early growth stage and crowded with products, business units tended often to select incompatible products for different projects. Today, organizations must choose either Microsoft Windows 2000/.NET Server or J2EE as their primary enterprise EAI or framework. You can find significant architectural similarity across both camps.

The promise of object-oriented, component-based development has been around for a long time, but the potential to deliver on that promise has only recently become a practical reality with contemporary application servers. Both Windows 2000/.NET Server and J2EE provide viable, practical, scalable, and robust application server architectures that can support integrated, object-oriented, and component-based application development.

Organizations must make a clear choice of a primary application server platform, even though they typically need to deal with more than one.

Microsoft's .NET application server is built into the Windows 2000/.NET Server software. Microsoft's application server platform now supports the development and use of software components written in most common programming languages. It is generally lower in cost and is available for use on any Intel-based server hardware platform.

Selecting the J2EE option means choosing from more than 20 vendors of J2EE application server products, knowing that some of these products are not 100-percent compatible with one another. As of this writing, BEA's WebLogic and IBM's WebSphere were the two most widely used Java application servers. The J2EE application server architecture is supported on most hardware platforms, including UNIX, mainframe, and Intel-based servers. However, this architecture generally costs more and requires that all software components be developed using the Java programming language.

In the early stages of deployment, the amount of code that is built or acquired to actually run on the default application server of choice is often significantly less than that required to integrate the newly created application server island with existing, monolithic applications and databases. As more new componentized application development, acquisition, and deployment occurs, the application server island will steadily expand to consume an increasing proportion of enterprise and line-of-business applications. Eventually, most applications become component assemblies running on the application server with only vestigial remnants of legacy applications and data sources.

Evaluation Criteria

Evaluating each component model platform against specific criteria weighted to corporate goals should drive effective choice. This assessment should include evaluating platform features, organizational skills, existing software assets, package solutions, and client strategies. It is important to note that a choice must be made.

Reliability, Scalability, and Availability. Because of Java's ability to run on a wide array of devices and operating systems, it has been viewed as having a more robust scale-up story than the Microsoft environment. However, many new application needs should be addressed by scale-out capabilities, not scale-up.

Integrating Existing Assets. Because no choice exists in a vacuum, it is important to evaluate both Windows 2000/.NET Server and J2EE on their ability to integrate with existing applications.

Microsoft has provided integration facilities for host systems via Microsoft Host Integration Server. Similar capabilities exist for other .NET-compliant languages and products. In addition, .NET and J2EE platforms have evolving integration stories based on XML. Microsoft appears to have an edge in XML technologies with the creation of SOAP and integration of XML support into its VisualStudio.NET and C# language.

Java's integration comes through the J2EE Connector API and vendor-specific integration technologies. Thus, the evaluation of Java platforms is specific to vendors. Sun plans to meet Microsoft's edge in XML technologies through electronic business XML from OASIS (ebXML) and by integrating XML into Java. Organizations that have large quantities of Windows-based application assets, such as Microsoft Exchange, COM+ components, and Microsoft SQL Server, are unlikely to find efficient integration with Java technologies.

Available Skills. Aside from the purely technical criteria, the most important issue in evaluating the two platforms is the existing pool of developers and the development strategy moving forward. Will the company rely on contract or outsourced development? Are existing developers skilled with Windows 2000/.NET Server and object-oriented programming (OOP) languages and techniques? Are their skills still focused on COBOL mainframe applications? How much of the future application load can be handled by software packages to reduce the number of skilled developers on staff?

Organizations with minimal OOP expertise should expect to spend six to twelve months developing these skills. This need for development will affect both the Windows 2000/.NET Server and Java platforms, though .NET provides easier entry paths, such as Visual Basic. Java tools, like Versata and Oracle Developer, continue to emerge, providing high-order abstractions and reducing the barrier to entry. However, these tools have smaller pools of available developers and lack the backing of university programs.

Java provides the simplicity of a single language that can be used on all platforms, for all applications, and in varying flavors such as Java, Enterprise Java Beans (EJB), and JavaScript. The advantage of Java lies in its ability to move developers between projects and hardware platforms. On the other hand, Windows 2000/.NET Server provides support for a broad variety of languages, and the new Common Language Runtime makes language choice a moot point. This language enables organizations that have developers with mixed skills (such as VB, Java, and COBOL experience) to develop for the platform with a less steep learning curve.

Creating a Map

Evaluation criteria such as these can provide a rational context in which to assess the two component architecture platforms. This choice must not be made in isolation, but must include the other architectural decisions behind adaptive infrastructures, such as networking and hardware standards.

Both Windows 2000/.NET Server and J2EE are viable alternatives. Most large organizations will need to deal with both to some degree and in some manner. However, both are not equally viable alternatives for any particular organization. On the contrary, a wrong choice can impair the ability of the enterprise's IT infrastructure to support competitive business requirements. An organization cannot reasonably expect to avoid a choice by shunning both or by trying to adopt both equally. The avoidance tactic amounts to having no middleware strategy at all. The adoption of two standards dissipates resources and impairs the effectiveness of both infrastructure and applications for the enterprise.

The choice of Windows 2000/.NET Server or J2EE represents a major fork in the road for each enterprise. The subsequent array of detailed product choices, despite significant overlaps, is substantially different, depending on the primary choice. Choosing .NET makes various Windows 2000/.NET Server products from Microsoft and other vendors the more likely direction for further infrastructure component product selections. A J2EE decision necessitates choosing from more than 20 J2EE-compliant application server vendor products and numerous Java-related secondary products.

Choosing the application server framework does not necessarily dictate product choices for other infrastructure layers. Both can be used with any Web server or database. In principle, .NET can be used as the primary application platform along with non-Microsoft database server software and Web-server software running on Linux. Similarly, choosing J2EE does not preclude using Microsoft SQL 2000 or Microsoft Internet Information Server.

In practice, however, the primary application server platform choice will typically lead to related infrastructure choices. Secondary choices motivated by a primary choice of J2EE will tend toward UNIX platforms, but a .NET choice implies a more substantial enterprise role for Windows 2000/.NET Server and Microsoft SQL Server 2000.

The decision for either .NET or J2EE as the primary application server platform foundation for the enterprise is crucial, with long-lasting consequences. Therefore, this choice should not be made casually, implicitly, or inadvertently by default. Every IT user organization should devote sufficient resources to a careful study and evaluation of both alternatives and make a clear choice. They should base that choice on explicit criteria individually evaluated and weighted by their relevance to the business requirements, as well as organizational constraints of the enterprise for which the choice is to be made.

User organizations must recognize that they must make an explicit choice of either .NET or J2EE as the primary application server platform framework for the enterprise. Then they must thoroughly study and evaluate both alternatives based on clear criteria weighted appropriately for the business requirements, capabilities, and constraints of the enterprise.

Refining Patterns in the Application Server Layer

Application servers enable 3/N-Tier Transact pattern designs and provide significant flexibility and scalability benefits beyond other transact pattern architectures. As such, this layer is absolutely critical to the design of this pattern, as reflected in Table 7.4.

Application servers provide substantial business benefits, but only when they are used effectively. Enterprises should move promptly to adopt best practices in the deployment and use of application servers to

Table 7.4 Application Server Layer Pattern Summary Chart

Layer or Service Component	Web Publish	3/N-Tier Transact
Application Server Layer		
Application Server	4	1

Key
1=Critical, All Cases
2=Highly Recommended, Most Cases
3=Optional, Some Cases
4=Optional, Fewer Cases

maximize benefits. Early adopters can gain a competitive advantage by employing these best practices.

The choice between .NET and J2EE is crucial. Larger organizations may be forced to support both. If so, restrict the J2EE version of the 3/N-Tier Transact pattern to a single integrated set of products used repeatedly, and be selective in the choice of J2EE-compliant products. Architecture standards will pay off only if amplified by technology and product (and even configuration) standards. This idea is the essence of the pattern design refinement process.

Early indications show many organizations are using application servers as just another way to build traditional monolithic applications without exploiting the opportunities application servers offer for more agile, lower-cost infrastructure. This trend will continue for the next few years, as IT organizations only gradually master and adopt best practices more suited to application servers and related technologies. Until then, early adopters have an ideal opportunity to gain a competitive advantage by adopting best practices for 3/N-Tier application deployment using application servers. Figure 7.9 shows a typical 3/N-Tier architecture.

Guidelines

Use the following guidelines when working with the application server layer.

Adopt 3/N-Tier Approaches. The most important best practice required to exploit application servers is to make a 3/N-Tier (not 2-Tier) server infrastructure the foundation for new application deployment. As shown in Figure 7.9, the 3/N-Tier Transact pattern essentially deploys applications across at least three distinct logical tiers of infrastructure.

- Presentation tier (Web or page server)
- Application tier (application server)
- Data access tier (database server)

Select a default platform. Use either Microsoft Windows 2000/.NET Server's built-in application server or a specific vendor's Java J2EE application server product as the default platform for new business logic development. Despite promises of write once, run everywhere and of attempted J2EE standardization, nontrivial applications are nowhere near 100-percent portable across Java application servers from different vendors. Regardless of whether you choose a Java or a Windows built-in application server, you should adopt only one vendor's product as the enterprise default.

Select a default integration server. A default integration server and related tools such as adapters and connectors can be used to create a complete integration infrastructure around the selected application server. To be effective, the 3/N-Tier Transact pattern infrastructure must supply integration components that are designed separately from the application server itself, even if vendors and products increasingly suggest that one product can do both. An application server is a critical core component of a modern adaptive infrastructure, but it alone is not sufficient. Linkage to legacy applications and business partners requires complementary integration services architecture and related infrastructure component choices as well. Refer to the "Integration Layer" section in this chapter for more details.

Limit compromises. Having chosen a default application server and complementary integration products, the fourth best practice is to limit compromises of these defaults to the absolute minimum. Ideally, you should always use default infrastructure choices. In practice, compro-

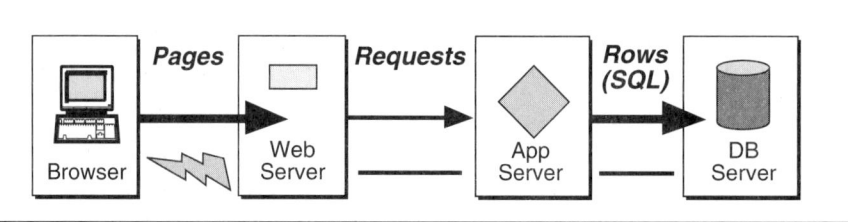

Figure 7.9 Contemporary 3/N-Tier Application Infrastructure

mises are sometimes necessary. Exceptions to the default choices should be strictly limited to only those instances where a clear business case can be made for an exception.

Exploit all opportunities. The prior best practices enable this one, which is to fully exploit all the opportunities that the 3/N-Tier Transact pattern offers, thereby gaining increased reliability, scalability, multiple POI support, business logic component reuse and externalization, business agility, and reduced time to market. The best way to reach your goals is to define the business benefits of each new application server deployment explicitly beforehand and to monitor results to verify that goals have been achieved.

Ensure reusability. Use a single approach to 3/N-Tier Transact pattern application servers to improve reusability, including reuse of business logic across multiple points of interaction. To achieve reuse at the highest level, program real APIs into applications from the start. This programming is a key differentiator between 3/N-Tier and 2-Tier architectures.

Buy (don't build). Not only should you avoid building your own application server, you should also purchase applications that avoid this need. While most applications are not yet on separate application servers, this trend will increase significantly over time—making it easier to buy applications that fit the infrastructure strategy.

Use scale-out architecture. For application server–based applications to scale, they must participate emphatically in a scale-out design for the 3/N-Tier Transact pattern. Build applications so that multiple application servers can be used interchangeably.

Avoid mixing application component logic with integration and presentation logic. Many developers say they're using 3/N-Tier architecture, when they're really still creating monolithic applications using 2-Tier architectures. Education and leadership are required for success. To achieve the full benefits of a 3/N-Tier Transact pattern approach, you must eliminate this mixing of logic. This step toward a more agile, component-based applications infrastructure is crucial. However, separation also provides direct business benefits. For example, you can more easily choose best-of-breed products for each tier and lower costs by using scale-out server hardware for the presentation and application tiers. Separation also allows better management of multiple points of interaction (POIs) for users. With this pattern architecture, it is much easier to support user access from various devices, including cell phones, personal digital assistants, and other "thin" devices, as well as from standard Web browsers and other PC-based clients.

Issues

Consider the following issues when working with this layer:

- Most applications, in practice, tend to mix business logic with presentation logic—thus reverting to the 2-tier transactional model. Avoid this tendency to take full advantage of the application server infrastructure.

- Many application server products are aimed at the Web exclusively and limit multi-POI support (only vaporware/vision stage). These products are not really being used as anything but Web application servers. They are not separate N-Tier application servers.

Summary

Now you understand the key functional components that contribute to an adaptive infrastructure. This chapter focused on solutions of particular value within the three main functional layers:

- In the database layer, components such as database servers and middleware are essential to the 3/N-Tier Transact pattern, and they are highly useful for Web Publish applications as well. For the 3/N-Tier Transact pattern, use direct integration with internal databases or applications to eliminate duplication. For the Web Publish pattern, establish a single data-replication solution based on your current data warehousing patterns, to avoid problems with timeliness or latency.

- In the integration layer, use of integration servers and related components is essential for 3/N-Tier Transact, but these components have less relevance in Web Publish patterns. For ultimate reusability, integration layer components should be bundled and offered to your organization as a formal and distinct Transactional Integration service.

- In the application server layer, use of application servers is becoming an essential component of most 3/N-Tier Transact applications. When used correctly, application servers can provide an important competitive advantage, since many organizations are still using them to build traditional monolithic applications without exploiting their ability to deliver a more agile, lower-cost infrastructure.

Following the basic precepts outlined in this chapter should help you pick the best-of-breed solutions for the functional parts of your infrastructure. The next chapter examines the presentation, API, and management layers of the Adaptive Infrastructure Platform.

Chapter 8

Interface and Management Components

This chapter provides details and criteria for designing the final layers of an adaptive infrastructure. Particular components in each layer are of special importance to infrastructure planners:

- In the presentation layer, components such as Web servers, wireless servers, and voice systems provide flexibility in presenting information to customers and other users.

- In the API layer, components such as Inter-APIs and Infra-APIs do the most to make applications reusable and to accelerate time-to-market.

- In the management layer, various components and techniques help ensure consistent delivery of contracted service levels within your organization.

This information can help you refine pattern designs so that they include the right mix of presentation, API, and management components. For a complete list of infrastructure components, including those used in both enterprise and e-Business computing, see Appendix A.

Presentation Layer

The presentation layer includes all the server-based components used to present information to users, including:

- Web servers
- Wireless Application Protocol (WAP) servers, including mobile application servers (MASs), Wireless Application Server Providers (WASPs), and Wireless Application Protocol (WAP) gateways
- Wireless services that communicate information to wireless devices, including cell phones, PDAs, and mobile computers
- Interactive Voice Response (IVR) systems, including speech recognition

Each of these components is discussed in greater detail on the following pages. Client-side components in the presentation layer are not covered in this book. These components include desktop PCs with appropriate Web-browser software or running "smart PC" applications, PDAs, and other wireless devices, as well as wired and wireless telephones.

Web Server

A Web server is a combination of:

- An HTTP listener/gateway
- A Hypertext Markup Language (HTML)–only Web/application server that offers a mix of Web-specific presentation services and e-Business logic

As discussed in Chapter 6, scale-out is the architectural trend in Web servers. Farms of smaller, less-expensive Commercial Off the Shelf (COTS) servers can be used to deliver Web services instead of more-expensive high-performance systems. Servers configured in farms work well for applications with limited state management requirements. Extra capacity can be added quickly or incrementally by integrating more servers. Farms enable organizations to minimize business risk by starting with small, inexpensive configurations and adding resources as the demand rises, rather than risking capital on an expensive large SMP cluster before demand proves itself.

Wireless Application Protocol (WAP) Server

In this new world beyond e-Business, information value increases in direct proportion to the speed of its delivery. Ever-present wireless access can supply critical information to mobile employees, accelerating business decisions and processes. Wireless access can also deliver information to customers, accelerating buying decisions or providing services in place at the right time. However, users can be promiscuous in their use of devices, working across multiple wireless platforms, including pagers, cell phones, palm computers, and laptops that use different operating systems, display types, markup languages, scripting capabilities, and wireless networks. Indeed, within a few years, half of business users will be mobile and carry several devices at one time. Consequently, best-practice enterprises must design for mobility, developing strategies that integrate the plethora of user interfaces and wireless networks. Tools available for doing this are summarized on the following pages.

Mobile Application Server (MAS)

As the wireless points of interaction (POI) market has emerged in the last few years, the WAP standard has led to the emergence of new wireless-focused, presentation middleware servers, also called WAP Servers. Organizations use these tools to take advantage of the new wireless devices by abstracting the device and network constraints from the core business logic of applications and using multiple POIs—for example, Web, WAP, and voice take advantage of the unique strengths of each medium.

A more complete mobile application server (MAS) approach is still evolving that will support WAP as well as other current and emerging wireless standards. As illustrated in Figure 8.1, a MAS helps you create business applications that can be viewed or navigated by many different types and models of client devices.

The main function of wireless middleware is to take presentation-neutral business logic, such as Extensible Markup Language (XML), from an application server and translate it into presentation-specific XML, while managing the state of the interaction. Typical presentation formats can include:

- Hypertext Markup Language (HTML)
- Wireless Markup Language (WML), formerly called Handheld Device Markup Language (HDML)
- Voice Markup Language (VoxML)

```
                    Business Logic
         ┌──────┬──────┬──────┬──────┐
         ▼      ▼      ▼      ▼      ▼
┌─────────────────────────────────────────┐
│ APIs: HTML, LDAP, OLE DB, MC SQL, XML   │
│      COM, CORBA, EJB, POP/IMAP          │
├──────────────────────┬──────────────────┤
│ Load Balancing and   │ Management       │
│ Failover             │ and Reporting    │
│ Session Mangement    │ Tools            │
│ Security/Authentication│                │
├──────────────────────┼──────────────────┤
│ Push Engine          │ Development      │
│                      │ and Testing      │
│ Personalization Engine│ Environment     │
├──────────────────────┴──────────────────┤
│ Device Adapters: WAP, Palm, SMS, RIM,   │
│        HTTP, cHTML, HDML, Voice         │
└─────────────────────────────────────────┘
```

Figure 8.1 Wireless Middleware Capabilities

Other services provided by wireless middleware include data compression, encryption or protocol translation, and a development environment.

Emerging wireless application middleware satisfies requirements to write business logic once and have it displayed many times on a variety of wireless devices. Wireless middleware provides a development environment to invoke and display application business logic through XML on various devices, while adding device-specific presentation logic. Most available products, primarily offered by smaller, emerging vendors, are server-based applications that can be accessed by wireless thin clients, such as WAP phones. Other vendors offer MAS solutions for creating client applications that can operate in disconnected notebooks and some of the new-generation personal digital assistants (PDAs).

Wireless Application Server Providers (WASPs)

A significant number of organizations plan to use wireless application server providers (WASPs) or systems integrators when building new wireless applications. WASPs generally provide systems integration and development, hosting services, MAS tools, and some prebuilt applications.

Outsourcers can provide rapid application development and minimize skill investments in transitional technologies. However, users should avoid a wireless hosting strategy that is completely separate from their existing Web hosting strategy. Furthermore, adopting a WASP proprietary MAS solution with limited industry support could constrain future sourcing options. Most WASPs eventually will embrace MAS products from the leading application server vendors. Figure 8.2 shows the wireless vendor market.

Wireless Application Protocol (WAP) Gateways

While the MAS server encompasses all mobile devices and includes numerous tools to develop and manage a multi-POI application, the Wireless Application Protocol (WAP) gateway is a much more primitive middleware server, primarily used by the wireless carriers to enable data interaction with WAP-compatible mobile phones.

WAP gateways perform the lower layer of translation for wireless phone applications or any personal digital assistant (PDA) with a WAP browser. Usually, the WAP gateway is located in the cellular carrier infrastructure at the intersection of the carriers' cellular network, and the Internet. Corporations do not need to have their own WAP gateway. However, security-conscious organizations might also put a WAP gateway in the demilitarized zone (DMZ) to avoid the security hole that exists when encryption protocols are changed in the WAP gateway. This limitation has been largely eliminated in WAP 2.0. Due to this development, as well as the evolution of MAS, WAP gateways will virtually disappear from the enterprise infrastructure over the next few years.

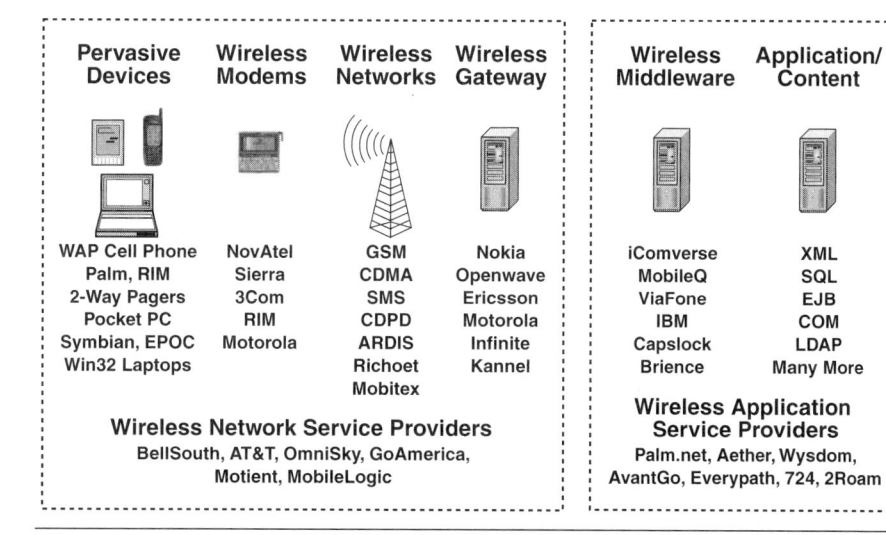

Pervasive Devices	Wireless Modems	Wireless Networks	Wireless Gateway	Wireless Middleware	Application/ Content
WAP Cell Phone Palm, RIM 2-Way Pagers Pocket PC Symbian, EPOC Win32 Laptops	NovAtel Sierra 3Com RIM Motorola	GSM CDMA SMS CDPD ARDIS Richoet Mobitex	Nokia Openwave Ericsson Motorola Infinite Kannel	iComverse MobileQ ViaFone IBM Capslock Brience	XML SQL EJB COM LDAP Many More
Wireless Network Service Providers BellSouth, AT&T, OmniSky, GoAmerica, Motient, MobileLogic				**Wireless Application Service Providers** Palm.net, Aether, Wysdom, AvantGo, Everypath, 724, 2Roam	

Figure 8.2 Wireless Vendor Landscape

Wireless Service

To access e-Business applications, wireless devices such as cell phones, PDAs, and laptops require a wireless network infrastructure that connects to the Internet. Many service providers supply this infrastructure, but continued market uncertainty has left some wireless application ideas without appropriate connectivity.

Despite the hype of wireless cellular carriers and the implementation of the WAP standard, cellular networks such as time division multiple access (TDMA), Global System for Mobil Communications (GSM), and code division multiple access (CDMA) remain ill-suited for corporate wireless data. Existing circuit-switched networks are also unsuitable because they are too expensive and lack sufficient bandwidth. Cellular networks won't improve until carriers start rolling out packet networks such as General Packet Radio Service (GPRS) or CDMA 1X. Until then, the alternative mobile wireless networks, such as CDPD from Verizon, ATT, Cingular, and Motient, remain the best source for providing mobile professionals with wireless access to the Web and corporate applications such as e-mail, or for exchanging real-time data from the field.

Wireless network operators are competing for the most densely populated centers, leaving large geographies uncovered. Consequently, the key selection criterion will be whether the wireless network offers a sufficient network footprint where you need it. Organizations requiring a national footprint are likely to be forced to patch together multiple networks, but they must also realize that not all users will be covered. Network costs can vary from $30 to $60 per user for unlimited usage, but you can also find discounts on bulk usage and off-peak system-to-system telemetry. The advent of the 2.5 generation (2.5G) packet cellular networks such as GPRS and CDMA 1X will drive incumbent wireless networks to discount heavily to remain competitive.

Domestic cellular voice carriers are currently building these networks and they expect to offer speeds up to 144 Kbps to replace existing circuit switched networks. However, actual speeds will remain between 40 and 80 Kbps without substantial price premiums, and coverage will be spotty for a few years until these networks are completely built.

Packet-switched networks allow carriers to offer per-bit or fixed-price charges instead of per-second charges, making cellular networks more attractive for business data. Bluetooth technology will allow cell phones to act as modems for laptops and PDAs, consolidating mobile wireless modems and service in one device, and thereby simplifying management.

Figure 8.3 shows the anticipated upgrade paths for next-generation technology.

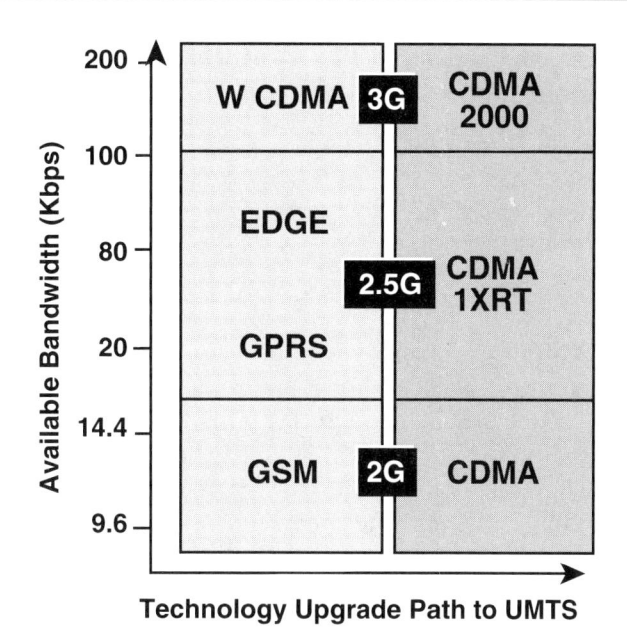

Figure 8.3 Technology Upgrade Paths

After 2.5G networks arrive, carriers plan to migrate to a third-generation (3G) standard. Original plans were to merge the disparate radio technologies into one worldwide 3G standard, called Universal Mobil Telecommunications System (UMTS). However, now it is more likely that two standards will coexist—WCDMA and CDMA2000—although both are based on the Code Division Multiple Access (CDMA) technology.

Despite the hype around 3G services, much of the technology required for data services over wireless networks is being implemented in 2.5G. The move to 3G will merely consolidate the voice and data networks and provide greater bandwidth, though not the originally proposed 2Mbps per user. Due to unresolved technical problems and the massive capital requirements for 3G networks, meaningful 3G services might not appear for another five years in the Americas, and no sooner than two years in parts of Europe and Asia. Japan remains the exception. However, its smaller geography, Nippon Telephone and Telegraph's (NTT) market dominance, and DoCoMo's iMode data services all set Japan apart from the global market.

Key Issues in Wireless: Location Tracking, Marketing, and Privacy

Two developments have had a major impact on domestic wireless service in the United States: the FCC-mandated Communications Assistance for Law Enforcement Act (CALEA) and the Global Positioning System (GPS).

With GPS, the ability to find wireless users and equipment anywhere has improved dramatically. However, this intrusive technology brings with it both personal privacy issues and new opportunities for direct sales and marketing.

The CALEA mandate requires all cellular carriers to have the ability to resolve a caller's location within 50 to 300 meters anywhere in North America when they make an emergency 911 phone call. In the near future, these location services will become new commercial product offerings available from existing cellular carriers.

In the commercial version of this service, when using E911-enabled phones, user location is transmitted to a wireless application service provider (WASP) each time the user enters a new geographic area. Ninety-five percent of all new handsets must have automatic locator information (ALI) capabilities by 2002. While this approach works for direct advertising, it is not a good solution for real-time monitoring. GPS service must be added to feed more accurate position data on demand. In this case, GPS provides positional data and conventional cellular carriers transmit that data back to a data-processing center that tracks the history of the user, vehicle or equipment.

Wireless location technologies could affect commercial operations in several ways. Most apparently is the business-to-consumer (B2C) space where location and demographics can be combined into marketing efforts. These technologies similarly affect the business-to-business (B2B) space, because mobile users can order supplies and materials directly from the field. This technology is important for big utilities, transportation, and warehousing companies in which knowing a customer's location means shorter delivery time, lower costs, and better customer relations. Location services can be easily added to wireless

Key Issues in Wireless: Location Tracking, Marketing, and Privacy *(continued)*

application service provider (WASP) product offerings, whether the location is derived from cell phones or GPS-based sources. The same is true with travel-routing and traffic-rerouting WASP portals.

While privacy is a concern, cellular carriers have no choice in implementing the FCC-mandated locator service. The service identifies the E911 caller's location for transmission to the public safety access center (PSAC) in an emergency. In this way, it is analogous to the automatic locator information data currently available to PSACs from terrestrial landline phone services. In both the US and Canada, users can control whether this data is available for commercial applications.

Voice

Voice data is carried by the telecommunications infrastructure, including PBXs, phone sets on premises, and services from long distance providers such as AT&T or MCI, or local phone companies such as regional Bell operating companies (RBOCs) or posts, telephones, and telegraphs (PTTs). While this book does not focus on the details of voice infrastructure, most B2C initiatives rely heavily on voice infrastructure for telemarketing and sales. By definition, e-Business has expanded interactivity beyond person-to-person to encompass more of a person-to-system paradigm, including Web browsers connecting over a phone line to Internet Web sites, or even XML Web service to XML Web service. Even voice interaction has become less person-to-person and more person-to-machine, as discussed in the next section on interactive voice response (IVR) and speech recognition.

Today, we see considerable movement toward merging voice and data infrastructure at the networking level. Nearly half of Global 2000 companies already have a converged staff responsible for both voice and data at some level, and momentum is building for converged cross-platform solutions that include voice, video, and data. Already, nearly half of large enterprises are testing Voice Over Internet (VoIP) systems.

However, despite continued vendor claims about their expertise and the maturity of their products, we see a continuing gap between reality and hype. Internal cross-pollination between voice and data disciplines remains a work in progress, with business units consolidating at the management level but operating independently at the worker level. The expertise offered by systems integrators, resellers, and distributors is even less mature since these companies basically rely on the vendors.

Within a few years, several top-tier vendors will offer Internet Protocol (IP) telephony for large enterprises. However, it will be some time before companies start to deploy converged solutions that enjoy the same degree of user acceptance and reliability, with a return on investment (ROI) that is comparable to existing PBX voice systems.

Interactive Voice Response (IVR)

Voice interaction is increasingly automated, with callers talking not to call center agents but to automated, interactive voice response (IVR) systems. In the United States, IVRs have been a call-center staple for more than a decade, and they have provided a way to automate customer service for almost as long. Most organizations had already invested in these solutions long before the Web-centric e-Business phenomenon arrived.

These devices automatically pre-answer calls, ask the caller for an account number or personal identification number (PIN). Then they allow the caller to access information automatically and to conduct transactions by keying in phone selections. Increasingly, these transactions are conducted through speech recognition, discussed later in this chapter.

Compared to live agents, IVR systems significantly lower the cost of providing service to callers. In addition, by identifying the caller through IVR, businesses can route calls to skilled call-center agents or knowledge workers, making person-to-person interaction more focused and effective.

Ultimately, building a network of geographically independent response centers will enable the integration of voice, data, and multimedia responses from multiple sources. For example, a Tokyo-based customer seeking support might be greeted by an agent in Los Angeles.

Simultaneously, the value of this customer assistance can be augmented by displaying a technical illustration and initiating a live chat session with an engineer in Munich.

The IVR concept has changed little over the years. An IVR port is an electronic customer service agent. The port identifies the caller by requesting an appropriate identification number and PIN and responds with appropriate information, while also acting as a portal for information. This capability results in intelligent call-routing to the appropriate live agent. Therefore, no person-to-person interaction needs to occur at all.

Profile data from customer relationship management (CRM) systems will increasingly be used to identify high-value customers and provide them with special skills or shorter wait times. For example, platinum-grade customers can be provided with premium service. Critical IVR technical issues include platform evolution, CRM integration, and ease of user management.

Global adoption of wireless devices such as mobile phones, PDAs, and two-way pagers has increased call-center traffic and increased customer expectations. This situation offers further potential to move these traditional interactions to nontraditional POIs. Voice customers with limited time do not want to wait in long voice queues, but they will opt for IVR self-service, preferably driven by speech recognition or voice portal applications to satisfy the immediate demand.

Wireless PDA applications must be intuitive and secure, with appropriate application programming interfaces (APIs) to the associated CRM profile indexes, so that platinum-grade customers can be presented with a platinum level of service. Then information about the transaction must be captured for reuse by the CRM system.

Speech Recognition

Historically, IVR use by telephone users has involved pressing keys on the phone dial—a decidedly tedious user interface. However, rapid advances in speech recognition technology are helping replace the phone dialing method with quickly recognized voice commands.

Speech recognition technology can translate spoken words or phrases into data queries transmitted through the IVR and then to the appropriate back-end system or database. Data returning from the system is translated into words and the IVR system speaks the requested information back to the caller. This technology is quite different from dictation.

Initially, users of speech-enabled IVR ports speak an instruction in response to a prompt. This response is met by a recognition client or "traffic cop," which hands the communication to a separate server for processing. This server provides load balancing, general health checks, failover services, and finally translation—all in a way that keeps the processing isolated from the host IVR. The user interface, or logic flow, guides the caller through the interaction, allowing a logical conversation that uses natural language.

The design of these applications is often outsourced to either a speech recognition vendor or the IVR partner for application development and integration. Outsourced, speech-enabled voice response will grow into voice portals for small- to medium-sized businesses as vendors start to adopt voice technology to augment Web-based portal infrastructure.

Streamlining IVR into a true information source has been a prime goal of many enterprises, driven by the trend toward self-service and by the goals of reducing costs and extending customer service touch points. Users have accelerated the addition of voice recognition applications and this trend will continue for the foreseeable future.

To implement these systems, enterprises typically rely on a phased approach, initially installing light versions that recognize numbers, letters, and a few common phrases.

These scaled-down versions enable speech recognition for a subset of applications at a comparatively cost-efficient price point. Light versions have the added benefit of easing the organization into the technology gradually, without a significant investment of time and money.

Refining Patterns in the Presentation Layer

Table 8.1 shows how each of the presentation layer components apply to the two main patterns of interest: Web Publish and 3/N-Tier Transact.

Presentation layer components will continue to improve and change as technology rapidly advances. However, as IT budgets tighten, managers will look for lower-cost options in components such as Web servers. Organizations will also move toward scale-out architectures, which allow them to add servers only when needed, thus saving costs and initial resources. Web-based applications will move to a 3/N-Tier architecture, which separates business logic from presentation logic, often using a MAS. The MAS is the critical component for creating and managing mobile applications. The MAS component maximizes reuse and extends the life of applications by isolating user interface, device, and network evolution from core business logic and vice versa.

Until cellular carriers deploy packet networks, alternative mobile wireless networks remain the best way to attain wireless access to the Web and to corporate applications. New FCC mandates have made it possible to find wireless users and equipment anywhere. However, privacy concerns continue to be an issue, as well as an area for commercial opportunities and growth.

As voice capabilities continue to change from person-to-person to person-to-system, a new trend of merging voice and data infrastructures

Table 8.1 Presentation Layer Pattern Summary Chart

Layer or Service Component	Web Publish	3/N-Tier Transact
Presentation Layer:		
Web Server	1	1
WAP Server	4	4
Wireless and Mobile Devices	4	4
Wireless Service	4	3
Voice	3	2
Integrated Voice Response (IVR)	1	1

Key
1 = Critical, All Cases
2 = Highly Recommended, Most Cases
3 = Optional, Some Cases
4 = Optional, Fewer Cases

could provide promising results. Integrated Voice Response (IVR) will remain the way to automate customer service and to lower the cost of providing services while allowing accurate delivery of calls to the appropriate destination. New advances in speech recognition will move IVR to the next level in the years to come.

API Layer

The API interface layer contains application programming interfaces (APIs) that allow advanced integration of applications. As such, this layer is crucial to the success of your organization in developing an adaptive infrastructure for e-Business and beyond. These various APIs expose business logic used within and between applications, as well as expose infrastructure services to application and infrastructure planners.

If applications do not provide APIs, they cannot be reused by other applications, which is the next stage of automation of business processes across corporate boundaries to business partners.

Understanding APIs

Figure 8.4 shows the various software components included in the API interface layer. Table 8.2 shows examples for each type of API.

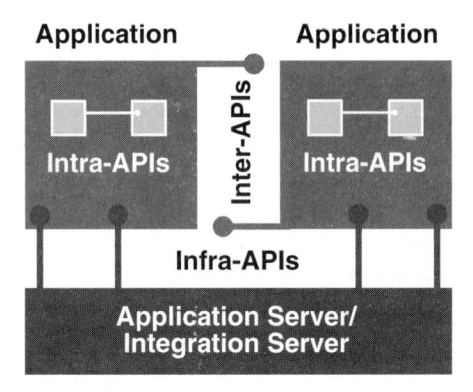

Figure 8.4 Software Components in the API Layer

APIs are separated into a distinct layer to highlight their importance, and not just for the integration or application servers and other infrastructure functions that use them to communicate.

In the past, programmers wrote applications from the business logic all the way down to the OS. Currently, however, most businesses insulate application developers from the OS by at least one layer of packaged infrastructure tools, such as application servers.

However, the application developer must still fill in the gap between the packaged infrastructure and the business logic at the core of the application. In addition, application developers must become adept at tuning and debugging the infrastructure itself.

Just as organizations separated the database administration function from application development in the past, adaptive organizations have now created a role that separates infrastructure development from application development and its corresponding APIs.

Table 8.2 API Types and Examples

Type	Purpose	Examples
Intra-API	Expose business logic used **within** an application	COM+ IDL and EJB IDL
Inter-API	Expose business logic used **between** applications	Rational Rose with a credit card verification service
Infra-API	Expose infrastructure services to application and infrastructure planners	J2EE, LDAP, ODBC

The new role of infrastructure developer relieves application developers from most infrastructure-related responsibilities. It enables each application developer to concentrate on the business analyst role instead of spending a lot of time working as a systems programmer. Moreover, infrastructure developers can focus on developing APIs that work across multiple projects and applications, thus becoming shared infrastructure to applications. This structure leaves application developers free to focus on other things, such as schedules, budgets, and quality.

In this new role, the infrastructure developer can take responsibility for selecting and configuring packaged infrastructures and even start building reusable extensions for it, including macros, custom wizards, code templates, and run-time libraries. This shared set of tools saves application developers time and relieves them of much of the tedium of infrastructure performance tuning and debugging.

Understanding Infra-APIs. Infra-APIs include the low-level technology services that application developers and infrastructure developers use to create business logic, such as security, naming, or object invocation. Increasingly, Infra-APIs and the services they encapsulate are considered industry standards, provided off-the-shelf as a built-in part of application servers, databases, or other components.

However, infrastructure developers still must create certain Infra-APIs for application developers to use in the development process. By this method, application components will actually tap into lower-level application services, which for the application server would include initialization, housekeeping, memory management, and failover. The low-level code has nothing to do with business logic—it just makes business logic execute more effectively.

Examples include container servers and integrated development environments (IDEs) that invoke off-the-shelf services and create new infrastructure services.

Understanding Intra-APIs. Intra-APIs are typically not exposed to other applications. Instead they help business logic communicate within individual applications. Since they are not reused outside a given application, they are created and managed only by the application's developers.

Examples of infrastructure solutions that support this kind of API development include visual modeling tools such as UML tools, which are offered as a built-in part of IDEs and container servers to promote productivity and single-source shopping.

Understanding Inter-APIs. Inter-APIs help business logic communicate between applications. They expose the application business logic that will be used by other applications. Since this logic affects other applications, Inter-APIs should be defined and managed by infrastructure developers. These APIs could include very coarse-grained or large-but-simple services, such as a credit card verification service offered by centralized IT to any business unit application needing the service. Additionally, Inter-APIs could be offered or consumed across business boundaries in an e-Business scenario.

Examples of solutions supporting the development of such Inter-APIs include container server IDEs, visual modeling tools, and adapter software development kits (SDKs).

Political and Organizational Impacts

Application and infrastructure developers must create a formal policy and framework for creating, cataloging, and storing APIs. Infrastructure developers must combine the application requirements and the principals generated by the architectural group, to design efficient, secure, and manageable interfaces.

Organizations must use the division of labor to increase componentized development with suitable architectural oversight to ensure reuse and compatibility. As application infrastructure moves toward component-based infrastructure platforms, businesses must evolve toward a more formal role for infrastructure developers and architects.

A main task for the infrastructure developer is to design the APIs that support multiple applications. Application developers are responsible for designing the Intra-APIs that work only inside of their applications. Developers who aren't solely focused on a single application can manage APIs built for multiple applications.

When managing APIs across multiple applications, several interesting issues arise:

- How do you set up an integration server to leverage Inter-APIs and create a service approach?
- What is the process used to develop APIs that will be used across multiple applications?
- Should infrastructure professionals be involved? The answer is an emphatic "Yes!"
- Most important, who determines whether the functionality behind a given API will be used solely within a single application or across

multiple applications? The former decision would make it an Intra-API for application developers to handle; the latter would make it an Inter-API, which would then be governed by infrastructure developers.

- What is the process to transition an API from an Intra-API to an Inter-API when its use changes to include multiple applications?

Getting infrastructure developers involved will be much more fruitful than allowing application teams to figure it out themselves, because application teams tend to produce an endless variety of APIs, with no central way of managing them all.

In any case, designing successful applications increasingly involves designing not only user interfaces, but programmatic interfaces for simpler, faster, and cheaper integration as well. Programmatic design vastly improves infrastructure, even when it is implemented with moderate success. This logic should become the foundation for a lot of standards-making and infrastructure planning.

Refining Patterns in the API Layer

Table 8.3 shows how the API Layer applies to refined designs in the two key patterns: Web Publish and 3/N-Tier Transact.

More than any other pattern, the 3/N-Tier Transact pattern should be designed from the ground up to offer the best reuse via APIs. Still, applications can use other attributes of 3/N-Tier architecture and not produce good APIs.

To do APIs well, you need to focus on more than just the structure of the application. A key infrastructure focus should be determining which APIs to open up to other applications or other businesses as application or Web services. Further consideration should determine how to manage them over time.

Management Layer

The management layer includes all the components necessary to plan and implement a management system to support your Web applications and services. Planning how to manage your Web applications is crucial. Important steps in this planning process should include using service level management (SLM) techniques, such as Web application monitoring strategies, and openly sharing metrics with your customers.

Table 8.3 API Layer Pattern Summary Chart

Layer or Service Component	Web Publish	3/N-Tier Transact
API Layer:		
APIs	3	2

Key
1 = Critical, All Cases
2 = Highly Recommended, Most Cases
3 = Optional, Some Cases
4 = Optional, Fewer Cases

Service Level Management (SLM)

All parts of an adaptive infrastructure must be managed while they are running, including components, layers, patterns, and services.

For e-Business and beyond, you should be less concerned about products that let you monitor and manage individual components and place more emphasis on service level management (SLM) solutions that let you track service levels for complete sets of components, such as full patterns. Likewise, you should focus on the end-user experience rather than only on metrics for individual systems, network devices, or components.

You can support these service level monitoring tools with tools such as traditional enterprise management systems and centralized event/alert consoles to help fulfill service level agreements (SLAs) and business-defined, rule-based policies. These separate systems management tools can help by reporting on the success or failure of individual components, as well as complete systems, in meeting business targets and assisting in problems, changes, and asset management functions.

As vendor solutions become more sophisticated, they will do a better job of measuring and reporting application response time, which closely matches the end-user experience. In turn, this data will help IT organizations demonstrate to the business how well all the components of the infrastructure work together to deliver business value. However, it is important to manage customer expectations carefully, because much less control usually is involved than application response reports would lead you to believe.

While the market for the management and reporting tools continues to evolve and consolidate over the next few years, IT organizations must evolve as well. The maturity of correlation tools will help bring about meaningful SLA measurements. Eventually, businesses will establish centers of excellence that bring application and infrastructure developers together for adaptive planning of the entire business lifecycle.

Web Application Monitoring Strategy

Service level management for Web-based applications is gaining increased attention, though the choice of available tools remains limited. Regardless, it is important to develop a cohesive monitoring plan for Web applications as soon as possible, to prevent the divergence of processes and technology that plagues distributed environments.

Managing Web applications is currently one of the biggest concerns of IT operations and support organizations. Application management (AM) is typically addressed one to two years after applications are initially deployed; e-Business and Web applications are no different. Most application management is done reactively rather than proactively, without a cohesive management plan or integrated tool choices. While many companies have deployed only their first few Web applications, IT planners in those organizations still have a chance to develop Web application monitoring plans before a multitude of tool choices and process definitions make the plethora of applications unmanageable.

Web management is a multivendor effort. Although vendors continue to pursue integrated AM, in the near future you must cobble together solutions from 10 or more vendors to have a complete AM solution. Such a solution should include response time monitoring, performance monitoring, content validation, content management, security monitoring, and clickstream analysis. Getting these solutions to work for non-Web POIs becomes equally problematic.

Bringing the problem under control requires a phased approach such as the one discussed on the following pages.

Phase 1: Monitor internal availability and response time

Site availability and response time are the first metrics to monitor. Active robots or clients can collect this data from within your DMZ and from internal nodes behind the firewall. These robots can simulate end-user activity along with internal response time. Although availability and response time are critical metrics, fewer than 10 percent of IT groups monitor them.

Availability should be monitored for the home page as well as key services or functions such as the search function or an ad server. At the same time, you should also measure the availability of required protocols such as HTTP and FTP. These metrics are ideal tools when defining service level agreements (SLAs). Most of the tools for measuring these parameters are standalone tools, not integrated with other monitors, but integrated tools should appear soon.

Phase 2: Monitor External Availability

The next step is to address external site availability: monitoring a Web site from the point of view of an external user by simulating page hits from different points on the Web. This activity should be used primarily to identify whether applications are visible to the Internet and also whether the Internet is the cause of slowdowns.

The best way to do this is to monitor site usage from no more than four or five external points. Although it is possible to get data from hundreds of external points, that data primarily identifies bottlenecks in the Internet and is not really useful.

Availability is the key SLA you should consider for external Web monitoring. As part of the SLA, you might agree on the length of time the application should be available to Web-based users. Obviously, you can skip this step for intranet applications but you should consider it for extranet applications.

Even if you can't publish a single response time number because of Internet variability, you will understand more what your customers actually see from different locations if your measurements are more geographically dispersed, or if you hire a service to do this for you. Moreover, these metrics can help you prove that the Internet is the culprit for availability problems, rather than the infrastructure components you have under your control.

In a crowded market, many products are available for this purpose. This situation in turn has helped reduce the purchase price of many solutions, particularly for the core monitoring service.

Phase 3: Monitor Internal Elements

Internal element monitoring tracks underlying hardware and software elements that support the Web application, such as servers, databases, and Web application servers. Initially, these elements should be monitored for availability; you should eventually track their performance as well. Performance monitoring of e-Business Web elements will receive plenty of vendor attention over the next few years, with Web and application servers receiving the most attention.

Phase 4: Monitor Key Transaction Response Time

In the next step, you should start monitoring the response times of key transactions. This assessment should be done first using internal monitors, looking at a fairly comprehensive set of transactions such as buying a product, accessing account information, and receiving a quote. You can also monitor response times externally but only for a subset of four to five transactions, for reasons outlined earlier. It will be critical to compare the different response times gathered from different measurement points with one another, because these comparisons will identify slowdowns more clearly. For example, if you find that the Internet is slow and the DMZ is slow, but internal response times are fast, you might start your analysis at the DMZ.

The ultimate goal is to correlate the data derived from all monitors. This correlation is critical in root-cause analysis and minimizing downtime, yet it is currently a manual process. Even though the correlation analysis is difficult, it increasingly improves customer satisfaction.

A Note on Metrics

You shouldn't measure something just because it can be measured; measure what matters. Many IT organizations report on metrics that are readily available such as router port utilization, packet loss, and network circuit capacity. These metrics often have little relevance to the business, so they confuse the issue and don't help determine how well the infrastructure supports the end user. By focusing on complete end-to-end monitoring of full patterns, rather than single components, you can achieve the important business goal of measuring from the user's perspective and improving the user experience.

SLAs should be agreements, not obligations. Most IT departments are told what level of service they must provide. They try to deliver on that expectation, realizing after the commitment was made that they need more bandwidth, servers, and personnel to deliver the level of support required. When the next year's IT budget is assessed, necessary spending far exceeds what was planned.

In many organizations, spending for network circuits has been increasing at 100 percent per year, so improving service levels has a definite cost. Often, the business does not understand what these costs are, because technical metrics rarely give insight into their value to the business.

Unfortunately, many IT directors haven't had an effective way to predict the network, management, and people costs associated with deploying a new business application. Predictive cost modeling, addressed in Chapter 4, can help you determine these costs early in the application lifecycle, when trade-offs on price/performance are best negotiated.

Most users want end-to-end application response. The good news is that this is getting easier to measure. However, offering these reports to customers contains a hidden danger. The unspoken assumption is that if you can measure something, you can control it. However, this assumption typically doesn't apply to application response time. If you're going to measure application response time, users must see that the component you're guaranteeing is network latency, not the entire end-user experience.

Consider setting up different services for monitoring versus management to make it clear that you are offering measurement, not control. Determine which metrics provide the best business value, and then advertise the metrics to end users as suggested in Table 8.4. For example,

Table 8.4 SLA Metric Categories

	Description	**Collection Point**	**Detail**	**Acceptable Ranges**
Availability	Monitoring the availability of a site's home page and key elements of the application (search function, shopping cart)	Internal agent	Site level Key services	98.0–99.99%
Response Time	Monitoring the response time in user terms for a site's home page, login, and key transactions	Internal agent	Home page User login Key transactions	1–5 seconds 5–10 seconds Varies
User Load	Number of users a site can handle during a set period of time	Load balancer or Web server	Number of user hits on a site home page; number of user transactions executed	Varies

metrics on network delay of critical business links would be more useful than information on individual router port utilization. It's good to know industry best practices, but it's better to have relative measurements that show performance improvements or that exceed stated objectives.

To show the benefits of sharing metrics data with customers, consider this example. One IT organization used to fix critical problems within two hours. When they sent a customer satisfaction survey to internal users, they were rated "fair" for the level of service and attention they provided.

Soon after, the IT group started a feedback system, which involved posting job completion times to an internal Web site for companywide viewing. Initially, this system caused a slip in job completion performance to about three hours. However, when the department polled the user community six months later, customer satisfaction ratings were up, even though absolute performance levels decreased, simply because users knew what to expect. Be prepared to advertise the service levels you track and or control. Show the good and the bad.

Refining Patterns in the Management Layer

Table 8.5 shows the importance of Service Level Management for the two key patterns discussed in this book.

Companies launching Web applications must plan application management proactively. Failure to plan results in fragmented technology, higher management costs, and longer resolution times when failures occur.

Moreover, you shouldn't be afraid to give customers information on performance metrics, even if they are below the industry average. Offer-

Table 8.5 Management Layer Pattern Summary Chart

Layer or Service Component	Web Publish	3/N-Tier Transact
Management Layer:		
Service Level Management (SLM)	2	2

Key
1 = Critical, All Cases
2 = Highly Recommended, Most Cases
3 = Optional, Some Cases
4 = Optional, Fewer Cases

ing clients a public view into performance helps establish trust and provides a baseline for measuring improved performance in the future.

It is better to underpromise and overdeliver, even if the metric doesn't beat the industry average for service. As in many business practices, communication is key. Listen to the user community to determine what service is requested, negotiate with users on the cost of providing requested service levels, negotiate how the improved performance will be generated, make it easy for everyone to see the reports, and be flexible by adapting service metrics over time to changing business conditions.

Using a Test Lab to Increase Performance

One way to predict and improve performance, particularly for 3/N-Tier applications, is by developing a test laboratory. Such a facility should include both equipment and procedures for investigating the infrastructure impact of various patterns and services.

Why test 3/N-Tier applications and infrastructure carefully? While you might assume that 3/N-Tier applications operate alike with similar infrastructure impacts, in practice they vary significantly. You should go beyond simple infrastructure pattern matching to gain a detailed understanding of a particular application's variance from its pattern's norm. If this doesn't happen, the 3/N-Tier application might stray far from the ideal pattern and might not exhibit the most efficient network response time or throughput. Failure to perform infrastructure impact assessments results in slower, less-successful application deployments, while your group shoulders the blame for being application ignorant.

Testing should focus on high-profile applications or those that traverse WAN or ISP links. While testing is often implemented only for enterprisewide initiatives, modules with problems in an otherwise efficient 3/N-Tier suite might be driven by just one line of business. To figure out how applications function, you should combine new skills and tools to better understand and predict specific application performance characteristics, particularly user response time, for enterprise WAN and Internet environments.

For example, inefficient database queries can result in a huge number of sparsely filled packet round-trips, which could affect user response time considerably in a WAN environment. For this reason, the test lab should include some physical WAN components. Some companies have added data channel simulators, which easily simulate error rates, latency, and bandwidth parameters. It is then simpler to test applications over a representative set of three to five branch offices or remote access user connections. While some companies install a frame relay link in their test labs, this method offers only a single branch office configuration without much flexibility.

Testing should also help ensure compliance with infrastructure plans. Besides learning about and simulating the application, more realistic stress testing should be performed in a physical test environment. If infrastructure impact assessment is performed at earlier stages, you will already know which applications are likely candidates for acceptance testing, and you can participate in understanding and optimizing these details earlier in the development and deployment process. Moreover, knowledge of application behavior by tiers improves your ability to perform post-deployment troubleshooting.

Summary

Now you understand the key presentation and management components of an adaptive infrastructure. This chapter focused on solutions of particular value within the following layers:

- In the presentation layer, components such as Web servers and IVR are equally important for any Web-delivered application, including those in both the 3/N-Tier Transact and Web Publish patterns. Other components such as voice and wireless can prove useful for some special cases. Over time, organizations will push for less costly options, especially those provided by scale-out designs.

- In the API layer, components such as Inter-APIs and Infra-APIs are highly recommended as a way to make your infrastructure highly adaptable and reusable. Having reusable APIs is one of the most powerful ways to gain agility and shorten time-to-market for critical business applications.

- In the management layer, companies launching Web applications must plan application management proactively. Failure to plan leaves you with fragmented technology, higher management costs, and longer downtimes. Offering clients a public view into performance helps establish trust and provides a baseline for measuring improved performance in the future. Use of a test lab can help ensure that your designs can perform "up to spec."

Following the basic precepts outlined in this chapter should help you pick the best solutions for each of these layers. Combined with the solutions discussed in the previous three chapters, you now have the information you need to build an innovative, agile, and highly adaptive infrastructure.

Appendix A

Component Catalog

This appendix lists some of the primary components contained in the adaptive infrastructure platform. Many of these components were discussed in detail in Chapters 5 through 8 of this book. This list provides additional information, including vendor/product examples, key patterns, and key services related to each component.

This list was current upon this book's publication. Changes in representative vendors and products should be expected, given continued market volatility and the normal pace of technical innovation. Vendor and product references in this appendix, as well as those appearing in the rest of this book, are intended to be used as examples for understanding more clearly the general points being made. Sometimes, seeing a familiar product makes a discussion much more clear and useful.

However, the use of any vendor and product names in this appendix (or the entire book) does not imply endorsement of any particular product. Such references are made for illustrative purposes only.

Appendix A: Component Catalog

Index to Components

Component	Page	Component	Page
Infra-API	302	Process Modeler	317
Inter-API	303	Data Access Middleware	318
Intra-API	304	Database Gateway	318
E-mail MTA	305	DBMS	319
Integrated Voice Response (IVR)	306	Voice Messaging Store	319
Interactive TV	306	Application Server HA	320
Streaming Server	307	Application Server HW	320
Terminal Server	307	Application Server OS	321
Voice	308	Database Server HA	321
WAP Server	308	Database Server HW	322
Web Server	309	Database Server OS	322
Application Server	310	Integration Server HA	323
Adapter Toolkit	311	Integration Server HW	323
Application Adapter	311	Integration Server OS	324
Computer Telephony Integration (CTI) Server	312	File Server and Network Attached Storage (NAS)	324
Integration Server	313	Web Server HA	325
EDI Gateway	314	Web Server HW	325
File Exchange Server	314	Web Server OS	326
Integration Transport	315	Business Continuance HW	326
Middleware Encryption	315	Business Continuance SW	327
Inter-Enterprise Integration (IEI) Server	316	Host Interconnect	327
Process Execution Engine	317	Storage Area Network (SAN)	328
Storage Server	329	Public Key Infrastructure (PKI)	337

Component	Page	Component	Page
Automatic Call Distributor (ACD)	330	Service Level Management	338
Content Delivery Network (CDN)	330	Smart Card	338
Content Security	331	SSL and Encryption HW	339
Directory Server	331	Traffic Shaper	339
Extranet Service Provider (ESP)	332	Two-Factor Authentication Device	340
Firewall	332	VPN Device	340
Hosting Service	333	VPN Service	341
Internet Access and Transport Service (ISP)	333	WAN Access Device	342
Intrusion Detection & Threat Management	334	WAN Service	342
Network Load Balancer	334	Web SSO	343
Network Pre-Routing (Voice)	335	Wireless & Mobile Device	343
Network Protocol & Address Management	336	Wireless Service	344
Proxy/Caching Server	337		

Infra-API

Purpose

Exposes low-level technology services, including security, naming, transactionality, and object invocation. Application and infrastructure developers consume these services during the creation of business logic. Increasingly, Infra-APIs and the services they encapsulate are provided off-the-shelf within application servers (J2EE/EJB/Java-based, CORBA, Microsoft COM+/.NET, and so forth). Infrastructure developers still need to augment application servers with higher-level frameworks, and then provide them to application developers for use during the development process.

Examples (Vendors and Products)

Technologies J2EE Enterprise Java Beans, Java Transaction Service, Java Messaging Service, Object Transaction Server, CORBA Messaging Services, and J2EE/EJB, Microsoft .NET, CORBA, and even DCE security services.

Products Container servers (provide off-the-shelf infrastructure services) and container server IDEs (used to invoke off-the-shelf services and create new infrastructure services).

Containers BEA WebLogic, IBM WebSphere, Microsoft COM+/.NET, Sun iPlanet/ONE, IDEs, IBM Visual Age, WebGain (a.k.a. Symantec Visual Cafe).

Layer Number	1
Component Layer	API
Priority	9
Key Infra Pattern	3/N-Tier Transact
Key Infra Service	Transactional Integration (EAI, IEI)

Inter-API

Purpose

Used in inter-application communication to expose application business logic for use by other applications. Since Inter-APIs affect other applications, they should be defined and managed by infrastructure developers.

Examples (Vendors and Products)

Technologies   X.12/Edifact EDI interfaces, user developed APIs into business process functionality, and ERP vendor provided APIs into packaged application functionality.

Products   Container server IDE, visual modeling tools (such as UML tools), and adapter SDKs.

Containers   BEA WebLogic, IBM WebSphere, and Sun iPlanet.

IDEs   IBM Visual Age and WebGain (a.k.a. Symantec Visual Cafe).

Modeling Tools   Rational Rose, Visio.

Integration Servers   IBM/New Era of Networks MQ Series Integrator (MQSI), SeeBeyond (formerly STC) e-Gate, and Active ActiveWorks.

Layer Number	1
Component Layer	API
Priority	4
Key Infra Pattern	3/N-Tier Transact
Key Infra Service	Transactional Integration (EAI, IEI)

Intra-API

Purpose

Used in intra-application communication to expose application level business logic that is used only within the context of a single application. Since Intra-APIs are not reused outside a given application, they are created and managed by that application's developers.

Examples (Vendors and Products)

Technologies   COM IDL, EJB IDL, CORBA IDL, RPC IDL, and Function calls.

Products   Container Server IDE, visual modeling tools (such as UML tools).

Containers   BEA WebLogic, IBM WebSphere, and Sun iPlanet.

IDEs   IBM Visual Age, WebGain (a.k.a. Symantec Visual Cafe).

Modeling Tools   Rational Rose and Visio.

Layer Number	1
Component Layer	API
Priority	9
Key Infra Pattern	3/N-Tier Transact
Key Infra Service	Transactional Integration (EAI, IEI)

E-mail MTA

Purpose

SMTP messaging (another POI) that is commonly used by e-mail response solutions for customer interaction or instant messaging. SMTP message transfer agents (MTAs), or gateways, are used to relay e-mail outside of the organization.

Examples (Vendors and Products)

SMTP gateways/MTAs   Exchange, Notes, and SendMail.

Response vendors   Kana, BriteWare, Egain, and Mustang/Quintus.

Instant messaging   AOL and ICQ.

Layer Number	2
Component Layer	Presentation
Priority	9
Key Infra Pattern	Store-and-Forward Collaborate
Key Infra Service	N/A

Integrated Voice Response (IVR)

Purpose

Also called Voice Response Unit (VRU), a device that pre-answers calls, asks for an account number or personal identification number (PIN), and enables the caller to access information, make transactions, etc. IVRs are another point of interaction (POI), whereby a server translates telephone Touch Tone (and going forward, speech) requests into data queries, which are then returned to the IVR with the result spoken back to the caller.

Examples (Vendors and Products)

Lucent Conversant, IBM DirecTalk, InterVoiceBrite, Edify, and Periphonics.

Layer Number	2
Component Layer	Presentation
Priority	9
Key Infra Pattern	3/N-Tier Transact
Key Infra Service	Voice

Interactive TV

Purpose

TV networks that run over cable, satellite, and broadcast, as well as Web networks. This interactive component should have bandwidth.

Examples (Vendors and Products)

BSkyB, Premier, etc.

Layer Number	2
Component Layer	Presentation
Priority	9
Key Infra Pattern	Stream Publish
Key Infra Service	N/A

Streaming Server

Purpose

Software that is used to stream out audio and video content to player clients, which may be proprietary protocols. It also supports IRC chat servers and shared whiteboarding solutions, including NetMeeting. The goal is to deliver real-time, or very near real-time, content that is usually multimedia.

Examples (Vendors and Products)

Audio/Video   Cisco WebTV, Real Networks Real Server, etc.

Shared whiteboarding   Cisco WebLine, Aspect WebAgent, Microsoft NetMeeting, and WebEx.

Layer Number	2
Component Layer	Presentation
Priority	9
Key Infra Pattern	Stream Publish
Key Infra Service	N/A

Terminal Server

Purpose

Software that services other specialized and/or proprietary terminal devices or protocols.

Examples (Vendors and Products)

Citrix Winframe/MetaFrame, Microsoft Terminal Server Edition, IBM 3174 remote controllers, and 3745 front-end processors (FEPs).

Layer Number	2
Component Layer	Presentation
Priority	9
Key Infra Pattern	2-Tier Transact
Key Infra Service	Desktop

Voice

Purpose

A collaborative POI that allows talking over voice networks to internal people, such as the customer interaction center (CIC) or call center.

Examples (Vendors and Products)

Plain old telephone services (POTS) and voice-over IP.

Layer Number	2
Component Layer	Presentation
Priority	9
Key Infra Pattern	Real-time Collaborate
Key Infra Service	Device

WAP Server

Purpose

Software that converts internal formats and protocols to those required to run over low bandwidth wireless networks. It also reformats the user interface (UI) to fit small screen sizes.

Examples (Vendors and Products)

Nokia, Ericsson, Phone.COM, Alcatel, and Motorola.

Layer Number	2
Component Layer	Presentation
Priority	3
Key Infra Pattern	3/N-Tier Transact
Key Infra Service	Device

Web Server

Purpose

A combination of two components:

- an HTTP listener/gateway (such as IIS with HTTP/ISAPI, Apache HTTP/CGI, and Netscape Enterprise Server with HTTP/NSAPI), and
- an HTML-only Web/app server that offers a mix of Web-specific presentation services (such as IIS ASPs and Apache JSPs) with the opportunity to incorporate business logic directly, rather than calling a separate application server.

Examples (Vendors and Products)

Technologies   HTTP, CGI, Active Server Pages, and Java Server Pages.

Products   Straight Web servers (including Microsoft IIS, Apache, and Netscape Enterprise Server).

Web/app servers (including Allaire ColdFusion, Haht HotSite, and IBM WebSphere Standard Edition).

Layer Number	2
Component Layer	Presentation
Priority	2
Key Infra Pattern	Web Publish
Key Infra Service	HTML

Application Server

Purpose

Software that executes business logic functions, allowing easy POI differentiation (3/N-Tier focused) or specific nailing to Web front ends (2-Tier). These software suites usually include a Web (or Web/app) server component. Previously, many solutions were built from separate execution, integrity, gateway, interaction, and toolkit services. Since single products now offer all these services as a bundle (even with standard service provider interfaces—for example, J2EE and .NET frameworks), those features are no longer split out as separate components of an application server. However, we still see enough differentiation in the integration server solutions to keep the separate component definitions.

Examples (Vendors and Products)

Technologies   TP Monitors, J2EE Enterprise Java Beans (EJB), Microsoft .NET (Web Services), CORBA, and Proprietary.

Products   BEA WebLogic Enterprise Edition, IBM WebSphere Advanced and Enterprise Editions, Sun iPlanet/ONE, Microsoft COM+/.NET, IBM CICS, and BEA Tuxedo.

Layer Number	3
Component Layer	Application
Priority	1
Key Infra Pattern	3/N-Tier Transact
Key Infra Service	N/A

Adapter Toolkit

Purpose

Software that enables development of application adapters, exploiting application or data-specific standards or proprietary APIs.

Examples (Vendors and Products)

Specific Adapter Toolkits of EAI vendors.

Layer Number	4
Component Layer	Integration
Priority	4
Key Infra Pattern	3/N-Tier Transact
Key Infra Service	Transactional Integration (EAI, IEI)

Application Adapter

Purpose

Software that connects integration rules engines and their transports to specific applications in a particular instance. This is accomplished by exploiting application or data-specific standards or proprietary APIs.

Examples (Vendors and Products)

Pre-built adapters from EAI vendors or ERP vendors.

Layer Number	4
Component Layer	Integration
Priority	4
Key Infra Pattern	3/N-Tier Transact
Key Infra Service	Transactional Integration (EAI, IEI)

Computer Telephony Integration (CTI) Server

Purpose

Software that integrates applications and telephony, and manages and routes (based on skills, wait time, etc.) telephone calls, e-mail, and agent-end user collaboration. CTI routing algorithms can be based on criteria supplied by customer databases (such as CRM), agent skills, wait time for an agent, and so forth.

Examples (Vendors and Products)

Genesys, Quintus, Prospect, IBM CallPath, TAPI, TSAPI, CSTA, and CT Connect.

Layer Number	4
Component Layer	Integration
Priority	3
Key Infra Pattern	3/N-Tier Transact
Key Infra Service	Voice

Integration Server

Purpose

Software that does basic routing (not workflow, and not transactional) and data transformation between applications, often running in a hub-and-spoke configuration. Previously, we have broken these two out into separate functions, but we rarely see them as independent products. Now, we have lumped them into a single component. Soon we expect to lump more of the remaining separate components in the integration layer into this overall integration server component.

Examples (Vendors and Products)

Viewlocity (was Frontec), NEON/IBM MQSI, SeeBeyond (formerly STC), and Mercator.

Layer Number	4
Component Layer	Integration
Priority	1
Key Infra Pattern	3/N-Tier Transact
Key Infra Service	Transactional Integration (EAI, IEI)

EDI Gateway

Purpose

Software that moves data and transforms it from flat format into standard data formats (such as X12 and EDIFACT) for use by business partners. Other services include scheduling, monitoring, acknowledgment, encryption, authentication, and non-repudiation.

Examples (Vendors and Products)

Sterling Commerce, IBM, Harbinger, St. Paul Software, GEIS, Telecom Finland, Actis, and Sun/Netscape Alliance.

Layer Number	4
Component Layer	Integration
Priority	9
Key Infra Pattern	3/N-Tier Transact
Key Infra Service	Transactional Integration (EAI, IEI)

File Exchange Server

Purpose

Software that moves data and schedules the move with some features for recoverability (including checkpoint restart). It may offer encryption, authentication, and other EB-oriented features and may also leverage OS-based FTP and scheduling (such as UNIX cron) capabilities.

Examples (Vendors and Products)

Sterling Software Connect:Direct, Connect:Mailbox, Micro-Tempus, IBM NDM, CA XCOM, and MLINK.

Layer Number	4
Component Layer	Integration
Priority	9
Key Infra Pattern	3/N-Tier Transact
Key Infra Service	Transactional Integration (EAI, IEI)

Integration Transport

Purpose

Software that enables particular application adapters to talk to centralized integration server hubs, where asynchronous (store and forward) and event-oriented behavior is critical. Often bundled with Integration (EAI) or IEI server.

Examples (Vendors and Products)

IBM MQ Series and Microsoft MSMQ (predominantly for internal EAI uses); SOAP (Simple Object Access Protocol that sends XML via simple RPC mechanism over HTTP and is most applicable to IEI uses).

Layer Number	4
Component Layer	Integration
Priority	3
Key Infra Pattern	3/N-Tier Transact
Key Infra Service	Transactional Integration (EAI, IEI)

Middleware Encryption

Purpose

Software that secures and protects middleware transports. Several products are specific to MQ Series as a system-to-system transport.

Examples (Vendors and Products)

Nanoteq, MQ Armour, Primeur DataSecure, and Candle MQSecure.

Layer Number	4
Component Layer	Integration
Priority	9
Key Infra Pattern	3/N-Tier Transact
Key Infra Service	Security (Isolation)

Inter-Enterprise Integration (IEI) Server

Purpose

Software that integrates business processes across business boundaries. Currently, IEI servers overlap the functionality provided by integration servers. However, they will evolve into mere inter-business adapters for those more general-purpose integration servers. Their primary focus is, and should be, community of interest management, XML formatting, and providing firewall-friendly transports.

Examples (Vendors and Products)

NetFish, WebMethods, Extricity, Bridges2Islands and Microsoft's BizTalk Server 2000.

Layer Number	4
Component Layer	Integration
Priority	2
Key Infra Pattern	3/N-Tier Transact
Key Infra Service	Transactional Integration (EAI, IEI)

Process Execution Engine

Purpose

Workflow software that executes workflow rules designed by a process modeler.

Examples (Vendors and Products)

Vitria BusinessWare, IBM MQ Workflow, New Era of Networks eProcess Enabler, Tibco IntegrationManager or InConcert, Mercator Enterprise Broker, webMethods Business Integrator, SeeBeyond [formerly STC] eBusiness Process Manager, Microsoft Biztalk Orchestration.

Layer Number	4
Component Layer	Integration
Priority	3
Key Infra Pattern	3/N-Tier Transact
Key Infra Service	Transactional Integration (EAI, IEI)

Process Modeler

Purpose

Workflow software that designs workflow processes for execution by the process execution engine.

Examples (Vendors and Products)

UML tools   Rational Rose and Visio.

Layer Number	4
Component Layer	Integration
Priority	3
Key Infra Pattern	3/N-Tier Transact
Key Infra Service	Transactional Integration (EAI, IEI)

Data Access Middleware

Purpose

Software that enables applications (including middle-tier app servers) to access DBMS-based data. Usually, this software provides a protocol to communicate across a network, not only a standard API like ODBC.

Examples (Vendors and Products)

Oracle SQL*Net and Net8, and ODBC drivers.

Layer Number	5
Component Layer	Database
Priority	9
Key Infra Pattern	3/N-Tier Transact
Key Infra Service	Database

Database Gateway

Purpose

Software that enables applications to access a variety of back end DBMS-based data, transforming calls into native calls for each DBMS supported.

Examples (Vendors and Products)

IBI EDA/SQL, Sybase OmniSQL, OLE DB and ODBC drivers.

Layer Number	5
Component Layer	Database
Priority	9
Key Infra Pattern	3/N-Tier Transact
Key Infra Service	Database

DBMS

Purpose

Software that stores data in formats to allow easy and fast retrieval, along with efficient writing of data, often relational in structure (RDBMS).

Examples (Vendors and Products)

Oracle, Sybase, Ingres, IBM DB2, and Microsoft SQL Server.

Layer Number	5
Component Layer	Database
Priority	4
Key Infra Pattern	3/N-Tier Transact
Key Infra Service	Database

Voice Messaging Store

Purpose

Software that enables voice-mail and messaging.

Examples (Vendors and Products)

Octel, Centigram, and Lucent.

Layer Number	5
Component Layer	Database
Priority	9
Key Infra Pattern	3/N-Tier Transact
Key Infra Service	Voice

Application Server HA

Purpose

High-availability solutions that are specifically for application server implementations. These are often options in the application server software, but may also include hardware solutions. If available, we recommend not using server (OS) layer HA solutions for EB situations (except in the case of DBMS servers).

Examples (Vendors and Products)

Clustering

Layer Number	6
Component Layer	Server
Priority	2
Key Infra Pattern	3/N-Tier Transact
Key Infra Service	N/A

Application Server HW

Purpose

Hardware platforms that support application server software.

Examples (Vendors and Products)

Sun, Compaq, IBM Intel, RISC, or S/390 servers.

Layer Number	6
Component Layer	Server
Priority	2
Key Infra Pattern	3/N-Tier Transact
Key Infra Service	N/A

Application Server OS

Purpose

Operating System (OS) software for platforms that support application server software.

Examples (Vendors and Products)

UNIX (Sun Solaris, HP-UX, IBM AIX), Microsoft NT and Windows 2000 server, and IBM OS/390.

Layer Number	6
Component Layer	Server
Priority	2
Key Infra Pattern	3/N-Tier Transact
Key Infra Service	N/A

Database Server HA

Purpose

High-availability solutions that are specifically for database server implementations. These are often options in the database server software, but may also include hardware solutions. If available, we recommend not using server (OS) layer HA solutions for EB situations (except in the case of DBMS servers).

Examples (Vendors and Products)

Oracle replication and clustering.

Layer Number	6
Component Layer	Server
Priority	9
Key Infra Pattern	3/N-Tier Transact
Key Infra Service	Database

Database Server HW

Purpose

Hardware platforms that support database server software.

Examples (Vendors and Products)

Sun, Compaq, IBM Intel or RISC or S/390 servers.

Layer Number	6
Component Layer	Server
Priority	9
Key Infra Pattern	3/N-Tier Transact
Key Infra Service	Database

Database Server OS

Purpose

Operating System (OS) software for platforms that support database server software.

Examples (Vendors and Products)

UNIX (Sun Solaris, HP-UX, IBM AIX), Microsoft NT and Windows 2000 Server, and IBM OS/390.

Layer Number	6
Component Layer	Server
Priority	9
Key Infra Pattern	3/N-Tier Transact
Key Infra Service	Database

Integration Server HA

Purpose

High-availability solutions that are specifically for integration server implementations. These are often options in the integration server software, but may include hardware solutions. They are generally used to avoid single point of failure for this component.

Examples (Vendors and Products)

Clustering and Microsoft Component Load Balancing (Windows 2000).

Layer Number	6
Component Layer	Server
Priority	2
Key Infra Pattern	3/N-Tier Transact
Key Infra Service	Transactional Integration (EAI, IEI)

Integration Server HW

Purpose

Hardware platforms that support integration server software.

Examples (Vendors and Products)

Sun, Compaq, HP, and IBM servers.

Layer Number	6
Component Layer	Server
Priority	2
Key Infra Pattern	3/N-Tier Transact
Key Infra Service	Transactional Integration (EAI, IEI)

Integration Server OS

Purpose

Operating System (OS) software for platforms that supports integration server software.

Examples (Vendors and Products)

UNIX (Sun Solaris, HP-UX, IBM AIX), Microsoft NT and Windows 2000 Server, and IBM OS/390.

Layer Number	6
Component Layer	Server
Priority	2
Key Infra Pattern	3/N-Tier Transact
Key Infra Service	Transactional Integration (EAI, IEI)

File Server and Network Attached Storage (NAS)

Purpose

File systems or storage subsystems that are connected *directly* to the network for direct access, either OS/HW combinations (NT/Windows 2000, NetWare, and UNIX) or in an appliance-style box without any standard OS to configure. Users access the system directly over TCP/IP and native protocols (such as NFS or CIFS) rather than with special storage channel protocols like SCSI. FTP servers are another example of a file-server component.

Examples (Vendors and Products)

Network Appliance, Auspex, EMC Celerra, MTI Vivant, or other NFS or Microsoft CIFS appliances and other OS/HW combinations (NT/Windows 2000, NetWare, and NFS).

Layer Number	6
Component Layer	Server
Priority	9
Key Infra Pattern	Store and Forward Collaborate
Key Infra Service	File System

Web Server HA

Purpose

High-availability solutions that are specifically for Web-server implementations. These are often options in the Web-server software, but may include hardware solutions. If available, we recommend not using server (OS) layer HA solutions for EB situations (except in the case of DBMS servers).

Examples (Vendors and Products)

Clustering and Windows NT/Windows 2000 Load Balancing Service (WLBS). See also network layer load balancers (not part of the Web server).

Layer Number	6
Component Layer	Server
Priority	2
Key Infra Pattern	3/N-Tier Transact
Key Infra Service	HTML

Web Server HW

Purpose

Hardware platforms that support Web-server software.

Examples (Vendors and Products)

Sun, Compaq, HP, and IBM servers.

Layer Number	6
Component Layer	Server
Priority	2
Key Infra Pattern	3/N-Tier Transact
Key Infra Service	HTML

Web Server OS

Purpose

Operating System (OS) software for platforms that supports Web-server software.

Examples (Vendors and Products)

UNIX (Sun Solaris, HP-UX, IBM AIX), Linux, Microsoft NT and Windows 2000 Server, and IBM OS/390.

Layer Number	6
Component Layer	Server
Priority	2
Key Infra Pattern	3/N-Tier Transact
Key Infra Service	HTML

Business Continuance HW

Purpose

Hardware devices that include disk storage and tape transports (often with robotics). Such devices support business resumption in the event of a failure, and day-to-day backup and recovery requirements.

Examples (Vendors and Products)

Tape transport vendors   IBM, Sony, STK, and Quantum.

Automation vendors   ATL, IBM, and STK.

Layer Number	7
Component Layer	Storage
Priority	9
Key Infra Pattern	3/N-Tier Transact
Key Infra Service	SAN

Business Continuance SW

Purpose

Software that enhances the ability to resume business functions in the event of a system or application failure. Remote mirroring of storage data is one type of software, along with server clustering software, which can reduce the time to recover data.

Examples (Vendors and Products)

Primarily from storage hardware vendors (such as CPQ, EMC, HDS, and MTI), yet often requires server clustering technologies.

Layer Number	7
Component Layer	Storage
Priority	9
Key Infra Pattern	3/N-Tier Transact
Key Infra Service	SAN

Host Interconnect

Purpose

Hardware device (such as a PCI card in a server) that connects the operating system servers for an application or database to a storage subsystem over copper or fiber optic cables (typically SCSI, Fibre Channel, or ESCON).

Examples (Vendors and Products)

Host bus adapter vendors   QLogic and Emulex.

Hardware platform vendors   Compaq and Sun.

Layer Number	7
Component Layer	Storage
Priority	9
Key Infra Pattern	3/N-Tier Transact
Key Infra Service	SAN

Storage Area Network (SAN)

Purpose

Physical implementation that separates and offloads storage and B/R traffic from the user/application network using various interconnect technologies. In addition to storage subsystems, traditional storage interconnects (such as Fibre Channel, Ultra SCSI, and ESCON) are typically used, although traditional network protocols like Ethernet can also be used.

Examples (Vendors and Products)

Hardware storage vendors   EMC, HDS, and MTI.

System vendors   CPQ, Hewlett-Packard, and Sun.

FC vendors   Ancor, Brocade, and McData.

Layer Number	7
Component Layer	Storage
Priority	9
Key Infra Pattern	3/N-Tier Transact
Key Infra Service	SAN

Storage Server

Purpose

External hardware device that houses storage (such as mechanical disk drives) separate from the application or database server platform. This device is used for information retrieval. Storage servers are typically connected via SCSI, Fibre Channel (potentially a fabric network), or ESCON over dedicated cabling.

Examples (Vendors and Products)

Hardware storage vendors   EMC, HDS, and MTI.

System vendors   CPQ, Hewlett-Packard, IBM, and Sun.

Layer Number	7
Component Layer	Storage
Priority	4
Key Infra Pattern	3/N-Tier Transact
Key Infra Service	SAN

Automatic Call Distributor (ACD)

Purpose

Facility that manages incoming calls based on the number called, agents available, and a database of handling instructions. Calls are lined up or queued accordingly. The ACD also gathers usage statistics, which include the balance use of phone lines, etc. It can run on PBX or separately for routing and load-balancing functions.

Examples (Vendors and Products)

Aspect; Rockwell Galaxy, Spectrum or Transcend; Lucent's CMS; and Nortel Symposium or ACD MAX

Layer Number	8
Component Layer	Network
Priority	9
Key Infra Pattern	Real-time Collaborate
Key Infra Service	Voice

Content Delivery Network (CDN)

Purpose

Networks that augment traditional forms of Web delivery by pushing content out to servers close to the user.

Examples (Vendors and Products)

Akamai, Sandpiper/Digital Island, iBeam, Skycache, and Adero.

Layer Number	8
Component Layer	Network
Priority	3
Key Infra Pattern	Web Publish
Key Infra Service	HTML

Content Security

Purpose

Software that provides content monitoring and filtering to implement security policies against viruses, Java/ActiveX, and inappropriate usage (including porn-site filtering).

Examples (Vendors and Products)

Firewall plug-ins for virus scanning (CA/Cheyenne, McAfee, Trend Micro), Web screening (Microsystems, SpyGlass, Secure Computing), and Java and ActiveX filtering (Finjan).

Layer Number	8
Component Layer	Network
Priority	3
Key Infra Pattern	Store and Forward Collaborate
Key Infra Service	Security (Isolation)

Directory Server

Purpose

Software that stores information about users and applications in a quickly retrievable format (such as a database). This type of storage makes data easily accessible via standard protocols (LDAP). It is often combined with Web SSO solutions and/or public key infrastructure to provide identity infrastructure.

Examples (Vendors and Products)

Novell eDirectory, Netscape iPlanet Directory Server, IBM SecureWay Directory Server, and Microsoft Active Directory.

Layer Number	8
Component Layer	Network
Priority	1
Key Infra Pattern	Web Publish
Key Infra Service	Security (Identity)

Extranet Service Provider (ESP)

Purpose

Services that offer a single point of contact for IP transport, firewall and VPN management, hosting, PKI, directory, middleware, professional services, and billing. Unlike pure hosting services, ESPs offer a mix of services specifically targeting B2B Extranets.

Examples (Vendors and Products)

No true ESPs currently exist, but emerging players include GE GES, Pilot, Aventail.net, and Telenisus.

Layer Number	8
Component Layer	Network
Priority	2
Key Infra Pattern	Web Publish
Key Infra Service	Web Hosting

Firewall

Purpose

Hardware/software that filters data and applications via a variety of mechanisms (including stateful packet inspection and application proxy) to prevent unauthorized users and applications from entering an organization's enterprise. It may also provide additional functions, such as virus scanning, encryption, network address translation, and virtual private networking capabilities.

Examples (Vendors and Products)

Checkpoint FireWall 1 and Cisco Pix.

Layer Number	8
Component Layer	Network
Priority	1
Key Infra Pattern	Web Publish
Key Infra Service	Security (Isolation)

Hosting Service

Purpose

Outsourced hosting offerings that support an organization's Web and application servers and/or provide high bandwidth connections to the "arteries" of the Internet.

Examples (Vendors and Products)

Exodus, Digital Island, Internap, UUNET, GTE, and Sprint.

Layer Number	8
Component Layer	Network
Priority	2
Key Infra Pattern	Web Publish
Key Infra Service	Web Hosting

Internet Access and Transport Service (ISP)

Purpose

Internet services (ISPs) that connect an organization's sites and individual users to the Internet via dedicated, dial-up, DSL, and cable modem access technologies.

Examples (Vendors and Products)

Uunet, PSInet, Sprint, AT&T, Terra, and Infonet (ISPs).

Layer Number	8
Component Layer	Network
Priority	3
Key Infra Pattern	Web Publish
Key Infra Service	WAN

Intrusion Detection & Threat Management

Purpose

Software and services that monitor an enterprise's firewalls and exposed hosts and reports any break-ins or security failures.

Examples (Vendors and Products)

Established products   Cisco/NetRanger and ISS/RealSecure.

Emerging products   Abirnet/SessionWall-3, Anzen/Anzen Flight Jacket, Axent/NetProwler, Internet Tools/ID-Trak, and Network Associates/CyberCop Network.

Layer Number	8
Component Layer	Network
Priority	3
Key Infra Pattern	Web Publish
Key Infra Service	Security (Isolation)

Network Load Balancer

Purpose

Switches or appliances that failover and balance traffic load across sets of servers, firewalls, and caches. The scope can cover server load balancing, as well as global or site load balancing.

Examples (Vendors and Products)

F5 Networks, Radware, Cisco Local Director, Arrowpoint, Alteon, Foundary, and Resonate.

Layer Number	8
Component Layer	Network
Priority	2
Key Infra Pattern	Web Publish
Key Infra Service	HTML

Network Pre-Routing (Voice)

Purpose

Service that uses the calling number, called number, or other database-influenced factors to determine the appropriate call treatments and routing of a voice call to a particular call center.

Examples (Vendors and Products)

GeoTel (now Cisco) and Genesys.

Layer Number	8
Component Layer	Network
Priority	9
Key Infra Pattern	Real-time Collaborate
Key Infra Service	Voice

Network Protocol & Address Management

Purpose

Protocol that is increasingly TCP/IP, though others may apply in non-EB situations (such as SNA and IPX) or specific channels. Wireless and direct voice are not usually over TCP/IP. Beyond this, software is required to enable users to determine and implement effective subnetting strategies, design DHCP and DNS server architectures (for example, clustering vs. distributed redundant servers), and distribute IP addresses to IP devices. Staff must publicly register DNS domain names and obtain public address ranges.

Examples (Vendors and Products)

Protocols   Implemented in OS software.

TCP/IP management solutions   Lucent (Quadritek) QIP, Nortel/Bay Networks NetID, Cisco Network Registrar, Check Point MetaIP, and Process Software IP Addressworks.

Layer Number	8
Component Layer	Network
Priority	9
Key Infra Pattern	Store-and-Forward Collaborate
Key Infra Service	Network (LAN, WAN)

Proxy/Caching Server

Purpose

Software/appliances that alleviate traffic across WAN components by storing frequently accessed https, streaming media, and objects that allow repeat requests to be served from inside the LAN. Proxy servers are less scalable than transparently installed caches. Appliance caches are preferable to software-only products.

Examples (Vendors and Products)

Cacheflow, Network Appliance, Cisco, Inktomi, Novell ICS (Dell, Compaq), Netscape, Squid, and Microsoft Proxy Server.

Layer Number	8
Component Layer	Network
Priority	2
Key Infra Pattern	Web Publish
Key Infra Service	HTML

Public Key Infrastructure (PKI)

Purpose

Public Key Infrastructure (PKI) that combines the database of keys with the ability to issue keys/certificates, enabling users, devices, and applications to gain authorized access to resources.

Examples (Vendors and Products)

Entrust, Verisign, Baltimore/Cybertrust, Netscape, and Microsoft.

Layer Number	8
Component Layer	Network
Priority	2
Key Infra Pattern	Store-and-Forward Collaborate
Key Infra Service	Security

Service Level Management

Purpose

Software platforms that enable users to monitor and track performance of an overall network and network components, also providing insight on service level management.

> **Note** A separate component per layer for element- or layer-specific management solutions may be required for completeness.

Examples (Vendors and Products)

HP Openview, Cabletron Spectrum (Platforms), Tivoli, Micromuse, Netcool, BMC, Candle, Inverse, Vitalsigns, and Keynote.

Layer Number	8
Component Layer	Network
Priority	2
Key Infra Pattern	3/N-Tier Transact
Key Infra Service	Management

Smart Card

Purpose

End user devices that contain a digital certificate used for authorization and authentication.

Examples (Vendors and Products)

Bull, Gemplus, and Keycorp.

Layer Number	8
Component Layer	Network
Priority	9
Key Infra Pattern	Store-and-Forward Collaborate
Key Infra Service	Security

SSL and Encryption HW

Purpose

Hardware products that accelerate encryption processing.

Examples (Vendors and Products)

Chrysalis, Rainbow, and Cylink.

Layer Number	8
Component Layer	Network
Priority	2
Key Infra Pattern	Web Publish
Key Infra Service	HTML, Security (Isolation)

Traffic Shaper

Purpose

Hardware devices and software enhancements to products (such as routers) that allow users to prioritize traffic by application, source, and destination via multiple techniques (including weighted-fair queuing and TCP rate control).

Examples (Vendors and Products)

TCP rate control   Packeteer

Queuing   Lucent/Xedia and NetReality

Layer Number	8
Component Layer	Network
Priority	9
Key Infra Pattern	3/N-Tier Transact
Key Infra Service	Network (LAN, WAN)

Two-Factor Authentication Device

Purpose

Physical tokens that generate onetime passwords.

Examples (Vendors and Products)

Security Dynamics SecureID cards.

Layer Number	8
Component Layer	Network
Priority	9
Key Infra Pattern	Store-and-Forward Collaborate
Key Infra Service	Security

VPN Device

Purpose

User-supplied products that enable telecommuters and road warriors to connect to internal resources across either the public Internet or VPN services (described above). VPNs may be deployed across dial-up links, cable modems, or DSL.

Examples (Vendors and Products)

VPN product vendors   Checkpoint, Nortel, and Cisco.

Layer Number	8
Component Layer	Network
Priority	2
Key Infra Pattern	Store-and-Forward Collaborate
Key Infra Service	Security (Isolation)

VPN Service

Purpose

Carrier-provided network services that link an organization's telecommuters and road warriors to internal resources. Remote access services may be extended to link outside entities (such as business partners, customers, and agents) to the organization.

Examples (Vendors and Products)

VPN service providers UUNET/Compuserve (MCI Worldcom) and AT&T Global Networking Services.

Layer Number	8
Component Layer	Network
Priority	2
Key Infra Pattern	Store-and-Forward Collaborate
Key Infra Service	Security (Isolation)

WAN Access Device

Purpose

Physical device that connects an organization's site to the outside world (via the Internet) and to other internal sites (via wide area network circuits and services). This typically includes WAN routers; and it may also include frame relay and/or ATM access devices. Routers may include quality of service and VPN functionality, but loading the router down with too many functions is not advised.

Examples (Vendors and Products)

Routers Cisco 7000 (for headquarters) 4500 and 2500 (for branch-office and remote sites); and Nortel products.

Layer Number	8
Component Layer	Network
Priority	9
Key Infra Pattern	All
Key Infra Service	Network (WAN)

WAN Service

Purpose

Physical network that links an organization's branch office, headquarters, and remote office sites together. Circuits and/or services are typically procured from the carrier.

Examples (Vendors and Products)

Frame relay, ATM services, or leased lines from AT&T, MCI Worldcom, Sprint, and Qwest.

Layer Number	8
Component Layer	Network
Priority	9
Key Infra Pattern	All
Key Infra Service	Network (WAN)

Web SSO

Purpose

Software that provides users with the ability to sign on to a Web server once and connect to multiple Web applications.

Examples (Vendors and Products)

Netegrity and Dascom.

Layer Number	8
Component Layer	Network
Priority	2
Key Infra Pattern	3/N-Tier Transact
Key Infra Service	Security (Identity)

Wireless & Mobile Device

Purpose

Mobile communication devices that currently include cell phones, PDAs, and laptop computers.

Examples (Vendors and Products)

Handheld products Nokia, Ericsson, Motorola, Palm, and Psion.

PC vendor products laptops.

Layer Number	8
Component Layer	Network
Priority	9
Key Infra Pattern	Real-time Collaborate
Key Infra Service	Voice

Wireless Service

Purpose

Satellite services (for example, VSAT or LEOS) and terrestrial services (such as digital cellular) that provide mobile communications.

Examples (Vendors and Products)

Digital cellular   Sprint, AT&T, Bell Atlantic, and Vodaphone/Mannesman.

VSAT services   Hughes.

LEOS   Iridium.

Layer Number	8
Component Layer	Network
Priority	3
Key Infra Pattern	Real-time Collaborate
Key Infra Service	Voice

Glossary

The following list contains many generic and specialized terms used in this book.

active server pages (ASP) A feature of a Microsoft Web server that allows scripting inside Web pages to be executed on the server side as the pages are being served. See also "Java server pages."

adaptive infrastructure Any infrastructure that demonstrates agility through reusable infrastructure components, patterns, and services. Adaptive infrastructure processes allow businesses to easily introduce new business initiatives while continuing to improve initiatives already under way.

application programming interface (API) Programming hooks that provide a way for external processes to communicate with and control a specific computer program. This book discusses three generic types of APIs used for different purposes. See also "Infra-API," "Intra-API," and "Inter-API."

application server layer The infrastructure layer that contains the business logic software. This layer includes the application servers themselves, as well as any related infrastructure planning and deployment tools.

application service provider (ASP) A third-party service company that provides customers with online Web-based applications.

ASP See "application service provider" or "active server pages."

back-end The part of the application that stores and processes data. In client/server computing, this usually refers to processes that occur on the server side. See also "front-end."

Border Gateway Protocol (BGP) A protocol used to exchange routing information between gateway hosts and routers on a network. The protocol helps network routing components look up table-based information to select the best available routing path.

business process automation (BPA) Systems that automate business processes.

business quality messaging (BQM) A set of technology standards devoted to providing a wide range of business-quality services, including guaranteed message delivery, failure notification and message journaling.

business-to-business (B2B) Any system or process that connects a business with its suppliers, partners, or corporate customers.

certificate authority (CA) A network-based authority that generates public keys for message encryption using public key infrastructure (PKI) technology.

certificate revocation list (CRL) A list of public key certificates that have been revoked, typically checked when verifying the authenticity of a certificate.

client/server computing A computing model in which the work is shared by multiple computers communicating over a network. Typically, the server accesses the data store and does most of the heavy processing work. The client receives only the portions of the data or application that it needs to do its work. "Thin clients" carry only a small part of the application load, with most of the work being performed on the server, while "smart PCs" carry a much larger load of application software, with most of the work performed on the client.

Client/Server Publish pattern An infrastructure pattern defined by the use of a smart PC, such as a sophisticated business intelligence client, with associated session-oriented protocols such as SQLNet inserted between the client and back-end database. This pattern is best used for implementing sophisticated data analysis capabilities for a small, well-defined user base.

clustering The process of grouping together a collection of servers or data in a central location to increase efficiency and effectiveness of security, performance, and administration.

code division multiple access (CDMA) A multiplexing technique used in second-generation (2G) and third-generation (3G) wireless technology, which optimizes available bandwidth by allowing a single channel to carry multiple signals.

Collaborate patterns Infrastructure patterns that use peer-to-peer communications to share documents. This book discusses three types of Collaborate patterns: Real-Time Collaborate, Structured Collaborate, and Store-and-Forward Collaborate.

commercial off-the-shelf (COTS) A term used in specification and procurement to describe any technology or product that is readily available and easily purchased from existing suppliers, with little or no customization.

Common Gateway Interface (CGI) A method used in some simple Web applications to move data from the client (Web browser) to the Web server using server-side applications or scripts. Typically, this method is used to process the contents of an online form by transmitting data or query strings embedded in a URL.

Common Object Request Broker Architecture (CORBA) An open, cross-platform, and cross-language framework that allows widely disparate programs to communicate with each other in a heterogeneous, distributed environment by using an "interface broker."

component Any hardware or software used in a computer system or application.

computer telephony integration (CTI) The process of connecting a PC to a telephone switch so that the computer can control the switch as needed.

content delivery network (CDN) An application or network service that provides content distribution and management.

cookies Small amounts of data stored on a user's computer, typically containing user-specific information such as preferences, automatic log-on data, or other configuration information.

customer interaction center (CIC) An enterprise resource planning (ERP) tool that provides an enterprisewide view of customer records.

customer relationship management (CRM) Applications or processes that help businesses manage customer relationships, typically by storing and analyzing extensive sets of customer data.

data warehousing A strategy in which data is extracted from large transactional databases and other sources and stored in smaller databases, to make data analysis easier.

database administrator (DBA) A person specifically responsible for maintaining databases.

database layer An infrastructure layer that includes all the software components used to deliver database services, including database management products, gateways, middleware, and voice messaging repositories.

database management system (DBMS) Any system designed specifically to store and manage data in an organized format.

demilitarized zone (DMZ) A portion of a network either immediately inside, outside, or between firewalls. Used for security purposes as a buffer zone between the internal network and external networks, such as the Internet.

denial of service (DOS) A network-based hacker attack that floods a server with bogus traffic, leaving it unable to conduct normal business. A DOS attack can disable a server by flooding its CPU with excessive requests, its memory through maintenance of excessive state information, or its disk capacity through excessive logging activity.

Direct access storage device (DASD) A magnetic disk drive, typically of the type used in mainframe or minicomputer environments, although the term may also encompass hard disk drives on servers and desktop PCs.

Directory Access Protocol (DAP) A predecessor of the Lightweight Directory Access Protocol (LDAP), used to locate and transmit information stored in user or customer directories.

directory service agent (DSA) Any server that handles LDAP directory requests from Web-based applications.

Directory Service Markup Language (DSML) A version of XML that provides a common format for network-based directories, allowing them to be accessed and shared by multiple Web-based applications.

discretionary costs Enhancements to a product that would be beneficial to complete, but can be pared down or postponed if there are budget or time constraints.

domain naming system (DNS) The system used to translate host computer names into IP addresses. DNS can also refer to the Domain Name Server, which implements the Domain Name System.

Dynamic Host Configuration Protocol (DHCP) A protocol used in TCP/IP networks to automatically provide static and dynamic allocation and management of IP addresses.

dynamic link library (DLL) A set of executable code stored as a separate module for processing purposes.

e-Business Any business conducted online over a public or private network using computer applications. e-Business traditionally was conducted using electronic data interchange (EDI) before the late 1990s, then became Web-based, and is now moving to multiple points of interaction (POI).

e-Commerce Any sales transactions conducted online. Typically considered a part of e-Business, but not the whole. e-Commerce applications often include online product catalogs, shopping carts, and credit card verification services.

Electronic Data Interchange (EDI) An early method of connecting businesses by using a common standardized format to exchange data, typically for transactional purposes (billing or payment).

e-mail A client/server application that involves distribution of formatted messages from computer to computer across networks. See also "Simple Mail Transfer Protocol (STMP)."

enterprise application integration (EAI) A message broker service that moves much of the responsibility for integrating applications out of the application and into a reusable, unified, systematic service that all applications can share. Also called *transactional integration*.

Enterprise JavaBeans (EJB) A server-side component architecture used to develop highly scalable and secure applications for the Java platform.

enterprise resource planning (ERP) A business management system that integrates all facets of the business, including planning, manufacturing, sales, marketing, and accounting.

enterprise systems Mission-critical systems on which the entire company depends, such as payroll, accounting, and inventory management.

Extensible Markup Language (XML) A subset of the Standard Generalized Markup Language (SGML) designed for use over the Internet. With XML, designers can create customized tags to provide functionality that is not available with HTML. Such tags can be codified as standards that business partners or industries can use to communicate and share data over the Internet. As a simple example, a specialized tag for "part number" can be used to identify part numbers in a set of Web-based information, for formatting or data analysis purposes.

Extensible Stylesheet Language Transformations (XSLT) A standard method for converting the structure of XML documents from one style sheet–based format to another.

extranet Any private network used for data exchange, typically between businesses, government agencies, or other organizations and their associated customers, suppliers, or business partners.

extranet service provider (ESP) A third-party company that specializes in providing hosting services for private extranets.

Federated Database Architecture (FDA) An architecture that provides autonomous, local processing for individual data stores, as well as a way to integrate the stores globally for applications.

Fibre Channel (FC) A set of standards for rapidly transferring data between workstations, mainframes, PCs, storage devices, and other peripherals at speeds up to 10 Gbps. Widely seen as a replacement technology for the Small Computer System Interface (SCSI) for data transfer between computers and storage devices.

File Transfer Protocol (FTP) A standard protocol for transferring files across TCP/IP networks, particularly the Internet.

front-end This part of the application displays data and provides user interaction. In client/server computing, the term usually refers to processes that occur on the client side. See also "back-end."

full-time equivalent (FTE) A term used when staffing resources to refer to several employees whose workload and work hours, when viewed as a whole, equals that of one full-time employee.

Global Positioning System (GPS) A satellite-based system that allows users of ground-based receiver equipment to determine the precise geographic location of any point on the globe.

graphical user interface (GUI) A display format that enables the user to operate in a visually rich environment, typically by using a mouse to point and click on icons, images, buttons, or lists of menu items on the screen.

Hypertext Markup Language (HTML) A set of standard tags used to mark up documents intended for use on the Web. The Web browser interprets the tags embedded in an HTML file and uses them as instructions on how to create the final formatted display.

Hypertext Transfer Protocol (HTTP) The protocol used for communication between Web servers and Web clients, or "browsers." This protocol, which is transparent to the user, allows the movement of data and documents across the Internet.

identity infrastructure An adaptive infrastructure service in which the entire authentication process and the components that this process relies upon are separated out into a common infrastructure service shared by all applications. As an example, the Identity Infrastructure might include a Web Single-Sign On (Web SSO) service, which helps avoid the need for users to maintain multiple user names and passwords to access multiple applications.

information technology (IT) A term often used in abbreviated form to generically describe the field of computing and all of its related technologies.

Infra-API Low-level technology services, such as security, naming, or object invocation, that application developers and infrastructure developers can use to create business logic. Increasingly, Infra-APIs and the services they encapsulate are provided off-the-shelf as a built-in part of application servers, such as EJB or .NET.

infrastructure The underlying structure of physical hardware, installed components, or services used to support a wide range of human activity, from transportation to power distribution to computing.

infrastructure developer A person responsible for designing or programming the shared portions of the infrastructure, particularly the APIs that are used to connect applications to shared infrastructure.

Infrastructure Impact Assessment (IIA) A set of techniques used to plan, build, and execute patterns. IIA involves measuring infrastructure patterns to see if they fit correctly during the project prototyping and operations phases.

infrastructure packaging A way of compartmentalizing, marketing, and funding infrastructure so that it provides easily identifiable value to the business.

infrastructure pattern A way of organizing infrastructure components that facilitates rapid mapping from business requirements to end-to-end infrastructure designs. Creating standard infrastructure patterns helps to streamline the process of providing infrastructure for application developers and business units. This book identifies three major types of infrastructure patterns: Transact, Publish, and Collaborate.

Infrastructure Pattern Matching (IPM) A set of techniques used to match infrastructure patterns to applications by asking who the users are, where they are located, and what work they will perform. Using IPM, infrastructure planners highlight business-critical design trade-offs and adjust infrastructure investment priorities.

infrastructure planner A person responsible for designing, implementing, and managing infrastructure.

infrastructure product A set of services packaged in such a way as to provide easily identifiable value to the business. See also "infrastructure packaging."

integrated development environment (IDE) Set of integrated tools that work together like a single application to automate many common programming tasks. Tools typically include a code editor, compiler, debugger, and GUI builder. Typical languages using IDE include Java, Visual Basic, and PowerBuilder.

integrated threat management (ITM) The ability to monitor and identify potential network intrusion threats by analyzing and correlating data from various sources, including host-based intrusion detection systems (IDS), network-based IDS, logs, auditing tools, and scanners.

integration administrator (IA) A person or group responsible for the selection of EAI technology and the creation of an agile EAI infrastructure.

integration layer An infrastructure layer containing all components that provide integration services between back-end applications and Web servers, application servers, or database servers. Typically, components include adapter toolkits, application adapters, integration servers, EDI gateways, file exchange servers, and more. The integration function could be internally focused, such as enterprise application architecture (EAI), or externally focused, such as inter-enterprise integration (IEI).

interactive voice response (IVR) Computer systems that react to remote, touch-tone telephones, using recordings for messaging. For example, when you call many businesses, you get a voice message asking you to press different numbers on the keypad to access various options.

Inter-API APIs that help the business logic communicate *between* applications.

inter-enterprise integration (IEI) Integration services that make it possible to communicate information and exchange data between organizations, such as in a business-to-business (B2B) context.

interface definition language (IDL) A language designed for describing the data structures passed between parts of an application, to provide a language-independent intermediate representation. Examples include CORBA or DCOM. Typical mainframe applications can be migrated into a component framework by wrapping them inside an IDL.

Internet The global public network used for data exchange between consumers, businesses, government institutions, and organizations.

Internet Protocol Security (IPsec) This emerging security standard provides higher-grade, packet-level security for IP networks. Typically, this security is implemented at the router level.

Internet service provider (ISP) A third-party company that specializes in providing Internet connectivity to business and consumers.

Intra-API Intra-APIs help business logic communicate *within* individual applications, and are typically not exposed to other applications. Since they are not reused outside a given application, they are created and managed only by the application's developers.

intranet Any private network used for data exchange, typically between employees of a particular business, government institution, or organization.

IP A generic term used to refer to networks, applications, or systems that use the Internet Protocol. See "Transmission Control Protocol/Internet Protocol (TCP/IP)."

IPsec See "Internet Protocol Security."

Java A programming language most often used for Web applications. It provides a level of presentation and processing sophistication not available through standard Web pages.

Java Database Connectivity (JDBC) A standard used to support communication between Java applications and back-end databases.

Java server pages (JSP) A feature of some non-Microsoft Web servers that allows scripting inside Web pages to be executed on the server side as the pages are being served. See also "active server pages."

Java 2 Enterprise Edition (J2EE) A version of the Java programming language designed for use in developing enterprise applications.

layers User-defined logical subdivisions of information or data.

legacy systems The older computing systems in a company, which typically do not represent the latest technology.

lifecycle The entire set of processes involved in creating and maintaining a computer system, typically involving several phases expressed as "plan, build, run, change, exit."

Lightweight Directory Access Protocol (LDAP) A standard protocol used to communicate customer or other user directory information across a TCP/IP network, such as the Internet. Because of the type of data it handles, LDAP is often employed by applications that require user authentication.

load balancing A technique used to improve reliability, performance, and manageability of server clusters by intelligently managing traffic into a cluster of servers and distributing the processing load using various strategies, such as "round robin," least connections, and CPU load.

local area network (LAN) A computer network that operates over short distances, such as a within a building. See also "wide area network (WAN)."

middleware Applications used to communicate or transfer data between front-end and back-end systems.

mobile application server (MAS) Middleware servers used to deliver data to wireless mobile applications. See also "Wireless Application Protocol Servers."

Moore's Law Gordon Moore's observation that a graph of chip performance as a function of time trended toward a doubling of transistor density (and therefore processing power) every 24 months.

Multiprotocol Label Switching (MPLS) A technology used to speed up traffic on networks by defining a specific path for each set of packets. This technology works on IP, ATM, and frame relay connections, thus the *multiprotocol* designation.

.NET A Microsoft standard designed to make many common applications interoperable over the Web. When fully realized, this platform will encompass servers, operating systems, software, and reusable services, including Web-based data storage and device software. Promised features will include automatic synchronization of remote data across platforms; increased XML support; and increased integration of e-mail, fax, and telephones.

network attached storage (NAS) Any hard disk storage that is accessible through a unique network address.

network layer An infrastructure layer containing all components that provide transport and networking services, including wires, optical fibers, firewalls, routers, switches, proxy servers, caching servers, load balancers, and VPN solutions.

network load balancing (NLB) See "load balancing."

network operating system (NOS) Any operating system that provides the services required by a network, such as user account management, peer-to-peer communication, file and print queuing, remote access services (RAS), and others.

network operations center (NOC) A central location used to manage networks.

non-discretionary costs Costs for those things that you must spend money on to keep the business going. For example, Internet service might be a non-discretionary cost if your business conducts a significant part of its business over the Internet.

object-oriented programming (OOP) A programming method that involves the creation and reuse of large blocks of code, called "objects." Typically, OOP is enabled by special programming languages such as C++ or Java.

1-Tier Transact pattern An infrastructure pattern that includes batch processing applications or online transaction processing (OLTP) applications, typically running on a mainframe. Although the application itself is fully centralized, users may be widely distributed over wide area networks (WANs) communicating with the host using data terminals or PCs.

online analytical processing (OLAP) Databases and systems that process and arrange large amounts of data into meaningful results used for high-speed analysis with data warehouses. Also called multi-dimensional databases.

Online Certificate Status Protocol (OCSP) A protocol used to check the current revocation status of a PKI certificate.

online transaction processing (OLTP) A generic term referring to any kind of online transaction, ranging from ATM transactions to issuing airline tickets online.

open database connectivity (ODBC) A Microsoft standard that provides a way for applications to easily transfer information to and from a wide array of common databases.

open source database (OSDB) A type of database that anyone can download and customize, such as MySQL.

operating system (OS) The underlying set of software that manages computer resources such as the display, keyboard, drives, network connections, and other operating components.

packaging See "infrastructure packaging."

patterns See "infrastructure patterns."

periodic process See "strategic infrastructure planning."

per-project process See "tactical infrastructure planning."

personal digital assistant (PDA) A handheld computing device used to store personal information such as address books, calendars, to-do lists, notes, media players, and calculators.

platform An organizational concept that refers to grouping individual component technologies into technical layers (or domains) to provide a base infrastructure for common technologies. A platform is a common infrastructure on which the hardware, software, and networking all function.

points of interaction (POI) Multiple interfaces used to communicate the same basic set of data to a user community, often through handheld devices such as cell phones and personal digital assistants (PDAs), but also through technologies such as interactive voice response (IVR).

Portable Document Format (PDF) A specialized file format developed by Adobe Corporation for presenting online documents, typically on CD, downloaded over the Web, or distributed as e-mail attachments.

portfolio An infrastructure planning tool that helps organize the process of identifying, cataloging, and managing patterns, platforms, and services on an ongoing basis.

Predictive Cost Modeling (PCM) Techniques that help planners quickly determine the cost of infrastructure development projects by taking Infrastructure Pattern Matching (IPM) processes and moving them to a higher level of detail on risks, resources, bills-of-material, and costs.

presentation layer An infrastructure layer containing all components that present data to the user, including Windows applications, Web pages and applications, mobile phones, PDAs, browsers, and telephones. Presentation server components are also in this layer, including terminal servers, streaming media servers, interactive TV, e-mail servers, and Web servers.

public key encryption (PKI) A technology that allows users of a public network, such as the Internet, to exchange data or transactions, privately and securely. PKI uses a cryptographic key pair containing a public key and a private key. The keys are issued by a trusted Certificate Authority (CA).

Publish pattern Any application that allows the user to download, view, listen to, or analyze data. Examples include reporting and analysis tools, Web brochure-ware, and streaming audio. This book discusses three types of Publish patterns: Client/Server Publish, Web Publish, and Stream Publish.

quality of service (QoS) A measurement of the level of service being supplied to a subscriber by a service provider.

rapid application design (RAD) tools Automated programming tools that help application developers design, build, compile, and test applications faster than they would be able to do using manual techniques.

Real-Time Collaborate pattern An infrastructure pattern that supports two-way transmission of audio and video in real-time. Applications in this category use streaming audio, video, graphics, or text to share information between users. The communication can flow either through a server for scalability, or directly from peer to peer. Common examples include Microsoft NetMeeting, Voice Over Internet (VoIP), AOL instant messaging, and videoconferencing.

Registration Authority (RA) A network-based service that verifies user requests for digital certificates and directs the Certificate Authority (CA) to issue them.

relational database management system (RDBMS) A database management system (DBMS) that provides relational capabilities, typically by storing data in cross-referenced tables.

remote access services (RAS) A network operating system feature that allows remote users to connect to the internal network system, typically using dial-up modems.

return on investment (ROI) The amount of profit returned as a proportion of the amount of money invested.

reusability The ability of infrastructure platforms, patterns, components, and services to be shared and reused by multiple applications. Reusability is a key concept in adaptive infrastructure.

scalability The ability of a computer system to handle increases in traffic or processing loads. The increased loads may be random and unpredictable, or planned out over time.

Secure Socket Layer (SSL) A standard software interface that provides authentication and data encryption security between a client and a server by sending data over a "socket," which is a secure channel at the connection layer in most TCP/IP applications.

Security Assertion Markup Language (SAML) A language related to XML that allows authentication and authorization information to be communicated across IP networks.

server layer An infrastructure layer containing both the server hardware and the operating system software that support applications.

server load balancing (SLB) See "load balancing."

service A set of reusable applications or processes delivered to an end user by a service provider.

service level agreement (SLA) A user requirement codified as a defined performance goal for service delivery. For example, to work properly, an application might require a TCP/IP network operating at T1 bandwidth (1.5 Mbps). These requirements are then defined as its "service level requirements."

Simple Mail Transfer Protocol (SMTP) A standard communications protocol used by e-mail servers to transmit e-mail messages sent by clients.

Simple Network Management Protocol (SNMP) This protocol is used in network management and monitoring.

Simple Object Access Protocol (SOAP) A lightweight protocol that allows different programs running in different environments to communicate with each other using HTTP and XML.

smart PC See "client/server computing."

SQLnet Software used to connect Oracle clients and servers and communicate using various protocols.

Starter Kit A set of components, patterns and/or services presented as an initial group to be considered by readers of this book.

storage area network (SAN) A network with its own dedicated set of servers and storage devices used specifically to store data for backup, mirroring, or redundancy purposes.

storage layer An infrastructure layer that handles short-term and long-term storage of data within the organization, including the backup and redundancies that are vital to data security and disaster recovery.

Store-and-Forward Collaborate pattern An infrastructure pattern that involves the basic transfer, replication, and storage of files or documents. Common examples include word processing files and spreadsheets distributed through files systems, e-mail attachments, or print queues. Most organizations also put desktop support and software distribution into this pattern.

stovepipe A term used to describe infrastructure components that are dedicated to specific applications, and not easily shared or reused.

strategic infrastructure planning A form of infrastructure planning that determines standard infrastructure patterns and services on a regular cycle, such as annually. Also called "periodic planning." See also "tactical infrastructure planning."

Stream Publish pattern An infrastructure pattern used for real-time publishing of streaming content, such as audio, video, and text. Content is published to a multimedia player and the file plays in near real-time as it downloads. See also "Real-Time Publish pattern." Common examples include Internet radio stations and film-clip Web sites.

streaming media Special audio or video files that play back simultaneously, as they are downloaded, as opposed to normal multimedia files that must be played back after downloading. Streaming media typically require special servers and file formats.

Structured Collaborate pattern An infrastructure pattern used to identify applications that provide shared access and automated, coordinated change to documents, files, or other data structures. Common examples include Lotus Notes groupware and workflow applications (except simple e-mail), document management applications, Web content management systems, many software development environments, and shared groupware calendars.

supply chain management (SCM) Applications or processes that help businesses manage their supply chains, typically by storing and analyzing extensive sets of vendor and inventory data.

tactical infrastructure planning A form of infrastructure planning that is completed on a per-project basis for each new application or technology being introduced into the organization. Also called "per-project" planning.

thin client See "client/server computing."

third generation (3G) A generation of wireless technology expected to provide advanced functionality for business applications, arriving in the 2003–2005 time frame.

3/N-Tier Transact pattern An infrastructure pattern consisting of a thin client communicating with a client-neutral, server-based application, which in turn communicates with a back-end database server. Common examples include PeopleSoft v8 and SAP R/3. With a Web server, the presentation is generated on another Web server tier, but still rendered by the Web browser. Since this design is truly N-tier rather than just 3-Tier, this pattern is called 3/N-Tier. This is the most scalable and flexible Transact pattern.

Total Cost of Ownership (TCO) The complete cost of a PC to the business, including not just the purchase price, but also any administration, maintenance, support, upgrade, and training costs needed to keep the PC operational.

Transact pattern Infrastructure patterns that support applications where user actions make durable changes to the state of the business or business processes. They include any application that writes structured information to a system or a data set. This book discusses three types of Transact patterns: 1-Tier Transact, 2-Tier Transact, and 3/N-Tier Transact.

Transactional Integration service See "enterprise application integration (EAI)."

Transmission Control Protocol/Internet Protocol (TCP/IP) A set of networking protocols that provides communication across a wide range of different network types and computing platforms. TCP handles data packaging and unpackaging, while IP handles data addressing and delivery.

2-Tier Transact pattern An infrastructure pattern that uses a smart PC on the desktop, communicating directly with a back-end database server. This category includes most traditional client/server applications that became popular earlier in the 1990s, but also includes Web applications that intertwine CGI/ASP/JSP presentation and application logic. Common examples include applications programmed using Visual Basic or Powerbuilder, and most Web applications using Microsoft active server pages (ASP) or Java server pages (JSP).

2.5 generation (2.5G) A generation of wireless technology associated with General Packet Radio Services (GPRS), which forms the intermediate step between 2G and 3G technology.

Universal Description, Discovery, and Integration (UDDI) A worldwide business registry that promotes e-Commerce by allowing businesses to register online, locate partners, and easily exchange data and online transactions using XML. The original registry was created through the efforts of Microsoft, IBM, and Ariba and now includes many Global 1000 companies.

User Datagram Protocol (UDP) An alternative to TCP often used with IP to transmit units of data (known as "datagrams") between computers on a network. UDP eliminates some of the data handling services provided by TCP, and thus works quicker for specific applications that don't need these services.

venture funding Funding by investors for projects that have a typically high risk factor. The theory of venture funding is that high-risk projects may create extremely high returns, effectively covering the cost of other less-profitable investments.

Very Small Aperture Terminal (VSAT) A system that uses satellite-based, point-to-multipoint data communications to provide wireless network services.

virtual LAN (VLAN) A network service that provides the functionality of a LAN on a basis other than geographic location. For example, a virtual LAN might connect a particular department or a certain group of users, regardless of their location.

virtual private network (VPN) A private network that operates across the Internet using secure communication. Typically used to connect remote users to an organization's internal networks without using dedicated lines, wide area networks (WANs), or remote access services (RAS).

Voice Markup Language (VoxML) A technology developed by Motorola that allows users to communicate with Web sites using a telephone and spoken commands.

Voice Over Internet (VoIP) A standard way of transmitting voice information over the Internet or other TCP/IP networks.

Web An Internet-based service used to transmit formatted documents and multimedia files, typically using HTML and HTTP, but also using PDF, XML, streaming media, and many other technologies.

Web browser A software application such as Microsoft Internet Explorer and Netscape Navigator used to view Web-based information over the Internet, intranet, or extranets.

Web Publish pattern An infrastructure pattern that uses HTML browsers and HTTP protocol to enable read-only access to structured HTML or XML documents.

Web Services Description Language (WSDL) An XML-based language used as part of UDDI to catalog the services that each UDDI subscriber has to offer.

Web Single Sign-On (SSO) A service that allows users to access multiple secure Web sites, Web applications, or online databases using a single user name and password.

wide area network (WAN) A network that connects users over a large geographical area, typically using dedicated lines supplied by local telephone companies.

Wireless Application Protocol (WAP) A standard protocol that allows Web applications to present information in a format small enough to fit on the screen of a cell phone, PDA, or other small wireless devices.

Wireless Application Server Provider (WASP) A third-party company that provides Internet-based applications in a way that is compatible with a variety of wireless presentation devices, including cell phones and PDAs.

XML See "Extensible Markup Language (XML)."

XML Query Language (XQL) A specialized language that allows Web applications to query data or text fields embedded inside XML documents.

XSLT See "Extensible Stylesheet Language Transformations (XSLT)."

Index

active directory services (ADS) 158
active server pages (ASP) 61
adaptability 20
adaptive cost 110
adaptive infrastructure 4
　selling it to upper management 18
adaptive infrastructure services 38
administration
　centralized and automated 143
agility 33, 39
　creating 40
analysis
　clickstream 291
　pattern analysis 222
　pattern-based 29
　root-cause 132, 293
appliances
　vs. switch-based products 172
application
　implementing and maintaining 88
application hosting 193
application management 198, 291
　planning 295
application programming interface (API) 32, 77, 92, 283
　understanding APIs 285
application programming interface layer 33
application server 220
application server layer 31

application service provider (ASP) 14, 103, 198
application subscriptions 103
application(s)
　externalization 207
applications
　extranet 154
　HTTP 135
　integrating 5
　Web-centric 139, 143
assets
　behind-the-wall 102
authentication 157
　cookie-based 142
　vs. authorization/b 150
authorization 150
automatic locator information (ALI) 280

bleeding edge 5
border gateway protocol (BGP) 174, 190
buffers 131
business
　negiotiating with 110
business vision refinement 101
business-to-business (B2B) 3, 135, 149, 193, 280
　integration of 5
business-to-consumer (B2C) 195, 280
business-to-employee (B2E) 195

365

Index

cache
  cache server 175
  forward cache 176
  proxy cache 176
  reverse caching 181
centers of excellence (COE) 89
certificate authority (CA) 147
certificate revocation list (CRL) 153
clusters 170
commercial off the shelf (COTS) 274
Communications Assistance for Law Enforcement Act (CALEA) 280
components
  cataloging 24
  identifying and cataloging 12
  organizing infrastructure 51
computer telephony integration (CTI) 32
consultants
  using them 8
content delivery network (CDN) 67, 73, 168, 179, 182, 208
corporate connectivity 189
cryptographic acceleration 138
customer expectations
  managing 290
customer interaction center (CIC) 206, 308
customer relationship management (CRM) 78, 283

data warehousing 28, 74
database layer 28
database management systems (DBMS) 128
decoupling 43, 46
defense in-depth 128
delegated administration 157
demilitarized zone (DMZ) 77, 120, 179, 277, 291
  extended vs. traditional 121
  multi-site 124
  parallel 124
design guidelines 48
digital receipts 149
digital signature 149
directory
  primary purpose of 158
directory server 153
directory service agent (DSA) 154
directory service markup language (DSML) 160
directory user agent (DUA) 154
distributed servers 183
DMZ Sandwich 122
dynamic link library (DLL) 42

e-Business 14, 23, 26, 148, 154, 206
  converging with business 92
  expectations of 1
  goal of 116
  hype vs. reality 2
  rapid ascendance of 31
e-Commerce 56, 154, 173
  consumer-centric 145
Edge Side Includes (ESI) 185
electronic document interchange (EDI) 5
encryption 132
enterprise application integration (EAI) 30, 77, 126, 155, 207
enterprise resource planning (ERP) 60, 158
enterprise systems management (ESM) 133
ethernet 167
expertise
  advanced ISP services 190
extensible markup language (XML) 5, 41, 71, 158, 174, 205, 221, 275
extensible stylesheet language transformations (XSLT) 75
extranet 193
extranet service provider (ESP) 193

fault tolerance 123, 125, 177
feedback system 295
Fibre Channel 209, 212, 218
file transfer protocol (FTP) 48
firewall 116, 138
  application proxy 116
  clusters 123
  dual 122
  serial, or DMZ Sandwich 122
  single 122
  stateful packet filtering 117
flash crowds 186, 202
full-time equivalent (FTE) 134

gap analysis 87
gateway
  SQL 47
gateways 28, 142
Global 2000 145
Global Positioning System (GPS) 280
graphical user interface (GUI)
  improving off-the-shelf 144

hackers 116, 121, 129, 133, 138, 148, 152
host pattern 60
host-based agents 131
hypertext markup language (HTML) 274, 275
hypertext transfer protocol (HTTP) 71

identity infrastructure
    purposes of 160
Infra-API 34
    understanding 287
infrastructure 7
    definition of 6
    identity vs. permission 159
    infrastructure patterns 27
    integration, reuse of 20
    organizing at the platform level 23
    permission vs. identity 162
    physical 198
    raw 23
    strategies 9
Infrastructure Pattern Matching (IPM) 14, 56, 83, 88, 90, 105
infrastructure planning 156
    strategic vs. tactical 15
inputs, tools, outputs, services (ITOS) 98
instant messaging 68
integrated agents 131
integrated development environment (IDE) 287
integrated threat management (ITM) 133
integrated voice response (IVR) 285
integration layer 30
Interactive Voice Response (IVR) 5, 32, 274, 282
Inter-API 34, 288
    understanding 288
inter-enterprise integration (IEI) 30
interfaces
    creating 48
Internet Protocol (IP) 282
Internet service provider (ISP) 14, 186
    consolidation of 204
Intra-API 34, 288
    understanding 287
intrusion detection system (IDS) 116, 128, 138
    network-based vs. host-based 129
IP multi-protocol label switching (MPLS) 190
IP transport 193
isolation infrastructure service 121
    definition of 115
isolation infrastructure service/b 116

J2EE 220
Java server pages (JSP) 61

key history management 147
key management 152
key pair 146
knowledge management 28

layer
    management 289
    presentation layer 274
layers 23
    creating separate 35
    organizing components into 24
legacy platforms 225
legacy systems
    integrating 5
lifecycles
    decoupling 40
lightweight directory access protocol (LDAP) 139, 154
load balancing 138, 168
load sharing 168
local area network (LAN) 166

manageability
    as factor in reverse caches 179
managed security service (MSS) 133
management
    data quality 157
marketing
    runaway campaigns 202
metadirectories 155
metadirectory 158
middleware 28
mobile application server (MAS) 274, 275
Moore's Law 219

network architecture 189
network attached storage (NAS) 206, 209
network IDS
    limitations of 131
network infrastructure 167
network latency 173
network layer 55
    best practices 208
network load balancer (NLB) 125, 135, 140, 168, 170, 173
    advantages of 172
    integrating SSL into 137
network operating system (NOS) 69, 154, 161
network traffic
    minimizing 76
networking 203
nodes
    importance of 189
non-repudiation 194
notifications
    attack 132

online analytical processing (OLAP) 64
online data stores (ODS) 74

online transaction processing (OLTP) 60, 73, 74, 168
operating system (OS) 225
organizations
    Global 2000 133
OSI stack 137
outsourcing 5, 21, 67, 74, 90, 104, 155, 192, 201, 203, 208, 276
    hosting services 195
    outsourcing patterns 50
ownership
    establishing 45

package and communicate 101
package pricing 104
partitioning 20
pattern
    1-Tier Transact 60
    2-Tier Transact 61, 126
    3/N-Tier Transact 29, 32, 63, 75, 122, 126, 127, 138, 168, 182, 192, 201, 220, 289
    Client/Server 63
    combination of Publish and Transact 74
    designing 104
    linking patterns with services 88
    maturity 58
    pattern design 201
    pattern refinement 88
    phasing out old 225
    Real-Time Collaborate 68
    refined 112
    scalability of a pattern as deciding factor 57
    selecting a pattern 111
    Store-and-Forward Collaborate 69, 80, 223
    Stream Publish 66, 220
    Structured Collaborate 70
    Web Publish 29, 50, 65, 71, 122, 137, 168, 182, 192, 216, 220
patterns 11, 23, 53
    defining 11
    identifying modular 13
PCI cards
    accelerating site performance 136
peering points 190, 194
performance drag
    minimizing 135
permissions management 150, 194
personal computer interface (PCI) 135
personal digital assistant (PDA) 5, 277
personal identification number (PIN) 152
planning
    assimilation 101
    per-project 100

strategic, or periodic 98
tactical, or per-project 98
platform 11, 23
point of interaction (POI) 208
    multiple 76
points of interaction (POI) 33, 119, 275
    multiple 90
points-of-interaction (POI) 56
policy
    compliance 133
portfolios 16
Predictive Cost Modeling (PCM) 83, 88, 106
presentation 77
presentation independence 19
presentation layer 32
private key infrastructure (PKI) 139
process 112
    getting the process defined 89
process model 45
process(es)
    repeatable 15
provider viability 191
public key encryption (PKI) 134
public key infrastructure (PKI) 146, 194
public safety access center (PSAC) 281

quality of service (QoS) 202, 205

redundant array of independent disks (RAID) 169
relationship-based management (RBM) 94
reliability vs. performance 174
request for proposal (RFP) 145
resource(s)
    dedicated 89
return on investment (ROI) 8, 80
reuse 20, 34, 42, 56, 92, 139, 146, 149, 156, 171
    reuse challenges 151
reverse proxies 179
risk management 118
robots 291
role
    application developer 17, 34, 46
    assigning roles 89
    business analyst 287
    business manager 87
    chief customer officer 96
    chief information officer (CIO) 86
    chief security officer 96
    chief technical officer (CTO) 96
    chief technology officer (CTO) 86
    infrastructure developer 17, 92, 102, 108, 287

role *(continued)*
  infrastructure manager 87
  infrastructure planner 9, 14, 20, 30, 74, 90, 165
  internal partner manager 96
  IT director 293
  programmer 34
  relationship manager 95
  vendor and sourcing manager 96
role identifiers 158
router 116
router hops 173
rule
  80/20 80

scalability 19, 72, 77, 125, 140, 142, 166, 170, 175, 220
  challenges of 152
  low-cost 168
  single-server 154
scale-out 165
  as architectural trend 274
scaling
  scaling up vs. scaling out 220
SCSI 209
secure HTTP 135
secure socket layer (SSL) 134, 147
secure sockets library (SSL) 73, 168
security 74, 77, 204
security assertion markup language (SAML) 145
server
  database 215
server cluster 172
server farm 169
server layer 27
server(s)
  server consolidation 221
  types of 221
service level
  defining 106
service level agreement (SLA) 204, 290, 292
service level agreements (SLA)
  negotiating 199
service level management (SLM) 289, 290
service levels 20, 39
  defining 48
service(s) 11, 18, 23
  adaptive 37
  bundling 198
  consumer 43
  creating 36
  decoupling 14
  defining adaptive infrastructure service 51
  defining service levels 45
  desktop 103
  externalizing 91
  full interface 43
  interface 43
  keeping the number low 46
  non-repudiation/b 149
  project 104
  provider 43
  security and directory 194
  Web edge 175
sharing 38
Simple Mail Transfer Protocol (SMTP) 205
Simple Network Management Protocol (SNMP) 134
Simple Object Access Protocol (SOAP) 41, 205, 221
single instance 214
single point of administration (SPA) 144
Single Sign-On (SSO) 140, 148
smart cards 151
smart PC 20, 61, 63
software development kit (SDK) 288
solution(s)
  bundling 146
SQLNet 63
SSL session ID 173
stability 38
Storage Area Network (SAN) 26, 206
  comparing with network-attached storage (NAS) 210
storage layer 206
stovepipes 11, 20, 54
  removing 14
  vs. adaptive infrastructure 42
strategy
  vs. strategic activities 87
supply chain management (SCM) 78
supply-side caching 138
switching 132
system partitioning 170

TCP/IP 14, 25, 42, 55, 68, 81, 205, 209
  definition of 166
test lab 296
threat management 133
tools
  Bluetooth 278
  Check Point FireWall-1 117
  CICS 34
  Cisco PIX 117
  ColdFusion 61
  COM+/.NET 34

tools *(continued)*
    Excel 69
    Forte 34
    freeware tools 120
    Haht 61
    J2EE 31, 34
    Kerberos 146
    metadirectory 155
    Microsoft IIS 126
    Microsoft Money 16
    Microsoft Windows 2000/.NET Server 31
    NetMeeting 68
    Passport 152
    Peoplesoft 63
    PowerBuilder 34, 61
    Quicken 16
    Real Application Cluster (RAC) 79
    RealPlayer 66
    SAP R/3 63
    Tuxedo 34
    Visual Basic 61
    WebLogic 31
    WebSphere 31
    Windows 2000/.NET 143
    Windows Media Player 66
    Word 69
total cost of ownership (TCO) 107, 119
    lowering 224
traditional DMZ 121
transactional systems 169
transactions per second (TPS) 135

trust
    challenges of 152

Universal Description, Discovery, and Integration (UDDI) 41, 205, 221
UNIX 212, 218
usability 132

videoconferencing 68
virtual private network (VPN) 25, 116, 167
voice markup language (VoxML) 275
voice messaging 28
Voice Over Internet (VoIP) 68, 281
voice response unit (VRU) 306

Web hosting 202
web management 291
Web server 121, 141, 154, 157, 169, 171, 172, 173, 202, 213, 215, 274
Web Services Description Language (WSDL) 41, 205, 221
Web Single Sign-On (Web SSO) 77, 139, 142, 145, 153, 154, 159, 162, 180, 194
wide area network (WAN) 166
Windows 2000/.NET 212, 218
wireless application protocol (WAP) 32, 274, 275, 277
wireless application server provider (WASP) 274, 276, 280, 281
wireless markup language (WML) 275

XML query language (XQL) 75